THE AMERICAN NEGRO
HIS HISTORY AND LITERATURE

THE SOUTH
SINCE THE WAR

Sidney Andrews

ARNO PRESS and THE NEW YORK TIMES

NEW YORK 1969

General Editor
WILLIAM LOREN KATZ

SIDNEY ANDREWS WAS ONE OF A NUMBER OF northern journalists who traveled South after the conclusion of the Civil War to report on conditions in the defeated Confederacy. His reports, which appeared in the *Chicago Tribune* and *Boston Advertiser,* attracted so much attention that they were quickly brought together into a volume originally published early in 1866. Together with Whitelaw Reid's *After the War* (1866) and John T. Trowbridge's *The South* (1866), this work by Andrews ranks as one of the three most significant travel books of that time dealing with the postwar South. It is a simply, but well-written and straightforward account that to this day remains an essential source on the subject.

From the point of view of the victorious North, the crucial problem of that postwar period was one of adequately defining and implementing the final results of the Civil War. By the fall of 1865, when Andrews undertook his tour, an extremely aggressive, if not arrogant, response on the part of former Confederates to the lenient Reconstruction policies of President Andrew Johnson was already clearly evident and of increasing concern to many in the North. Like other travelers, Andrews was invariably concerned with this problem, and his reports were to be of some importance in determining the final stance of the dominant North. Andrews was appalled at the demands of recent rebels, at their continuing domination within the South, and at their prevalent and unconcealed prejudice against black ex-slaves, southern unionists, and Yankees. His consequent portrayal provided a most informative picture of such conditions and represented a type of suspicious and dissatisfied northern response that would culminate a year later in the Congressional enfranchisement of the South's black freedmen.

Sidney Andrews was born thirty-one years before he wrote his influential account of the postwar South and spent his early childhood in Massachusetts. Following the death of his father in 1846, he moved to Dixon, Illinois, to live with relatives. In the late 1850's he attended the University of Michigan for three years but because of financial difficulties withdrew before graduating. Having previously been active for some years in newspaper work, he became an assistant editor and then editor of the Alton, Illinois, *Daily Courier*. Early in the Civil War he moved to the nation's capital where he worked as a Senate attendant and continued his career in journalism. In 1864 he became a special correspondent, using the pseudonym "Dixon," and it was in this role that he initiated his fourteen-week investigation of conditions in the South in September, 1865.

Beginning his tour in Charleston, South Carolina, to which he had traveled by sea, Andrews proceeded by railroad and stagecoach through much of the eastern half of the two Carolinas and concluded his tour with a somewhat amplified territorial coverage of Georgia. Altogether he spent about six weeks in South Carolina, three in North Carolina, and five in Georgia. Corresponding to an expressed political focus, he had undertaken his trip at a most opportune time, for in each state visited he was able to attend the state convention summoned to affect restoration under President Johnson's plan of Reconstruction. He was also able to report upon an important state convention of freedmen that was held in North Carolina during this time.

There can be little doubt that the most valuable portion of Andrews' work consisted of his various convention reports. These reports were filled with proceedings and speeches and include a highly informative analysis of a variety of prevalent southern political issues and attitudes. In addition to effectively depicting the intricacies associated with achieving sectional iv

reconciliation, Andrews also focused on important class, sectional, and ideological conflicts within the South; and it was from the convention proceedings in particular that he derived his well-founded suspicions of the real southern attitudes respecting their military defeat and the treatment of their former slaves.

When Andrews ventured beyond political matters, which he seldom did, his work was less satisfying. Although he was, it is true, a man "of intelligence, of kindly sentiments, honest, shrewd, and fair minded," his more general observations on southern people and life show a certain lack of sensitivity. And despite his stated intention to avoid a northern bias, he did not always succeed in doing so. He was clearly intolerant of conditions or values other than those that he identified with New England or the North. He showed little of the humility appropriate to a visitor, and he was, perhaps, a bit too free in condemning the South for a variety of faults ranging from poor hotels and cooking to excessive drinking, dirt, and sloth.

The real concern of his work throughout, however, was political, and it concluded with a stern warning against any immediate readmission of the South to her former status in the Union. Instead, advised Andrews, the victors should

. . . temper justice with mercy, but see to it that justice is not overborne; keep military control of these lately rebellious States till they guarantee a republican form of government; scrutinize carefully the personal fitness of the men chosen therefrom as representatives in the Congress of the United States; and sustain therein some agency that shall stand between the whites and the blacks and aid each class in coming to a proper understanding of its privileges and responsibilities.

For some time the North did follow a path similar to that recommended by Andrews, but by 1867 it turned to the enfranchisement of the black freedmen as a simpler and final solution. This was a measure that Andrews had flatly endorsed only once in his writings. He had done so in response to the suggestions of an unusually astute southern lawyer and former Confederate army officer, who advised that the real need of the former slaves was not the ballot but some form of economic independence. Like a number of northern radicals, this Georgian advised the confiscation and distribution of southern plantation land as the only promising solution to the social ills of the South. The North, of course, would refuse to endorse any such violation of the sacred right of property, and Andrews' response to this suggestion typified the traditional faith of the North, and of the nation, in the adequacy of the democratic electoral process. "But put into the negro's horny palm the simple right to vote," said Andrews, "and he is at once installed into ownership of houses and lands and comforts and luxuries, from which only his own idleness or improvidence can dispossess him." Time would tragically disprove that facile assumption.

Several times in his dispatches from the South, Andrews had indicated some difficulty with his health, and four years after his trip he was forced by illness to give up a successful newspaper career. Thereafter he resided in Massachusetts, where he did some occasional writing and editorial work and also served for several years as secretary of the State Board of Charities. He died in 1880, at a rather early age, his most significant accomplishment having been the work reprinted here.

Otto H. Olsen
DEPARTMENT OF HISTORY
NORTHERN ILLINOIS UNIVERSITY

THE

SOUTH SINCE THE WAR:

AS SHOWN BY

FOURTEEN WEEKS OF TRAVEL
AND OBSERVATION

IN

GEORGIA AND THE CAROLINAS.

BY

SIDNEY ANDREWS.

BOSTON:
TICKNOR AND FIELDS.
1866.

UNIVERSITY PRESS: WELCH, BIGELOW, & CO.,
CAMBRIDGE.

INTRODUCTORY NOTE.

——◆——

I SPENT the months of September, October, and
November, 1865, in the States of North Carolina,
South Carolina, and Georgia, as the Correspondent
of the Boston Advertiser and the Chicago Tribune,
and a considerable portion of the matter of this
book has appeared in letters to one or the other
of those papers.

MARCH, 1866.

CONTENTS.

———◆———

THE SOUTH SINCE THE WAR.

I.

CONDITION AND PROSPECTS OF THE CITY IN WHICH REBELLION BEGAN.

CHARLESTON, September 4, 1865.

A CITY of ruins, of desolation, of vacant houses, of widowed women, of rotting wharves, of deserted warehouses, of weed-wild gardens, of miles of grass-grown streets, of acres of pitiful and voiceful barrenness, — that is Charleston, wherein Rebellion loftily reared its head five years ago, on whose beautiful promenade the fairest of cultured women gathered with passionate hearts to applaud the assault of ten thousand upon the little garrison of Fort Sumter!

"The mills of the gods grind slow, but they grind exceeding small." Be sure Charleston knows what these words mean. Be sure the pride of the eyes of these men and women has been laid low. Be sure they have eaten wormwood, and their souls have worn sackcloth. "God's ways seem dark, but soon or late they touch the shining hills of day." Henceforth let us rest content in this faith; for here is enough of woe and want and ruin and ravage to satisfy the most insatiate heart, — enough of sore humiliation and bitter overthrow to appease the desire of the most vengeful spirit.

Who kindled the greedy fire of December, 1861, whereby a third of the city was destroyed? No one yet knows. "It was de good Jesus hisself," said an old negro to me when I asked him the question, — "it was de Almighty Hand workin' fru de man's hand." Certain it is that the people were never able to discover the agency of the fire; though, so far as I can learn, no one doubts that it was the work of an incendiary, — "some man," say the ex-Rebels, "who wanted to do you Federals a good turn."

Recall last winter's daily bulletin about the bombardment, — so many shells and no damage done, — so many shells and no damage done, — day after day the same old story, till one almost believed it true. Yet ex-Rebel officers will tell you now that our aim was so perfect that we killed their sentinels with our Parrott guns; and go where you will, up and down the streets in almost any portion of the city, and you find the dumb walls eloquent with praises of our skill.

We never again can have the Charleston of the decade previous to the war. The beauty and pride of the city are as dead as the glories of Athens. Five millions of dollars could not restore the ruin of these four past years; and that sum is so far beyond the command of the city as to seem the boundless measure of immeasurable wealth. Yet, after all, Charleston was Charleston because of the hearts of its people. St. Michael's Church, they held, was the centre of the universe; and the aristocracy of the city were the very elect of God's children on earth. One marks now how few young men there are, how generally the young women are dressed in black. The flower of their proud aristocracy is buried on scores of battle-fields. If it were possible to restore the broad acres of crumbling ruins to their foretime style and uses, there would even then be but the dead body of Charleston.

The Charleston of 1875 will doubtless be proud in wealth and intellect and rich in grace and culture. Let favoring years bring forward such fruitage! Yet the place has not in itself recuperative power for such a result. The material on which to build that fair structure does not here exist, and, as I am told by dozens, cannot be found in the State. If Northern capital and Northern energy do not come here, the ruin, they say, must remain a ruin; and if this time five years finds here a handsome and thriving city, it will be the creation of New England, — not necessarily the pattern of New England, for the influences from thence will be moulded by and interfused with those now existing here; but yet, in the essential fact, the creation of New England.

It was noted on the steamship by which I came from New York that, leaving out the foreign element, our passengers were from Charleston and from Massachusetts. We had nearly as many Boston men as Charleston men. One of the Charleston merchants said to me that when he went North the passengers were also almost equally divided between Massachusetts and South Carolina; and he added, that, in Eastern Massachusetts, where he spent some days, he found many men who were coming to Charleston.

Of Massachusetts men, some are already in business here, and others came on to "see the lay of the land," as one of them said. "That's all right," observed an ex-Rebel captain in one of our after-dinner chats, — "that's all right; let's have Massachusetts and South Carolina brought together, for they are the only two States that amount to anything."

"I hate all you Yankees most heartily in a general sort of way," remarked another of these Southerners; "but I find you clever enough personally, and I expect it'll be a good thing for us to have you come down here with your money, though it'll go against the grain with us pretty badly."

There are many Northern men here already, though one cannot say that there is much Northern society, for the men are either without families or have left them at home. Walking out yesterday with a former Charlestonian, — a man who left here in the first year of the war and returned soon after our occupation of the city, — he pointed out to me the various "Northern houses"; and I shall not exaggerate if I say that this classification appeared to include at least half the stores on each of the principal streets. "The presence of these men," said he, "was at first very distasteful to our people, and they are not liked any too well now; but we know they are doing a good work for the city."

I fell into some talk with him concerning the political situation, and found him of bitter spirit toward what he was pleased to denominate "the infernal radicals." When I asked him what should be done, he answered: "You Northern people are making a great mistake in your treatment of the South. We are thoroughly whipped; we give up slavery forever; and now we want you to quit reproaching us. Let us back into the Union, and then come down here and help us build up the country."

Every little variation from the old order of things excites the comment "Yankee notion," in which there is sometimes good-natured querulousness and sometimes a sharp spice of contempt. Stopping a moment this afternoon in a store where were three or four intelligent men, one of them asked me the use of the "thing" I had in my hand. It was one of the handle-and-straps so common in the North for carrying shawls, cloaks, overcoats, &c. Seeing that none of them had any idea what it was, I explained its use. "Well, now, what a Yankee notion!" "Yes," answered another, "but how handy it is."

To bring here the conveniences and comforts of our Northern civilization, no less than the Northern idea of right and wrong, justice and injustice, humanity and inhumanity, is the work ready for the hand of every New England man and woman who stands waiting. There is much prejudice to overcome, and some of it is bitter and aggravating; but the measure of success won by Northern men already in the field is an earnest of the reward for others. Self-interest is a masterful agent in modern civilization.

Business is reviving slowly, though perhaps the more surely. The resident merchants are mostly at the bottom of the ladder of prosperity. They have idled away the summer in vain regrets for vanished hopes, and most of them are only just now beginning to wake to the new life. Some have already been North for goods, but more are preparing to go; not heeding that, while they vacillate with laggard time, Northern men are springing in with hands swift to catch opportunity. It pains me to see the apathy and indifference that so generally prevails; but the worst feature of the situation is, that so many young men are not only idle, but give no promise of being otherwise in the immediate future.

Many of the stores were more or less injured by the shelling. A few of these have been already repaired, and are now occupied, — very likely by Northern men. A couple of dozen, great and small, are now in process of repair; and scores stand with closed shutters or gaping doors and windows. The doubt as to the title of property, and the wise caution of the President in granting pardons, unquestionably has something to do with the stagnation so painfully apparent; but very much of it is due to the hesitating shiftlessness of even the Southern merchant, who forever lets *I dare not* wait upon *I would*. Rents of eligible storerooms are at least from one fourth to one third higher than before the war, and resident business men say only Northern men who intend staying but a short time can afford to pay present prices. I 'm sure I can't see how any one can afford to pay them, but I know the demand is greater than the supply.

I queried of the returning merchants on the steamship how they were received in the North. An Augusta man complained that he could get no credit, and that there was a disposition to be grinding and exacting. One Charleston

man said he asked for sixty days, and got it without a word
of objection.   Another told me that he asked for four
months, was given three, and treated like a gentleman
everywhere.   Another showed me the receipt for a debt
of about fifteen hundred dollars contracted before the war,
which he had paid in full; and when he asked for four
months on a bill of eight thousand dollars, it was readily
given.   Still another settled his old indebtedness with one
third cash and eight and twelve months notes for the balance, while he got ninety days on three fourths of his new
bill.   One man said he had many friends in the North, and
they all knew him for a thorough Rebel; he expected some
taunts, but tried to carry himself like a gentleman, and was
courteously received, " even in Boston."

I judge that such of the merchants as first went North
and settled with their creditors made more favorable terms
than those who went later.   If it be said that those were
men who had loved the Union, while these are men who
had not; that those were men of keen sense of commercial
honor and integrity, while these are men who cared less
for an adjustment; that those are men who deserved favors,
while these are men who have forfeited all claim to special
consideration, — if this be said, the pith of the matter will
probably be hit so far as regards most of those who now
complain of their reception.

Yet there are men who deserved better than they have
received.   These are they who, whatever their views on the
questions at issue in the war, meant to pay all their debts.
Most of them are men who loved the Union and hated
secession.   That there were such men in all parts of the
State is beyond question.   When the negroes say any one
was a Union man during the war, the fact is established;
from their judgment and testimony there is no appeal.
These men, having no faith in the Confederacy, put everything they could into cotton or rosin or turpentine, — hop-

ing to save something from the general wreck they saw impending, — only to find in the end that they are scarcely richer than those who invested everything in Confederate bonds.

It would seem that it is not clearly understood how thoroughly Sherman's army destroyed everything in its line of march, — destroyed it without questioning who suffered by the action. That this wholesale destruction was often without orders, and often against most positive orders, does not change the fact of destruction. The Rebel leaders were, too, in their way, even more wanton, and just as thorough as our army in destroying property. They did not burn houses and barns and fences as we did; but, during the last three months of the war, they burned immense quantities of cotton and rosin.

The action of the two armies put it out of the power of men to pay their debts. The values and the bases of value were nearly all destroyed. Money lost about everything it had saved. Thousands of men who were honest in purpose have lost everything but honor. The cotton with which they meant to pay their debts has been burned, and they are without other means. What is the part of wisdom in respect to such men? It certainly cannot be to strip them of the last remnant. Many of them will pay in whole or in part, if proper consideration be shown them. It is no question of favor to any one as a favor, but a pure question of business, — how shall the commercial relations of the two sections be re-established? In determining it, the actual and exceptional condition of the State with respect to property should be constantly borne in mind.

Yet when all this is said in favor of one class of merchants, it must, in good conscience, be added, that by far a larger class is showing itself unworthy of anything but stringent measures. "How do you find the feeling?" said I to a gentleman of national reputation, who is now here settling the affairs of a very large New York house. "Well, there are a good many merchants who don't mean to pay anything more than they are obliged to," said he in reply. I asked of one of the leading merchants this morning, "Are your people generally disposed to settle their accounts?" His answer was, "Those who expect to continue business must of course do so." "How about the others?" I queried. "I 'm afraid there is n't so much commercial honor as there should be," he replied. I am told of one firm which represented itself entirely ruined, when subsequent investigation showed that it had five thousand pounds sterling to its credit in Liverpool; and of another which offered only thirty cents on the dollar, when its property in New York alone will cover over seventy cents on the dollar of its entire indebtedness.

That Rebellion sapped the foundations of commercial integrity in the State is beyond question. That much of the Northern indebtedness will never be paid is also beyond question. What is desirable is, that creditors should become cognizant of all the facts in the case before fixing terms. For the rascal there is but one set of terms; for the honest man there should be every possible consideration.

The city is under thorough military rule; but the iron hand rests very lightly. Soldiers do police duty, and there is some nine-o'clock regulation; but, so far as I can learn, anybody goes anywhere at all hours of the night without molestation. "There never was such good order here before," said an old colored man to me. The main street is swept twice a week, and all garbage is removed at sunrise. "If the Yankees was to stay here always and keep the city so clean, I don't reckon we 'd have 'yellow jack' here any more," was a remark I overheard on the street. "Now is de fust time sence I can 'mem'er when brack men was safe in de street af'er nightfall," stated the negro tailor in whose shop I sat an hour yesterday.

On the surface, Charleston is quiet and well behaved; and I do not doubt that the more intelligent citizens are wholly sincere in their expressions of a desire for peace and reunion. The city has been humbled as no other city has been; and I can't see how any man, after spending a few days here, can desire that it shall be further humiliated merely for revenge. Whether it has been humiliated enough for health is another thing. Said one of the Charlestonians on the boat, " You won't see the real sentiment of our people, for we are under military rule; we are whipped, and we are going to make the best of things; but we hate Massachusetts as much as we ever did." This idea of making the best of things is one I have heard from scores of persons. I find very few who hesitate to frankly own that the South has been beaten. " We made the best fight we could, but you were too strong for us, and now we are only anxious to get back into the old Union and live as happily as we can," said a large cotton factor. I find very few who make any special profession of Unionism; but they are almost unanimous in declaring that they have no desire but to live as good and quiet citizens under the laws.

For the first two months of our occupancy of the city scarcely a white woman but those of the poorer classes was seen on the street, and very few were even seen at the windows and doors of the residences. That order of things is now, happily, changed. There does n't yet appear to be as much freedom of appearance as would be natural; but very many of what are called the " first ladies " are to be seen shopping in the morning and promenading in the evening. They, much more than the men, have contemptuous motions for the negro soldiers; and scorn for Northern men is frequently apparent in the swing of their skirts when passing on the sidewalk.

One does n't observe so much pleasantness and cheerfulness as would be agreeable; but the general demeanor is

1 *

quite consonant with the general mourning costume. A stroller at sunset sees not a few pale and pensive-faced young women of exquisite beauty; and a rambler during the evening not unfrequently hears a strain of touching melody from the darkened parlor of some roomy old mansion, with now and then one of the ringing, passionate airs with which the Southern heart has been fired during the war.

Mothers yet teach their children hate of the North, I judge; for when I asked a bright-eyed girl of half a dozen years, with whom I walked on a back street for a block or two, whose girl she was, she promptly answered, "A Rebel mother's girl." Patience, good people who love liberty, patience; this petty woman's spite will bite itself to death in time.

Down in the churchyard of St. Philip's, one of the richest and most aristocratic of churches in this proud city, is a grave which every stranger is curious to see. There are only the four plain panelled brick walls about three feet high, and on them a mottled white marble slab, some nine feet by four in size. At the head of the grave is a single sickly ten-foot-high magnolia tree. At each corner of the foot is a sprawling and tangled damask rose-bush, and about midway on the right there is also a small white rose-bush. All around the little plat is a border of myrtle, sweet in its rich greenness, but untrimmed and broken and goat-eaten. It is the grave of the father of the Rebellion, and on the marble slab there is cut the one word, —

"CALHOUN."

This churchyard symbolizes the city of Charleston. Children and goats crawl through a convenient hole in the front wall, and play at will among the sunken graves and broken tombstones. There is everywhere a wealth of offal and garbage and beef-bones. A mangy cur was slinking among the stones, and I found a hole three feet deep which he had dug at the foot of one of the graves. Children were quarrelling

for flowers over one of the more recent mounds.   The whole
yard is grown up to weeds and brush, and the place is desolate and dreary as it well can be; more desolate because
cruel hands have broken away the corners of the great
marble slab of Calhoun, — for mementos, I suppose.   Time
was when South Carolina guarded this grave as a holy spot.
Now it lies in ruin with her chief city.   When Northern
life shall rebuild and revivify that city, let us pray it may
also set chaste and simple beauty around this grave; for
there is no need to wish the brave but bad spirit of Calhoun
greater punishment than it must have in seeing the woe and
waste and mourning which the war has brought the region
he loved so well.

II.

MANNERS AND CUSTOMS IN THE INTERIOR OF SOUTH CAROLINA.

ORANGEBURG C. H., September 7, 1865.

FROM Charleston to Orangeburg Court House is seventy-
seven miles.   Route, South Carolina Railroad.   Time,
seven and a half hours.   Fare, five dollars.   There is one
train per day each way.   Our train consisted of five freight-
cars, the baggage-car, a box freight-car with seats for negroes, and one passenger-coach.   The down train, which we
met at Branchville, — where Sherman's army was to find its
doom, — consisted of seven freight-cars, four of which were
filled with troops on the way to Charleston and home, the
baggage-car, and two passenger-coaches.   Our one car was
uncomfortably full when we started; but only eleven of the
passengers came through.

"What sort of accommodations can I get at Orangeburg?"
I asked of a friend in Charleston.

"You 're not going to stop up there? O you can't do it!"

"Well, I shall try it, at all events."

"Don't do it; Orangeburg is just as good as any of these towns; but I advise you to shun all of 'em. The accommodation's are awful: push right on to Columbia."

I was n't to be put down that way, for I had consulted a gazetteer, and learned that "Orangeburg is a pleasant and thriving town on the northeast bank of the north fork of the Edisto River. It is in the midst of a farming district, and is the centre of a large cotton trade. Population two thousand seven hundred." That was before the war, and I knew the place had been partly burned; but I felt confident that my friend exaggerated.

We left the city at seven and a half o'clock in the morning. Twenty miles out, the conductor came through the car, and collected our fares; for no tickets are sold at Charleston. In front of me sat a good-looking young woman, of about twenty-two, I judged. Hearing her very plainly say that she was going to Orangeburg, I determined to ask her about the town and its hotel accommodations.

"Yes, I live there," she said.

"Is there a hotel in the town, or any place at which a person can stop?"

"O yes, there 's a hotel," she said; and after a pause, she added, "but it 's hardly such a place as a gentleman would choose, I think."

She spoke pleasantly enough, and, having answered my question, might have dropped the conversation; instead of which, she went on to say that persons who had occasion to stop in town for some days frequently took a room at a private house, and were much better suited than at the hotel.

I did the only thing I well could do, — the thing that it was perfectly natural I should do. I asked her if she could mention one or two private houses at which I might ask for accommodations, if the hotel proved unendurable.

I fully expected that she would say her mother sometimes accommodated gentlemen; and I may as well own that I had determined what reply I should make to that announcement.

Instead, however, she turned in her seat so as to face me, and said, with considerable vim, " Are you a Yankee ? "

The question surprised me; and I simply answered, " From the North."

" By what right do you presume to speak to me, sir ? " she asked, in a clear and snapping tone, that caught the ears and eyes of most of the passengers.

The strangeness of the question, no less than the remarkable change in her manner, coupled with the fact that I knew myself to be under the observation of thirty or more persons of Southern birth and feeling, embarrassed me to such degree that I could only stammer, " By the right which I supposed a gentleman always had to ask a lady a civil question."

" Well, sir, I don't choose to talk with you."

And she settled herself sharply into her seat, jerked her little body into a very upright position, and squared her shoulders in a very positive manner, — while I sat flushed and confused.

What should I do about it ? That was a question I asked myself twenty times per hour for the next thirty miles. I was seriously inclined to apologize, though I hardly knew for what; but did n't, for I feared the little Rebel might snub me again, if I gave her an opportunity. In front of her sat a young man who had been a captain in the Rebel army. Him she soon engaged in conversation, and they cheered the slow miles with most lively chat. Surely, thought I, this is beginning the three months' journey unfortunately. I could have borne her indignation quite easily; but each individual in the car soon made me aware that my Yankee baseness was well known and thoroughly appreciated.

The forenoon wore away, and the crazy old engine dragged itself along. Little Miss was vivacious and entertaining; the ex-officer was evidently in a cheerful frame of mind; I sat alternating between repentance and indignation. Finally the whistle sounded for Branchville.

Missy rose in her seat, shook out her skirts, drew on her small thread glove, turned to me, — mind you, not to the ex-officer, but to me, — and asked me if I would be good enough to hand out her basket for her.

Here was another surprise. Queer creatures, these little Rebels, said I to myself, as I followed her out, — carrying the not heavy basket. She did n't stop when we reached the platform of the station-house, but walked on towards its upper end; and I followed, demurely, but wonderingly. Fifteen or twenty yards away from the car, she suddenly stopped, and turned quickly upon me with " Thank you ; I want to apologize to you ; I was rude."

And here was the greatest surprise of all ! It caught me in confusion; but I managed to say something to the effect that perhaps I was too forward in asking the question I did.

" No, you were not. It was right that you should ask it, and I was rude to answer you so uncivilly. But you caught me at a disadvantage ; I had n't spoken to a Federal since Sumter was taken."

" Well, it did n't hurt you very much, did it ? " said I. Whereat she laughed and I laughed, and then the engine whistled.

" I 'm going to stop here a day or two," she remarked ; and then, " You 'll shake hands, won't you ? " as I started for the car. So we shook hands, and I left her standing on the platform.

I had n't learned much about my chances for comfort in Orangeburg, however.

We got here at three o'clock in the afternoon. I was determined to stop, let the accommodations be what they would, and firmly said "No" when the stage agent at the depot urged me to take a seat for Columbia.

There were five passengers with baggage. Twenty-five negroes crowded around us, and troubled the hot air with harsh clamor. "Give yer baggage here, sir." "Luf dis yer nig tote yer plun'er, Mass'r." "Have yer balese toted to de hotel, sah?" "Tuk a hack up town, Mass'r?"

There was the man I wanted. He proved to be a strapping boy of thirteen or fourteen, who tossed my valise to the top of his head and strode off with both hands swinging.

I found the "hack" to be a rickety old short-boxed spring wagon, with two rough board seats, on the back one of which was a worn-out cushion, over both being a canvas supported on sticks nailed to each corner of the box. This establishment was drawn by a scrawny lame mule, and we were seventeen minutes in accomplishing the half-mile, which the boy called it, up to the hotel.

I was a little distrustful about the hotel; and learning from the driver that boarders were sometimes taken at another house, I stopped there and asked the white girl of fifteen, whom I found on the piazza, if they could give me meals and lodgings for about three days. She thought they could, but would call her mother. So much of the house and grounds as I could see presented an inviting appearance, and I indulged in visions of a pleasant chamber and many dreamy hours on the broad piazza. Presently "mother" appeared. She was a plump woman of thirty-three, perhaps.

"Yes, sir, we have a couple of rooms, and we sometimes take transient boarders," said she, answering the question I put to the girl.

"I am stopping three or four days in town, and had much rather be at a pleasant private house than at the hotel," I said.

"Are you a Yankee or a Southerner?"

"O, a Yankee, of course," I answered, smiling, though I saw breakers ahead.

"No Yankee stops here! Good day, sir!" And she turned and walked into the house.

The negro boy, who stood with my valise on his head, volunteered the remark, "Haf to go to de hotel, sah"; and I followed him back to the "hack."

At the "hotel" was a negro boy washing the steps from the piazza into the basement. I told him what I wanted. He would call the Missus. She was somewhere in the lower part of the house; and after her head came into sight above the level of the floor on which I stood, she stopped and washed her hands in the dirty water with which the boy had just finished scrubbing the stairway, smoothing her hair with them and wiping them on her apron.

I made known my desires, paid my driver his charge of seventy-five cents, and was shown by Robert — him of the wash-rag and scrubbing-brush — to room No. 8, the figure being at least a foot in length and rudely done in white chalk.

The room is about fourteen feet square, has one window fronting the southeast, and is in the third story. Lath and plaster there are not, on this floor at least. The partitions are of rough unmatched pine, with strips of cloth over the larger cracks, and a cheap wall paper on the boards all round. The ceiling is also of wood, and was once painted white, but is now, like the wall paper, of a smoky yellow. The paper is much broken by the shrinkage of the boards, and large patches of it have been torn off in a dozen places. The walls and ceiling are handsomely decorated with wasp's mud nests and sooty-branched cobwebs. The bed is a dirty cotton mattress in an old-fashioned high-post bedstead. There are no sheets, and in fact nothing but a cotton-stuffed pillow and a calico spread. This establishment is the abode of a numerous and industrious colony of the Improved Order of

Red Men, to whom I nightly pay a heavy blood tribute. Beside the bed there is for furnishing of the room one cane-seat chair, a seven-by-ten looking-glass, and a three-foot-square and breast-high plain pine table, on which are a cracked wash-bowl and a handleless and noseless water-pitcher, to which I prevailed on Robert to add a cracked tumbler. In the window are six sound panes of glass, four cracked ones, and the remnants of five panes more. I suppose I should add also to the furniture several very social and handsome mice, and a healthy and lively swarm of uncommonly large mosquitoes.

The house has three stories and a basement dining-room. The first and second floors have broad piazzas on each side of the house. The first floor has four rooms, and the second and third have five each. Robert says mine is the best on the upper floor, — in which fact there is much consolation. Glimpses into the second floor rooms have not bred in me any desire to move down. In the so-called drawing-room there are three old chairs, a round and rickety centre-table, a sort of writing-desk, the wreck of a piano, and several pieces of carpet. In the dining-room are two twelve-foot plain pine tables, and twenty-three chairs of five different patterns. The table-spread of this noon was the same we had on the evening of my arrival, three days ago, and it was horribly filthy then. The dining-room itself is airy and clean. In the hall, and pasted to the wall, are a set of "rules for the hotel," twice as long and formidable as any I ever saw in any Northern house, whether first or fourth class. The hotel register, a book fully equal to the necessities of any Boston house for six months, is, with a lead pencil, handed round at the supper table each day for the reception of the names of persons who have arrived since morning.

The hotel grounds consist of a large yard, the gate of which is always open, and within which all the stray stock

B

of the town has free ramble. At the bottom of the broad
steps on the upper side of the house is a large mud-puddle,
in which dogs and hogs alternately wallow, there being at
least five of the former and nine of the latter running about.
The dogs are gaunt and wolfish, — the hogs are slab-sided,
half-grown, and very long of nose. There is in the yard
about everything one can name, except grass and cleanliness, — bits of wood and crockery, scraps of old iron, wisps
of straw and fodder, old rags, broken bottles, sticks, stones,
bones, hoofs, horns, nails, etc., etc., *ad infinitum.* The barber throws the sweepings of his shop on one side the house,
and the cook is equally free with her slops on the other side.

The "Missus" is the head of the house. She is tall and
angular, with a complexion sallow to the last degree of sallowness, eyes in which there is neither life nor hope, hair
which I am sure has not felt either comb or brush during
my stay. Her dress is a greasy calico, of the half-mourning
variety, to which she sometimes adds an apron which is n't
more repulsive only because it can't be. She is a type of
women, thank God, without counterpart in the North. She
goes about the house in a shuffling, shambling manner, with
the cry "Robert — Robert — Robert," or "'Manda — 'Manda — 'Manda," always on her tongue. There is no variety
of accent in this cry, but only one of length, as "Robert —
Ro-be-rt — R-o-b-e-r-t." During meals she stands at the
head of the table, and serves out the allowance of tea or
coffee, and sugar and milk, with an unending string of such
talk as this: "Robert, tend the hominy"; "Gal, get the
gemman's cup and sasser"; "'Manda, mind the flies";
"Goodness gracious, nigger, why don't ye pass them biled
eggs"; "Now, Robert, do see them flies"; "'Manda, look
arter them squeet pertaterses"; "Now, ye good-for-nuthin'
nigger, can't ye brush away them flies?" She complains,
in whining, listless fashion, to everybody, about the "niggers," telling how idle, shiftless, and ungrateful they are.

She has a husband, who takes special pains to inform everybody that he has n't anything to do with the hotel; and whose sole occupations, so far as I can see, are smoking, complaining about "the niggers," and doctoring a poor old blind, spavined horse.

The genius of the house is Robert, who stands on his head as well as on his feet; who is trim, pert, wide-awake; who picks out a Northern man with unerring instinct, and is always ready and prompt to serve him; but who is forever out of the way, or very busy when that cry of "Robert — Ro-be-rt — R-o-b-e-r-t" shuffles up through the house. What trick of stealing sugar he has n't learned is n't worth learning. "*She* talk about the niggers, — bah!" he exclaims, as he goes about his work.

When I was ready last evening to go to my room, I sent Robert for a light, and told him to bring me a whole candle. He came back directly and said, throwing his finger over his shoulder, "She says can't have it." I followed him into the dining-room, where she sat whining at 'Manda.

"Madam, I should like a light."

She told Robert to bring her a candle, and was about to cut off a piece two inches long.

"I should like a whole candle to-night, if you please," said I.

"Want a whole candle, sir?"

"Yes, ma'am, I 'm going to write in my room awhile this evening."

"Want a long candle? What yer goin' to write? Want all this candle?"

"Can't I have the candle?"

"The whole candle? Gemmen allers takes a short light and goes to bed right soon."

"Shall I take that candle, or shall I send Robert out to buy me one?"

"I reckon ye can havè this. I 'll send Robert up for it arter a while."

I did n't stop to argue that point, but when I reached the hall I said to Robert, "You 'll find the door locked if you come up"; to which he responded, "I sha'n't come."

The table is wretched. The tea, eggs, and waffles are the only articles even passably good. Bread and biscuit are alike sour and leaden, and all the meats are swimming in strong fat. The cook is a large and raw-boned negro-woman, who is aided by the "Missus," the boy Robert, and the girl 'Manda. I suppose Sarah cooks quite to the satisfaction of her mistress; but I doubt if it would be possible for any Northern girl, even with twenty years of training, to make of herself a cook so utterly bad as Sarah is. She certainly exhibits most remarkable ability in spoiling everything in the line of eatables.

The general management of the house, I scarcely need add, is hopelessly miserable. Everything is forever at sixes-and-sevens, and the knowledge of where anything was yesterday gives not the least indication of its present whereabouts. The establishment, not less in its several parts than in its aggregate whole, is an unclean thing. Shiftlessness has here his abode, and there is neither effort nor desire to dispossess him. And the traveller's bill is three dollars and a half per day!

I have not drawn this picture except for a purpose. I hear, already, in this Southern trip, a great deal about the superior civilization of the South. This hotel is a part of its outgrowth. Orangeburg was a place of twenty-five hundred to three thousand inhabitants. It is the county seat. Here is the State Orphan Asylum. The place is midway between Charleston and the capital. Let any one consider what is the character of the only public house in any Northern town of the same size, and similarly situated, and then the quality of this boasted Southern civilization will be apparent. Nor can it be said that the war is responsible for the condition of things here, for the house was full from the beginning, and has not suffered any loss from either army. It could not receive a week's support in any community of any State from Maine to the Rocky Mountains. Yet here it lives on and on, year after year, a witness for Southern civilization. Let us call things by their right names, — then shall we say *Southern barbarism*.

III.

THE SITUATION WITH RESPECT TO THE NEGRO.

ORANGEBURG C. H., September 9, 1865.

RECALLING how persistently the whites of this State have claimed, for twenty-five years, to be the negro's special friends, and seeing, as the traveller does, how these whites treat this poor black, one cannot help praying that he may be saved from his friends in future. Yet this cannot be. Talk never so plausibly and eloquently as any one may of colonization or deportation, the inexorable fact remains, that the negro is in South Carolina, and must remain here till God pleases to call him away. The problem involved in his future must be met on the soil of which he is native; and any attempt to solve it elsewhere than in the house of these his so-called special friends will be futile.

The work of the North, in respect to South Carolina, is twofold: the white man must be taught what the negro's rights are, and the negro must be taught to wait patiently and wisely for the full recognition of those rights in his own old home. He waited so long in the house of bondage for the birthright of freedom, that waiting is weary work for him now; yet there is nothing else for him and us, — nothing but faith, and labor, and waiting, and, finally, rest in victory.

The city negro and the country negro are as much unlike

as two races. So, too, the city white man and the country
white man differ much from each other.   The latter, however, is just what he chooses to be, while the country negro
is just what slavery and his late owners have made him.
Tell me what you will derogatory of the country negro, and
very likely I shall assent to most of the language you use.
He is very often, and perhaps generally, idle, vicious, improvident, negligent, and unfit to care well for his interests.
In himself, he is a hard, coarse, unlovely fact, and no amount
of idealizing can make him otherwise.   Yet, for all that, he
is worth quite as much as the average country white.

The negro, one may say, is made by his master.   I even
doubt if he is, in many cases, morally responsible for his
acts.   With him there is no theft when he takes small property from the white ; there is, of course, crime in the eye of
the law, but there is none in the design or consciousness of
the negro.   Has not every day of his existence taught him
that robbery is no crime ? So, too, if this uncouth freedman,
just from the plantation, falls into a passion and half kills
somebody, you will utterly fail in your effort to make him
understand that he has committed a grave crime.   Has not
his whole life been witness of just such right and lawful outrage on humanity ?   This language may indicate a bad state
of affairs ; but it points out certain conditions with respect to
the negro that must be taken into account by any one under-
taking to deal with him as a freedman.

Everybody talks about the negro, at all hours of the day,
and under all circumstances.   One might in truth say —
using the elegant language of opposition orators in Congress — that " the people have got nigger on the brain."
Let conversation begin where it will, it ends with Sambo.

I scarcely talk with any white man who fails to tell me
how anxious many of the negroes are to return to their old
homes.   In coming up from Charleston I heard of not less
than eleven in this condition, and mention has been made

to me here in Orangeburg of at least a score. The first curious circumstance is, that none of them are allowed to return; and the second is, that I can't find any of those desirous of returning. I presume I have asked over a hundred negroes here and in Charleston if they wanted to go back and live with their old masters as slaves, or if they knew any negro who did desire to return to that condition, and I have yet to find the first one who hesitates an instant in answering "No."

I spoke of this difficulty I have in finding a single negro who loved slavery better than he does freedom to an intelligent gentleman whom I met here last evening, — a member of the Rhett family. "I am surprised to hear that," said he; "but I suppose it 's because you are from the North, and the negro don't dare to tell you his real feeling." I asked if the blacks don't generally consider Northern men their friends. "O yes," he answered, "and that 's the very reason why you can't find out what they think."

They deserve better treatment than they get at our hands in Orangeburg, at least; and I am told that what I see here is a forecast of what I shall see in all parts of the State. Theoretically, and in the intent of Congress, the Freedmen's Bureau stands as the next friend of the blacks; practically, and in the custom of the country, it appears to stand too often as their next enemy. That General Saxton is their good friend does not need to be asserted. Very likely the district commissioners under him are wise and humane men, and unquestionably the general regulations for the State are meant to secure justice to the freedmen.

The trouble arises from the fact that it is impossible for the State Commissioner or his chief deputies to personally know all, or even half, their various local agents. Take the case right in hand. Head-quarters for this district are thirty miles below here; and the ranking officer of the bureau has, probably, agents in at least forty different towns, the majority of whom are doubtless lieutenants from the volunteer forces of the army. They are detailed for this duty by the military commander of the post or the district, — sometimes after consultation with the district commissioner, but quite generally without. As the post garrisons are constantly changing, there may be a new agent of the bureau once a month in each town of the district; and I need not add, that the probabilities are that half the aggregate number on duty at any given time are wholly unfit for the work intrusted to them.

Again, take the case right in hand. The acting agent here at present is a lieutenant from a New York regiment. He is detailed by the colonel commanding, and has been on duty several weeks. Yet he never has seen the district commissioner of the bureau. His duties are to examine, and approve or disapprove, all contracts between the planters and the negroes, and to hear and determine all cases of complaint or grievance arising between the negroes themselves, or between the whites and the negroes. He treats me courteously, but he has no sympathy with the poor and lowly; and his ideas of justice are of the bar-room order, — might makes right. He does n't really intend to outrage the rights of the negroes, but he has very little idea that they have any rights except such as the planters choose to give them. His position, of course, is a difficult one; and he brings to it a head more or less muddled with liquor, a rough and coarse manner, a dictatorial and impatient temper, a most remarkable ability for cursing, and a hearty contempt for "the whole d—n pack o' niggers." I speak from the observation of a good deal of time spent in and around his office.

I found Charleston full of country negroes. Whites of all classes concur in saying that there is a general impression throughout the back districts that lands are to be given the freed people on the sea-coast; and this, I am told, renders them uneasy and unreliable as plantation hands. Whites of all classes also concur in saying that they will not work.

"I lost sixteen niggers," said a Charleston gentleman; "but I don't mind it, for they were always a nuisance, and you'll find them so in less than a year." I asked, as usual, what they are now doing. Two or three of the men went into the army, one of the women had gone North as a cook, another is chambermaid on a steamer, and he found three of the men at work on one wharf the other day. " But," said I, laughing, " I thought the free negro would n't work." " O well, this is only a temporary state of affairs, and they'll all be idle before winter; and I don't look for nothing else when cold weather comes but to have them all asking me to take them back; but I sha'n't do it. I would n't give ten cents apiece for them."

Many of the private soldiers on duty here tell me that the planters generally overreach the negroes on every possible occasion; and my observation among such as I have seen in town tends to confirm this assertion to a considerable extent.

Coming up in the ears from Charleston I had for seat-mate part of the way one of the delegates to the Convention which meets at Columbia next week. He was a very courteous and agreeable gentleman, past middle age, and late the owner of twenty-two negroes. He was good enough to instruct me at some length in respect to the character of the negro. " You Northern people are utterly mistaken in sup-posing anything can be done with these negroes in a free condition. They can't be governed except with the whip. Now on my plantation there was n't much whipping, say once a fortnight; but the negroes knew they would be whipped if they did n't behave themselves, and the fear of the lash kept them in good order." He went on to ex-plain what a good home they always had; laying stress on the fact that they never were obliged to think for themselves,

2

but were always tenderly cared for, both in health and sickness; "and yet these niggers all left me the day after the Federals got into Charleston!" I asked where they now are; and he replied that he had n't seen anybody but his old cook since they ran away; but he believed they were all at work except two, who had died. Yet I am told constantly that these ungrateful wretches, the negroes, cannot possibly live as free people.

Yesterday morning while I sat in the office of the agent of the Freedmen's Bureau there came in, with a score of other men, a planter living in this district, but some sixteen miles from town. He had a woful tale of an assault upon himself by one of his "niggers," — "a boy who I broughten up, and who 's allers had a good home down ter my place." While the boy was coming in from the street the man turned to me and explained, " It never don't do no good to show favor to a nigger, for they 's the most ongratefullest creeturs in the world." The dreadful assault consisted in throwing a hatchet at the white man by one of a crowd of negroes who were having a dispute among themselves, and suddenly discovered, in the early evening, somebody sneaking along by the fence. The boy said it was n't a hatchet, but a bit of brick; and added, that the man was so far away that no one could tell whether he was white or black, and that he did n't throw the brick till after he called out and told the man to go away. I followed the negro out after he had received his lecture from the officer, and had some talk with him. " D—n him," said he, referring to his employer, " he never done nufin all his d—n life but beat me and kick me and knock me down; an' I hopes I git eben with him some day."

Riding with an ex-Confederate major, we stopped at a house for water. The owner of the property, which was a very handsome one, was absent; and it was in charge of a dozen negroes, former slaves of the proprietor.

" Now here," said the late officer, " here is a place where

the negroes always had the pleasantest sort of a home, — everything to eat and drink and wear, and a most kind master and mistress."

Pompey, aged about twelve, came to bring us the water.

" Pompey," said the Major, " Pompey, how do you like your freedom ? "

He hung his head, and answered, " Dun know, mawssa."

" O, well, speak right out; don't be afraid; tell us just how it is now," said he again.

Whereupon Pompey: " Likes to be free man, sah; but we 's all workin' on yer like we did afore."

" That 's right, Pompey," said I; " keep on working; don't be a lazy boy."

" It won't do," said the Major; " he 'll grow up idle and impudent and worthless, like all the rest."

" No, sah," answered Pompey, " I 's free nigger now, and I 's goin' to work."

There is much talk among the country people about a rising of the blacks. A planter who stopped here last night, and who lives twelve miles to the west, told me that it was believed in his neighborhood that they had guns and pistols hid in the timber, and were organizing to use them. His ideas were not very clear about the matter ; but he appeared to think they would make serious trouble after the crops are gathered. Another man, living in Union district, told the company, with evident pleasure, that they 'd been able to keep control of the niggers up to his section till 'bout three weeks ago ; he 'lowed thar 'd bin some lickin', but no more 'n was good fur the fellows. Now the Federals had come in, and the negroes were in a state of glad excitement, and everybody feared there would be bloody business right away.

A thing that much shocks me is the prevalent indifference to the negro's fate and life. It is a sad, but solemn fact, that three fourths of the native whites consider him a nuisance, and would gladly be rid of his presence, even at the expense of his existence. And this in face of the fact that all the planters are complaining about the insufficiency of labor. Thus, in Charleston, a merchant told me, with relishing detail, a story to the effect that, soon after the promulgation of the order against wearing Confederate buttons, a negro soldier doing duty in the city halted a young man, informed him of the regulations, and told him that if he was seen on the street again wearing the obnoxious buttons, he would probably be arrested; whereupon the hopeful scion of the Charleston aristocracy whipped out a large knife, seized the negro by the beard, and cut his throat. The soldier died in about a week; but nothing had been done with the man who killed him. So, too, a man who seems to be acting as stage-agent here says "a d——d big black buck nigger" was shot near Lewisville about three weeks ago; and the citizens all shield the man who shot him, and sanction his course. All the talk of men about the hotel indicates that it is held to be an evidence of smartness, rather than otherwise, to kill a freedman; and I have not found a man here who seems to believe that it is a sin against Divine law.

IV.

SCENES IN THE TRACK OF SHERMAN'S ARMY.

COLUMBIA, September 12, 1865.

THE war was a long time in reaching South Carolina, but there was vengeance in its very breath when it did come, — wrath that blasted everything it touched, and set Desolation on high as the genius of the State. "A brave people never before made such a mistake as we did," said a little woman who sat near me in the cars while coming up from Charleston; "it mortifies me now, every day I live, to think how well the Yankees fought. We had no idea they could fight half so well." In such humiliation as hers is half the lesson of the war for South Carolina.

Columbia is in the heart of Destruction. Being outside of it, you can only get in through one of the roads built by Ruin. Being in it, you can only get out over one of the roads walled by Desolation. You go north thirty-two miles, and find the end of one railroad; southeast thirty miles, and find the end of another; south forty-five miles, and find the end of a third; southwest fifty miles, and meet a fourth; and northwest twenty-nine miles, and find the end of still another. Sherman came in here, the papers used to say, to break up the railroad system of the seaboard States of the Confederacy. He did his work so thoroughly that half a dozen years will nothing more than begin to repair the damage, even in this regard.

The railway section of the route from Charleston lies mostly either in a pine barren or a pine swamp, though after passing Branchville we came into a more open and rolling country, with occasional signs of life. Yet we could not anywhere, after we left the immediate vicinity of the city, see much indication of either work or existence. The trim and handsome railway stations of the North, the little towns strung like beads on an iron string, are things unknown here. In the whole seventy-seven miles there are but two towns that make any impression on the mind of a stranger, — Summerville and George's, — and even these are small and unimportant places. Elsewhere we stopped, as it appeared, whenever the train-men pleased, — the "station" sometimes existing only in the consciousness of the engineer and conductor.

Branchville was, however, noticeable because of the place it once occupied in Northern anxiety. There is where Sherman was to meet his fate. Have we forgotten how the Richmond papers of early February spoke? They were not at liberty to mention the preparations, etc., but they might say, etc., and the Yankee nation would have sore cause to remember Branchville, etc. Unfortunately, however, Sherman flanked Branchville, just as he had other places of thrice its importance, and it missed the coveted renown. It is nothing but a railroad junction in a pine barren, with a long, low station-house and cotton warehouse, and three or four miserable dwellings.

I found the railroad in better condition than I supposed that I should. The rails are very much worn, but the road-bed is in fair order for nearly the entire distance. The freight-cars seemed in passably good repair; but the passenger-coaches were the most wretched I ever saw, — old, filthy, and rickety. On our train was one new feature, — a colored man and his wife, whose duty it was to wait on the passengers.

I came up from Orangeburg, forty-five miles, by "stage," to wit, an old spring-covered market-wagon, drawn by three jaded horses and driven by Sam, freedman, late slave, — of the race not able to take care of themselves, yet caring, week in and week out, for the horses and interests of his employer as faithfully and intelligently as any white man could. There were six of us passengers, and we paid ten dollars each passage-money. We left Orangeburg at four, P. M.; drove eight miles; supped by the roadside; drove all night; lunched at sunrise by a muddy brook; and reached Columbia and breakfast at eleven, A. M., thankful that we had not broken down at midnight, and had met only two or three minor accidents. I am quite sure there are more pleasant ways of travelling than by "stage" in South Carolina at the present time. Thirty-two miles of the forty-five lie in such heavy and deep sand that no team can travel faster than at a moderate walk. For the other thirteen miles the road is

something better, though even there it is the exception and
not the rule to trot your mules. The river here was formerly spanned by an elegant and expensive bridge, but the
foolish Rebels burned it; and the crossing of the Congaree
is now effected in a ferry, the style and management of
which would disgrace any backwoods settlement of the West.

The " Shermanizing process," as an ex-Rebel colonel
jocosely called it, has been complete everywhere. To
simply say that the people hate that officer is to put a fact
in very mild terms. Butler is, in their estimation, an angel
when compared to Sherman. They charge the latter with
the entire work and waste of the war so far as their State
is concerned, — even claim that Columbia was burned by
his express orders. They pronounce his spirit "infernal,"
"atrocious," "cowardly," "devilish," and would unquestionably use stronger terms if they were to be had. I have been
told by dozens of men that he could n't walk up the main
street of Columbia in the daytime without being shot; and
three different gentlemen, residing in different parts of the
State, declare that Wade Hampton expresses a purpose to
shoot him at sight whenever and wherever he meets him.
Whatever else the South Carolina mothers forget, they do
not seem likely in this generation to forget to teach their
children to hate Sherman.

Certain bent rails are the first thing one sees to indicate
the advent of his army. They are at Branchville. I looked
at them with curious interest. "It passes my comprehension
to tell what became of our railroads," said a travelling acquaintance ; "one week we had passably good roads, on
which we could reach almost any part of the State, and the
next week they were all gone, — not simply broken up, but
gone; some of the material was burned, I know, but miles
and miles of iron have actually disappeared, gone out of existence." Branchville, as I have already said, was flanked,
and the army did not take it in the line of march, but some
of the boys paid it a visit.

At Orangeburg there is ample proof that the army passed that way. About one third of the town was burned. I found much dispute as to the origin of the fire; and while certain fellows of the baser sort loudly assert that it was the work of the Yankee, others of the better class express the belief that it originated with a resident who was angry at the Confederate officers. Thereabouts one finds plenty of railroad iron so bent and twisted that it can never again be used. The genius which our soldiers displayed in destroying railroads seems remarkable. How effectually they did it, when they undertook the work in earnest, no pen can make plain. " We could do something in that line, we thought," said an ex-Confederate captain, " but we were ashamed of ourselves when we saw how your men could do it."

We rode over the road where the army marched. Now and then we found solitary chimneys, but, on the whole, comparatively few houses were burned, and some of those were fired, it is believed, by persons from the Rebel army or from the neighboring locality. The fences did not escape so well, and most of the planters have had these to build during the summer. This was particularly the case near Columbia. Scarcely a tenth of that destroyed appears to have been rebuilt, and thousands of acres of land of much richness lie open as a common.

There is a great scarcity of stock of all kinds. What was left by the Rebel conscription officers was freely appropriated by Sherman's army, and the people really find considerable difficulty not less in living than in travelling. Milk, formerly an article much in use, can only be had now in limited quantities: even at the hotels we have more meals without than with it. There are more mules than horses, apparently; and the animals, whether mules or horses, are all in ill condition and give evidence of severe overwork.

Columbia was doubtless once the gem of the State. It is

as regularly laid out as a checker-board, — the squares
being of uniform length and breadth and the streets of uniform width.   What with its broad streets, beautiful shade-
trees, handsome lawns, extensive gardens, luxuriant shrubbery, and wealth of flowers, I can easily see that it must
have been a delightful place of residence.   No South-Carolinian with whom I have spoken hesitates an instant in
declaring that it was the most beautiful city on the continent; and, as already mentioned, they charge its destruction
directly to General Sherman.

It is now a wilderness of ruins.   Its heart is but a mass
of blackened chimneys and crumbling walls.   Two thirds
of the buildings in the place were burned, including, without exception, everything in the business portion.   Not a
store, office, or shop escaped; and for a distance of three
fourths of a mile on each of twelve streets there was not a
building left.   " They destroyed everything which the most
infernal Yankee ingenuity could devise means to destroy,"
said one gentleman to me; " hands, hearts, fire, gunpowder,
and behind everything the spirit of hell, were the agencies
which they used."   I asked him if he was n't stating the
case rather strongly; and he replied that he would make
it stronger if he could.   The residence portion generally
escaped conflagration, though houses were burned in all
sections except the extreme northeastern.

Every public building was destroyed, except the new
and unfinished state-house.   This is situated on the summit
of tableland whereon the city is built, and commands
an extensive view of the surrounding country, and must
have been the first building seen by the victorious and
on-marching Union army.   From the summit of the ridge,
on the opposite side of the river, a mile and a half
away, a few shells were thrown at it, apparently by way
of reminder, three or four of which struck it, without
doing any particular damage.   With this exception, it was

unharmed, though the workshops, in which were stored
many of the architraves, caps, sills, &c., were burned, — the
fire, of course, destroying or seriously damaging their con-
tents. The poverty of this people is so deep that there is
no probability that it can be finished, according to the original design, during this generation at least.

The ruin here is neither half so eloquent nor touching
as that at Charleston. This is but the work of flame, and
might have mostly been brought about in time of peace.
Those ghostly and crumbling walls and those long-deserted
and grass-grown streets show the prostration of a community, — such prostration as only war could bring.

I find a commendable spirit of enterprise, though, of
course, it is enterprise on a small scale, and the enterprise
of stern necessity. The work of clearing away the ruins is
going on, not rapidly or extensively, to be sure, but something is doing, and many small houses of the cheaper sort
are going up. Yet, at the best, this generation will not
ever again see the beautiful city of a year ago. Old men
and despondent men say it can never be rebuilt. "We shall
have to give it up to the Yankees, I reckon," said one of two
gentlemen conversing near me this morning. "Give it up!"
said the other; "they've already moved in and taken possession without asking our leave." I guess the remark is
true. I find some Northern men already here, and I hear
of more who are coming.

Of course there is very little business doing yet. The
city is, as before said, in the heart of the devastated land.
I judge that twenty thousand dollars would buy the whole
stock of dry goods, groceries, clothing, &c. in store. The
small change of the place is made in shinplasters, printed
on most miserable paper, and issued by the various business
men, "redeemable in United States currency when presented
in sums of two dollars and upwards." "Greenbacks" and
national currency notes pass without question in the city,

but are looked upon with suspicion by the country people. " Having lost a great deal by one sort of paper, we propose to be careful now," they say. Occasionally one sees a State bank-note, but they pass for only from twenty-five to sixty or sixty-five cents on the dollar. There is none of the Confederate money in circulation ; though I judge, from what I hear, that considerable quantities of it are hoarded up in the belief that things will somehow take such a turn as to one day give it value.

There is a certain air of easy dignity observable among the people that I have not found elsewhere in the State, — not even in Charleston itself. Something of this is probably due to the fact that the capital is located here ; but more of it, probably, to the existence of Columbia College. It was before the war a very flourishing institution, but has been closed during the last three years. The old but roomy buildings are in part occupied by the military authorities, partly by the professors and officers of the college, and are partly closed. No indication is given as to the time of re-opening the school. It is said by residents that the city contained some of the finest private libraries in the South ; but these, with one or two exceptions, were burned.

The women who consider it essential to salvation to snub or insult Union officers and soldiers at every possible opportunity do not seem as numerous as they appeared to be in Charleston ; and indeed marriages between soldiers and women of the middle class are not by any means the most uncommon things in the world ; while I notice, in a quiet, unobservant manner, as even the dullest traveller may, that at least several very elegant ladies do not seem at all averse to the attentions of the gentlemen of shoulder-straps. Can these things be, and not overcome the latent fire of Rebellion ?

In coming up from Charleston I learned a great many things, by conversation with persons, and by listening to conversation between people; and these are some of the more important facts thus learned.

Thus, one man insisted with much vehemence that cotton is king, and that a resolution on the part of the South not to sell any for a year would bring the North upon its knees.

Another man was very confident that the North depends entirely upon the cotton trade for a living, and that a failure to get at least one million bales before spring will bring a tremendous financial crash.

Another gravely asserted that a state of anarchy prevails in the entire North; that the returned soldiers are plundering and butchering indiscriminately; and that there has recently been a most bloody riot in Boston.

Another, and a man of much apparent intelligence, informed me that the negroes have an organized military force in all sections of the State, and are almost certain to rise and massacre the whites about Christmas time.

Another had heard, and sincerely believed, that General Grant's brother-in-law is an Indian, and is on his staff, and that the President had issued an order permitting the General's son to marry a mulatto girl whom he found in Virginia.

A woman, evidently from the country districts, stated that there had been a rising of the negroes in Maryland; that a great many whites had been killed; and that some considerable portion of Baltimore and many of the plantations had been seized by the negroes.

And, finally, an elderly gentleman who represented himself as a cotton factor, declared that there would be a terrible civil war in the North within two years; that England would compel the repudiation of our National debt and the assumption of the Confederate debt for her guaranty of protection.

The people of the central part of the State are poor, wretchedly poor; for the war not only swept away their stock and the material resources of their plantations, but also all values, — all money, stocks, and bonds, — and generally left nothing that can be sold for money but cotton, and only a small proportion of the landholders have any of that. Therefore there is for most of them nothing but the beginning anew of life, on the strictest personal economy and a small amount of money borrowed in the city. It would be a benefit of hundreds of millions of dollars if the North could be made to practise half the economy which poverty forces upon this people.

They are full of ignorance and prejudices, but they want peace and quiet, and seem not badly disposed toward the general government. Individuals there are who rant and rave and feed on fire as in the old days, but another war is a thing beyond the possibilities of time. So far as any fear of that is concerned we may treat this State as we please, — hold it as a conquered province or restore it at once to full communion in the sisterhood of States. The war spirit is gone, and no fury can re-enliven it.

The spirit of oppression still exists, however, and military authority cannot be withdrawn till the relation between employer and employed is put upon a better basis. On the one hand, the negro in the country districts must be made to understand, what he has already been taught in the city, that freedom does not mean idleness. On the other hand, the late master should specially be made to understand that the spirit of slavery must go to the grave with the thing itself. It will not be an easy work to teach either class its chief lesson. We must have patience, — patience, and faith that neither faints nor falters.

V.

ORGANIZATION OF THE SOUTH CAROLINA CONVENTION.

COLUMBIA, September 13, 1865.

IN obedience to the proclamation of Provisional Governor Perry, the delegates of the people of South Carolina assembled at noon to-day in State Convention for the purpose of repealing the ordinance of secession and remodelling the State Constitution. The Convention met in the Baptist Church, in which the Secession Convention of 1860 originally assembled; though that, after two sessions, adjourned to Charleston, where the ordinance of secession was passed. That Convention numbered 168 members. This has but 124, — that is, the proclamation fixes this as the number. In point of fact, however, the number present will not probably exceed 115; for it is known that three parishes held no elections, while Bishop Lynch, of Charleston, is in Europe, and Wade Hampton is not expected here. There were present to-day 101 delegates.

Five parishes are entirely unrepresented. There were two or three precincts in each of three districts where, so far as can be learned, there was no voting; but there is not even a pretence on the part of anybody that there was anywhere in the State any interference with, or restraint upon, the elections by the military. The Convention is the free choice of the people. In one district, Anderson, the various candidates were called upon to show their hands; elsewhere the canvass passed off without speech-making, and only the four delegates from that district — "district" answering to "county" in the North — are bound by any pledges.

Four at least of the delegates have national reputation, — James L. Orr, late Federal representative, ex-Rebel colonel, and ex-Confederate senator; F. W. Pickens, late Federal

representative, and the first Secession governor; Alfred
Huger, postmaster at Charleston for the last twenty-five
years; and Samuel McGowan, late major-general in the
Rebel army, and one of the bravest officers this State gave
the Confederacy. One delegate, James Farrow, was four
years a member of the Rebel Congress. Twelve, namely,
David L. Wardlaw and Thomas Thomson of Abbeville
District, James L. Orr of Anderson, J. J. Brabham of Barnwell, John A. Inglis and Henry McIver of Chesterfield,
James Conner and J. Du Pre of Charleston, J. P. Richard-
son of Clarendon, R. G. M. Dunovant of Edgefield, William
R. Robertson of Fairfield, and John W. Carlisle of Spartanburg, were also delegates in the Secession Convention.

The people have cut loose from many of their old leaders,
and others of that class have found their graves since the
war began; but there are perhaps a score of delegates whose
faces are more or less familiar to persons who have attended
the sessions of the South Carolina General Assembly any
time within a dozen or fifteen years. Of those who have
some time been United States officers other than postmaster
there are, I believe, four. Of those who were officers in the
Rebel army there are not less than twenty-five or thirty, including at least four generals and six colonels. The half-
dozen fellows — of the blunt and blotchy nose, beefy and
bloated face, shining and swallow-tailed coat — who always
attend conventions as delegates are here, and occupy the
chief seats. So are also here the half-dozen country justices
of the peace, no less knowing than usual, and fruitful with
platitudes and resolutions.

For the rest, three fourths of the delegates have titles, —
captain, major, colonel, judge. It is the fashion of the South,
as of the West, I suppose. There are a dozen young men,
and about the same number of very old men; but otherwise
they range mostly from forty-five to fifty-five years of age.
Gray and grayish heads are numerous. It is n't by any

means a prepossessing body.   The average Southern head
does n't show near as much intellectual force and vigor as
the average Northern head; and the beauty of the South
is solely in the faces of its young women, — half of it at
least in the faces of its mulatto and quadroon girls.   A few
of the delegates are clad wholly, and very many of them
partly, in homespun.   Many coats show Confederate buttons, — from the necessity of poverty rather than the choice
of disloyalty, I judge.   Many of the members are rough,
ignorant country fellows, and the Convention will be managed by less than a score of delegates.   The difference between the two classes of delegates — those who lead and
those who are led — is much greater than could exist in any
Northern body of the same numbers; not that the one class
is any way superior to the best class of a Northern State, but
that the other class is almost immeasurably inferior.   Half
these men are so deficient in capacity and knowledge that
scarcely one of them could by any possibility get into a New
England convention.

    That, in the stress of war, South Carolina should implore
to be made a colony of Great Britain does not now seem
half so strange to me as it did nine months ago.   Her government was republican in name, but not in fact; while the
whole under-current of her society set toward monarchical
institutions.   Everybody, even now, dreads popular elections; dozens of delegates have said to me that it is n't well
to allow the people to elect their own rulers; and this Convention will no more than give the election of governor,
lieutenant-governor, representatives, members of the General
Assembly, and Presidential electors, to the people, leaving
the great host of other officers to the appointment of the
Governor or the election of the Legislature.   Many of these
delegates were elected, not because they represented the
will of the parish or district, but because they represented
the will of some great family.   It was the English system

reproduced here, with scarcely a variation. A dozen or
more boast of their twenty years in the Legislature. It
was not a republican form of government; but, more than
that, it was not, is not, and will not soon be, a republican
community. "It will not do," say the leaders, — men who,
personally, are easy, agreeable, and abundant in courtesies
to the stranger, — "it will not do to put power in the hands
of the common people." Two delegates have said to me at
different times, "It was a great mistake when we passed our
free-suffrage law."

The delegates were called to order by Judge Robertson
of Fairfield District, on whose motion Franklin J. Moses,
of Sumter District, was made temporary chairman. Judge
Robertson was one of the members of the Convention of
1860. Mr. Moses is of Hebrew descent, and has been a
member of the State Senate for over twenty years.

The Convention at once proceeded to business, without
any remarks from the chairman. Two gentlemen were
appointed temporary secretaries, and the delegates then
presented their credentials and signed the roll of the Convention; after which about a dozen who had not taken the
amnesty oath advanced to the space in front of the platform
and were sworn thereto. They were, without an exception,
men whose appearance marked them as from the back
country.

The election of a permanent President was called; and
leave being given, several gentlemen were nominated.

Hon. C. M. Dudley, of Marlboro District, who has been
known from the beginning as a Union man, though he took
but little part in public affairs, was presented by James L.
Orr. The Charleston delegation nominated Hon. David L.
Wardlaw, of Abbeville District, who was originally opposed
to secession, but acquiesced in the action of the State. Mr.
T. M. Dawkins, a delegate from Union District, was also
nominated, but rose and asked his friends not to use his

name.   Wade Hampton, of cavalry fame, who is one of the
Columbia delegates, was suggested; but before the voting began, Mr. Huger, of Charleston, and postmaster there during
Buchanan's administration, inquired if General Hampton
was nominated by permission; adding, that his veneration
for him was such that he could not consent to seeing his
name put up unless by his express desire.   That produced
its withdrawal.   He has not been in the city since the Convention was called.   The contest was, therefore, narrowed
down to one between Mr. Dudley and Mr. Wardlaw, both
of them men of unexceptionable private character.   The
first ballot was Wardlaw, 42; Dudley, 36; Dawkins, 12;
Hampton, 5; Scattering, 5.   The second call gave Wardlaw, 55; Dudley, 35; Dawkins, 9; and blank, 1.   Judge
Wardlaw was thereupon declared elected.

He is a small and kindly mannered gentleman, well along
in years, and one of the judges of the Court of Sessions
and Common Pleas.   He has served many years in the
General Assembly, and has often been elected speaker of
the lower House.   He was one of the Union men of the
fall of 1860, accepted the decree of the State, was a delegate in the Secession Convention and chairman of the Committee on Revision of the Constitution.   His home is in
the northwestern part of the State, beyond the route of
Sherman's army.   Delegates say there is no particular sig-
nification in his election over either of the other candidates.
His remarks on taking his seat were very brief, and also
without any special significance.   He hoped the Convention
would soon restore the State to the Union; and urged the
delegates to do their duty in sincere and earnest spirit, that
Peace and her blessings might once more abide in the whole
land.

It seems that the fire-eaters are not yet all dead; for as
soon as a committee had been appointed to wait on the Governor and tell him the Convention was ready for business,

Mr. A. P. Aldrich, a delegate from the district of Barn-well, in the central part of the State, and in which there was a slave population of 17,400 to a white population of 12,000, offered the following resolution, which he asked might be printed, and made the special order for to-morrow: —

Resolved, That, under the present extraordinary circumstances, it is both wise and politic to accept the condition in which we are placed; to endure patiently the evils which we cannot avert or correct; and to await calmly the time and opportunity to effect our deliverance from unconstitutional rule.

In this resolution there is, of course, the very essence of Rebellion. More than one delegate saw the point at the first reading by Mr. Aldrich himself, and when it had been re-read by the President, a sharp running debate of half or three quarters of an hour took place, in which the mover was opposed to four or five of the ablest men in the Convention.

Mr. Dudley protested briefly against the passage or print-ing of any such resolution, and moved that it be laid on the table.

Mr. Aldrich responded, that he did not ask debate now, but would be prepared to defend the resolution to-morrow.

Judge Frost, of Charleston, also expressed the idea that the resolution was very objectionable. He believed it indi-cated a spirit at war with the best interests of the State, and repugnant to the feelings of the great body of her citizens.

Ex-Governor Pickens tersely said, in a very feeling man-ner: "It does n't become South Carolina to vapor or swell or strut or brag or bluster or threat or swagger; she points to her burned cities, her desolate plantations, her mourning hearths, her unnumbered graves, her widows and her or-phans, her own torn and bleeding body, — this, she says, is the work of war; and she bids us bind up her wounds and pour in the oil of peace, — bids us cover her great naked-ness; and we must do it, even if it needs that in so doing we go backwards!"

Mr. Aldrich replied, that he was not satisfied with the condition of things; that there had always been in the country an unconstitutional Republican party and a constitutional Democratic party; that the South had always acted with the latter, and that her hope and salvation lies only in an immediate union with the Democratic party of the North; that the State is now ground under the iron heel of a military despotism, repugnant alike to her people and the spirit of the Constitution; that for his part, he would not submit without an indignant protest; that he hoped for the speedy overthrow of the party now in power; and that he meant just what the resolution says, — to be quiet till we are strong enough, through the aid of the Democratic party of the North, to get a constitutional government.

Mr. McGowan, of Abbeville District, late major-general in the Confederate service, and bearing the marks of several wounds, denounced the resolution in a brief speech of thrilling eloquence, which brought hearty applause from the delegates and the galleries. " I protest with all the earnestness of my nature against this resolution. It is not true that South Carolina carries a dagger underneath her vestments; not true that she stands with obedient words on her lips and disloyal spirit in her heart. The work she begins to-day she begins in good faith. She was the first to secede, and she fought what she believed to be the good fight with all her energies of heart and head and hand and material resources. Whatever may have been charged against her, no one has ever dared charge her with double-dealing. Her word is her bond. She is so poor that it is no figure of speech to say she has lost everything but honor. Pass this resolution, and you rob her of her honor, and bow in the dust the head of every one of her true sons. She has seen enough of war; in God's name I demand that she shall not be made to appear as if she still coveted fire and sword."

The Aldrich resolution went to the table with only four dissenting voices, being refused even the poor privilege of going to the printer or to a committee.

Some debate followed on the question of rules for the Convention, in which a member having suggested that the rules of the Convention of 1860 were specially adapted for the government of such bodies, and might therefore be adopted for use now, Mr. Orr pointedly remarked that he thought as little reference as possible to that Convention would be desirable. A committee was therefore appointed to prepare rules, and the Convention then adjourned.

COLUMBIA, September 14, 1865.

The Provisional Governor sent in his message to the Convention at noon. It was read by his son, who is one of the delegates, and its reading occupied about twenty-five minutes. What he has to say on the subjects of slavery and negro suffrage appears in the following paragraphs : —

" Under the war-making power, the military authorities of the United States have abolished slavery in all of the seceding States. The oath you have solemnly taken to ' abide by and faithfully support all laws and proclamations which have been made during the existing Rebellion, with reference to the emancipation of slaves,' requires you, in good faith, to abolish slavery in your new or amended Constitution. The express terms on which your pardons have issued stipulate that you shall never again own or employ slave labor. Moreover, it is impossible for South Carolina ever to regain her civil rights and be restored to the Union till she voluntarily abolishes slavery, and declares, by an organic law, that neither ' slavery nor involuntary servitude, except as a punishment for crime, whereof the party shall have been duly convicted,' shall ever again exist within the limits of the State. Until this is done we shall be kept under military rule.

" The radical Republican party North are looking with great interest to the action of the Southern States in reference to negro suffrage ; and whilst they admit that a man should be able to read and write and have a property qualification in order to vote, yet they contend that there should be no distinction between voters on account of color. They forget that this is a white man's government, and intended for white men only; and that the Supreme Court of the United States has decided that the negro is not an American citizen under the Federal Constitution. To extend universal suffrage to the 'freedmen' in their present ignorant and degraded condition would be little less than folly and madness. It would be giving to the man of wealth and large landed possessions in the State a most undue influence in all elections. He would be enabled to march to the polls with his two or three hundred 'freedmen' as *employés*, voting as he directed, and control all elections. The poor white men in the election districts would have no influence, or their influence would be overpowered by one man of large landed estate. That each and every State of the Union has the unquestioned right of deciding for herself who shall exercise the right of suffrage is beyond all dispute. You will settle this grave question as the interest and honor of the State demand."

After the reading of the message, the organization of the Convention was completed by disposing of the only contested-seat case. It was that of St. Luke's parish, which includes Hilton Head Island. It appears that Mr. David McGregor received the vote of one precinct, the voters, eighty-two in number, being mostly like himself, of Northern birth, but resident on the island for three or four years, and legally qualified under the laws of the State as electors. Mr. L. F. Youmans received seventy-five votes, — the aggregate of the three other precincts in the parish. The island people were unable to learn the names of the regular managers of elections, or, in fact, that the other precincts of the parish intended voting; and after much fruitless effort to find the proper authorities to receive the poll, they held a meeting and appointed their own managers. Mr. McGregor brought the certificate of these managers, — Mr. Youmans that of the regular managers. The case was referred to a special committee of three, who reported in favor of Mr. Youmans, on

the ground that he alone held the proper certificate of election. The case was decided on its merits, without regard
to the fact that Mr. McGregor is a Northern man; and he
expresses himself fully satisfied with the decision.

<hr />

VI.

THE LEADERS OF THE CONVENTION AND THE REPEAL
OF THE SECESSION ORDINANCE.

COLUMBIA, September 16, 1865.

IN Charleston and on the route hither I several times
asked what would be the probable length of the State
Convention, and was generally answered, "Not over a week,
at most." I even found some gentlemen who thought it
could finish its work in four days. The four days are gone,
and the work is but fairly begun.

"It is the reproach of South Carolina abroad that her
Constitution is less popular and republican in its provisions
than that of any other State in the Union," says Provisional
Governor Perry in his message to the Convention. If the
sea-coast members could generally have their way this Constitution would scarcely be popularized in the least. The
Convention could easily have done what they desired should
be done in even less than four days. The upper-country
members, however, have from the first said that no one need
look for an adjournment under two weeks, unless the coast
delegates gave them their way without much debate.

In fact there is as much difference of sentiment between
the two classes of delegates as though one class came from
this State and the other from Indiana. There has been a
conflict going on between the two sections of the State for
thirty years, which rages now with the more vigor because

outside difficulties have compelled unity of action for the
past five years. It grows mainly out of what is technically
called the parish system of representation, whereby the legislation from the beginning of the century has practically been
controlled by the city of Charleston, and has actually been
in the hands of the members of the General Assembly from
that city and county and three other counties. Under that
system, which originated soon after the settlement of the
State, and was indorsed in the formation of the original
and all subsequent State Constitutions, half a dozen counties
on the sea-coast cast as many votes in the Legislature as the
balance of the State. In the early days of the State's existence, when nearly all the wealth and population were in
these counties, the system worked no serious injustice; but
of late years it has proved injurious to the interests of the
up-country, and has kept up an ever-increasing feud between
the two sections. Originating chiefly in this cause, there are
now a dozen different questions of State policy in respect to
which there is more or less bitterness of feeling between
the two classes of delegates. Those from the up-country
are determined that a full and fair settlement shall now
be had. "We have drawn the sword and thrown away the
scabbard," said one of them on the floor of the Convention.
"I verily believe our people will fight on it," said another to
me last evening. Of course this talk is of the die-in-the-last-
ditch sort; but it serves to show the existing feeling between
the two sections of the State.

The record of the first four days of the Convention shows
that there is a good deal of life in the body. It also proves
that the delegates are generally well disposed toward the
government. That they have fallen in love with President
Johnson or with the Union party of the North, or with those
whom everybody down here styles Yankees, no one even
pretends. They are subdued Rebels, some of them are
even conquered Rebels; but few are anything more. They

have a very wholesome fear of the government, and a very wholesome respect for the power of the North. The whole crew of pestilent fellows does not number over a dozen. There are also about the same number who go to the other extreme, and are disgustingly servile and abject. With these exceptions, the delegates are generally frank, plain-spoken men, owning that the South is beaten, desiring nothing so much as long years of peace, acquiescent in the overthrow of slavery, and mostly disposed to make the best they can of the freedman, but utterly without faith in his capacity to labor and take care of himself; anxious to be again in full fellowship in the Union, and ardently longing for the reopening of trade with the North.

The chief man in the Convention is Benjamin F. Perry, Provisional Governor of the State; not that he himself is on the list of delegates, but that his position, in the peculiar circumstances of the hour, makes his word and wish of very unusual significance. The executive office has been removed here for the time being; the rooms of the Governor at the hotel are full at all hours when the Convention is not in session; the Governor sometimes spends the whole day at the Convention; his son and private secretary is one of the delegates; it is an almost every-hour occurrence, in the debates, that the question is asked, "Is that view approved by the Provisional Governor?" or that the remark is made, "I think we had better consult the Governor first." So it may be said that he is the leader of the Convention. He is a tall, large, straight man, who carries a gold-headed cane and wears gold-bowed spectacles. Beside this, he has a very long, large nose, and a very long, large, prominent chin. He wears a wig, and has a smoothly shaven face. He looks like a man of power, and has an inoffensively self-satisfied appearance.

James L. Orr has a great deal to do with matters and things, and is at the head of one of the eight standing com-

3   D

mittees, — that on the Executive Department of the Constitution. His public life is well known. He was considered
one of the coolest-headed and soundest-hearted Union men
in the State five years ago this summer ; but, for all that,
he was one of the leading members in the Secession Convention, and in the Rebel Senate during the whole existence
of the Confederate government. Now he is one of the leading reconstructionists. Many of the delegates distrust him,
— they say he changes from one side to the other too easily.
Yet he has much influence in the body. He is over six feet
in height, and of at least one hundred and ninety pounds
weight. His face is florid and rubicund to the last degree.
His nose is short, but prominent ; his forehead high and
bald. He is ready and forcible in debate, and carries himself
with a very democratic air.

Francis W. Pickens, ex-Governor of the "Independent
State of South Carolina," as it was called at his inaugura-
tion, is a battered old wreck, — short and squarely built,
with a large and squarish head, a broad and flat face, a
small and insignificant nose, round and piggish eyes, and
broad and high forehead. He has bristly iron-gray moustache and chin whiskers, and wears a brown wig, — whereby
there is a very peculiar and noticeable contrast. His voice
is feeble, his manner colloquial, his air jaunty. He is third
on Orr's committee, and is on his feet oftener than any other
man. He eats his humble pie with some ostentation, and is
specially solicitous that nothing shall be done to offend His
Excellency the Provisional Governor, or His Excellency
the President of the United States. His course and language are such as to call from delegates in private conversation frequent reference to the day when Fort Sumter surrendered, and to the speech he made on that occasion, —
" The Independent State of South Carolina has humbled the
flag that no nation on earth ever before humbled ; it has
been brought down in obedience to the behest of a sover-

eign State, on whose soil it shall never again be raised," &c., &c.

John A. Inglis is at the head of the committee on the Legislative Department, and is, perhaps, the most clearly intellectual man in the Convention. He is one of the three Chancery judges of the State, — a medium-sized man, trim, compact, without an ounce of superfluous flesh, erect, lithe, clear-headed, clear-eyed, clear-voiced, always ready, self-possessed, marvellously impassioned on occasion, — a man whose face shows forty-five years while his hair indicates sixty. He was a member of the Convention of December, 1860; introduced the original resolution declaring it the duty of South Carolina to secede from the Federal Union; moved to exclude the reporters of Northern papers from the floor of the hall; was chairman of the Committee on Federal Relations; and, as such, reported the ordinance of secession, and carried it through with swift energy. He is of spotless personal integrity, frankly admits the defeat of the South, has no love for the Yankees, swears by South Carolina, and lost by the war a handsome house and one of the choicest private libraries in the State.

C. M. Dudley is at the head of the committee on General Amendments to the Constitution, — is tall, ungainly, awkward, round-shouldered, slab-sided, shambling in his step, and homely of face as a man well can be. With all this, he is a man of much ability and rare good sense, and is unquestionably looked up to as a leader by at least a third of the delegates. He is pre-eminently the advocate of the strictest economy in public affairs, and is mentioned as a strong Union man so long as there were any Union men in the State.

A. P. Aldrich is the leader of the impracticable, unconquered element, — the men who are sullen or spiteful, the untamed fire-eaters. They number less than a dozen, though there are a dozen more who would like to follow his lead. He was a quartermaster in the Rebel army. "He 'd feel

differently if he 'd met as many of your troops on the
battle-field as I have," said one of the delegates, when
I asked him about Mr. Aldrich. He is noticeable for his
long and tumbled hair, and his long full whisker and moustache. He is able and forcible in debate, and " a real good
fellow," personally.

The first ordinance introduced into the Convention was
the following : —

" We, the delegates of the people of the State of South Carolina, in General Convention met, do ordain, That the ordinance
passed in Convention, December 20, 1860, withdrawing this State
from the Federal Union, be, and the same hereby is, repealed."

This ordinance came from ex-Governor Pickens, on the
first day of the session, when it went over under the rules.

On the second day he called it up for immediate action,
with the single remark that he thought it the first business
for the Convention, in order that the country might see that
South Carolina is in earnest in her profession of a desire to
conform to the results of the war.

Mr. Huger, the old postmaster of Charleston, seconded
the motion for immediate action, and made a rambling, old
man's speech of twenty minutes' length, which the house
applauded out of personal feeling for him, probably. He is
over eighty years of age, is tall, and not much bent, has a
face indicative of great force and strength of character, and
wears long white hair, — the general appearance of his face
reminding one of the pictures of Calhoun, whom the old
man eulogized. The noticeable feature of the speech was
its language of devotion to South Carolina. " She is my
mother; I have all my life loved what she loved, and hated
what she hated; everything she had I made my own, and
every act of hers was my act; as I have had but one hope,
to live with her, so now I have but one desire, to die
on her soil and be laid in her bosom. If I am wrong in
everything else, I know I am right in loving South Caro-

lina, — know I am right in believing that, whatever glory
the future may bring our reunited country, it can neither
brighten nor tarnish the glory of South Carolina. She has
passed through the agony and the bloody sweat; and as we
now return her to the Federal Union, let every man do his
duty bravely before the world, trustfully before God, remembering each man for himself that he is a South-Carolinian. She has been devastated by the invader, reviled by
the hireling, mocked by the weak-hearted; but she has accepted the invitation to return, — accepted it in good faith,
with the assurance of a word better than a bond; and now,
no matter what she gives up, no matter what there is to
endure and to forget, let us all do our duty as becomes her
children, counting it our chiefest honor to stand by her in
evil report as well as in good report, honor alike to live
with her and to die with her!"

The scene was in the highest degree dramatic, — the
venerable old man standing between the platform and a
table, with a supporting hand on each, and speaking in the
most impassioned manner, with a clear, resonant voice that
easily filled the whole church; every member of the Convention sitting with strained attention; the galleries bending over in silence, the better to see and hear; a clerk
standing near the feeble Huguenot Carolinian to pass the
glass of water while he spoke, and reach for him his staff
when he had concluded.

Rev. Dr. Boyce, of Greenville, and President of the
Baptist Theological Seminary at that place, thought the ordinance insufficient in terms for the desired purpose; and at
his suggestion it was sent to a special committee of three,
consisting of Governor Pickens, General McGowan, and
Judge Lesesne.

On the following day, the third of the session, it was
reported, by Governor Pickens, in this form: —

"We, the people of the State of South Carolina, by our delegates in Convention met, do ordain, That the ordinance adopted by us in Convention on the twentieth day of December, in the year of our Lord one thousand eight hundred and sixty, entitled, an ' Ordinance to dissolve the union between the State of South Carolina and other States united with her under the compact entitled " The Constitution of the United States of America," ' is hereby repealed."

Immediately after the report was read, the Governor called for action on the ordinance, and it was at once put on its passage, without debate. The recorded vote was, — Yeas 105, Nays 3.

And so, on the 15th of September, 1865, the State of South Carolina, after nearly five years of rebellious absence, in which she has destroyed all her living and very nigh destroyed herself, comes home. There are no cheers or huzzas, no salvos of artillery and clanging of glad bells, as when she set up the proud palmetto standard, — only suggestive silence and the eloquent catching for breath of a multitude of men.

The three nays were Messrs. A. P. Aldrich, J. J. Brabham, and J. M. Whetstone, the delegates from Barnwell District. Mr. Aldrich explained, that, as the conquering party had carried on the war for four years on the theory that the States were not out of the Union, he could n't see any sense in repealing an ordinance of secession. His tone and manner were those of petty spite.

By a curious coincidence, immediately after the passage of this ordinance, there came to light the following very remarkable resolutions, which were introduced by William Wallace, one of the delegates from this city : —

"*Whereas*, By the fortunes of war, our former noble and beloved Chief Magistrate, Jefferson Davis, is now languishing in prison, awaiting his trial for treason; and

"*Whereas*, The fanatics of the North, not satisfied with the widespread ruin and desolation which they have caused, are shrieking for his blood; —

" *Resolved*, That it is the paramount duty of South Carolina, who led the way in our late struggle for independence, and for which struggle he is now suffering, to use every lawful means in her power to avert the doom which threatens him.

" *Resolved*, That to this end, a deputation of members of this body be sent to the city of Washington, in behalf of the people of South Carolina, to ask of His Excellency the President of the United States to extend to the Honorable Jefferson Davis that clemency which he has shown to us, who are equally the sharers of his guilt, if guilt there be, and which is accomplishing so much toward restoring the peace and harmony of the Union."

The fluttering began before the reading of these resolutions was finished, and several members were on their feet at once. Mr. Dudley got the floor, and quietly suggested that this was scarcely appropriate language for a body which had just returned the State to the Union, and was relying on the generosity of the North for full admission again into the sisterhood of States. Two or three other delegates made remarks to the same effect; and Mr. Wallace then accepted as a substitute a simple resolution appointing a committee to memorialize the President in favor of the pardon of Davis, Stephens, Magrath, and Trenholm.

In this connection, I cannot forbear quoting the remarkable language in which the little daily paper of this city, edited by the novelist William Gilmore Simms, who has always been called a Union man, speaks of this matter. It is as follows : —

" These appeals are eminently proper, coming, not merely from the people of South Carolina, but from those of all the several States of the Confederacy. How should any of their people be able to lift their heads if harm should come to any of their leaders ? President Johnson must perceive that to save these people from shame, he must shelter these, their representative men, from harm. We have no doubt that he will do so, and we are willing to leave this matter in his hands. He can entertain no base or little revenges. We take for granted that he will dismiss, without impediment or bond, all these eminent persons of state;

that he will give to Mr. Davis the freedom of the country or the use of a frigate to convey him to foreign shores. He can do no less."

During the four days of the Convention a large number of resolutions have been presented and referred to the appropriate committees. They touch almost every conceivable question of State policy, but are merely representative of individual views, and need not, therefore, be given in this record. They are indicative, however, of a disposition to make some sweeping and radical changes in the Constitution.

The attendance on the sessions of the Convention is not large, but it is increasing daily. Possibly one hundred persons were in the galleries of the church to-day. No ladies were present on the first day ; on the second day there were four, evidently of the middle class of society ; yesterday the number from that class was increased; and to-day there were also present about a score of those who evidently number themselves among the *élite* of the city.

VII.

ACTION OF THE CONVENTION ON THE SLAVERY QUESTION.

COLUMBIA, September 19, 1865.

THERE were two things which, in a national point of view, it was essential that this Convention should do as soon as possible, — declare the abolition of slavery, and repeal the Ordinance of Secession. Ex-Governor Pickens, of swift repentance, saw this so clearly, that he introduced an ordinance, on the first day of the session, to accomplish both these things. I have already related how the Ordinance of Secession was repealed. The slavery question was settled to-day, not by an ordinance, but by the adoption of a clause for the Constitution.

" It is impossible," said Governor Perry in his message, —

"it is impossible for South Carolina ever to regain her civil rights and be restored to the Union till she voluntarily abolishes slavery, and declares by an organic law that neither slavery nor involuntary servitude, except as a punishment for crime whereof the party shall have been duly convicted, shall ever again exist within the limits of the State." The several steps by which this consummation was reached may properly be shown in considerable detail.

There are two or three delegates who will not so much as admit that slavery is overthrown, hoping, I judge, that the general government will one day be glad to settle the question by paying a certain compensation for the sake of quiet. There are two or three more who think the whole matter ought to be referred to the Legislature. The great body, however, were ready on the opening day of the session to take action upon it in some form. Propositions embracing clauses for the new Constitution were therefore submitted by several members, in form as follows : —

By ex-Governor Pickens, of Edgefield District: "The fortunes of war, together with the proclamations of the President of the United States and the generals in the field commanding, having decided that domestic slavery is abolished; therefore, under the circumstances, we acquiesce in said proclamations, and do hereby ordain implicit obedience to the Constitution of the United States and all laws made in pursuance thereof."

By James H. Ryon, of Fairfield District: "The slaves in South Carolina having been *de facto* emancipated by the action of the Federal authorities, neither slavery nor involuntary servitude, except as a punishment for crime whereof the party shall have been duly convicted, shall ever be reestablished in this State."

By James L. Orr, of Anderson District: "Slavery, except as a punishment for crime after due conviction, is forever prohibited in this State."

3 *

By Henry D. Lesesne, of Charleston: "Slavery having been abolished by the military power of the United States, it shall never be re-established in this State."

By James Winsmith, of Spartanburg District: "Slavery having been abolished by the proclamations of the President of the United States and the military authorities of the same, neither negro slavery nor involuntary servitude shall hereafter exist in this State, except as a punishment for crime of which the party shall have been duly convicted by law."

By Samuel McGowan, of Abbeville District: " The emancipation of slaves having actually taken place, slavery shall not hereafter be re-established in this State."

By William H. Perry, of Greenville District: "Slavery and involuntary servitude are hereby abolished in South Carolina, and shall not again exist in the State except as a punishment for crime whereof the party shall have been duly convicted."

These various paragraphs show in what form the subject originally presented itself to the minds of such members as were specially interested in it. It will be observed that five of these seven delegates deemed it necessary to recite the manner in which the overthrow of slavery was accomplished.

Some of these propositions went to one committee, and some to another; and, curiously enough, their reports showed that one committee represents that wing of the Convention which insists that the method of the abolition of slavery shall be declared, while the other is willing, like a small number of delegates, to accept the fact without any explanatory words. These reports were as follows : —

By the Committee on Amendments to the Constitution: " Slavery having ceased to exist in this State, it shall not hereafter be permitted or re-established."

By the Committee on Ordinances: "Slavery having actually been destroyed by the military force of the United

States, it is hereby declared that slavery no longer exists in
the State of South Carolina, and that all persons heretofore
held as slaves are free; and it is further declared and ordained, that slavery shall not again be established in this
State; provided, however, that the General Assembly may
adjudge involuntary servitude as a punishment for crime
whereof the party shall have been duly convicted."

It seemed to an outsider like myself that there was no
essential difference between these two propositions, but that
the former, being the more direct, was to be preferred.   The
action of the Convention, however, was to prove that the
happiness of a people, not to say the preservation of a State,
may depend upon a nice observance of the distinction be-
twixt tweedledee and tweedledum.

The latter of the foregoing reports came first on the cal-
endar, and was therefore taken up as the order of the day.
The discussion that followed had two branches and a side
issue.   The first branch turned on the question whether the
necessary action should be taken by the Convention or by
the Legislature ; the second had to do with the phraseology
of the ordinance, regard being had to the peculiar sensibili-
ties of the people, and to the "historical fact" that the slaves
were emancipated by Federal authority ; while the side issue
concerned the subject of negro suffrage.

Mr. L. W. R. Blair, a delegate from Kershaw District,
a very tall and very homely man, with remarkably retreating
forehead, an immense and immensely red nose, no chin to
speak of, and a weak and straggling grizzly whisker and
moustache, whose misfortune it is to be ignorant of the fact
that he lives in the nineteenth century, and also of the other
fact that there has been a great war, and who, of course sublimely ignores all such things as emancipation proclamations,
Congressional enactments, military orders, etc., gravely rose
in the back part of the church and proposed the following as
a substitute for the Ordinance Committee's report : —

"*Resolved*, That the question of slavery and all questions connected therewith be referred to the Legislature of the State, whose duty it shall be to consult with the proper authorities of the United States, and learn the intention of the government in respect to the institution of slavery ; and authority is hereby given to the Legislature to take such action as seems conducive to the best interests of the State of South Carolina, and such action, when taken, shall be final and conclusive ; and the Legislature shall have power to make laws applicable to colored persons alone, and shall enact such laws as are needful to prevent negroes and persons of color from engaging in any business or pursuit but such as involves manual labor, mining, road-making, agriculture, and the production of naval stores."

Mr. Blair proceeded to support this astounding proposition in a speech of half an hour's length. He was willing, he said, to give up slavery, but he was not willing to do it without some guaranties. He had great confidence in the President, but none in the party now in power in the North. That party was already clamoring for concessions which the South could never grant. Every true son of South Carolina would die rather than grant the right of suffrage to the negroes of the State. He was opposed to making a full surrender of slavery till the State had some guaranty that such surrender would bring full restoration of political rights to her people. Moreover, might it not hereafter appear that some pecuniary compensation would be adjudged as due to the South for the destruction of her slave property ? He would not take any action till the whole subject had been considered in all its bearings, and the Legislature was the only body that could do that.

Mr. Dawkins, of Union District, chairman of the committee which made the report, said the committee had endeavored to choose language which would accomplish the end he believed all men desired, and would be as little distasteful as possible to the people of the State. The ordinance simply declared that slavery had been actually destroyed by the military force of the United States. Nothing was said as to the right of that force to thus act ; and, on the other hand, there was nothing in the ordinance to preclude any man or the State from asking compensation, or from sharing in it if it was voluntarily tendered. He was not wedded to the particular language of the report, but would accept any other that would accomplish the same end. He was, however, wholly opposed to the proposed amendment. I feel certain that it is to the last degree impracticable. We shall have no Legislature till we declare slavery abolished. However it may displease any of us to admit it, the fact is that we are at the mercy of the authorities at Washington. We have been beaten in the contest, and we can have no government but such as is agreeable to them. We are now under military rule. True, we have a provisional governor, but he is, after all, only a military governor with another name. I am glad to bear testimony to the fact that the military authorities are disposed to concede to us every possible advantage consistent with their views of public safety, and to see that there is a prospect of the speedy restoration to us of our civil rights. But I am confident that such restoration will only follow prompt and graceful acquiescence on our part in the action of the authorities on the slavery question ; and I repeat, that I believe we can have no Legislature till we declare that slavery is abolished and shall never again be established. What, then, is the part of wisdom and good sense ? Is it to be stubborn and obstinate ? There is but one condition of society worse than military rule : shall we recklessly provoke that ? Shall we not the rather do what the plain duty of the hour requires, and thus relieve ourselves, as soon as may be, from military rule ?

Mr. Orr said he would accept the report of the committee, though he would have chosen fewer words. The election of Mr. Lincoln, five years ago, was taken by the people of the South as an evidence that the people of the North were

not disposed to allow them what they believed to be their
plain rights. The State seceded. We went out to save
slavery. Other States followed the example of South Carolina. The Confederacy was formed, and its Constitution
showed that the saving of slavery was the common purpose
of all the Southern States. Slavery was made the corner-
stone of the new government. The result was what any
man ought to have expected : it was not reasonable to suppose the North would allow a disruption of the Federal
Union without war. The whole matter was referred to that
tribunal. It was decided against us. Shall we try the issue
again ? Who is so mad as to even dream we could be more
successful than we have been already ? We first failed at
the ballot-box, and now we have failed on the battle-field.
Nothing remains for us but to come forward and meet
the new issue. We must put it in the Constitution that
slavery is dead, and that we will never attempt to revive it.
Unless we do that, we shall have no Legislature. I don't
presume to speak by authority, — I only take cognizance of
the fact that the case has been tried in the last possible tribunal, and has been decided against us, and I see that we
must now submit, whether it be easy or painful for us to do
so. Shall we obstinately, persistently, and stubbornly refuse
to acquiesce ? Is that the part of wisdom ? I don't know
how far the conqueror may go with his victory. There have
been cases in which whole peoples were swept from the
face of the earth : is that what we covet ? The war has
made the North victor : is it remarkable that the victors
should fix the terms of our restoration to political rights ?
They have done no more than we expected. We said in all
our speeches at the beginning that slavery was in danger ;
that if the dominant party succeeded in their efforts, slavery
would be destroyed. They succeeded at the ballot-box, and
we then made the issue on the battle-field. We were defeated there as we had been elsewhere, and the institution

of slavery is hopelessly destroyed. Now the conqueror makes his terms, — abolish slavery by your own enactment, declare that it shall never be re-established, treat your freed people well, popularize your Constitution. Are these terms hard? Might they not have been much harder? Are they not, on the whole, very liberal? We are to retain nearly all our civil rights and most of our property other than slaves: might we not have fared much worse? It may be hard in our judgment to concede these terms; but what is it in their judgment? If we fail to do our duty according to their judgment, what will be the consequence? Do we covet military rule as the chief good? There have been states in which military governors made it their duty, if not their pleasure, to break the spirit of the people: are we anxious for such authority over us? If we reject the boon now offered us, — and I tell you it is a boon for a subjugated people to be allowed the restoration of most of their personal and political rights, — if we reject this, what then? Let gentlemen consider. I refer you to the speech of the Honorable Thaddeus Stevens, recently made. I know him as a man of great ability, and as a leader among the radicals. He proposes to confiscate the property of seventy thousand leading men in the South to pay the national war debt; and if the radicals were in power, I don't doubt but that some such policy would prevail. We seem to forget where we stand; we forget that we made the war and have been beaten; we forget that our conquerors have the right to dictate terms to us. And I tell you, it is to the good favor of Andrew Johnson that our terms are no worse, — nay, are so liberal. He is the dike between us and the waves of Northern fanaticism. Let us be wise men. Let us strengthen his hands by graceful and ready acquiescence in the results of the war. So shall we strengthen ourselves, and soon bring again to our loved State the blessings of peace and civil rule.

Mr. Dunovant, of Edgefield District, denied that the war

was on the question of slavery. It was waged in the interests of State rights. We were whipped, and the issue on
that question is forever settled. But I deny the right of any
one to dictate to us in respect to matters not in issue in the
war. I deny that slavery is abolished. The relation of
master and slave is disrupted, but that relation returns as
soon as you restore the civil authority. I will not admit
that we are rightfully under military rule; the President
has no warrant in the Constitution for keeping a standing
army among us, and I will not submit my will to him in this
matter. I don't mean to be understood as opposing the abolition of slavery, but I think it is the business of the Legislature and not of this Convention.

Mr. McGowan, of Abbeville District, said one of the
chief things for which the Convention was called was to declare the abolition of slavery. He asserted as a historical
fact, that the war was forced upon the South, but did not
care to argue the point now. The war left us in the dust, —
it put us at the mercy of the North. The conqueror had
the right to prescribe the conditions of our restoration to
civil and political rights. These conditions I accept in all
fidelity, in all good faith, in all sincerity, with one condition
in return, — that we are hereafter to be left political masters
in the State. We must be left free to legislate for all the
people here, white or black, otherwise I would accept martyrdom before I would acquiesce in the demand made upon
us respecting slavery.

The discussion on the general subject rested here, and
the Blair substitute was tabled with only two or three
dissenting voices.

A two hours' wrangle then ensued as to the phraseology
which should be adopted to gain the desired end. The
various propositions on which votes were taken during this
debate were the following: —

From the Committee on Ordinances, Mr. T. N. Dawkins,

of Union District, chairman: "Slavery having been actually destroyed by the military force of the United States, it is hereby declared that slavery no longer exists in the State of South Carolina, and that all persons heretofore held as slaves are free; and it is further declared and ordained that slavery shall not again be established in this State, but involuntary servitude may be adjudged by the General Assembly as a punishment for crime." The vote in Convention on this form of words — it being the aforementioned order of the day — was 46 Yeas to 61 Nays.

From the Committee on General Amendments to the Constitution, Mr. C. M. Dudley, of Marlboro District, chairman: "Slavery having ceased to exist in this State, it shall not hereafter be re-established or permitted." The vote of the Convention on accepting this phraseology was 35 Yeas to 72 Nays.

Substitute proposed by John A. Inglis, of Chesterfield District: "Slavery is hereafter and forever prohibited in this State." On the question of adopting this form, the vote was 25 Yeas to 80 Nays.

Substitute proposed by Rev. Dr. James P. Boyce, of Greenville District: "Neither slavery nor involuntary servitude, except as a punishment for crime whereof the party shall have been duly convicted, shall ever be re-established in this State." This was also rejected by a vote of 45 Yeas to 58 Nays.

It will be judged from this record of votes that the Convention was determined that it should appear in the Constitution that slavery was not abolished by the voluntary action of the State.

Judge Lesesne, of Charleston, would not stultify the State of South Carolina by leaving it possible for any one to suppose that, after four years of such devastating war as we have known, she did this thing of her own accord.

Mr. Dudley could see no necessity for attempting to say

E

through what agency slavery had been lost. He thought there was no occasion to use language that might be offensive. Moreover, it was possible that the condition of slavery might be re-established as a punishment for crime; and he would not leave the purpose of the Convention with regard to this matter in any doubt.

Judge Frost thought it ought to be understood by this time that South Carolina was not omnipotent; and that there were some things she could not do, — one of these being to re-establish slavery.

Colonel Rion said he did all he could for the South while the war lasted, and was now thoroughly whipped; yet he was not afraid to declare the historical fact that slavery had been destroyed by the Federal government.

Mr. Melton declared that he would oppose all amendments that claimed to recite the historical fact, for the Constitution is not intended as a text-book on history.

Chancellor Inglis would also vote against such amendments, because a Constitution should simply enunciate general principles: history was n't at all likely to lose or forget the facts.

General McGowan asked if there were ten men in the Convention who would favor the abolition of slavery as an independent proposition aside from the events of the last four years.

Mr. Dudley responded that there was need to remind the Convention that they were suppliants for mercy, though he believed that proper self-respect, aside from all other considerations, demanded that they should abstain from the use of needless words.

General McGowan retorted that he would not vote for the proposition at all, unless it recited the truth and the whole truth.

Rev. Dr. Boyce said it seemed to him that the Convention should have respect for the dignity of the work it was doing and the document it was making; the historical fact would appear in a thousand other places.

The Convention was determined, however, to have the so-called "historical fact," and finally, by a vote of 59 to 43, agreed upon the following language : —

"The slaves in South Carolina having been emancipated by the action of the United States authorities, neither slavery nor involuntary servitude, except as a punishment for crime whereof the party shall have been duly convicted, shall ever be re-established in this State."

The occasion — the abolition of slavery in South Carolina — had lost its superficial interest, because of the senseless wrangle over a form of words. The fine audience of the early part of the day had wearied and gone away. Only the delegates and a few spectators whom nothing could disgust into forgetfulness of the import of the work in hand remained. The dull equinoctial afternoon was fading into a dark and dreary evening.

Finally the vote on the main question — the passage of this clause as Sect. 11 of Article IX. in the new Constitution — was called. In all parts of the church men kept tally of those who voted "Nay." They were Messrs. A. P. Aldrich and J. M. Whetstone, of Barnwell District; R. G. M. Dunovant, of Edgefield District; T. J. Goodwyn, of St. Matthew's Parish; J. H. Morgan, of Orange District; Edward Porter, of Williamsburg District; H. S. Sheridan, of St. Bartholomew's Parish; and L. F. Youmans, of St. Luke's Parish. The vote stood 98 Yeas and 8 Nays.

So the fact was accomplished beyond all cavil, and so South Carolina stepped into the ranks alongside Massachusetts, — joining hands with her to bear aloft the banner of freedom, — bowing to the logic of events rather than that of free speech, — convinced by cannon-balls rather than by arguments; yet, under the circumstances, turning from the things of slavery to the things of liberty with commendable grace.

At the gateway of the church, as I came out, I met an old negro woman, — neat, prim, deferential. "Well, Auntie," said I, "the Convention has just said ·there shall be no more slavery in South Carolina." "How's dat ar?" I repeated the idea in more familiar terms. "Is dat ar true, Massa?" "True as the Bible, Auntie." "Wall now tank de Lord fur dat ar. I's dun gone pray fur dat dese yer forty years. I's hope he come in my time; but 'pears like he idle by de way. Now he come, and I's ready fur my ole man in de hebens. Tank de Lord, tank de Lord!"

VIII.

THE BASIS OF REPRESENTATION.

COLUMBIA, September 21, 1865.

WHAT is the true basis of representation in a republican form of government? This is the profound question over which the Convention has to-day spent a session of about seven hours. Everybody expected a struggle when this matter was reached, for the first day's resolutions showed a very prevalent desire to at least discuss the subject in all its bearings. Yet that the negro could be brought into that discussion seemed never to enter the minds of even some of the oldest and ablest delegates; and his introduction into the assembly this afternoon was followed by scenes both ludicrous and humiliating.

The basis of representation in the Legislature of this State has always been unusual, not to say complex. In the House it was property and population, taxation and white inhabitants, — half the members being apportioned on the basis of white population, and the other half on the value of all property, slaves included. In the Senate it was geographical area and territorial extent, modified by the parish system, under which the area occupied by the major part of the slave population received not less than three times as great a representation as the same area mainly occupied by white population.

The committee to which the legislative article of the Constitution was referred reported in favor of retaining the old basis of representation in the House, and of abolishing the parish system of representation in the Senate.

The debate to-day was upon that section fixing the basis of representation in the House; but such range was given it that it embraced, as I have already indicated, the whole question of the true basis of republican representation. The adoption this morning, by a vote of 73 to 36, of a rule limiting each delegate to fifteen minutes in speaking, gave the debate a fragmentary character, and doubtless killed half a dozen lengthy speeches.

Mr. James L. Orr advocated this basis of representation, — white population in the House, and white population and taxation in the Senate, — and moved to so amend the article under debate, fixing white population as the basis for the House. The proposition was pretty closely debated on its merits, and the scheme was rejected — by Yeas 24, Nays 83.

Mr. Cadwallader Jones, of York, wanted the basis of representation in the Senate to be property, and in the House white population, and submitted a series of amendments to carry out his view. This question was also debated on its merits, with some reference to its advantages for the different sections of the State, and finally rejected — by Yeas 20, Nays 85.

Mr. Robert Dozier, of Georgetown, proposed that the basis for representation in the House should be property, and all the inhabitants, white and black.

This proposition dragged the poor negro right in by the ears. His appearance was either very alarming or very dis-

tasteful, for the Rev. Dr. Boyce sprang to his feet, and, with
indignant haste, moved to lay the amendment on the table,
saying he believed every man was ready for instant action.
Much to his surprise, apparently, several of the oldest and
strongest delegates protested in warm terms against this gag
movement, and the Reverend Doctor was forced to withdraw
his motion. He renewed it three times during the afternoon,
but was obliged to three times more withdraw it; and the
discussion upon the right and expediency of admitting the
negro into the body politic as an element of representation
ran through five long hours. It was no proposition to allow
him to vote, or even to allow any one to vote in his name,
or for him; but simply a proposition to allow ten thousand
whites living in a district where there are twenty-five thousand negroes, to send as many representatives to the General
Assembly as are sent by twenty-five thousand whites living
in a district with only ten thousand negroes.

There was during the day a great deal of frothy talk,
through which it was found that the proposition stood upon
three principal legs, and had several side-supports.

Its effect in State affairs was the medium through which
a majority of the speakers saw it. The discovery was soon
made that it would ultimately give the control of the House
to the low-country. Sectional feeling was, therefore, at once
enlisted for or against it; and some of the up-country members made furious speeches against it, while some of the
Charleston delegation endeavored to win votes by appealing
to the magnanimity of up-country friends who had broken
their power in the Senate by the overthrow of the parish
system.

The bearings of the amendment upon the question of Congressional representation were also of much interest to various gentlemen. Mr. Dozier himself appeared to be chiefly
concerned in this regard. He argued that as negroes are
an element in the Congressional representation, it would be

inconsistent to exclude them from the body politic as represented in the State Legislature. On what ground can we ask Congress, said he, to allow us four representatives now, and probably seven, and at least six, after the next census, when our present white population gives us but two, if we deny the right of the negroes to be represented in our local government? This argument, in other phraseology, was used by a dozen or more delegates. On the other hand, it was argued that there is no connection between the two matters; that the apportionment of four representatives — two for whites and two for three fifths of the negroes — must stand till after the next census; and that then the whole population, black and white, must be counted in assigning the representation, unless Congress meantime amends the Constitution, which it is not at all probable can be done.

The just claim of the negro to representation was advocated by a few members, including three or four of the ablest delegates in the Convention. It was argued that he had heretofore been represented in both houses, — directly as property in the lower house, and indirectly through the parish system in the upper house; and that it would be unjust to now cut him off from all representation. "It will be outlawry to do so," said Chancellor Inglis. On the other hand, it was held that if the negro be admitted into the body politic at all, he must be given a vote. "This is but the entering wedge of negro suffrage," said Colonel Rion, "and I oppose it as such." "I am sure the mover does not mean it as such, and I am also sure none of those who support it mean it as such," said Mr. Thomson, of Abbeville; "but I am convinced it is but the stepping-stone to negro suffrage." "You cannot, in my judgment, pass this amendment," said Mr. Orr, "till you are prepared to follow it with one giving the negro the elective franchise, and I shall vote against it on that ground." "Adopt this amendment," said General McGowan, "and you pass the political power of the State

over into the hands of the negro." "The measure of our own
necessities should be the measure of our recognition of the negro as an element in the body politic," echoed Mr. Thomson.
" This is a white man's government," re-echoed Dr. Boyce.

Those to whom the Convention is accustomed to look for
leadership were about equally divided on the question, and
the discussion indicated that delegates were inclining to favor
the proposition more and more with each hour's delay of the
final vote. That was at length reached, and the amendment,
much to the surprise of Rev. Dr. Boyce, failed by only seven
majority; the votes standing — Yeas 52, Nays 59.

This was considered as settling the dispute; and, without
amendment, the section was agreed to as it came from the
committee.

The end had not, however, been reached. The Convention took a recess till this evening, during which the discussion among the eighty or ninety delegates at the hotel was
kept up with even more intensity than on the floor of the
church. Several were not satisfied with the vote they had
given, and it was determined to return to the section. Accordingly, as soon as the Convention came together after the
recess, a motion was made to recur thereto, which was carried — by Yeas 52, Nays 48.

Mr. Aldrich, chief of the fire-eaters, moved an amendment
providing, in effect, that three fifths of the negroes shall be
counted, with the whites, in fixing the population-represen-
tation of the lower house, the property-representation being
also retained.

This proposition was debated two hours, and many of the
younger and third-rate members committed themselves to it
as a compromise between no-negro representation and full-
negro representation. The older heads then took the floor,
and made a dead set against it on the ground that the principle of negro representation is either right or wrong, — if
wrong, then this amendment should not be adopted even to

benefit the low country, where the negro element will ultimately reside; and if right, then no compromise was admissible. Wherefore Mr. Aldrich was constrained to withdraw his amendment, to disembarrass the Convention.

Mr. Norwood, of Darlington, then moved a reconsideration of the vote by which Mr. Dozier's amendment had been rejected at the morning session. He said he was opposed to negro suffrage, but neither he nor his people were afraid of a discussion of the subject.

Judge Edward Frost, of Charleston, an aged gentleman of high standing, got the floor, and supported the motion to reconsider, making the only creditable speech of the whole debate. He said the chief error of the South had been that she was not favorably disposed toward discussion of questions affecting the welfare and relations of the negro; and he was very sorry to see such undue sensitiveness upon the subject in this debate. The events of the last four or five years have settled a great many things, and one of the things thus settled is that South Carolina is not omnipotent. It is effectually determined that we cannot have our own way in everything. We assumed that we knew all there was to know about the negro; and that where the world differed from us in opinion, it was wrong. Events would seem to indicate that we were wrong in at least some very important particulars. The world insisted that the negro is a man, and we have even been brought to that acknowledgment. The world now demands that we fix the political status of the negro; and we must consider the question, whether it does or does not please us so to do. The old relation of master and slave is abolished. What new relation shall be given to the negro? We cannot ignore him. We cannot give him suffrage, — he is not fit to exercise it; but if the community in which he lives has a representation on his account, he will be in one sense represented. Gentlemen talk about his ignorance, and plead that as a bar to his

4

admission into the body politic in any form. He is ignorant; I grant you that; but how came he so? Did he
make himself ignorant? Did he ever have a chance to
choose his station in life? Was it not an act of insubordi-
nation for him to ask instruction? We may as well admit
it first as last, — slavery made him what he is. Ignorance
is the natural and inevitable result of our former system of
labor. Let us do the negro justice: he is mainly what we
of the ruling class made him. In one sense, we still stand
in the relation of master to him, as the educated and intelligent are always the masters of the ignorant and feeble-
minded. It is our duty to consider his condition and help
him to become a better man. Take away his ignorance,
and you take away some of the burdens and some of the
dangers of society. If no higher considerations will move
us, let us consult our own material interests, and give him a
fair chance. Treat him as a free man, as an element of
prosperity in the State, and you soon make him such an element. We cannot any more maintain the opinion of South
Carolina against the world. The negro has civil rights, as
we all have; political rights he will be slow to ask for, I
think, if we treat him fairly. His natural temperament is
such that he shuns responsibility. Fully and freely concede his rights as a man, and he will be willing you should
make his laws. I have not known him to ask for suffrage
except when influenced by bad or designing men; but it is
the part of wisdom for us to open our eyes and see where
we stand. We must concede that the negro is a free man,
having civil rights, having property rights, having the right
to be represented in the body politic, and unquestionably
destined at no very distant day to have political rights."

"Why, he's a Black Republican!" exclaimed a man who
sat in the seat with me at the church, while Judge Frost
spoke. "Well, he's the only one who has spoken," said I,
in reply. "Yes, and d—n him, he's the only one here, I

reckon," continued my seat-mate. "You are sitting next to one !" I answered, with some asperity of tone, I 'm afraid. "You?" "Yes." I had the whole seat to myself soon after the close of the conversation.

The motion to reconsider was carried by a vote of 55 to 51 ; but, a little later, Chancellor Inglis rose and said, that reflection had convinced him it would not be wise at this time to admit the negro as an element in any form into the body politic, and he therefore moved to lay the pending amendment — originally offered by Mr. Dozier — upon the table. The nobodies followed the Chancellor's lead, and the amendment went to the table by 75 to 24.

Therefore the basis of representation in the lower house of the General Assembly stands as it always has since the original Constitution was adopted, — white population and taxation.

I was not sorry to see the Dozier proposition finally killed. So far as granting any right to the negro, it was a sham and a cheat. In the mouths of one or two men it meant good-will to him ; but it would have proved worse than the apples of Sodom had it been ingrafted into the Constitution.

IX.

THE GREAT CONTEST BETWEEN THE UPPER AND LOWER SECTIONS OF SOUTH CAROLINA.

COLUMBIA, September 23, 1865.

THERE has long been strife between the two sections of the State locally known as the "up-country" and the "low-country." Just how it originated, and by what jealousies it has been fed, probably no one could satisfactorily explain to an outsider. A dozen gentlemen have volunteered to elucidate the whole matter for me, and so long as I listened only to one side I thought I understood it ; but, having heard both parties, I am convinced that no one really comprehends it. That there is ill-blood is patent enough. " I hate the saints of New England in reference to national affairs, and I hate the saints of the low-country in State affairs," said one of the up-country men to me yesterday. " The low-country has overridden us long enough," said one of the delegates, " and now we 've drawn the sword, thrown away the scabbard, and are going to have a settlement." The hostility of the one section to the other five years ago was scarcely less than the State hostility to the general government ; and the up-country now charges the low-country with having brought on the war. " Disunion was born in the parishes," is the public remark of one delegate.

The opening day of the session of this Convention found the political power of the State where it always had been, — in the low-country. The second day's session made it apparent to everybody that the up-country had marshalled its forces for a struggle, and meant to depose the king and take the reins of government into its own hands. The end of this, the tenth day's session, sees this purpose accomplished, — sees the low-country at the feet of the strong and innovating up-country.

To show the successive phases of the conflict in the Convention whereby this result was gained is the purpose of this letter.

The origin of the parish system of representation in the upper house of the General Assembly dates with the formation of the original Constitution. Theoretically the senatorial representation was one from each district. Practically this was the case only in the upper and back portions of the State. The sea-coast districts were divided into parishes, and each parish was entitled to a senator, even if it contained no more than one hundred voters. Therefore, as some of the districts were divided into several parishes, a few districts on the coast, — Charleston, Colleton, and Beaufort, for instance, — if they did not have an actual majority in the Senate, certainly were strong enough to control the vote of that body; and that they did so control it, and generally for their own benefit, is beyond question. Forty or fifty years ago, when nearly all the wealth and population were in the sea-coast districts, this parish system constituted a check on the tendencies of the up-country, which, if not founded in any right, at least did not operate to any serious disadvantage. For the last twenty years or more, however, it has been an oppressive burden on the State, of which it seemed utterly impossible to get rid; for it could not be reached except through an amendment to the Constitution, and a convention for that purpose could only be called by the Legislature; and legislatures so virtuous that they readily vote themselves and their constituents out of power are not numerous — in South Carolina at least. A convention, therefore, called by other authority than the Legislature, and without restriction as to the questions upon which it should act, was to the up-country partial compensation for the overthrow of the Confederacy. The issue of the elections there, if issue it can be called when everybody favored it, was "death to the parishes."

The first onset in behalf of the up-country was made by the Provisional Governor, who says in his message: "The parish representation in the Senate is unequal and unjust, contrary to all republican principles; for twenty or thirty voters in one of the parishes, whose population and taxation combined entitle it to only one member of the House of Representatives, have the same representation in the Senate that three thousand voters have in Edgefield District, whose population and taxation entitle it to six members in the House."

The only hope for the parishes was that the Convention

would limit itself to a narrow range of action. The low-country was in favor of doing as little work as possible; the up-country was in favor of doing as much as possible.

On the first day of the session one of the low-country delegates offered a resolution calculated to define and limit the province of the Convention. It was unceremoniously sent to the table.

The quarrel between the two sections next came to the surface on the question of appointing the standing committees. Few committees meant narrow range of work and a speedy adjournment; and of course that view was supported by the sea-coast members. Many committees meant a thorough revision of the Constitution, and that was what the up-country members wanted. The latter carried the day, after a good deal of skirmishing, getting eight committees.

On the second day, Judge Lesesne introduced a resolution reciting that the action of the Convention should be restricted to those measures which are necessary for the reinstatement of the State in the Union, and the restoration to her of a civil government. This may be called the first movement of Charleston; but it amounted to nothing, for the resolution was instantly tabled.

On the third day, that city made a reconnoissance in force, under the lead of John Conner, late a general in the Confederate service, whose chief of staff on the occasion was Judge Frost, also of the delegation from that city. General Conner's force consisted of the troops used on the previous day by his colleague Judge Lesesne; but it was marshalled in such a manner as to present a much more imposing front, and was handled with consummate skill. Two hours' spicy debate served, however, to send his resolution to the table; and he then retired and left the field to the up-country enemy.

On the fourth day, the three low-country members of the Committee on the Executive Department made a report, stating, " We are of the opinion that the Convention, not having been called according to the forms of the Constitution of the State, can only exercise such powers as are absolutely necessary to restore the State to the Union with a Constitution republican in its character; and that any fundamental change in the said Constitution is not within the exercise of such powers." This was signed by Messrs. Aldrich of Barnwell District, and Conner and Simonton of Charleston; but these names were not enough to secure the acquiescence of the Convention in the opinion, and the report also went to the table.

On the fifth day, the St. Helena Parish election case came up. The applicant for a seat was a young man originally from Philadelphia, but resident about three years on the island, and to all intents and purposes a citizen of the State. His constituents are, like himself, mostly new-comers, though all legal voters. There was no pretence of fraud, or that the election did not fairly represent the will of the people of the parish. The term of office of the managers of election appointed by the Legislature in 1860 – 61 had expired, and there were neither managers nor legislative delegation to appoint new ones. Therefore the people did the best thing they could in the emergency, — held a mass-meeting, and chose their managers. The technical question involved in the case was, whether the certificate of managers thus appointed could be received. The special committee of three to which the matter was referred, and of which Mr. Perry, the Governor's son and private secretary, was chairman, decided that it could, and reported in favor of the admission of the delegate. The debate was sharp and spirited. The informality of the election and certificate were admitted on all hands. The committee and most of their supporters argued that, as the will of the people had been fairly expressed, the informality could be overlooked. Mr. Orr would admit the delegate as an earnest of the good faith and good

disposition of the people of the State in their relation to the
Union.   Judge Thomson, of Abbeville District, would admit
him as an earnest of the welcome he stood ready to extend
to all Northern men who are willing to cast their fortune
with South Carolina in this hour when she so much needs
help.   On the other hand, the chief argument of the opposition rested on the facts that the delegate is a Northerner,
that the owners of the island have been driven from their
homes, and that the constituency now there is from the
North.   The report of the committee was sustained, and
the delegate was admitted by a vote of 56 to 53 ; and the
action of the Convention in this regard was generally con
sidered as another repulse to the low-country.

On the seventh day, the parish system was brought out
for trial, condemnation, and execution ; and the work was
so thoroughly accomplished, that hardly enough of its friends
were found to give the mourners a respectable appearance.
The question came up indirectly, on a proposition to give
the city of Charleston two senators instead of one, as recommended by the Legislative Committee.   The debate was
long and earnest, and called out the ablest men of the Convention.   The merits and demerits of the parish system
were discussed in all their length and breadth, and the
amendment was finally adopted by a vote of 78 to 30.

In this vote was the grand defeat of the low-country.   It
swept away the system which made South Carolina the
leader in the Rebellion, and in a moment transferred the
political power of the State from the conservative hands of
the low-country to the progressive hands of the up-country.
This fact is of grave importance.   The parishes governed
the State in the one sole interest of slavery ; and though the
up-country will not govern it just yet in the interest of freedom, the proportion of negroes in the low-country districts
is very much larger than in the up-country districts.   The
inhabitants of the low-country are of direct foreign descent,

with monarchical and aristocratic tendencies; those of the up-country came originally from the North, and have republican and democratic tendencies.

The people of the State are wretchedly poor; but on the evening of the day in which this great victory was gained, I heard — and for the first time since the Convention met — heard, in the rooms of the leading up-country delegates, a lively and long-continued fire of champagne corks. Peace to the ashes of the parish system!

George D. Tilman, a man of immense frame and very considerable abilities, genial and off-hand, who has lived in South America and California, and now hails from Edgefield District, who has served six years in the State Legislature for honor, and two years in the State Penitentiary for manslaughter, who quotes philosophy from De Tocqueville, and historical maxims from Gibbon, — this man, who makes friends with everybody, and at whom the "gentlemen," so called, of the low-country, affect to sneer, is a genuine Red Republican in his disregard of what are called "ancient rights and privileges." Sitting with great blue-gray eyes that seem always half asleep, he is always alert and wide-awake; slouching along with a rolling gait, he is careful and earnest; utterly wanting in the power of oratory or rhetoric, he has made more points than any other member of the Convention, and has carried all of them but one, and that of minor importance. He is the leader of the advance line of the up-country delegates, not so much by any election as by the inherent force of necessity; for he fights independently, and leaves them no choice but to follow. He is fairly entitled to the honors of the day in the open-field fight against the Conner resolution, and has been from the first the restless and untiring and self-possessed and good-humored enemy of the parish system, or, to use his own phrase, "the Chinese conservatism of Charleston." His object has been, and still is, to cripple the power of the low-

4 *   F

country in every possible way. He will take no bond of fate, but builds his walls of offence and defence in the Constitution itself.

On the eighth day, the low-country attempted by strategy to recover what it had lost in a shoulder-to-shoulder contest. Power through control of the Senate had been taken away, but power might be regained through control of the House. Therefore the sea-coast delegates generally supported the scheme for including three fifths of the blacks as an element of population in establishing the basis of representation. I have already reported the action on that question, — how it was debated through five long hours, lost by 52 to 59, reconsidered by 55 to 51, and finally tabled by 75 to 24. There were various times during the day when it seemed as if the low-country would win the battle; but the final vote showed its strength to be relatively about the same as in the struggle on the parish representation. This was its last effort, — the sceptre has departed from Judah.

On the tenth day, Tilman smote the routed enemy once more; he called it "reaping the just fruits of victory." His blow came in the form of an amendment to the Constitution, providing that, after 1869, no district in the State shall have more than twelve representatives. This was aimed at the city of Charleston, which now has twenty. The low-country was exhausted, and the amendment was adopted after a brief debate by 61 to 43.

This record closes with to-night. I see no chance for again striking the low-country. The end of the Convention is near. The up-country has won in every point it made. Hereafter it will be responsible for the legislation of the State. The first Legislature will be elected under the old system. Thenceforward the new Constitution will govern; under it South Carolina cannot be the haughty and exclusive creature she was in ante-Rebellion days.

X.

MINOR WORK OF THE STATE CONVENTION.

Columbia, September 25, 1865.

THE Convention has about finished its labors. I have reported its action in regard to all the more important questions, and have now to speak of but three subjects, — first, the miscellaneous business; second, the attitude of the Convention toward the general government; third, its talk and action in respect to the freedmen.

And, first, of the miscellaneous business, including thereunder the chief unmentioned amendments to the Constitution.

The Convention can scarcely be said to have amended the old Constitution; it has, the rather, been making a new one. The more important changes not already given, as well as the action on certain rejected propositions, are indicated as follows : —

The election of Presidential electors is taken from the Legislature and given to the people. This change created considerable debate, some twenty-five or thirty of the older delegates being seriously opposed thereto.

The election of Governor is taken from the Legislature and given to the people; the term of office is changed from two years to four years; he is declared ineligible for two consecutive terms; and the fifteen hundred pounds sterling freehold qualification is abolished. The questions involved in the action on this section have been much canvassed by the people, and there is a considerable body in the Convention strongly opposed to the change. It was, however, so well understood that this was one of the particulars in which the President required that a more republican form should be given the Constitution, that the section passed without a division.

The Lieutenant-Governor, elected like the Governor, and having the same qualifications and term of office, is made *ex officio* President of the Senate.

A proposition to give the appointment of Secretary of State, and Treasurer and Comptroller-General, to the Governor, with the consent of the Senate, led to a protracted and somewhat excited debate, and was finally lost by 39 to 72. Their election remains as heretofore, — with the Legislature.

The property qualification — a freehold of three hundred pounds sterling for State senator; a freehold of five hundred acres of land and ten negroes, or a real estate valued at one hundred and fifty pounds sterling, for State representative; and a freehold of fifty acres, or a town lot, for a voter — has been abolished. The first-mentioned change prevailed by a vote of 59 to 47; the others were made without division.

The effort to provide that no man should vote unless he could read the Constitution was, of course, a failure. " It would disfranchise at least a quarter of the people," said one cautious delegate. " More than that," said another. " I have known a grand jury within the last ten years of which only one man could write his name," echoed a third. The proposition came from Delegate Thompson, of St. Helena Parish, and found the table within five minutes of its presentation.

The veto power is given to the Governor, but a majority of the whole representation in each house may pass any bill over his veto.

A District Court is created to take jurisdiction of all civil cases wherein one or both the parties are persons of color, and of all criminal cases wherein the accused is a person of color. The judge of this court is elective by the Legislature, holds his office for four years, and is eligible to a re-election.

A resolution was passed, expressing the opinion that the Legislature ought, at its next session, to adopt the Constitutional amendment submitted by Congress at its last session. There was no debate upon the matter.

The General Assembly is forever prohibited by ordinance from passing "any law imposing civil disabilities, forfeiture of property or of other rights, or punishment of any kind, on any citizen or resident of the State, or person owning property herein, for the relation of such citizen, resident, or person to, or his or her conduct in reference to, the late secession of this State from the Federal Union or the war which grew out of the same, or for any participation, aid, counsel, or assistance therein."

The new Congressional districts are established by counties, and are as follows : —

First District, — Lancaster, Chesterfield, Marlboro, Darlington, Marion, Horry, Georgetown, Williamsburg, Sumter, Clarendon, and Kershaw.

Second District, — Charleston, Colleton, Beaufort, and Barnwell.

Third District, — Orangeburg, Edgefield, Abbeville, Lexington, Newburg, Richland, and Fairfield.

Fourth District, — Anderson, Pickens, Greenville, Lawrence, Spartanburg, Union, York, and Chester.

And, second, with respect to the attitude of the Convention toward the general government.

The debate on the Aldrich resolution, on the Jeff Davis pardon-memorial question, on the St. Helena election case, on the slavery clause of the Constitution, and on the Congressional-representation ordinance, showed very clearly the political standing of the delegates. They have no special love for the Union, but war has taught them a hearty respect for the United States. They talk very little and very mildly about State rights, but not one of them was able to see that the secession ordinance should have been annulled instead of repealed, — for does not a mere repeal amount to a practical reaffirmation of the right to secede? However, the question never will be of special consequence so far as this State is concerned ; for the whole Confederacy, late and so-called, could not coerce her into again taking up arms against the general government.

And, third, of the talk and action of the Convention in respect to the freedmen.

The temper of the Convention toward the negro is very far from being what the friends of humanity desire. The delegates, generally speaking, are probably better disposed toward him than the majority of their constituents, for I suppose they represent the best intelligence of their respective districts; but even their views, as a body, are extremely narrow and supremely selfish, not to add of the most fancifully fearful character.

Governor Perry, of whom I have heretofore spoken as the leading man in the Convention, began the hue and cry against the poor African in the message delivered on the second day of the session. True, he says slavery is gone, — "dead forever" is his tautological phrase; but he rails against the negro soldiers, actually has the face to quote the Dred Scott decision against the negro's right to citizenship, and indorses the dreary and absurd falsehood that "this is a white man's government, intended for white men." I submit that this sort of talk, admissible from a sixth-rate ward politician, is entirely out of character for even a Provisional Governor, can do no possible good to any living man, and is productive of nothing but increased ill-feeling between the two classes of people who now occupy the State, and must continue to occupy it during this generation at least.

There has been a great deal of this white-man's-government talk, in face of the fact that the negroes in the State number one third more than the whites, and the fact that they have almost to a man desired the success of the Union in the war, and the further fact that the whites of some sections are asking that soldiers may be kept in the State to protect them. Such men as James L. Orr, Thomas Thom-

son, General Sam McGowan, Rev. Dr. Boyce, Dr. Robert
Dozier, George D. Tilman, to say nothing of a dozen men
of less note, have allowed themselves indulgence in passionate declamations by way of echo to the message.

Obnoxious and short-sighted as the Convention is in this
regard, — for the men who were going to fight the Yankees
from street to street of all their cities and chief towns, and
finally die in the last ditch, seem to have learned little wisdom of language, — there is something still worse. " The
negro is an animal whose character the North seems utterly
unable to comprehend," said one of the sea-coast delegates.
In that phrase lies the key of the Convention's sentiment
and judgment, — the negro is an animal; a higher sort of
animal, to be sure, than the dog or the horse, but, after all,
an animal.   Even so taciturn a man as Mr. Chancellor Inglis felt it necessary to rise and gravely argue that the negro
is a human being, has the right of life and protection by the
laws, and must receive attention even from men who make
Constitutions.   Ask any given delegate if the negro is a
human being, and you of course insult his intelligence; but,
for all that, the Convention treats him like an animal whose
presence is endured, but is no way desirable.   Individual
men there are who sincerely sympathize with him in his
anomalous and trying condition, — men who contemplate
the labor question with as much grave anxiety as any man
in the North; but these are the exception, not the rule, and
they only serve to make more hideous the general average
sentiment and political judgment.

The general debate in respect to the abolition of slavery,
and the leading points of the debate in respect to the proper
and expedient basis of representation in the General Assembly, have been given; and there remains only to report
what was said and done regarding negro evidence and negro
suffrage.

Mr. Mayor Macbeth, of Charleston, introduced the ordinance giving the negro the right to testify. " I consider it proper," said he, " that the Convention should act on this subject. It is not a question as to our opinion on the propriety of allowing him to thus give evidence, but a question of retaining military courts or permitting him to appear in our civil courts." No word, you see, for the inherent right of every man to be heard in his own defence, but simply a cold question of policy. Yet even this raised a storm. Nothing more was asked than that it be sent to a committee for their report; but this common courtesy was denied by a sharp and decisive vote. The temper of the Convention was unmistakable; but Mr. Orr rose and rebuked the delegates, saying a proposition to refer for inquiry was rarely rejected, and to reject the present motion would be a very grave matter. This brought the question again before the house, when a bare majority allowed it to go to the Committee on the Judiciary Department, from which it finally came with a recommendation that it be passed, in the following form : —

" We, the people of the State of South Carolina, by our delegates in Convention met, do declare and ordain, and it is hereby declared and ordained, that hereafter colored persons shall be permitted to testify in all the courts of this State, in all cases where the rights of person or of property of persons of that class are involved."

The report was received with a great deal of disfavor, and action on it was from time to time postponed, without debate, till to-day, when it was called up and ordered before the freedmen's code commission, which the Governor has been instructed to appoint, — only three delegates — Judge Edward Frost of Charleston, Dr. A. P. Wylie of Chester, and J. G. Thompson of Beaufort — being prepared to vote at once for the ordinance.

" How long do you suppose the agitation of the question of negro suffrage can be staved off in the State?"

said I to an up-country delegate of high standing. "Till the taking of the next census, I hope," he answered. "Do you really believe it can be kept down five years?" "Yes, I think it will be," was his final reply. That the Convention would show any favor to the question I presume no one really expected. Even South Carolina, with all her desolation, does n't yet fully comprehend that there has been a deluge. I did hope, however, that I should find half a dozen men at least in favor of giving suffrage to some negroes, as many more in favor of abolishing the barbaric color qualification, and still as many more ready to admit that suffrage would be the right of the negro as soon as he is able to use it understandingly. Vain hope! If there are six men who so much as admit that it will probably be right or politic to give suffrage to any negro of their State within ten years, four of them must be among the thirty or thirty-five whose views I have not personally learned.

Perhaps a score of delegates have taken occasion to express themselves in very strong terms as now and forever opposed to negro suffrage in any form, no matter what the limitations. Mr. Dawkins said the freed people were clearly unfit to vote now, and he did n't think the Convention was called upon to express any opinion as to what they might be in the future. Mr. Orr would vote against giving them the ballot, but presumed the fanatics of the North would not be content till they had secured it for them. Mr. Dozier would accept negro suffrage when the moral and intellectual character of the negro has been so elevated that he is fit to take part in government. Mr. Inglis said negroes were no more qualified to vote now than children. Judge Frost said the negro was to be treated as a human being who had civil rights, and unquestionably would, at no very distant day, have political rights. Mr. Melton, of Chesterfield, said the idea that South Carolina might, within five years, admit negro suffrage, was not more startling than the idea would have been, in 1860, that she would within five years declare slavery abolished. With these six exceptions, I believe no expression has been made indicating any degree of tolerance for the bare idea of negro suffrage.

POSTSCRIPT.

The Convention adjourned *sine die* on the evening of September 27th, having held a session of thirteen days. A proposition to adjourn subject to the call of the President of the Convention was lost by a vote of 24 to 57.

Much has been said about the so-called Hammond resolutions, and I find an impression prevailing in some quarters that the Convention repudiated the State-rights doctrine. On the contrary, however, it was very careful to do nothing of the sort, as a brief statement will show.

On the fourth day of the session Mr. Paul H. Hammond, a son of the late United States Senator of that name, introduced a series of resolutions "declaratory of a national policy." They were referred to the Committee on Ordinances and Resolutions, which, on the seventh day of the session, reported them back in the following form : —

" Inasmuch as a fundamental difference of opinion in reference to the character, powers, and policy of the government of the United States and of the State governments, existed in the Convention which framed the Constitution, and, after more than three quarters of a century of political contest, resulted in a bloody and exhausting war; and, whereas, when a people draw the sword, appealing to the last and highest tribunal known to man, they should abide by its decisions in good faith; and, whereas, it is neither wise nor politic in the people of the South to continue any longer a contest in which they have been twice defeated, once by political majorities and once by the sword : therefore, we, the people of South Carolina, in Convention assembled, accept, as the results of the war, the principles embraced in the following resolutions, and will sustain them fully and faithfully as a national policy : —

" *Resolved*, That the Union is the first and paramount consideration of the American people.

"*Resolved*, That it is the true policy of the American people to confine the general government strictly within the limits of the Constitution, and to acknowledge the inalienable right of each State to regulate its own affairs in its own way.

" *Resolved*, That it is an incontrovertible fact that slavery has ceased to exist through the exercise of the military power of the Federal government, and that any attempt by us to revive it would be impolitic, unwise, and not only futile, but disastrous.

" *Resolved*, That the late war arose from an apprehension, on the part of the weaker section, of oppression and tyranny in the future, and was carried on under an honest conviction, coexistent among statesmen in every part of the country, with the adoption of the Constitution itself, that a State had the reserved right to revoke the powers it had delegated to the general government, whenever, in the judgment of such State, there might be danger that those powers would be used to its disadvantage. The war, therefore, not having been strictly in the nature of rebellion or insurrection, we most respectfully suggest to His Excellency the President the justice and wisdom of not enforcing the pains and penalties affixed to those crimes by the laws of the United States.

" *Resolved*, That we indorse the administration of President Johnson, and will co-operate with him in the wise measures he has inaugurated for securing the peace and prosperity of the whole country."

These resolutions, with the accompanying introduction, are substantially, so far as they go, the same as those introduced by Mr. Hammond, — the changes made by the committee being few and verbal and wholly unimportant.

It is a very curious and suggestive fact, however, that the committee rejected the second of Mr. Hammond's series, which was in these words : —

" *Resolved*, That sovereignty, a unit absolute and indivisible, which, in all nations, must exist somewhere, resides in the American people ; and its authorized representative within the limits of the organic law — i. e. the Constitution — is the Federal government."

The resolutions as reported from the committee were made the special order no less than four different times; but, strangely enough, on each occasion something else was found to be more pressing, and their consideration was never reached.

On the last day of the session, however, the Convention took up, and unanimously passed, the following resolution, which was introduced by Colonel Henry G. Simonton of Charleston :

"*Resolved* by the delegates of the people of South Carolina in Convention assembled, That we indorse the administration of President Johnson, that we cordially approve the mode of pacification proposed by him, and that we will co-operate with him in the wise measures he has inaugurated for securing the peace and prosperity of the whole Union."

XI.

SUMMARY OF FOUR WEEKS' OBSERVATIONS.

CHESTER, September 27, 1865.

THE attitude of the people toward the general government is, on the whole, pretty good. I am convinced that even in South Carolina there was a large body of men who never favored Rebellion. I do not make this assertion except after much inquiry and conversation. State pride, State pride, — that is what ruined South Carolina. Men went into Rebellion, not of original choice, but because the State did. These men say now, — said in the Convention to those who talked of conservatism in changes of the Constitution, — "O yes, if you'd had a little more conservatism five years ago, we shouldn't be where we are now."

It is already a question how the State got into Rebellion. "Disunion was born in the parishes," said an up-country delegate. "The political leaders carried us out," said one merchant to me. "The Rebellion came from the people," urged a man who had been a colonel in the Rebel army. "We went out to save slavery," argued Delegate Orr. "We went out for State rights," responded Delegate Dunovant. "The woman tempted us, and we did eat," answered Delegate Summer. It is a good sign that the people are found thus differing. "I begin to wonder, after all," said the mayor of one of the back cities, "if there was any real occasion for us to go to war." "You never'll get us into another war till we know exactly what it is about," remarked a Columbia merchant in my hearing.

There has been a great deal said about the existence of a sullen spirit in the State. I have not discovered much of it. The famous Aldrich resolution was an expression in that direction; but in a body of one hundred and ten members, it found but four supporters, even in a *viva voce* vote. Aldrich afterward made a speech in the same vein as his resolution, and the galleries applauded him heartily; but when I saw it I could not help recalling that the same gallery had previously heartily applauded McGowan's indignant speech against the resolution. The applause of a crowd of young loafers counts for very little, any way. I don't believe there are many Aldrich men in the State. Daily intercourse for over three weeks with all sorts of people and under very many different circumstances has failed to reveal them to me, if there are. The people have a prejudice against the Yankees, and they avow it without any hesitation. They are somewhat disposed to boast of their martyrdom. "The State is nothing now but a county of the United States," is a remark I have heard scores of times, as though there were pride even in recalling other days. The pride is perfectly harmless. They exult in their war record. "We believed we were right," they say, "and we fought for our belief with every possible energy." Remembering that the

State is a part of our nationality, shall we not, in other fashion though it be, also exult in the heroism of her people ? They are poor enough, but there is no humiliation in their poverty. "Incurred as ours was, it is no blame and no disgrace, but rather a glory and a boast," passionately exclaimed Chancellor Inglis one day when some one impliedly said the State ought not to admit her poverty. However it may be with other States, South Carolina is conquered, and has great respect for the power of the North. Love is something which must grow as respect did. All these various sorts of pride abound, but any widespread sullenness or obstinacy in respect to the general government there is not, unless my observation is wholly at fault.

Something has also been said about the existence of a fawning, cringing spirit. On the steamer I met a fellow from Charleston who had been to Washington with a pitiful story, in order to get pay for property destroyed. One of the up-country Convention delegates went before General Ames, whose head-quarters are at Columbia, and indulged in some tear-shedding while he told his story and asked for favor. Old Governor Pickens, as I have before said, was nervously sensitive that nothing should be said or done that could possibly give offence to His Excellency the President, or His Excellency the Provisional Governor. These are exceptions, however. The people at large have not that spirit.

Some persons like to show why the Rebel defeat occurred. Delegate Youmans impliedly says Davis was obstinate in keeping men in power whom the people would not trust; an up-country merchant with whom I travelled thought the negroes were not used as they ought to have been; a Charleston cotton-factor assured me the officials starved the army; a Columbia lady was confident victory went with us because we had the old banner, which the South might just as well have claimed; while an Orangeburg miss of eighteen or twenty said the Yankees had been deceitful, and were able to fight a great deal better than the South ever supposed they could. These diversions of why and wherefore are harmless enough ; let persons indulge in them if they will. The fact remains, that almost every man, woman, and child will readily own that the South is whipped. " We did the best we could in war, and were beaten; now we are going to do the best we can in peace," is the conclusion.

" Is there anything of defiance among the people ? " some one asks. " Who is so mad as to talk of further war ? " asks Delegate Inglis. " Who is crazy enough to dream of resistance by any power on this continent to the will of the United States ? " interrogates Delegate Orr. " If the youngest of you lives to my age even, you will not see another musket shouldered in the South against the Union," observes venerable Delegate Huger, with the weight of his eighty years bending him toward the grave. " Whose voice could raise a regiment, nay, a company, in the whole State for further resistance ? " exclaims Delegate McGowan. " The conqueror has the right to make the terms, and we must submit," say dozens of men everywhere.

It is idle and foolish, more, it is false and cruel, to urge or argue that there is danger of further armed resistance to the authority of the government in South Carolina. The argument against the restoration of the State to political fellowship must rest on other grounds. It can rest on other bases without losing any of its strength, too.

I know there were a score of ex-Confederate officers in the Convention. " Does n't that indicate a rebellious spirit ? " may be queried. For my part, I wish every office in the State could be filled with ex-Confederate officers. It is the universal testimony of every officer of our own troops with whom I have conversed, from the commanding general down, as well as of every Northern man two months resident in the State, that the late Rebel soldiers are of better disposition toward the government, toward Northerners, toward progression, than any other class of citizens.

The delegates of the Convention have mostly united in asking Colonel James L. Orr to allow himself to be voted for as Governor. He replies that he does not desire the office, but will accept it if elected. That he will be elected I do not doubt. A few men are advising that Wade Hampton be also brought into the field. He has many warm personal friends, and is popular with the masses; but I think the people will not elect him, even if he is a candidate. Mr. Orr never was very heartily in the Rebellion. "We always rather distrusted him," said a prominent ex-Rebel to me yesterday. The merit of his election will not, however, lie in his former relation to the war, but in his present views of State and National policy. He is pre-eminently the leader of the progressives, and is of far more liberal and sensible views, I think, than Governor Perry. When, four days ago, one of the Convention delegates, who mourns for the olden days, expressed his pride in the great men and the general hospitality of the State, Mr. Orr retorted that she never had anything else to be proud of; and then burst out into a passionate eulogy of the many-sided life of the North, and a scathing criticism of the narrow, inert, centralizing policy of South Carolina, which I shall not soon forget. " I am tired of South Carolina as she was," said he; " I covet for her the material prosperity of New England. I would have her acres teem with life and vigor and industry and intelligence, as do those of Massachusetts."

The white man and the negro do not understand each other, and consequently do not work together so harmoniously as it is desirable that they should. It would seem that, one party having work to do and the other needing work, there would be such community of interest as leads to unity of purpose and action ; but the fact is, that each party distrusts the other, and therefrom results bickering and antagonism.

That there are many kind-hearted planters — men who

made slavery in very truth a sort of patriarchal institution, and who are now endeavoring in all sincerity and earnestness to make the negro's situation not only tolerable, but comfortable — is as true as it is that there are many negroes who cling to the old places and the old customs, and are doing their work just as faithfully and unselfishly as ever. These men, on either side, are, I am convinced, the exceptions.

The fault unquestionably, it appears to me, lies with the white man. He is of the ruling race, and might, I feel very certain, have established a different order of things if he had pleased to do so, and had exercised good common sense in the beginning. That there are some planters who find the free negroes honest and faithful is positive proof that there might have been many more, and if many more, then without number.

Most of them began by assuming, however, that it was right to keep the negro in slavery just as long as possible, and by adding thereto the assumption that the free negro would not work. Military power has compelled the recognition of his freedom in every district, I believe, though in some of them not till within the last six weeks ; but this almost universal belief that he will not work is doing a good deal to prove that he will not ; and troubles which are dimly foreshadowed will come from this cause alone, — the brutal assumption that the negro cannot be controlled except by fear of the lash.

There is among the plantation negroes a widely spread idea that land is to be given them by the government, and this idea is at the bottom of much idleness and discontent. At Orangeburg and at Columbia, country negroes with whom I conversed asked me, " When is de land goin' fur to be dewided ? " Some of them believe the land which they are to have is on the coast ; others believe the plantations on which they have lived are to be divided among themselves.

5   G

One of the Convention delegates told me that an old negro man, who declined going away with some of the hands bound for Charleston, gave as his reason for remaining, that " De home-house might come to me, ye see, sah, in de dewision." There is also a widely spread idea that the whites are to be driven out of the lower section of the State, and that the negroes are there to live by themselves. That so absurd ideas as these could exist I would not believe till I found them myself. This latter notion I even found in Charleston among negroes.who had just come in from the back country. Other absurd notions well known to prevail are, that freedom can only be found "down-country," i. e. in the neighborhood of Charleston ; that it is inseparable from the presence of the army, etc.

Some of these ideas, it was, of course, natural the negro should have, — they are born of his blind and passionate longing for liberty, born of his weary waiting in the house of bondage. Where the poor creature got the others, and most dangerous, I'm sure I don't know. The whites charge the demoralization to the negro soldiers. However this may be, it is painfully certain that, next to teaching the whites that the negro is a free man and not an animal, the hardest work before the North now is to teach the negro what constitutes his freedom.

As I have already intimated, the negroes are drifting down toward the coast in great numbers. In the night of travel between Orangêburg and Columbia, we met scores of them trudging along with their whole earthly possession in a bundle on the head. Walking in the bright moonlight seventy or eighty rods ahead of the hack, I spoke with many. They had but few words ; " Goin' to Char'ston," was often their only reply. Whether talkative or taciturn, there was a firm foot and an unruffled voice for the coast. " What are you going to do there ? " I asked, — only to get for my answer, " Dun know." I never shall forget the scenes of that two or three miles' walk between one and two o'clock in the morning of that 11th of September. There had recently been some robberies of travellers on that road, and guerillas suggested themselves with every outline seen in the sheeny distance. Yet it was only the exodus of the negroes, going out ignorantly and mistakenly, yet seeking nothing less noble and worthy than freedom.

Despite the fact that nearly everybody tells me the free negro will not work, the experience of some of the better class of planters convinces me that he will work, if he is treated like a man. He is unquestionably sensitive about his freedom, — it is the only thing he has that he can call his own.

Some of the blacks are working along as heretofore, under private arrangements with their former masters ; but in most cases there is a written contract between the employer and the employed, — one copy in the hands of the planter and the other at the Freedmen's Bureau office. I hear of very few cases in which the compensation is in money ; in nearly all instances it is a part of the crop. The laborer's share ranges from one tenth to one half; on some small farms, where special privileges are given the negroes in the way of clothing, use of land, use of team, use of time, the share may not be over one sixth to one tenth of the regular crop ; in the lower part of the State, where most of the labor is done by hand, and where there are no special privileges, the share is from one third to one half; in the upper part of the State, where horses or mules are more in use, the share is from one fourth to one third. The contracts generally expire at New Year's.

It is beyond question that but little work has been done in the State this season. The free negro is the scapegoat on which the whites lay the burden of this wrong, of course ; but it seems to me that the disturbed condition of the country in the early summer and through all the spring is extenuation enough.

It is, however, true that the lately freed negro has not
generally been made to comprehend that there are six laboring days in each week.   The railroad companies complain that they can get but three or four days' work per week
from the blacks engaged in rebuilding the roads; and the
contract officers of the Freedmen's Bureau quite universally
concur in the statement that five days make a plantation
negro's week for work.   Instances in which the contract
officers have been called on to go out into the country and
convince the negroes that work must be done on Saturday
as well as on other days are not at all rare.

The indifference which so many of the people feel and
express as to the fate of the negro is shocking and to
the last degree revolting to me.   He is actually to many of
them nothing but a troublesome animal; not a human being,
with hopes and longings and feelings, but a mere animal,
valuable, but altogether unlovable.   " I would shoot one
just as soon as I would a dog," said a man to me yesterday
on the cars.   And I saw one shot at in Columbia as if he
had been only a dog, — shot at from the door of a store, and
at midday!   " If I can only git shet of 'em I don't care
what becomes of 'em," said one of my two stage companions in the ride from Columbia to Winnsboro, while speaking of the seventy negroes on his plantation.   Of course
he means to " git shet of 'em " as soon as possible.   There
are others who will follow his example.

There has been much talk to the effect that the planters
are, now that the main work of the season is over, turning
the negroes adrift.   It will not be easy to do this on any
large scale, nor can I believe that many employers will attempt it.   Indifference most heartless is one thing, — downright active cruelty is quite another.   The one may prevail;
but, aside from all other considerations, fear of the military
will prevent the other.   The facility with which the negro
can bring his late master before the provost-marshal is
something not wholly unpleasant to see.

The whole labor system of the State is in an utterly demoralized condition. How soon it can be thoroughly reorganized, and on just what basis that reorganization will take place, are questions of no easy answering. The labor question, and not reconstruction, is the main question among intelligent thinking men of the State. Scarcely one in a dozen of the best of them have any faith in the negro. " The experiment of free negro labor is bound to be a failure; and you of the North may as well prepare for it first as last," is substantially the language of hundreds. And thereafter follow questions of, " What shall then be done with the negro?" and, "Where shall we then get our labor?"

Look at the figures for a few districts. In Sumter there were, in 1860, of whites, 6,857, and of negroes, 17,012; in Fairfield, 6,373 whites, and 15,736 negroes; in Colleton, 9,255 whites, and 32,661 negroes; in Beaufort, 6,714 whites, and 33,339 negroes; and in Georgetown, 3,013 whites, and 18,292 negroes. Is it any wonder that the white population of these districts is nervously sensitive about the negro? The proportion of blacks is even greater now than these figures indicate; for war has taken out the whites and brought in the negroes to such an extent that one delegate told me there were in his parish but twenty-two voters and over two thousand negroes. What is to come of such a condition of affairs?

The question is not to be whistled down the wind with the answer, "It will regulate itself"; for straightway on its heels follows this, How will it regulate itself? Suppose you give suffrage to the negro in a State whose population now must be about one third white and two thirds negro? It is no question of punishment for those who have fought against the government; over that fleeting and insignificant matter is the great problem of the good of the two races, the advancement of humanity, and the lofty democratic right of every man to a voice in choosing his rulers.

XII.

THE GREAT MILITARY PRISON OF NORTH CAROLINA.

SALISBURY, September 29, 1865

SALISBURY, — of hateful notoriety, of sharp and painful memory to a hundred thousand hearts! Salisbury, — cursed of men dying of cold and starvation, cursed of men driven mad by fiendish torture! Salisbury, — one of the horrible names an unclean and infamous usurpation carved on its sinful and loathsome monument!

It is a comely enough little town, lapped in a pleasant country, but one can never forget its slaughter-yard. You see its site from the car window as you come up from the south. Its southwestern corner came down to within fifty feet of the railroad track. Its northwestern corner came up to the town line, and is scarcely eighty rods from the principal hotel.

The Salisbury military prison was established in the summer of 1863. At first, and for more than a year, it was occupied as a penitentiary for the confinement of what were called State prisoners, — Southern Union men, captured naval officers, deserters from the Union armies, and Northern men held on suspicion or as hostages. It was first used as a place of confinement for soldiers captured in battle in the fall of 1864. Previous to that time persons confined here were treated much better than at the majority of the Rebel prisons; but some time in the summer of that year Major John H. Gee, of Selma, Alabama, a coarse and brutal wretch, was made commandant; and his cruelties not only soon balanced the account, but made the prison the terror of our army, and only less dreadful than Andersonville.

The prison proper was a brick building, forty by one hundred feet in size, and four stories in height, formerly a cot-

ton factory. Connected with it were six small brick buildings, — formerly offices and tenement houses, — and a small
frame hospital, large enough for no more than fifty or sixty
beds.

At a later day these buildings were enclosed in a yard
of about six acres, and, after the fall of 1864, were entirely
used for hospital purposes. The stockade wall was a stout
board fence some twelve feet in height, on which sentinels
were stationed fifty feet apart. Inside the wall was a ditch,
varying in width from six to ten feet, and in depth from
three to six feet.

In the spring and summer of 1864 respectable citizens
were allowed to visit Northern men confined here, and the
condition of the prisoners at that time was comparatively
good. I am satisfied that there were some genuine Union
people resident in the town, and many more in the counties
to the westward. These never wearied in good offices to
the prisoners, and for a while they did much to mitigate the
rigors of confinement. All this was changed, however, when
Gee became commandant, and particularly after the Rebels
began to confine soldiers here.

In the fall and winter of 1864 not less than fourteen
thousand men were herded within this small enclosure like
sheep, tortured with infernal malignity, cheated of food when
the storehouses half a mile away were bursting with rations,
cheated of shelter when fifty or sixty thousand feet of lumber
originally intended for this use was lying useless at the upper end of the town, cheated of fuel when magnificent forests
were almost within rifle-shot! The poor wretches fought
for bones like dogs. One boy went crazy, and ate nearly
all the flesh from his arm below the elbow! To save themselves from storm and cold, they burrowed in the earth like
wild animals; and the keeper went round of a morning and
stirred up the mass in each hole to see how much of it had
died during the night! It is beyond all human comprehen-

sion why Divine Mercy permitted these things to be. The
number of deaths ran as high as seventy-five per day; in
one period of eight days, five hundred and twenty-six were
tumbled out for the dead-wagon; for three months the daily
average was not less than forty. In the aggregate the Rebellion murdered here over seven thousand men!

The prisoners, thanks to the tender mercies of their cap-
tors, came to the place generally without shoes or blankets,
rarely with overcoats, and often without blouses. The buildings in the stockade were soon overflowing with the sick.
For those not admitted to the hospital there was very little shelter, though it is said by negroes that the prisoners
begged again and again for the privilege of going out under
guard to cut logs to use in building barracks. The winter
of 1864–65 was unusually severe in this latitude, and snow
fell here to the depth of three inches on several occasions
between the 1st of November and the 1st of March.

It is beyond all question that the wretch Gee deliberately
starved many of the prisoners. Men who were Rebels during the war admit as much. I am told that the commissary
warehouses were full of provisions, which the commandant
again and again refused, in shockingly profane terms, to
issue even to the poor creatures in hospital. Much of the
time only half-rations were allowed, and on more than one
occasion hundreds of men got nothing for forty-eight hours.

The sufferings of the prisoners were so great that efforts
were constantly making to escape. That many of them did
escape we all know. "Golly, I seed a-many of 'em come
down fru ole Mas'r's fiel' to Pete, hes cabin," said an aged
negro man whom I met yesterday. He lived thirty miles
west of the town last winter, and had been horsewhipped for
feeding the Yankees. That the prisoners were sometimes
aided in escaping by officers of the prison is at least believed
by not a few persons living hereabouts.

Concerning the insurrection which took place here last

November, one can learn but little. That a small body of prisoners rushed upon the guard for the purpose of overpowering them, that they succeeded in this endeavor, that they failed to get out of the stockade, that the gun of the fort at the corner was turned upon the prison and fired, that at least one hundred men were killed or severely wounded, — so much my persistent inquiries seem to establish.

"Does ye call dis yer hor'ble?" said a negro man whom I met this morning as I walked over the stockade; "I calls it beautiful since Stoneman polished it up." Indeed, flame and wrath did their work well, and the Salisbury military prison is a thing of the past, which man nevermore can see.

The walls of the old factory building stand intact, but roof and floors and windows are all gone. The small brick buildings exist only as half a dozen irregular piles of rubbish. Some of the hundred great oak-trees within the stockade are already dead and others are dying. The fence shows only a line of post-stumps and post-holes. The ditch has been partially filled. The well which supplied the prison is no more used. Three fourths of the great pen is covered with a sprawling fireweed, offensive alike to sight and smell. There is satisfaction in all this; yet signs many remain of the dreary days of last winter. You find, in strolling about, the broken bowl of an earthen pipe, the well-worn blade of a belt knife, even the regulation button of a soldier's coat. Here is where the earth was scooped away to make a bank in which bricks could be laid so as to give draft for a fire; there you see where other bricks were laid to furnish a heated surface for cooking purposes.

Treading at random over ground on which there is neither grass nor vegetation, you seem often to find yourself walking on yielding soil. Here were the holes in which men lived. They were all filled by Stoneman's troops; but the filling of a few was done so imperfectly that it is easy enough to see what they were. From three to five feet

5 *

deep, irregularly circular in shape, from two to six feet in diameter on top, with sides so scooped under that the bottom diameter was generally half larger than the other, — this is what they were. In them lived all the negro and many of the white prisoners, for months. They were in the lower part of the stockade, and could scarcely have been dry even in the dryest season of the year; while one shudders at the thought of what they were in the stormy months of winter and spring. It was in such mud-holes as these that Rebellion murdered our soldiers.

Night and morning the dead wagons came. "I saw'd three and four and five big wagons loaded of a mornin' right often," said the barber under whose hands I sat; "and they dragged 'em about by the legs and arms just like as if they 'd been dead hogs; and none on 'em had much clothes on; and their hair was all full of red mud; and their heads swung over the sides of the wagon; and the fellers they 'd crack a head with their whips, and say out loud, 'Lie still there, you d—d Yankee,' and then laugh; and they did n't take no more care on 'em than 's if they 'd been dead hogs."

Down the road where those poor bodies were thus hauled I walked to the place of their burial. There is a good view of the pleasantest part of the town, as you go, and full sight of hundreds of acres of very heavy forests. It is a long slope to the southwest, a little muddy brook, a sharp ascent of forty or fifty feet, and there they were tumbled out into the trenches. "I heerd how 't was done," said an elderly white man who came along while I sat on the fence, — "I heerd how 't was done, an' I cum over yer one Sun'ay to see was it so bad as the soldiers said 't was. 'T was a cold an' nasty evenin', sir, an' they jist caught 'em up, one man to the arms and one to the legs, an' slung 'em in from the wagon; an' some on 'em said one man was n't dead, but they jist flung him in with the rest. I never cum yer no more, sir, till the Yankees got this yer fence built."

I told an ex-Confederate captain, whom I talked with at
the hotel, what stories I had heard about the treatment of
the dead bodies, and asked him if he supposed they could
be true in whole or part.   " Well, you see, we had our best
men all in the field, and there were a good many Alabama
fellows up here, and the Major in command was a d—d vil-
lain any how, and I reckon there were some right bad things
done.; but our people here protested against it to General
Lee and Mr. Davis, and 't was better after that."   I suppose
he meant after Major Gee was superseded, about last New-
Year's, by General Johnson.   Yet no man would dare put
into print all the stories told here about the outrages on
poor stark dead bodies during the months of November and
December last.

The cemetery is a quiet, retired, and lonesome spot, forty
rods east of the railway, seventy or eighty rods southwest
of the stockade, and half a mile or so south of town.   The
enclosure is nearly square, and about an acre in extent.
Around it is a neat, plain, high, and strong board fence, built
by Stoneman's orders, — the oak posts having already done
some service in the wall of the stockade.   The ground slopes
gently to the eastward ; in the northeastern corner are two
or three small oaks ; in the southeastern some twenty or
twenty-five small pines.   The bodies were laid in thirteen
long trenches.   No headboards were used, no record was
kept, and it is therefore impossible to tell where any particular soldier lies.   There are thirteen great graves.   As the
heartless Rebel guards filled them, so they must forever
remain.

XIII.

AFFAIRS IN WESTERN NORTH CAROLINA.

GREENSBORO, September 30, 1865.

THERE were three of us in the stage from Columbia to Winnsboro on the evening of the 25th, — a North Carolina planter, and an ex-Rebel colonel, beside myself. The planter was a coarse, vulgar fellow, whose whole thought seemed to be given to an effort to outwit the officers of the Freedmen's Bureau, and " git shet " of some sixty negroes on his tobacco plantation. The colonel was a man of much travel, liberal culture, and good heart, — glad the war is over, anxious to hereafter live in peace with everybody, and fearful that the negroes of the State will see very sore times before spring. We made the thirty-two miles in eight hours, at an expense of nine dollars apiece.

The trip hither from Winnsboro is made by railway, one hundred and sixty-four miles, in sixteen hours, at a cost of twelve dollars, exclusive of meals.

On that section of the road from Winnsboro to the Catawba River the rolling stock is passably good, and our train consisted of a baggage car, a negro car, a passenger car, and two freight cars. Our passengers were about a dozen negroes, twenty soldiers, three ladies, and ten citizens. Stoneman burned the long bridge over the Catawba, and it is not likely to be rebuilt before next summer.

Half a mile below the river we left our train, and were brought to this bank in a comfortable covered wagon, crossing the wide stream on an insecurely fastened pontoon bridge. It so happened that when the railroad bridge was destroyed most of the cars were below the river ; and our new train consisted of an old freight car, into which negroes and baggage loaded, and a miserable second-class passenger car, with a plain wood bench on each side in place of the ordinary seats. There were neither curtains nor blinds for the windows, and the mercury stood at about ninety.

On the section of railway from Charlotte to Greensboro the rolling stock is comparatively good, many of the cars just having been thoroughly repaired and repainted. The road-bed is also in much better condition than that of any South Carolina road, though the iron is badly worn, and must soon be in great part replaced. The line runs two passenger trains per day each way, with an express freight car attached to the morning train.

Sleeping cars are apparently an unknown thing on Southern railways, and bid fair to be so for some time to come. One can't help wondering frequently how it is possible for any one to be so stupidly opposed to comfort as are large numbers of Southern persons.

If sun and compass were both at fault, general observation would give ample assurance that I had moved northward. Much of the country through which one travels in Western North Carolina is suggestive of Pennsylvania, though occasionally there are oak openings like those of Minnesota and high plains like those of Iowa. Moreover, it abounds in small farms rather than in large plantations; and corn, not cotton, is the principal product. There are apple orchards and many peach-trees, some fences, and occasionally a comfortable and pleasantly situated farm-house. The ability of cooks for ruining eatables whilst preparing them for the table is also something less up here than in the low country, though they apparently labor to their utmost even in this State. Salvation for any one from the North lies in the fact that the average white of North Carolina is less intelligent than the average white of the other State, and therefore the effort to ruin the negro cook has not been as successful here as there.

Winnsboro and Chester in South Carolina, and Char-

lotte and Salisbury and Greensboro in North Carolina, are
five towns after one pattern.   Each is a county town of three
or four thousand inhabitants, and each has two hotels of such
character that the chance traveller stopping at either wishes
he had gone to the other.   Each town is noticeable for extreme length and an extreme absence of width.   There is a
main street, broad and dirty, about a mile in length, with a
deep well and great pump in the middle of the carriage-way
toward each end, and another about half-way between ; one
narrow and dirty street on each side the broad avenue ; about
a dozen narrow and dirty cross-streets.   In each town the
business is mainly done on the principal street, and in each
town the best private residences are at either end of this
principal street.

Inquiry and observation have satisfied me that the ten
hotels in these five towns are not unlike one another in many
features.   Give whatever directions you may in the evening, you are sure to be roused up half an hour after
daylight.   The servant wants your boots ; leave your boots
outside on retiring, and he wants to bring in fresh water ;
leave your boots and pitcher outside, and he wants to come
in to brush your clothes ; leave your boots and pitcher and
clothes outside, and he insists on waking you to see if you
don't want something ;   call him to your room five minutes
before retiring, assure him that you wear cloth shoes, don't
use water, can shake out your own coat, and will not want
anything in the morning but sleep, and just as surely as
next morning comes, so will that negro boy, who straightway
pounds at your door till you are wide awake, and then asks
if you are going in the early train !   At each of the hotels
where I stopped there was plenty of coffee at supper, but
neither request nor direction of mine could bring tea ; while
at one place a boarder told me he had made diligent effort
daily for a week to get it, and then had given up in despair.

I begin to meet avowed Rebels.   It is a mistake to suppose that this class of creatures is confined to South Carolina, even a mistake to suppose that it resides in that State in any considerable numbers. There are half a dozen here to one down there. Sherman visited that State; his army swept through it like a demon of devastation and destruction. No pen could tell how the pride and beauty thereof are laid in ruins. Yet that treatment was what the haughty little State needed. Let no man ever extenuate or apologize for his course. Less fire would have spared more property, but also more rebellion. More fire would have made more healthy spirit in this State. The people in the western part scarcely know, so far as their material interests are concerned, that there has been a war.

In South Carolina every man was ready to take the oath; he made no professions of Unionism, but he owned that he had been fairly beaten, wanted peace and privilege of trade, and would sincerely obey the government hereafter. Here there is a great deal of talk about " our rights," a great deal of complaint at the action of the government, and a great deal of that spirit which still refuses either to acquiesce or to be comforted. The manner of speech there in regard to the " Yankees " — meaning thereby all the people of the North — was respectfully appreciative even when indicative of bitter personal hatred. With the Rebel population of this section a " Yank " is spoken of in terms not only of dislike, but of contempt.

I was somewhat curious to see the Unionism of Western North Carolina of which we heard so much during the war. Considerable of it, I am convinced, was less a love for the Union than a personal hatred of those who went into the Rebellion. It was not so much an uprising for the government as against a certain ruling class. This is, of course, a general remark; for I find many intelligent men, whose Unionism is of the judgment and affection, and whose speech on almost every phase of the question at issue would do no discredit even to the radicalism of Massachusetts. Yet a rebellion against the little tyranny of local politicians was unquestionably at the foundation of much of the opposition to the Davis government.

For a man who wholly and passionately hates a Rebel, — hates him without the least allowance for any extenuating circumstance, — give me, however, one of these North Carolina Unionists.

At Charlotte I found one of them. He was something like sixty years of age, but seemed vigorous as most men at forty. "There's six or seven creeturs up in my deestric' as can't live there a gret while, now I tell ye," said he to me when I asked him how the Union men and the late Rebels got along together; "our deestric' 'll git shet of 'em putty soon. Ef they's fellers as can't taken a wink, we'll jest haf ter giv' 'em a nod." And he brought his arms and head into position for sighting a gun.

"You don't mean that there'll be any shooting done," said I.

"Don't I, though?" he answered.

"But the military will look after such things, and the county militia will very soon arrest any man who is lawless."

"Jes' so; but thar's jest six G—d d—n infernal sneakin' Rebels up in my deestric' as can't no how at all live thar six weeks longer. That thing's settled, Mister, and thar ain't no use talkin'!"

"But is there such feeling against the Confederate soldiers all through your county? Can't you let bygones be bygones, and all live in peace, and all turn in to improve the country and work on the farms?"

"It's jest here, Mister: I don't speak fur nothin' but my deestric', an' what I tell ye is what me an' my neighbors 'll stand to."

State the question to him as I would, he had only the one answer. He had nothing to say for any other part of the county. The word "district" is unusual hereabouts, and I could get from him no definite idea of the extent of territory it included, though he said there was a matter of five hundred people lived there.

The old man was singular only in his expression of the idea that there can be no fellowship with the ex-Rebel soldiers. In other forms I have heard it from at least a score of men since coming into the State. The feeling of hostility does n't seem so much founded in cool judgment as in passionate instinct. I know words are very cheap; but so many men from such different sections of the western half of the State could not speak to the same effect unless there were a general public feeling to that effect.

I made many inquiries, having in view the purpose of learning if the return of Rebel soldiers has been prevented by force or threats, or if there have been any outrages upon their persons or property. I found all men disinclined to converse upon the subject. A countryman from near Morgantown said a Rebel lieutenant was found dead near his house one morning three weeks ago, shot from behind through the head. An intelligent negro man from the section thirty miles back of Salisbury told one of the merchants of that town, in my hearing, that a certain Mr. Benson, formerly of that county, who had been in the Rebel army, was shot two weeks ago to-day by some person unknown. Men of character in Salisbury and Charlotte, as well as in this town, tell me that they have no doubt the ex-Rebel soldiers, those who were in any sense leaders, will fare hard at the hands of the mountain Unionists.

On the other hand, an out-and-out unconquered Rebel who introduced himself to me at Salisbury, by asking "Which way did you come from, stranger?" to which question I simply answered "From below," and who therefrom seemed to conclude that I must be a Rebel also, — this man said to me substantially that the Union men of the western

H

portion of the State, whom he invariably called "nigger Yankees," are the "meanest set of men the sun ever saw"; did n't go into the army because they "are cowards and d—n fools," and "will have to lower their tail-feathers a good deal or get into trouble." So, too, an ex-Rebel captain, on the cars between the Catawba River and Charlotte, said to a gentleman sitting next me on the bench, that he did n't propose to allow any "stay-at-home cuss" to lord it over him when he got there. One of the officers on duty at district head-quarters at Salisbury told me that some of the returning Rebel soldiers were disposed to make trouble with the men who did n't go into the war, and particularly with the few who had been in our service.

The temper of a large number of men in this end of the State appears to be indicated by the remark of a man opposite whom I sat at dinner one day in Salisbury. His neighbor asked him for whom he would vote in the coming Congressional election.

" I sha'n't vote at all."

" O yes, vote for somebody, — vote for me if you can't vote for any one else."

" No ; I won't vote. I don't know as I 'll ever vote again."

" Why, man, how you talk ! What do you mean ? Not vote when so much depends upon who is sent to Congress this winter? Not vote?"

" No, I 'll be d—d if I do ; and I 'll not vote again till I can do so without asking any d—d Yankee who I may vote for!"

Gentlemen who appear to be careful calculators assure me that in this section, — say the central part of the western half the State, — not more than one half, and some even say one third, of the legal voters appeared at the polls to vote for Convention delegates last week, for the reason that they knew that they could not vote for whom they pleased.

In South Carolina, as I have previously said, there was no-where, so far as I could learn, any pretence of military inter-ference with the election; and the composition of the Con-vention of that State was such, that I presume every man freely voted for his first choice. Here, however, while there is no complaint of direct interference by the military, it is charged that certain men are not elected because it was understood that the commanding officer of the district or sub-district would not allow any leading Rebel to serve.

In the South Carolina Convention there were a score of men whose record for Unionism was as bad, and for Rebel-lion as good, as that of any man in this State; and if their election could be permitted there, it would seem there could be no good reason for disallowing the election of such men here. Yet I see that even the Raleigh papers assert that not more than half the vote of the State was cast, and that many counties send so-called Union delegates, which, under a free election, would have sent men of an entirely different stamp. It would appear, therefore, from all I hear up this way, that while the South Carolina Convention represented the actual sentiment of the people of that State, the North Car-olina Convention will represent the sentiment of only one class of people, and that the class which calls itself the Union element.

In just what the military control or interference consisted it is impossible to learn. Two weeks before the election the department commander, General Ruger, issued orders to the effect that on election day officers and soldiers would not only be kept away from the polls, but within their re-spective camps, and that any person guilty of attempting to interfere with the election would be promptly and severely punished. So far as I can hear, there was neither violation of the letter nor the spirit of this order.

The complaint goes behind the order, and alleges from hundreds of mouths that certain men in every county whom the people desired to elect were compelled to refuse the use of their names. Did General Ruger, of the department, or General Heath, of the district, or Governor Holden, ever issue an order, or ever say directly or indirectly, or authorize any one else to say, that certain men must not be elected or would not be allowed to serve in the Convention? is a question I have, in one form or another, asked of fifty or sixty different men. I can get no tangible evidence of interference or dictation, though it is asserted and reasserted that there was an "understanding" that some men would, and others would not, be allowed to serve as delegates.

The poor whites could be relied upon during the war because their instincts led them in a path parallel to that taken by the government. Now, however, say many of our officers on duty in this section, they give us more trouble than the real Rebels, — those who voluntarily went into the Rebel army. They have very little judgment, and their instincts do not now lead them toward the ends the government is pursuing. Not a few of them claim that the farms of the leading Rebels should be apportioned out among those who fought Rebels.

I have already spoken of the somewhat savage disregard of the lives of those who have been known as Rebels. There is, further, an almost utter contempt of the property rights of Rebels in the country districts. It is a remark one often substantially hears, — "Every d—n thing in South Carolina ought to be destroyed, and every d—n man driven out of the country, and every d—n woman hung." Unquestionably these North Carolina Unionists have suffered much from Rebels before the war as well as during the war. I am not arguing a case against them, but only stating facts. The root of the matter is, that they are making the readjustment just what they made the Rebellion, — a personal issue with another class of the people. However satisfactory this fact may be to any man or any body of men in the North, it is one which gives trouble to our troops.

I did not anywhere in South Carolina, however, find Union men such as are to be seen even in Salisbury of bitter memory. The best Unionism of that State is more or less overgrown with the rank weed of State rights, but there are men here whose loyalty is as clean as that of Andrew Johnson. That they are numerous I cannot say, — I have neither seen many nor heard of many; but that there are even a score whom any ordinary traveller can find, is a sign of the times full of encouragement. One of the Convention delegates from Rowan County is a man whom the Rebels had in prison for his Unionism. "The government has been a great deal more lenient towards us than we should have been toward the North under similar circumstances," said a Union man to me here this afternoon, thus repeating almost the very words of an ex-Rebel surgeon with whom I talked at Charlotte.

I saw to-day for the first time a man who would not take "greenbacks" in payment for property. He came in from the country with a load of wood, and actually hauled it out of town this evening because no one would pay him for it in gold. Much inquiry in South Carolina discovered only two or three localities in which there would be probable difficulty in travelling without gold; but one of our majors, whom duty has called through over a dozen of these western counties within the last six weeks, tells me that the localities in which paper money would be taken are the exception rather than the rule; and a surgeon of our army whose home is fifty miles back of this place, and who has been up on two weeks' leave, said to me this forenoon that he lost the opportunity to make several good trades while there, because he had only legal-tender money. The people say, he observes, that having lost so much by one sort of paper money, they don't propose to take any of the other sort just at present.

The local police militia system is in full force through this section. "How does it work?" I asked of a smart lieutenant at Concord. "Hinders rather more than it helps," said he. I asked the same question of a smart negro man from the country back of Lexington, and he replied, "'Pears like it be ruther hard on de poor nigger." Yet, on the whole, I am satisfied that it has proved beneficial.

I saw one of the officers who organized the force in half a dozen counties. It is in companies of about seventy-five men, with officers approved or appointed by the district commander. Arms and ammunition are furnished by the government, the officers of the company being under bond for the proper use of the latter and the careful keeping and ultimate safe return of the former The force is under control of the military, and receives its orders from the assistant provost-marshals. In organizing it, this captain said he endeavored to get the best men he could find, — men of property and mature years, whose interest it would be to preserve order and not oppress the negro.

Special cases there have been, I am sure, in which the negro was abused, even by members of this force. Thus in Concord, on the day of the election, a gang of rowdies from the country made a wholly unprovoked attack on the negroes with clubs and stones, and the militia was not only found worthless for the preservation of order, but some of its members actually joined in the brutal assault upon the blacks. Apple-jack and whiskey were at the bottom of the row, which resulted in the flight of the negroes, the serious but not dangerous injury of three or four of them, the calling out of a company of troops, the arrest of about forty whites, of whom about half were discharged, about a dozen released on bail, and six or seven are yet in confinement for a further hearing.

This case is, however, exceptional; and whilst the aggregate of reported cases in which individual negroes have been maltreated by individual members of the militia is much larger than one would like to find it, there is no question but that the force has done very much to keep down the antagonism between the ex-Rebels and the non-Rebels which is so dangerous to the ultimate good of the negro. With proper military authorities hereabouts, and proper weeding out of the companies of militia from time to time, as the disposition of its members comes to light, I am satisfied that this local police force will become a strong influence on the right side, and be productive both of general good order and general protection to the negro.

XIV.

THE NORTH CAROLINA FREEDMEN'S CONVENTION.

RALEIGH, October 3, 1865.

" HAVE you been into both Conventions?" said I to an ex-Congressman from the North whom I met here this evening, referring to the Freedmen's Convention just closed, and the Constitutional Convention two days old.

" Yes, I've attended two sessions of each. I stopped down at the other hotel when I got here, and I took some pains to talk with a good many of the delegates to the Governor's Convention."

" Well, how do they talk about things in general and State affairs in particular?"

" There is n't loyalty enough in that whole house to hurt anything; and as for brains, they 're pretty much all over here at the African church."

Thus said the ex-Congressman, who has a national repute, and is not classed among the so-called " radicals."

In sober truth, the Freedmen's Convention was a body of which the negroes of this or any other Southern State might well be proud, and which no Northern man could see without feelings of hearty respect.

Just what reasons certain colored men had for calling a Convention of their people do not appear of record. This Convention has, however, proved its own justification for being; and has done a good work, not alone for the Freedmen of this State, but for the Freedmen of the entire South.

The call came from a committee of three, appointed at a meeting held in Wilmington about a month ago : —

" Let the leading men of each separate district issue a call for a meeting, that delegates may be chosen to express the sentiments of the Freedmen at Raleigh on the 29th of September, and let each county send as many delegates as it has representatives in the Legislature. Rally, old men, we want the counsel of your years and experience; rally, young men, we want your loyal presence, and need the ardor of youth to stimulate the timid; and may the spirit of our God come with the people to hallow all our sittings and wisely direct all our actions.

"A. H. GALLOWAY,
JOHN RANDOLPH, JR.,
GEORGE W. PRICE,
Committee."

The Convention met on Friday last, and terminated its labors to-day, after a four days' session. The sittings were held in the African church of this city. It is a plain, white, wooden building, with floor accommodations for about three hundred persons, and gallery accommodations for about one hundred more. Its floor is carpeted and its seats cushioned. The noticeable feature in it is a large and elegant and life-like plaster-of-Paris bust of Mr. Lincoln, standing on a bracket, and against a dark background in the farther end and over the pulpit seat. Over the bust is a canvas, bordered with black, on which is neatly inscribed the last paragraph of Mr. Lincoln's last Message : " With malice toward none, with charity for all, with firmness in the right, as God gives us to see the right, let us strive on to finish the work we are in, to bind up the nation's wounds, to care for him who has borne the battle, and for his widow and orphan; to do all which may achieve and cherish a just and everlasting peace among ourselves and with all nations."

The call provided for one hundred and twenty-two delegates. On the assembling of such as appeared on Friday, it was found that but about half the counties in the State were represented. In some I presume the call has never been seen, for the newspapers entirely ignored it till within a few days of the time set for the Convention. Aside from this supposition, though, there was reason enough, in the cost of travelling and the condition of the freed people out of the towns, for the small attendance from the western section. "We should have counted it a decided success, if even only a quarter of the counties had been represented," said one of the leading delegates; "as it is, we think we have achieved a great victory."

Many of the delegates had regular credentials from the proper county officers, but others were certified only by local organizations, church societies, &c. The difficulty of the occasion was met by resolving the affair into a general mass Convention of those who had credentials of any sort from any organized body of freedmen. The aggregate of delegates was one hundred and seventeen, representing forty-two counties, — all sincere, earnest men, and most of them here in "the spirit of our God." The great majority of them were freedmen, not freemen, though some of them have hardly yet been given by their late masters a realization of the fact they are even freedmen.

The temper of the body was exceedingly good, and was in general accord with the speech of the permanent President, — Rev. John W. Hood of Newbern, of Northern birth, but of some years' residence in this State, — who, on taking the chair, spoke as follows : —

6

"GENTLEMEN OF THE CONVENTION, — I hardly know how to express my thanks for the high honor you have conferred upon me; an honor I could scarcely have dreamed of enjoying, for I consider that there has never been and never will be a more important assembly than this now convened here. We have met to deliberate in a Christian spirit upon the best interests of our people, — holding up before God and men as our motto, 'Equal rights before the law,' yet understanding it to be wise and proper that, whether in doors or out of doors, we should bear ourselves respectfully toward all men. Let us avoid all harsh expressions toward anybody or about any line of policy. Let us keep constantly in mind that this State is our home, and that the white people are our neighbors and many of them our friends. We and the white people have got to live here together. Some people talk of emigration for the black race, some of expatriation, and some of colonization. I regard this as all nonsense. We have been living together for a hundred years or more, and we have got to live together still; and the best way is to harmonize our feelings as much as possible, and to treat all men respectfully. Respectability will always gain respect, not from ruffians, it is true, but from gentlemen; and I am convinced that the major part of the people of North Carolina are gentlemen and ladies. I do not mean one class alone, but the major part of the people, both white and black. That being the case, if we respect ourselves we shall be respected. I think the best way to prepare a people for the exercise of their rights is to put them in practice of those rights, and so I think the time has come when we should be given ours; but I am well aware that we shall not gain them all at once. Let us have faith, and patience, and moderation, yet assert always that we want three things, — first, the right to give evidence in the courts; second, the right to be represented in the jury-box; and third, the right to put votes in the ballot-box. These rights we want, these rights we contend for, and these rights, under God, we must ultimately have."

The Convention was very much like the mass Convention of white folks, "only a little more so." There were parties, cliques, demagogues, ambitious men, — there was "log-rolling," "wire-pulling," and a general exhibition of most of the arts by which would-be leaders attempt to carry their ends against the will of the mass. It was pleasant to see, however, that the great body of the delegates not only had a pretty clear conception of what they wanted to do, but, as is not always the case with convention delegates, also of what they wanted not to do. The men who, by virtue of some education, some travel, and some association with Northern people, aspired to rule matters for their own interest and aggrandizement were very quietly shelved on the second day, and thereafter found that their power was gone. So, too, those of passionate nature and demagogical spirit, who undertook to uplift themselves on the breakers of angry epithet and inflammatory declamation, were also put aside after the first day. That there were some droll scenes is, of course, true. Many of the delegates were like great noisy, ignorant children, and acted very much as a drove of such children do when they "play" convention. Others knew nothing of any meetings but the religious gatherings of their own people, and appeared to imagine that tears and shouts and sobs and ejaculations were as much in order here as in the prayer-meetings of the rural districts. The natural habit of the negro to exaggerate showed itself on the first day and in the first hour in a scramble for a seventh Vice-Presidency, and afterwards worked itself into furious speeches either about nothing or on wholly immaterial points. The dramatic element of the negro character came to the aid of his vivid imagination, and there were touches of pantomime that would have been instructive even to old Gabriel Ravel himself. Moreover, in the line of comedy-acting, a dozen of these delegates were competent to give lessons to Warren, or Clarke, or Jefferson; and three or four of the eight sessions were, as pure entertainments, better than two hours with Gough or any other master of humor known to the Northern public. The President's place was no office of mere honor, and the most diligent use of his powers would have been unequal to the task of keeping quiet and uniform good order.

Yet, when all these things are admitted, there is to be commended the sincere earnestness of the delegates as a body, the liberal spirit of their debates, the catholicity of their views of duty in the present emergency, the patient and cheerful tone of heart and head which prevailed, and the unfailing good-humor which bridged all chasms and overcame all difficulties. Their extra passion came only from extra zeal; their turbulence at times was merely the sudden flashing of warm good-will for their people; their unseemly drollery was but a manifestation of their natural disposition to enjoyment even under the most adverse circumstances.

Perhaps a dozen of the delegates were not native to this State; but, with few exceptions, those who took part in the debates or were in any way responsible for the action of the Convention, were not only North-Carolinians by birth, but slaves by growth, — men who have always lived and expect to continue living in the State. It is also worth remarking that it was really a Convention of colored men, not a colored men's Convention engineered by white men. It was even so strictly a Convention of the negroes of North Carolina, that there was some sensitive jealousy toward one or two delegates born in this State, but educated in the schools and under the influences of the North. "We meant it for a Convention of our own people," said one of the committee to me, "and these outsiders from Wilmington and Newbern shall not control us." The deficiencies of the Convention will, of course, be charged to the negroes of the State: its excellences, properly and in simple justice, also belong to them.

The leader of the body was Mr. John H. Harris, of this city; a man of scarcely one eighth white blood; a former slave who did his daily task with other farm negroes, and sat for hours, year in and year out, after that task was accomplished, in the fireplace, with a pine knot in one hand and a book in the other; who is, in the true sense, self-educated; an upholsterer by trade, and, latterly, a teacher by profession; a plain, patient, unassuming man, whose wise judgment, catholic views, genuine culture, and honest manhood, fit him to adorn any station in any society.

Others of the principal delegates were Mr. A. H. Galloway, of Fayetteville, of some service in our army, much association with Northern people, and of exceedingly radical and Jacobinical spirit; Mr. John P. Sampson, of Wilmington, a young man of ability, liberal education in Northern schools, and somewhat wordy radicalism; Mr. Isham Swett, barber, of Fayetteville, of rare dramatic talent, mature years, ready speech, moderate views; Mr. John R. Good, barber, of Newbern, of thoughtful heart and gray head and simple gentlemanhood; Mr. John Randolph, Jr., of Greensboro, carpenter by trade and teacher by profession, radical in desire, but conservative in action, longing for much, but content to make haste slowly; Mr. J. P. Shanks, of Charlotte, of few public, but many private words, and all of them words of soberness; Rev. Alexander Barr, of Raleigh, diffident and unassuming, but of weight in all councils; Sergeant Foster, of the First North Carolina Heavy Artillery, a good soldier, of few words and careful deeds; Rev. George A. Rue, late chaplain of the Thirty-second United States Colored Troops, a pure African, of six years' ministerial service in Massachusetts, whom Northern favor has made neither foolish nor haughty.

A great many unimportant matters were needlessly brought before the Convention, and there was much talk on trivial affairs, and a deal of wordy debate in respect to some legitimate business. Yet even all this was not without its value; for it brought out many facts and opinions of general use to the delegates as individuals, and served to help them to closer fellowship and more unity of sentiment in respect to the future. On the whole, the Convention did its work with commendable directness; and there were a number of speeches, and one or two somewhat lengthy debates, that would have been creditable to any white man's convention, with even picked delegates.

A dozen resolutions were reported and adopted, some of which, as usual, were unimportant. It must be said, however, that they all meant something, — which is more than can be said of resolutions often adopted at conventions in the North, — and that their general sense was wise, liberal, and appreciative.

The chief resolution declares that it is not the policy of the colored people to flock to the cities in too large numbers, and urges them to remain at their old homes and at their old employments, unless good reasons exist for changing; advises them to live soberly and honestly, work faithfully and industriously, save money and buy a few acres of land as soon as possible; build themselves houses, and sacredly observe the marriage relation; avoid quarrels, and cultivate friendly relations with the white people; help each other, and educate themselves and their children.

Other resolutions which were adopted express reverence for the memory of " those heroes, John Brown, Robert G. Shaw," numerous others of less note, " and last and greatest, Abraham Lincoln "; hail with satisfaction the passage of the Constitutional amendment, the organization of the Freedmen's Bureau, the establishment of schools for the education of seventy-five thousand colored children, the admission of John S. Rock to the bar of the Supreme Court, the issuing of the Emancipation Proclamation, and the recognition of Hayti and Liberia; thank the good people of the North for their aid so freely extended to the freedmen in a thousand ways; thank that portion of the Republican party led by Messrs. Chase, Greeley, Sumner, and others, for its efforts to secure to the colored man his rights through Congressional action; and declare that any colored man who will not do for another colored man what he would for a white man under similar circumstances is unworthy of respect.

A considerable part of one afternoon was given to debate upon a resolution which advised colored teachers for colored children and colored preachers for colored congregations. The resolution was supported by Messrs. Harris, Sampson, Bass, and others, and opposed by Messrs. Galloway, Rue, Randolph, Good, Sweat, and others. The argument for its passage was, that it would tend to stimulate education among the young men and women; that against it was, that it would serve to set up another wall between blacks and whites. Several delegates favored the general policy enunciated in the resolution, but opposed its passage, on the ground that some of the more ignorant of their people would look upon it as a recommendation not to send their children to the schools established by the Freedmen's Bureau and the Aid Societies of the North. This argument carried the day, and the resolution was tabled.

The chief thing done by the Convention, however, was to adopt an address for presentation to the State Convention which met yesterday, and to the Legislature which meets in November. How this address should be prepared was a subject of anxious consideration. There was some fear at the close of the first day's session that the Convention had fallen into control of the unwise and hot-headed faction. The excitement natural to the hour wore off, however, before the next session, and the drawing up of the address was intrusted to a committee of five elected *viva voce* by the delegates. Five better men could not have been selected. It was certain that their action would be wise and judicious; and the real good sense of the Convention showed itself in the hearty unanimity with which it adopted the following very noteworthy paper: —

" To the Constitutional Convention of North Carolina and the Legis-
lature to assemble thereafter : —

" Assembled as delegates from different portions of the State of
North Carolina, and representing a large body of the colored population, we most respectfully and humbly beg leave to present to
you, and through you to the people of the State, something of our
situation and our wants as a people.

" Earnestly disclaiming all wish to forestall your action or to
dictate in the solemn and important duties which have been intrusted to you at this most critical period, and confiding in your
justice, wisdom, and patriotism to guard the interests of all classes,
and more particularly of that class which, being more helpless,
will most need your just and kind consideration, we but exercise the right guaranteed to the humblest citizen in thus peti-
tioning.

" It is with reverent and grateful acknowledgment of the Divine power and interposition, that we accept the precious boon
of freedom, resulting, as it has, from a prolonged and sanguinary
struggle between two great powers; and finally decreed as it has
been by the national will, we look forward with confidence to see
the decree ratified by the whole people of this State.

" Though it was impossible for us to be indifferent spectators
of such a struggle, you will do us the justice to admit that we
have remained throughout obedient and passive, acting such part
only as has been assigned us, and calmly waiting upon Providence.   Our brethren have fought on the side of the Union, while
we have been obliged to serve in the camp, to build fortifications,
and raise subsistence for the Confederate army.   Do you blame
us that we have, meantime, prayed for the freedom of our race ?

" Just emerging from bondage, under which our race has
groaned for two hundred and fifty years, and suffering from its
consequent degradation, we are fully conscious that we possess
no power to control legislation in our behalf, and that we must
depend wholly upon moral appeal to the hearts and consciences
of the people of our State.

" Born upon the same soil, and brought up in an intimacy of relationship unknown to any other state of society, we have formed
attachments for the white race which must be as enduring as
life, and we can conceive of no reason that our God-bestowed

freedom should now sever the kindly ties which have so long united us.

"We are fully conscious that we cannot long expect the presence of government agents, or of the troops, to secure us against evil treatment from unreasonable prejudice and unjust men. Yet we have no desire to look abroad for protection and sympathy. We know we must find both at home and among the people of our own State, and merit them by our industry, sobriety, and respectful demeanor, or suffer long and grievous evils.

"We acknowledge with gratitude that there are those among former slave masters who have promptly conceded our freedom, and have manifested a just and humane disposition towards their former slaves. We think no such persons, or very few at least, have lost their working-hands by desertion.

"At the same time, it must be known to you that many planters have either kept the freedman in doubt, have wholly denied his freedom, or have grudgingly conceded it; and while doing so have expelled his family from the plantations which they perhaps cleared and enriched by their toil through long and weary years. Some have withheld a just compensation, or have awarded such pay as would not support the laborer and his family. Others have driven their hands away without any pay at all, or even a share of the crops they have raised. Women with families of children, whose husbands have been sold, have died, or have wrongfully deserted them, have in some cases been driven away from the homes where, under slavery, they have spent a lifetime of hard service. Is it just or Christian thus to thrust out upon the cold world helpless families to perish? These grosser forms of evil we believe will correct themselves under wise and humane legislation; but we do most respectfully urge that some suitable measures may be adopted to prevent unscrupulous and avaricious employers from the practice of these and other similar acts of injustice towards our people.

"Our first and engrossing concern in our new relation is, how we may provide shelter and an honorable subsistence for ourselves and families. You will say, work; but without your just and considerate aid, how shall we secure adequate compensation for our labor? If the friendly relations which we so much desire shall prevail, must there not be mutual co-operation? As our

6 *   I

longer degradation cannot add to your comfort, make us more
obedient as servants, or more useful as citizens, will you not aid
us by wise and just legislation to elevate ourselves?

" We desire education for our children, that they may be made
useful in all the relations of life. We most earnestly desire to
have the disabilities under which we formerly labored removed,
and to have all the oppressive laws which make unjust discrimi-
nations on account of race or color wiped from the statutes of the
State. We invoke your protection for the sanctity of our family
relations. Is this asking too much? We most respectfully and
earnestly pray that some provision may be made for the care of
the great number of orphan children and the helpless and infirm,
who, by the new order of affairs, will be thrown upon the world
without protection; also that you will favor, by some timely and
wise measures, the reunion of families which have long been
broken up by war or by the operations of slavery.

" Though associated with many memories of suffering, as well
as of enjoyment, we have always loved our homes, and dreaded,
as the worst of evils, a forcible separation from them. Now that
freedom and a new career are before us, we love this land and
people more than ever before. Here we have toiled and suffered; our parents, wives, and children are buried here; and in
this land we will remain, unless forcibly driven away.

" Finally, praying for such encouragement to our industry as
the proper regulation of the hours of labor and the providing of
the means of protection against rapacious and cruel employers,
and for the collection of just claims, we commit our cause into
your hands, invoking Heaven's choicest blessings upon your deliberations and upon the State.

                              " J. H. HARRIS,
                                JOHN R. GOOD,
                                GEORGE A. RUE,
                                ISHAM SWETT,
                                J. RANDOLPH, JR.,
                                        " Committee.'

This address, in which the action of the Convention finally
crystallized, I regard as one of the most remarkable documents that the time has brought forth. When I consider

the untutored condition and manifold discouragements of this people, the sudden revolution in their social and political relations, all that they have suffered, all that they have cause to fear, and all that they hope for, the wisdom and propriety of their action challenges admiration. This is their first political act; and I do not see how they could have presented their claims with more dignity, with a more just appreciation of the state of affairs, or in a manner which should appeal more forcibly either to the reason or the sentiment of those whom they address.

Scarcely a quarter of these late delegates to this, the first negro convention in a Southern State, can read and write. Some of them have hardly yet been allowed to realize that slavery has been overthrown, — were obliged to leave their homes in the night, are asking safe-conduct papers from the military authorities, and will even then quietly return home in the night. They are dressed in the very cheapest of homespun, are awed by the very atmosphere of a city, speak a language that no Northern white man can understand. To them, as to all men, by travel and association there has come enlargement of view, enlargement of desire and aspiration, a new sense of freedom, and a new purpose to labor for their rights. To them and to all others there has also come, I am convinced, a new sense of the responsibilities of manhood, and a new sense of the manner in which they must meet these responsibilities. They came up "in the spirit of our God," — they have not forgotten God in all their labors; who shall doubt that He will bless this work of theirs?

XV.

THE ORGANIZATION AND *PERSONNEL* OF THE NORTH CAROLINA STATE CONVENTION.

RALEIGH, October 5, 1865.

IN obedience to the proclamation of Provisional Governor Holden, the State Convention met at noon on Monday, the 2d instant. The third day's session has closed, and no business of importance has yet been done. The delegates begin their work as though they expected to be here three or four weeks. In South Carolina, where the whole Constitution was to be remodelled, but nine committees were appointed, while here thirteen have been already ordered, and the Committee on a Division of Business has not yet concluded its labors.

The Convention is composed of one hundred and twenty delegates, all of whom are present but three, detained at home by sickness, as is understood. Of the number there are six of Governor Holden's eight provisional judges, five of his eight provisional solicitors, and two members of his personal military staff.

The sessions of the Convention are held in the hall of the House of Commons, — that is, the lower house of the Legislature, — in the north end of the State Capitol. The room much needs cleaning and painting. Its only ornament is a full-length copy of Stuart's Washington, which hangs at the right of the Speaker's chair, and has been retouched by a daubing artist, I judge. The sessions of the Secession Convention of May, 1861, were also held in this hall.

In point of average ability, I think the delegates here rank above those in the South Carolina Convention; though in that body were half a dozen men whose standing is equalled by not more than one or two delegates in this. In that, however, were a great many fifth-rate or sixth-rate men; while here the majority are second-rate or third-rate men as compared with those. There half a dozen men controlled the action of the whole body in respect to most questions; here there are a score or more who deem their opinions of some special importance.

The temporary President of the body was Lewis Thompson, of Bertie County, a man sixty years old, of straight figure, with a pleasant and wrinkled face, white up-standing hair, reddish gray throat and chin whiskers. He is pointed out as the richest man in the State prior to the war, and is one of the real out-and-out Union men of the Convention.

The permanent President is Honorable E. G. Reade, of Person County. He is a tall, slim man, with iron-gray hair, whiskers, and moustache; is quiet, easy, precise; has a thin face and a particularly thin nose, and wears kid gloves during the sessions of the Convention. He is regarded as one of the best jurists in the State, was a Whig and an opponent of secession and State rights, and is now provisional judge of the eighth circuit by appointment of the Governor. The proceedings of the Convention indicate that he was the only nominee for the Presidency. The question was settled in a preliminary meeting, at which he received twenty-seven out of one hundred and three votes, the remaining seventy-six being distributed among eleven candidates. Mr. Reade, having the highest number of votes, was unanimously agreed upon for the office. His speech on taking the chair contained one passage which, for touching felicity of expression, is not often excelled in public speeches: —

" Fellow-citizens, we are going home. Let painful reflections upon our late separation, and pleasant memories of our early union, quicken our footsteps toward the old mansion, that we may grasp hard again the hand of friendship which stands at the door; and, sheltered by the old homestead, which was built upon a rock and has weathered the storm, enjoy together the long bright future which awaits us."

After the delegates had presented their credentials, they were called forward in groups, and sworn to "support the Constitution of the United States." I recall that at Columbia only a few delegates were sworn, and that they were required to take the amnesty oath.

The Governor's message came in on the second day. It was so brief that its reading occupied no more than five minutes. He takes it for granted that the Convention will recognize the abolition of slavery, provide that it shall not be re-established, and submit the amended Constitution to a vote of the people. He quotes the paragraph which I have given from President Reade's address, and further says: —

"North Carolina attempted, in May, 1861, to separate herself from the Federal Union. This attempt involved her, with other slaveholding States, in a protracted and disastrous war, the result of which was a vast expenditure of blood and treasure on her part, and the practical abolition of domestic slavery. She entered the Rebellion a slaveholding State, and emerged from it a non-slaveholding State. In other respects, so far as her existence as a State and her rights as a State are concerned, she has undergone no change.

"Allow me to congratulate you, gentlemen, upon the favorable circumstances which surround you, while engaged in this great work of restoring the State to her former and natural position. It is my firm belief that the policy of the President in this respect, which is as broad, as liberal, and as just as the Constitution itself, will be approved by the great body of the people of the United States; and that the period is not distant, if we are true to ourselves, and properly regardful of the reasonable expectations of our friends in other States, when our senators and representatives will resume their seats in Congress, and when our State will enjoy, in common with the other States, the protection of just laws under the Constitution of our fathers."

From Columbia I had occasion to report that there was a sharp struggle in the Convention concerning the number of committees that should be appointed, wherein the up-country carried the day in favor of eight, as against the low-country, which wanted but two or three. This Convention does things differently. It appointed one business committee of nine, which cuts out work for the Convention, and recommends the appointment of various special committees for certain designated purposes. As I have already said, thirteen of these special committees have been ordered and selected.

I note, too, that in Columbia the floor of the Convention was gladly made free to correspondents of Northern papers. Here, however, Colonel C. C. Clarke, late of the Rebel army, moved on the first day to admit only five reporters, being the number present from this State. Other delegates came to the rescue of the six from the North; Mr. Clarke's resolution went to the table; and the hall is opened to the representatives of all papers.

I further note that the United States flag has been ordered raised on the Capitol here while the Convention is in session. At Columbia it was not named in the Convention; and Head-quarters flag, on the hotel at which most of the delegates boarded, was such an unpleasant sight that three or four of them expressed a desire for its removal.

I find that I, in common with many other persons of the North, was entirely wrong in supposing that the Whig party and the Democratic party, as distinct political organizations, died at least ten years ago. I saw nothing in South Carolina to convince me of my error; but here, in North Carolina, I discover, with proper amazement, that the old parties are both alive, and neither of them a whit older or less pugilistic than it was twenty years ago. To be an " old line Whig" is to be a perfect gentleman, while to be an " old line Democrat" is to be a vulgar fellow outside the pale of good society; or, on the other hand, to be an " old line Democrat" is to be a man of good sense and sound

opinions, while to be an "old line Whig" is to be a conceited
fool and bloated aristocrat.

This old party spirit is, — I write it with questioning of
To-Day if this really is the year 1865, and if there really
has been a world-astounding war of four years' duration, —
this old party spirit is the foundation-stone of this North
Carolina Constitutional Convention.   Delegates talk of the
Whig party and of the Democratic party, even during grave
and serious debates on the most important questions.   It is
the Democratic party, one class affirms, that made secession
a possible thing, and brought the State to the verge of ruin.
It is the Whig party, the other class retorts, that was half
disloyal to the State, and caused disaster by its supineness
and coldness in behalf of the war.   These things are publicly spoken on the floor of the Convention, while in private
conversation half the delegates have no measuring-rule for
a man but the fact that he is either a Whig or a Democrat,
and no judgment for a measure but that it originates with
one of these parties.   When I found that the old parties
appeared to flourish in the western part of the State, I supposed the appearance due either to some local cause or to
the fact that I happened to meet only the one man in fifty
who clung to the old style of expression ; but I observe that
delegates and hangers-on from all sections use the words of
twenty years ago as glibly as ever, whence I conclude that
Whigs and Democrats flourish as in other days from one end
of the State to the other.

Of the one hundred and seventeen delegates in this body, I
judge that there are about eight or nine who, in the winter of
1860 – 61, really believed in the constitutional right of a State
to secede ; about twenty more who desired North Carolina
to secede, and did n't trouble themselves to settle the question whether she had a right to do so ; and about a dozen
more who wanted her to go out, but recognized that it
would be an act of rebellion for her to do so : leaving sev-

enty-five or eighty who were not believers either in secession or revolution. Of these, I judge, about twenty-five
quietly acquiesced in the work of the Secession Convention ;
about forty submitted to Confederate rule, but were always
its avowed enemies ; and about eight or ten stubbornly refused to acknowledge any allegiance to the Rebel government. This, I believe, may be taken as a fair statement of
the record of the delegates. The progress and result of the
war, however, changed the views of many of those who
originally favored rebellion or secession ; and of the whole
number, not more than the odd seventeen were, I judge,
known as " Secessionists " at the close of hostilities. Of these
seventeen, I doubt if more than half a dozen are to any extent believers in the State-rights doctrine, and Judge Manly,
of the Supreme Court, is the only one who has avowed his
belief publicly in that dogma.

Nine of the delegates in this body were members of the
Secession Convention, viz. : — Giles Mebane of Alamance
County, E. J. Warren of Beaufort, D. D. Ferrebee of Camden, Bedford Brown of Caswell, George Howard of Edgecombe, R. P. Dick of Guilford, W. A. Smith of Johnston,
John Berry of Orange, and A. H. Joyce of Stokes. Of this
nine, four held positions, civil or military, under the Rebel
government : and two, Messrs. Dick and Warren, are now
provisional judges.

In the Secession Convention, Mr. Dick, present judge of
the seventh circuit, was chairman of the Committee on General Amendments to the Constitution, and the mover of the
long-debated proposition for submitting the ordinance ratifying the Constitution of the Confederate States to a vote of
the people, which was lost by thirty-four to seventy-two.
Mr. Warren, present judge of the second circuit, was the
mover, in that Convention, of the exceedingly troublesome
proposition, that the powers delegated to the Confederate
government might be at any time withdrawn by the people

conferring them, — a proposition embodying the very quint-essence of State-rightsism, on which, I believe, a direct vote was never reached; the usual method of procedure having been to postpone it from time to time, by an average vote of about two to one, for the consideration of some other measure.

B. F. Moore, of this city, is not only one of the ablest men in the Convention, but also in the State. His standing is indicated by the fact that he was put at the head of the committee appointed to prepare business for the Convention. He is a clear-headed and comprehensive lawyer, of short and stocky person, round and strongly marked face, rosy complexion, white hair, clean-shaven chin, and, though carrying at least sixty-five years, stands as straight and square as a boy of twenty. Intellectually he is tough and pugnacious; politically he is a Whig, and an uncompromising opponent both of Secession and Rebellion.

"Uncle Nat Boyden," though not one of the ablest men, should be set down as one of the leaders of the Convention. He lives at Salisbury, and must be near seventy years of age. His hatred of Secessionists and "the infernal heresy of secession," as he terms it, is something charming to see. He is at the head of the Committee on the Ordinance of Secession. In appearance he is one of the cleanly, precise gentlemen of the old school: in manner he is blunt and courteous. He is of slight and bent figure, and has a delicate and scholarly face, noticeable for its small chin and exceedingly high, full, and broad forehead. His plain, hard, practical good sense, rather than any particular ability or acumen, gives him a good deal of power among the average men of the Convention; and he stood next to Mr. Reade in the informal ballot for the Presidency.

Honorable Thomas Settle, Jr., of Rockingham County, of some years' service in the Legislature, and for one or two sessions Speaker of the lower house, was given the chairmanship of the regular committee on the slavery question, and afterwards that of the special committee on the State debt. He is a man about six feet in height, one hundred and ninety pounds in weight, and thirty-eight years of age; erect, broad-shouldered, with full face, firm mouth, bronzed and rosy cheeks, large black eyes, and black hair and whiskers. He speaks with force and unmistakable emphasis, gesticulates with a full sweep from the shoulder, and adds a sincere love of the Union to a hearty hatred of Secessionists.

M. E. Manly, of Craven County, is perhaps the leading Calhoun man of the State, as he certainly is the only member of the Convention who has courage and frankness enough to openly avow his belief in the doctrine of State rights. "I still believe in that doctrine, as expounded by Mr. Calhoun," said he, this afternoon, "and still hold that it is necessary, to save us from centralization and secure to us our rights under the Constitution." Mr. Manly is a tall, spare man of about fifty-three, I judge, with a noticeably long, thin face, much cut up with fine wrinkles. He has a firm mouth, thin Roman nose, and square forehead, almost covered with the reddish gray hair which falls from above and is combed up from the sides. Forget everything else about him you might, but, having seen him even but once, you never could forget his eyes, — small, steely, restless, incisive, half-closed, set far back under jutting frontals, — eyes that at first glance seem to see nothing, but that unquestionably do see everything. Mr. Manly is a poor speaker, a very able jurist, and was one of the secession leaders, and a judge under the Rebel government. "I am willing," he now says, "to vote for a resolution declaring that the arbitrament of the sword has decided against the right of a State to secede from the Federal Union."

John Pool, of Bertie County, is called one of the ablest lawyers in the State. He is said to be a very strong and clear-headed Union man, and is mentioned as a probable

candidate for the United States Senate. He is a short
and thick-set man of forty-five or thereabouts, has a round
and genial face, prominent nose, small gray eyes, broad and
wrinkled forehead, short and grizzly whiskers, and thin dark
hair. He speaks with ease and freedom, and appears to have
a passion for good cigars.

XVI.

DEBATE AND ACTION IN RESPECT TO THE ORDINANCE OF SECESSION.

RALEIGH, October 7, 1865.

THE Convention has been five days in session, and has
done but one thing. That thing, however, it did in the
most thorough manner, — did so decisively that it will not
ever again need doing in this State.

When Mr. Boyden was announced as chairman of the
Committee on the Ordinance of Secession, everybody understood that the Secessionists would get no favor from that
committee. There was little surprise, therefore, when he
reported the following : —

"*Be it declared and ordained by the delegates of the good
people of the State of North Carolina in Convention assembled,
and it is hereby declared and ordained,* That the ordinance of
the Convention of the State of North Carolina, ratified on the
21st day of November, 1789, which adopted and ratified the
Constitution of the United States, and all acts and parts of acts
of the General Assembly ratifying the same, are now and at all
times since the adoption and ratification thereof have been, in
full force and effect, notwithstanding the supposed ordinance of
the 20th day of May, 1861, declaring that the same be repealed,
rescinded, and abrogated ; and the said supposed ordinance is
now, and at all times hath been, null and void."

When this came in, an effort was made to get immediate action by a suspension of the rules ; but Judge Manly said its phraseology was very objectionable to him, and he hoped the usual method of business would be adhered to, in order that he might have time to prepare an amendment. It was accordingly laid over. When it came up in regular order yesterday, Mr. D. D. Ferrebee, of Camden County, announcing that he concurred in view with Judge Manly, offered the following as a substitute and a compromise : —

"*We, the delegates of the good people of the State of North Carolina, in Convention assembled, do declare and ordain, and it is hereby declared and ordained*, That the ordinance of the Convention of the State of North Carolina, ratified on the 21st day of November, in the year 1789, which adopted and ratified the Constitution of the United States, is in full force and effect; and the ordinance of the late Convention of the State of the 20th day of May, in the year 1861, is hereby declared to be null, and the same is hereby repealed, rescinded, and abrogated."

Judge Manly said he would accept the substitute, though he did not altogether like it. He very briefly argued that the language of the original was both unusual and unnecessary, and that it gravely reflected upon the able body which passed the ordinance of secession.

Thereupon the debate began, and the end was not reached till ten long hours had been consumed in talk. Twelve gentlemen advocated the original report, and eight favored the substitute. The difference between the two propositions lies in a single sentence, — the one simply repeals the ordinance of secession, while the other declares that ordinance to have been always null and void.

All that was said on the actual merits of the question in issue did not occupy more than two hours. Several sterling Union men, whose lips have been sealed for four or five years, took the opportunity to lash certain Secessionists and pound the dogma of secession ; and what they had to say was by no means the least relishable part of the discussion, though it had no relevancy directly to the matter in hand. There were more, however, who " had no intention of speaking," &c., but would " take the opportunity," &c., " to say a few words," &c., " to define my position," &c. I suppose it was all right, but I own that I could n't see the need for so much explanation, if all the Unionism has such age and purity as it claimed for itself! Half the twenty speakers professed themselves unable to see any very essential difference between the two propositions, and of course could n't understand why the leaders should manifest such interest in the debate.

Mr. Nathaniel Boyden, of Salisbury, chairman of the committee, defended the ordinance which he had reported. He thought it of the utmost importance to declare that the secession ordinance had always been null and void, and that the ordinance of 1789 had always been in force. Before the passage of the ordinance of 1861 the State occupied her true position, and all her rights under the Constitution were granted to her. It is now of the greatest importance that we should affirm that we have always been entitled to those rights, and only deprived of them by illegal military force. I desire to put her in such position that no one in Congress can set up a denial of her equality when her representatives present themselves there. You may say that the President admits that we have never been out of the Union. I answer that it is not sufficient for him to admit it, — we cannot fairly claim our rights unless we here so affirm. Before 1861 our people never felt the Constitution of the United States except through its blessings. I pray to God that it may be at once fully restored to us. I want the secession ordinance buried so deep that even the Day of Resurrection can't find it. Who clings to it now? Have we not had enough of it? Are not all our hearts heavy with loss and sorrow, — is not the land red with the death-blood of our bravest and best? God give us clearness of sight and strength of will to do our duty like men! There never was anything more than a pretence for secession, and it becomes us now to make an end of the infernal heresy. The wording of this ordinance is not intended to be discourteous, and only those will deem it so who are tinctured with the heresy at which it is aimed. If it be said that the phraseology is unusual, I answer, so is this assembly, so is the order under which we meet here, so is the history of the last four years, so was the action of that body which assembled here in May, 1861.

Colonel Ferrebee, a gentleman of fine figure, good looks, courteous manner, moderate abilities, and forty-five years, said he had always opposed secession, but had voted for it in the Convention of 1861, because he believed the situation of affairs at that time made it necessary for the State to withdraw from the Federal Union. She took a course which she may regret, but of which she has no cause to be ashamed. And I maintain that the ordinance of the committee casts a stigma upon every son of North Carolina who took up arms in her defence, and is an insult to every member of the Convention of 1861. Its language does not indicate calm and deliberate action, but only *malice prepense.* I am as tired of the war and as anxious to return to the Union as anybody. Why not go back with kindly feelings? We can all vote for the substitute which I have proposed. Why not accept it, and have harmonious action? Whether the principle of secession is true or not, thirty thousand North Carolina soldiers are in their graves in attestation of the validity of the ordinance of May 20, 1861. In their names I come forward with the olive-branch.

Mr. John B. Odom, of Northampton County, said the principle of coercion is as well established as if it were written in the Constitution. The war has taught us that the government of the United States is something more than a rope of sand, — it has given the lie to despots who say that republicanism has no inherent life. I have no fear that any faction will ever again attempt a dissolution of the Union; but secession has wellnigh ruined the country. It is odious to me, and I care not how strong the language in which I express my detestation of it. Give me the committee's ordinance, — I will accept that if I can get nothing more pungent. The leaders of the Rebellion were men who wanted to steal from us the freedom of the ballot-box. Mr. Lincoln was the Mordecai sitting in their gate, and they undertook to play the part of Haman. I am for helping them through. I had much rather they would rule in hell than serve in heaven. Since the war began they 've made me swallow many a bitter pill; now I want them to take this dose without the least sweetening.

Mr. George Howard, of Edgecombe County, one of the circuit judges of the State during Confederate times, said he voted heartily for the ordinance of secession, as an act of revolution. So far as the United States is concerned, he admitted that the ordinance has always been null and void; but so far as the people of the State are concerned, it is the charter under which they have acted and carried on a government *de facto* for four years, and he would not wrong them by tearing it ruthlessly away. He denied that military power had taken the State out, or kept it out, and said it did not follow that those who oppose the ordinance of the committee are Secessionists. The declaration that it was necessary to make secession odious, implied that some were hostile to the general government. He felt sure there was not a man in the State but came back heartily and cheerfully.

Mr. John Pool, of Bertie County, a prominent candidate for United States senator, said he believed the action of the Convention to be of the utmost importance. The State is in the Union or out of it. If in the Union, then she has the high powers and privileges belonging to the States under the Constitution. If she is out of the Union, she is a conquered province. It is no small matter which of the two propositions presented is accepted. The one declares that we have rights which illegal acts have not taken from us; the other makes us subjects, kneeling at the feet of the conqueror. There is a vast difference between the two propositions. It was intended by the fathers that the Constitution of 1789 should be binding forever. I dissent *in toto* from the doctrine that a State has the right to secede. I even go further, and say that I do not believe one fourth of the delegates in the Convention of 1861 held that the ordinance of secession was constitutional. They voted for it under constraint of the military status then existing. They believed it a rebellious or revolutionary measure, and at once prepared for war. In their words they tried to make us believe that their course was legal, and that we should come peaceably through the difficulty; but their every act told a different tale, and bade us expect bloodshed. I mean to assert no more, now, than that they knew they were doing what was revolutionary and unconstitutional. For myself, I don't hesitate to admit that I have always believed the secession ordinance null and void. It is said that the ordinance of the committee is unusual. It is a most unusual thing for a State to rebel, a most unusual business that we have to settle, and it demands unusual remedies. I have yet to learn that any course is wrong because it is unusual. Shall we admit that we are a conquered province? We do that if we accept the proposed substitute. There are those in the States never in rebellion, who affirm that the rights of the conqueror are over us. Shall we furnish them with arguments in support of that doctrine? Not so. The act of the Convention of 1861 was revolutionary, — the ordinance of secession has always been null. I appreciate the scruples of gentlemen here who voted for it; but if they believed it

7   J

constitutional, they must now vote against the ordinance before the house, as I shall, with my views, vote against the proposed substitute. It is the old question of the right of secession, on which I cannot compromise.

Colonel Ferrebee interrupted, and said that both ordinances declared the act of secession null.

Mr. Pool continued, and answered, not so. One says it *is* null: the other says it *was* null. Of course, it is null now: the result of the war has made it so; but I demand that you shall say it always was null. Can we compromise there? If gentlemen want a smooth road, let them take the stones from the path marked out by the committee. We are told not to throw obstacles in the way: the first obstacle comes from the men who raise the cry. This is n't a mere question of language, but a question of principle; and I warn gentlemen not to overlook this fact. I am proud as any one can be of the valor and patriotism and devotion of the sons of North Carolina, who battled for what their leaders taught them was right. If there is a stigma on any one, it is on us and not on them.

Colonel Ferrebee asked if the Convention of 1861 did not obey the voice of the people in passing the secession ordinance.

Mr. Pool answered that he did not now believe, and never had believed, that a majority of the people of the State ever favored secession or revolution.

Mr. Edward Conigland, of Halifax County, would vote for the substitute because he believed the functions of a Convention were legislative, and not judicial. He did n't believe this body had a right to go back and pass upon the doings of a former Convention. He thought it useless to declare that North Carolina never favored secession. She would go down to posterity as having been for it almost unanimously.

Mr. Giles Mebane, of Alamance County, who gesticulated

much with his right hand, between the thumb and first finger of which he held an immense quid of tobacco, taken from his mouth when he rose to speak, thought the original report only a commentary on the Constitution of the United States, which neither the people of the State nor the authorities at Washington required from the Convention.   As for killing the doctrine of secession, he thought Grant and Sherman had buried that long ago.   He believed the act of 1861 an act of open rebellion, but should favor the substitute because it went to the desired point in a plain way.

Mr. Samuel F. Phillips, of Orange County, said that as the Convention of 1861 had expressed an opinion one way on the question of the right of secession, he thought it very important that a body of equal rank should put on record a counter opinion, and he therefore favored the committee's ordinance.   He thought the functions of the Convention both legislative and judicial, — in its legislative capacity it could repeal what a former Convention had done, and in its judicial capacity it could also declare it null from the beginning. He held that the doctrine of secession was a creature of the mind, which the success or failure of an army could not affect.   Therefore it was necessary to declare the counter proposition to that declared in 1861.

Mr. D. F. Caldwell, of Guilford County, said he had been mobbed, inhumanly assaulted, rotten-egged, shot at repeatedly, dragged into the army, and forced into double duty continually, because he was an avowed Union man ; and he admitted that he could n't have much sympathy for the fine scruples of gentlemen who desired such tenderness of treatment for the Secession Convention.

Mr. Alex McIver, of Mecklenberg County, would accept the substitute as a compromise.   He thought there was no occasion for this Convention to sit in judgment on the work of the Convention of 1861, particularly as that was so cheerfully acquiesced in by the people.

Mr. Lewis Thompson, of Bertie County, temporary president of the Convention, said this was no time to be led astray by sentiment. Personally he had none but kindly feelings for the gentlemen who made appeals for compromise, but there was a principle involved here on which he never could compromise. The government of the United States is not a mere compact, as it is called in the ordinance of secession; and this Convention should solemnly indorse the decision of the battle-field. This the proposed substitute does not do: it is a subterfuge, and says nothing on the great point in issue. He was anxious that the State should set herself right. Her people had never favored secession, and the work of the Convention of 1861 was an open insult to them. He wanted gentlemen to meet the fair question, — is the government of the United States nothing more than a mere compact, that may be dissolved at any time on the whim of any one of the thirty or forty parties thereto? If they were willing to own that, then, of course, they could very readily compromise on the substitute; but if they believed, as he did, that the fathers of 1789 intended their ratification of the Constitution of the United States to be forever binding on the whole people of the State, they could not poison their souls with such miserable sophistry.

Mr. William Eaton, of Warren County, who took much pains to proclaim that he had opposed secession since 1850, thought the original harsh in its terms, while the substitute would accomplish the desired end without hurting anybody's feelings.

Judge E. J. Warren, of Beaufort County, — a man forty years old, of medium size, having a dark skin, dark brown hair and whiskers, long nose, projecting chin, large, deeply sunken and sluggish brown eyes, and serious, half-sad cast of countenance, — said secession is an abominable heresy. I was in the Convention of 1861, and voted for the act which makes it necessary for us to come here. I denied then, as I deny now, that any State has a Constitutional right to secede. A people may always attempt a revolution, and this the dominant party in North Carolina had already well begun before that Convention met. The passage of the original ordinance reported to-day from your committee will only be an act of pure justice to those of us who were forced into voting for the so-called secession ordinance. Talk to me of courtesy to that body! To whom did they show courtesy? To the venerable Judge Badger, the brightest intellect and the purest heart of the State? To Judge Ruffin, who threw his great ability and commanding influence on the side of moderation? Their counsels were swept away like feathers by the mad leaders of the majority. If it be argued that the language of this ordinance is unusual, we respond that the occasion is unusual; if it be said no other State has gone so far in respect to the secession ordinance, we respond that the Old North State sets a bright example of devotion to the Union of the fathers; if we are called discourteous, we demand why courtesy should be shown to a body which would listen neither to age nor wisdom, but, with hot-headed haste, passed an ordinance tearing the State away from the Union within two hours after assembling, and then resolved itself into a mob amid the firing of cannon and the ringing of bells! Yet these sensitive gentlemen, with a courtesy all their own, now come here and charge us with *malice prepense!* How admirably the charge comes from them; how appropriate are the words in their mouths! And they tell us we shall insult the brave soldiers of our State if we agree to the committee's report! I tell them, and I tell the country, that a large majority of those who bore aloft the standard of North Carolina in this pitiful conflict — carried it with rare honor to themselves, but with shame to the judgment of their political leaders — have their opinions expressed in the language of this original ordinance, not in the lying terms of the substitute! These gentlemen who talk so feelingly of discourtesy are afraid to unmask their real position. If there is nothing at issue but a question of courtesy, how does it happen that the committee's report is so much criticised? If there is no essential difference between the two propositions, why is there so much talk about compromise? I charge that the whole purpose of these gentlemen is to hoodwink this Convention into an indorsement of the legality of secession. The original ordinance of the committee speaks my opinion as a judge on that question, my sentiments as a man on our duty in the present emergency; and I do not doubt that it will speak the sentiment of our children for all time to come.

Honorable Bedford Brown, of Caswell County, — once a member of Congress, an excessively patronizing and Pecksniffian gentleman, — told, at some length, the story of his efforts to prevent secession, and of his sufferings as a Union man during the war. There were two ways, however, he said, of doing a thing, — one becoming, and one unbecoming. The proposed substitute accomplishes enough, — the original ordinance too much; because it is not respectful to the people who elected the Convention of 1861 in the full expectation that it would pass an ordinance of secession. For that reason he should vote for the substitute.

Mr. B. F. Moore, of Raleigh, said he drew the ordinance now before the house. It indicated his political faith, and what he believed to be the political faith of the people of North Carolina. The real question is whether we have or have not been out of the Union. Gentlemen on the other side are willing to say we have not been citizens of the United States since 1861. I claim that we never have been anything else. If you simply repeal the ordinance of secession, you admit that our relationship as citizens was taken away by that act. If so, how has it been restored? If so, by what right do we sit here under the United States flag? How have we regained our citizenship? Who has restored it to us? General Grant has n't, General Sherman has n't. Has Congress? has the President?

Mr. Howard said he thought the passage of the ordinance would make void all acts of the courts and the Legislature since 1861.

Mr. Moore responded that he did not so believe. He had talked with President Johnson on that question, who held the opinion that all acts of the State since 1861 were void in any event. He himself could not indorse that opinion; but to meet all possible objections, he had prepared an ordinance legalizing all acts not in conflict with the Constitution of the United States.

Judge Manly argued that the act of secession created a government *de facto*, even if it did not a government *de jure*, and therefore had not always been null; and he, moreover, thought this Convention was not called upon to express a judicial opinion on the doings of the Convention of 1861. The exact legal status of their work must be left to the decision of the courts. He denied that he favored the substitute because he believed in the right of secession, for he was willing to vote for a resolution declaring that the result of the war had decided against any such right. He did not, however, desire to mix that question — that abstract question — with questions affecting the restoration of the State to the Union.

Mr. Boyden said he had very recently been North, and while in Washington called on the President, the Secretary of State, the Attorney-General, the acting Secretary of War, and other officers of the government. I alluded to reports which had been made by representatives of the Northern press in our State, regarding the loyalty of our people; and I assured these officers that the statements were mostly false and often malicious, and that the citizens of our State are entirely cured of any love they ever had for secession, and would in all respects demean themselves as good and sincere and loyal men. The language I have heard during this two days' debate, the bitter opposition that this ordinance has encountered, has convinced me that I was wrong in my assurances to the President and his associates. The correspondents have comprehended the spirit of some of our people more clearly than I did. Yet I am satisfied that the great body of them will sanction our passage of the original ordinance. However the leaders may talk, I don't believe you can ever get the masses into another fight with the general government. Still, this debate has more and more convinced me that it is necessary for us to declare that the ordinance of secession never had any binding effect whatever. It was an act of open rebellion, and of course falls with the end of the Rebellion; but I want a positive declaration that no body of men ever had a right to pass such an act. I should be glad to have a unanimous declaration to that effect, but I can't accept the substitute for the sake of harmony; I cannot compromise here, for there is a weighty principle involved. Unanimity in a good cause is a grand thing, but in any other it is a grave misfortune. It has been well said that we are going home. As we knock at the door of the old homestead, let us present this ordinance. It will give assurance that neither principalities, nor powers, nor life, nor death, nor any other thing, shall hereafter separate us from the sisterhood of States.

The secession heresy died hard, but the Convention was determined to kill it. Finally, when an hour and a half beyond the usual time of adjournment had passed, when the second day of the contest fell low in the west, and the shafts of sunset lay silvery and horizontal in the sombre chamber, Colonel Ferrebee, with a last scattering and damaging shot into the ranks of his personal assailants, grounded arms and gave up the battle.

The substitute was rejected by Yeas 94, Nays 19. The

test vote, on the second reading of the original ordinance, immediately followed, resulting Yeas 105, Nays 9. The nine who were found utterly opposed to the report were W. A. Allen of Duplin County, T. J. Faison of Sampson, D. D. Ferrebee of Camden, George Howard of Edgecombe, H. Joyner of Warren, M. E. Manly of Craven, A. A. McCoy of Sampson, H. F. Murphy of Wilmington, and R. H. Ward of Rockingham.

It was late in the day, and everybody was tired. " Let's suspend the rules, and put the ordinance on its passage to-night," cried Settle, the fair, of Rockingham. Nobody objected, the rules were suspended, and the President stood up and demanded in a loud and measured voice, "This ordinance having been three times read, the question is, shall it pass?" Somebody raised the question that, not being an ordinance to amend the Constitution, it did not need three readings, and was already passed. Several delegates vociferated clamorous advice, and Mr. President, new in his duties, stood half bewildered. Settle cut the knot with his sonorous, "It's a good thing, and let's give it three readings, anyhow!" So the measured voice again demanded, "Shall the ordinance pass?" There was a strong and exultant "Aye," the clear and emphatic "No" of Howard and McCoy, the suggestive silence of Manly and Ferrebee, — and then the President's word of announcement, "The ordinance is passed."

Thus did the State set her heel on the head of the viper of secession; and thus was the mild sovereignty of the old banner reaffirmed and re-established, never more to be defied or denied in North Carolina.

XVII.

ACTION IN REGARD TO SLAVERY AND THE FREEDMEN.

RALEIGH, October 11, 1865.

THE curse of North Carolina is a sort of petrified Hunkerism. The best men in the Convention stand unblushingly in their places and repeat, one after another, the short creed of the Hunkers: "I believe in the white man only. I believe that this country was made for white men only. I believe this is the white man's government, and no negro should have any part in it." Thus they justify their individual action, and the collective action of their constituents. And they fortify their justification with the result of the recent vote in Connecticut, of course. Thus Mr. Thomas Settle, late District Attorney, and Speaker of the lower house of the Legislature, and now candidate for a seat in Congress, one of the ablest of the delegates: "This is a white man's government, and intended for white men only, as even Connecticut, in New England itself, has just decided."

The action of the Convention on the slavery question, under the leadership of Mr. Settle, was, however, as prompt, decisive, and radical as any man could desire. The committee to consider the subject made its report on the third day's session, and it came up next in order after the report respecting the secession ordinance. The clause for the new Constitution is substantially in the words of the ordinance of 1787, and is as follows: —

" Slavery and involuntary servitude, otherwise than for crimes, whereof the parties shall have been duly convicted, shall be and hereby are forever prohibited within the State."

In South Carolina a long time was spent in determining the phraseology of the slavery clause. Exceeding sensitiveness was manifested in regard to the matter by many gentlemen, three or four of whom even went so far as to say that they would not vote for it at all unless it recited the "historical fact" that the abolition was by the United States authorities. That a question of this sort would be raised here was certain enough, but that it would find less than a dozen supporters was unexpected.

Mr. John B. Odom, of Northampton County, proposed to amend by inserting so that the clause should read : " The institution of slavery having been destroyed in North Carolina, it is hereby declared that slavery and involuntary servitude," etc. He very briefly said that he fully accepted the terms of the President for restoration to political rights, and would not only cheerfully vote for the prohibition of slavery, but would oppose any attempt to retain control of the subject ; but he thought it advisable to declare the historical fact about the matter.

Mr. Settle favored the language of the report, as being plain, simple, and direct. If it were necessary to insert the historical fact, let the mover go on and recite that slavery was killed by secession, which a majority of the people of the State always opposed ; that it might have been partially retained if the Davis government had not been obstinate ; and that it received its death-thrust when the Confederate government adopted the policy of taking negroes into the army. He could n't see any occasion for putting into the clause a looking-glass in which future generations might see the gaping wounds of this.

Mr. Bedford Brown also opposed the qualifying phrase. He wanted the clause to stand as it came from the committee, pure and simple ; he wanted it to appear that the people of North Carolina now, wiser for the result of the late war, of their own free choice abolish and forever prohibit slavery.

Probably these arguments would have proved sufficient to

kill the amendment; but its little show of vitality vanished in an instant when a member of the Smith family moved to insert in it after the words "North Carolina," the words, "by the Secessionists." This palpable hit caused an explosion of laughter, which carried it to the table with only six or eight opposing voices.

Colonel Thomas J. Faïson, of Sampson County, in manner and appearance the leader of a gang of guerillas, and in fact a Rebel of the most virulent and malignant type, proposed to strike the word "forever" from the ordinance, "so as to let the next generation," he explained, "do what it pleases about the matter." Half a dozen delegates were on their feet demanding the yeas and nays; and poor Faison, dumfounded at the storm he had unwittingly raised, withdrew his amendment, and followed that action by withdrawing himself in confusion from the chamber.

This closed the debate, which had not occupied over fifteen minutes. It was twenty minutes before noon on the 7th instant. One hundred and nine delegates answered to their names on the call of the roll. William Baker, of Ashe County, plumply responded "No"; but every other name in the list was against him, and he changed his vote before it was announced.

And so, by a unanimous vote of her delegates in Convention assembled, the State of North Carolina, acting under the force of necessity, declared slavery abolished and forever prohibited within her limits. In how large and humane a sense this prohibition is declared, let the future show.

The question of negro suffrage does not either directly or indirectly come before the Convention; yet three or four delegates have not failed to find occasion to show their standing. One of them, to be sure, was tipsyish when he did so; but in this case, as I learned in private conversation, Philip sober did not differ in opinion from Philip drunk.

"I am unalterably opposed to negro suffrage," said one delegate; "the negro was not intended to use a ballot." "I am opposed to negro suffrage, because this is a white man's government," said another. "The legislation of the State should be conceived in full and unreserved conformity to existing relations, rather than to any scheme of social and political equality," said a third. "I can't see what people mean who advocate negro suffrage," observed a fourth. It is all of that sort, — no one takes cognizance of the fact that there has been a deluge, nor of the other fact that the whole superstructure of Southern society rests on the back of the negro.

There is in the Convention, as in some sections of the State, a good deal of talk the drift of which I do not understand. Said one delegate: "It is uncharitable and unkind to feel any resentment toward the negro for anything that happened during the war; it is not his fault that he was made free; he was faithful and obedient to the end." Said another: "The negro had no agency in establishing his freedom, and we must not condemn him for that which he made no effort to produce." As if it were a sin to be free! Or, as if in getting freedom the negro had got a great evil! What means this pseudo sentiment for the freedman?

Of course colonization finds favor, and finds it in some unexpected quarters. General Alfred Dockery, venerable of years and venerated for his public and private character, is its leading advocate. He urged it in a half-hour's speech, illustrating his argument with much reference to the colonization of the Indians. "The blacks have ceased to be producers, and the whites cannot support them," he argued; "therefore it would be better for both races that they be separated." Here again the North was made to do duty. Mr. Caldwell, of Greensboro, wanted an equal distribution of the negroes to all parts of the country; "and when that is done, North Carolina will do as much for the negro as

Connecticut does." Mr. Settle was extremely glad that
General Cox had dared to come out in Ohio in favor of colonization, and expressed the belief that the country would
finally settle down on the Cox and Connecticut basis. It
was pleasant to find in the *Progress* newspaper of this city,
the editor of which is a Southerner and a former slaveholder,
the following vigorous editorial paragraph concerning this
miserable colonization business : —

"If there is any one Christian duty more binding upon the
Southern people than any other, it is the duty to take hold of
this unfortunate race and educate, Christianize, and elevate them.
If they are now licentious, ignorant, vicious, lewd, and generally
depraved, it is the result of slavery, and of itself is sufficient argument against the institution ; and it should be the pride of those
who are responsible for their present condition, and who have
grown rich and prospered on their labor, to treat them with justice and kindness. The mob may throw up their hats and sing
hosannas to those political leaders who advocate running the
negroes away and oppressing them now ; but right, honesty, and
justice will finally triumph, and the verdict of a virtuous, Christian people will bring them to shame. When the blacks could
be put upon the block and sold like other merchandise, and parents and children, husbands and wives, separated like cattle, the
poorest non-slaveholder had no objection to their remaining here,
and no one felt, not even the poor whites, who were kept poor
and degraded by the 'institution,' that they were in the way ;
but now that, in the order of Providence, they have been lifted
from the degradation of slavery, and a prospect of moral and
intellectual improvement is opened up to them, the mob cries,
'Away with them!' And, to our shame be it said, the mob finds
leaders among those who claim to be foremost in their devotion
to the Union."

Propositions to protect the freedman from drunkenness,
by levying upon every gallon of liquor the same tax as is
levied upon each two hundred acres of land, and to provide
for the support of pauper freedmen, by levying a capitation
tax upon the able-bodied, were more or less debated, and

gave various delegates an opportunity to declaim against the ignorance and general shiftlessness of the poor African, — only one or two being fair enough to admit that slavery was in some degree responsible for his character.

The Convention spent six hours in trying to agree upon a proposition fixing the matrimonial status of the freedmen and freedwomen; and then, by a vote of 68 to 42, agreed to leave the matter for settlement by the Freedmen's Code Commission. In the debate there was something of the stale stupidity about a white man's government, but the manner of its enunciation was not so offensive as it might have been; and its inherent offensiveness was somewhat redeemed by the ardent desire of two or three delegates to see the freedmen educated and elevated. For, give them education, and all other good things must come in its train, — give them that, and the shackling name "freedmen" will vanish like a ghost of the night, as it is, and they will stand before the world in their own right as freemen.

The address of the Freedmen's Convention was sent in through Governor Holden, courteously received, and referred to a special committee of five, of which John Pool, of Bertie County, one of the ablest lawyers of the State, is chairman. That committee had the subject under consideration for four or five days, and then made the following report, which the Convention at once adopted: —

" The Committee to which was referred the Address of the Freedmen's Convention, asks leave to submit the following report: —

" The subject-matter of the address and petition could be more appropriately acted on by the Legislature than by this Convention; but the importance of the subject, and the necessity for careful and considerate action, are so great that it may be proper for the Convention to take some initiatory steps towards its adjustment.

" The former relations of master and slave having ceased in

North Carolina, new and mutual rights and duties have super-
vened, which require corresponding legislation. A large class of
the population, ignorant and poor, has been released from the
stringent restraints of its late social and political position, and
from its dependence upon the individual obligations of another
class for its support, government, and protection; and it now
becomes the duty of the State to assume their charge, and enact
such laws as right and justice may require, and as may be most
conducive to the general welfare.

" The abolition of slavery has been adopted in good faith, and
with full determination that it shall not again exist in the State,
either in form or substance; but the consequences of its former
existence will inevitably affect the state of society for years to
come. In consequence of his late condition as a slave, the freedman is ignorant of the operations of civil government, improvident of the future, careless of the restraints of public opinion,
and without any real appreciation of the duties and obligations
imposed by the change in his relations to society. It is the interest of the white race, if he is to reside among us, to improve
and elevate him by the enactment of such laws, conceived in a
spirit of fairness and liberality, as will encourage him to' seek his
true welfare in honest industry and the faithful discharge of the
duties of his life. His intelligence and social condition must depend upon his industry and virtue.

" Prejudices of a social character will probably forever exist.
They are not confined to this State, nor to those States or countries where the institution of African slavery has been recognized,
but have pervaded every society where the two races have been
brought in contact.' However unjust such prejudices may be
deemed in theory, wisdom and prudence require that they should
be so far recognized and respected by legislators as to avoid rash
attempts at measures that might serve only to inflame and
strengthen them. Although we cannot hope for the entire cor-
rection of many of the evils under which we now labor, yet time
will materially modify them, and much may be safely trusted to
its silent but effective operation. Hasty and inconsiderate action
should be avoided; and above all things, should the delicate
questions evolved from the new relations among us be kept from
the arena of party politics.

" There are, at present, in North Carolina, some real bonds of attachment between the two races. Families have been brought up and nurtured together under our former domestic relations, — faithful servants have gained the esteem and confidence of their former masters, and possess and reciprocate tender feelings of affection from those whose infancy they have watched, and in the pleasures and sports of whose childhood they have participated. Their services and sympathy in affliction are remembered, and the dearest memories of the dead are associated and shared with them. From such ties, and from the common feelings of interest, justice, and humanity, more is to be hoped for their improvement and welfare than from the assertion of impracticable claims for social and political rights or from the aid of those whose interference is likely to be regarded with jealousy and met with resentment. We deplore the premature introduction of any schemes that may disturb the operations of these kindly feelings, or inflame the inherent social prejudice that exists against the colored race. The necessary legislation should be conceived in a spirit of perfect fairness and justice, and in full and unreserved conformity to existing relations; but it should be suited to the actual condition of the parties, and be aimed rather to their material and moral welfare, and to the general peace and prosperity of the State, than to any theoretical scheme of social and political equality.

" Those of our laws that are inapplicable to the changed relation of master and slave, and those that are in contravention of it, should be repealed. Many new laws are now indispensably necessary to meet the present condition of things; and these should be drawn with great care and with the most mature consideration.

" The committee therefore recommends that the Provisional Governor of the State be requested to appoint and constitute a commission of three gentlemen, eminent for legal ability, to propose and submit to the consideration of the Legislature at its next session a system of laws upon the subject of freedmen, and to designate such laws or parts of laws now in force as should be repealed in order to conform the statutes of the State to the ordinance of this Convention abolishing the institution of slavery.

" For the committee,

" JOHN POOL, *Chairman.*"

K

There is one admission in this report for which we may give sincere and heartfelt thanks: "In consequence of his late condition as a slave, the freedman is ignorant, careless, improvident," etc. See how, in an instant, a word of manly truth knocks away all the texture of that web of sophistries about the natural inferiority of the negro!

It was hardly possible for the Convention itself to revise the entire code of laws relating to the colored man; and therefore it was best to ask the Governor "to appoint and constitute a commission of three persons, eminent for legal ability, to prepare and submit to the consideration of the Legislature, at its next session, a system of laws upon the subject of freedmen." The injustice of the action lies in the fact that neither the Convention as a body, nor any delegate as an individual, was wise enough to see that there must be no laws for white men, no laws for black men, but only laws for all men alike.

In the Freedmen's Convention, something was one day said about the ignorance of the negro, and one of the members repeated the remark of an ex-Rebel, to the effect that "the nigger has no business to talk of his 'rights under the Constitution,' for he don't know what the word means." "It may be," said Mr. Isham Sweat, barber at Fayetteville, with a passionate burst of eloquence, — "it may be that we are so ignorant we don't know what the word 'Constitution' means; but none of us are so ignorant that we don't know what the principle of justice means!" Is the North less wise than this negro barber who stands and pleads for his people?

XVIII.

THE WAR-DEBT QUESTION AND THE MINOR WORK OF THE CONVENTION.

RALEIGH, October 14, 1865.

I HAVE already referred to the fact that, while travelling in the western part of the State, I was often told that the Convention would of course be strongly Union, because the Rebel element did not vote, — shielding itself behind the assertion that the " authorities," either military or provisional, would not allow Southern men to run as delegates.   I received these reports as to the sullen character of a considerable portion of the people with much allowance ; but conversation with the officers on duty here, and with the members and hangers-on of the Convention, has convinced me that they are substantially true.

If " hatred of Secession " and " love of the Union " were synonymous phrases, there would be cause for sincere rejoicing in the position of affairs here ; for the action of the Convention in respect to the secession ordinance was something more than respectable, — it was admirable.   The passage of the ordinance declaring that it had always been null and void was not, it is true, received with any manifestation of gratification, though, considering the crazy joy on the passage of the ordinance of May, 1861, some common congratulation would have been admissible.

The spirit of the Convention, however, was none the less unmistakable for this omission.   The delegates, as a body, took a sort of savage delight in insisting on the yeas and nays on every vote respecting the matter.   " We 'll get these d—d Secesh on the record good and strong," said a delegate of the Smith family to me.   They boast of their soldiers, and of the heroic record of the North Carolina regiments,

but they very rarely indorse the cause for which those soldiers fought. They are prolific in assertion to the effect
that the " geographical position " of the State forced her into
an alliance with the Confederacy. " My situation, and not
my will, consents," appositely quoted one delegate ; and they
are at much pains to convince strangers that, whatever it
may be necessary to do with respect to other States, North
Carolina should at once be restored to her old position in
the government. If this impalpable something that calls
itself Unionism had for even one of its component parts a
broad love of impartial justice, there might be reason for
untroubled hope of the future. As it is, there needs to be
careful discrimination between the little leaven and the
whole lump ; and it will be a sad thing if the President pins
his faith to everything in North Carolina that throws stones
at Secession and boasts of its Unionism.

The Convention has substantially closed its labors, though
it will probably hold a couple of brief sessions next week.
I have reported its action in respect to the freed people, the
slavery question, and the secession ordinance ; and there
remains for me now only the duty of very briefly showing
its record in regard to other matters of minor general interest.

With characteristic observance of the order in which their
work should be done, the delegates, immediately after passing the slavery ordinance, took up that for re-establishing
civil government, which was amended, briefly debated, and
then passed. It provides for an election of Governor, members of the Legislature, and representatives in Congress.

All persons, otherwise qualified according to the Constitution now existing, will be allowed to vote who have taken
the amnesty oath prescribed by President Lincoln, or that
prescribed by President Johnson, and, if of the excepted
classes, have been pardoned. An effort was made to so
amend the ordinance as to allow all to vote, whether they

have or have not been pardoned, and have or have not taken an amnesty oath. The mover of this section professed extreme loyalty, but that did n't carry his amendment, which was tabled without a division.

A proposition to abolish the property qualification for members of the General Assembly was considerably debated, but finally defeated by a very decisive vote ; as was also, at a later stage of the proceedings, an ordinance creating the office of Lieutenant-Governor.

After much debate, an ordinance was passed vacating all State offices which, since May 20, 1861, have been held by persons who have taken an oath inconsistent with the official oath to support the Constitution of the United States ; and the Legislature is directed to cause them to be filled, according to law, at its first session.

The Convention spent the best part of two days upon the ordinance giving force to proceedings since the passage of the so-called secession ordinance. All laws enacted since that day are ratified, except such as relate to slavery, and such as are incompatible with the Constitution of the United States and with the allegiance of the State to the general government. Validity is given to all judicial proceedings, all contracts, all marriages, and the acts of all civil officers of the State, except as hereinbefore recited. No civil or military officer of the State or the so-called Confederate States shall be held liable for the proper discharge of any duty imposed on him by any authority purporting to be a law of the State or Confederate States governments.

There is, on the part of many delegates, an extreme nervousness on the subject of the Congressional representation. " I think we ought to take up the ordinance redistricting the State as soon as possible," says Colonel Love, " so that gentlemen who are likely to be sent to Congress may have full time for preparation." " The passage of this resolution," says the venerable delegate from Caswell, Mr. Brown,

" will, in my humble opinion, be of great aid to our Congressional delegation." " It is of the utmost importance," says Mr. Boyden, " that you declare the secession ordinance null and void, now and always, so that no just claim may be set up for refusing admission to our representatives in Congress." " It is a part of the public policy of the State that our Congressional delegation should be in Washington on the first day of the session," says Mr. Moore, who would like to have it appear that he speaks for Governor Holden. " Pass this as it comes from the committee," — the ordinance regarding secession, — " and you take the game out of the hands of the Northern fanatics when our senators and representatives apply for admission into Congress," says a delegate from one of the back counties. " They must demand, and insist upon having, all the rights and privileges now given to the members from Massachusetts or any other State," responds another.

The ordinance redistricting the State was therefore, at the proper time, taken up and promptly passed. The new districts are as follows, by counties : —

First District, — Currituck, Camden, Pasquotank, Perquimans, Gates, Chowan, Hertford, Northampton, Halifax, Martin, Bertie, Washington, Tyrrell, Hyde, and Beaufort.

Second District, — Pitt, Craven, Jones, Lenoir, Wayne, Green, Edgecombe, Wilson, Onslow, Carteret, Duplin, and New Hanover.

Third District, — Brunswick, Columbus, Bladen, Sampson, Cumberland, Robeson, Richmond, Harnett, Moore, Montgomery, Anson, and Stanley.

Fourth District, — Warren, Franklin, Nash, Granville, Orange, Wake, Johnston, and Chatham.

Fifth District, — Alamance, Randolph, Guilford, Rockingham, Davidson, Forsyth, Stokes, Surry, Person, and Caswell.

Sixth District, — Rowan, Cabarrus, Union, Mecklenburg, Iredell, Davie, Yadkin, Wilkes, Alexander, Catawba, Lincoln, and Gaston.

Seventh District, — Ashe, Alleghany, Watauga, Yancey, Mitchell, McDowell, Burke, Rutherford, Cleveland, Polk, Henderson, Buncombe, Madison, Haywood, Jackson, Macon, Cherokee, and Caldwell.

The "basis of representation" question with respect to the lower house of the Legislature, which excited so much debate at Columbia, could get attention from but one delegate here, — Love, of Jackson County, — who was allowed to make a speech of an hour's length in favor of making that basis the white population of the State. It remains as heretofore, i. e. "Federal population, — that is, all free persons and three fifths of all other persons."

The attendance on the daily sessions of the Convention has been very meagre. I doubt if one hundred persons of the resident population have, from first to last, looked into the chamber.

I have only to add, further, that the ordinance declaring secession null and void, and that prohibiting slavery, are to be submitted to a vote of the people of the State.

For my final judgment with regard to the Convention, I adopt the words of Judge Howard, and say that I have " more faith in those who, without making loud professions of what they have always felt and believed, honestly give up all their past ideas, and avow themselves henceforth good citizens of the United States, than in those whose fierce zeal for the Union slumbered during all the years of secession, and only broke out in the hour of the triumph of the Union cause," — or, in other words, a conquered Rebel will, to my thinking, be much more easily converted into a good citizen than most of these North Carolina Unionists.

POSTSCRIPT.

The Convention was in session sixteen days. At the beginning of the second day's session, it ordered the United States flag to be raised on the State House. At the beginning of the last day's session, the President made the announcement that the order had not been executed because no flag could be obtained in the city. Possibly the strict letter of the order required that one should be bought, though the delegate who offered the resolution supposed one would be borrowed of the military. A hearty acquiescence in its spirit would have suggested an application to the general commanding the department, whose head-quarters are here, or would have permitted the acceptance of one of those tendered to the Convention through individual delegates. The facts in the case are somewhat suggestive when coupled with the professed Unionism of the Convention.

When I left Raleigh, it was generally understood that the Convention would not take any decisive action in respect to the war-debt question. There was an extreme sensitiveness in regard to the matter. The secession ordinance had been emphatically declared null and void from the beginning; but I believe the debt incurred in the endeavor to support that ordinance would have been assumed, had it been possible to get a vote upon the direct proposition ! It was comparatively easy to repudiate an act which the result of the war had already repudiated; but the debt was a question of pocket instead of principle, and very many of the so-called Union leaders were unable to see its illegality.

On the second day's session a resolution was offered calling on the Governor for information as to the specie-value of the war-debt of the State at the time when incurred. It was a simple inquiry; but the purpose of the Convention to take no steps at all in relation to the matter was apparent enough by its almost unanimous vote in sending the resolution to the table.

On the fourth day, a resolution was offered asking the Provisional Governor if he had any information or intimation from the President as to the course that should be pursued by the State relative to the debt contracted for the prosecution of the war. The purpose of the Convention to assume this debt was further apparent by the decisive manner in which it rejected this resolution.

On the fifth day there came an ordinance declaring that no tax should be laid, and no money appropriated, to pay any part of this debt. It was sent to its grave without debate.

On the sixth day, Mr. Settle introduced an ordinance providing for the payment of all just debts of the State, and also declaring that no part of the Rebel war debt should be paid. He asked that this might be made the special order for the following day, but was pressed to allow it to go to the Finance Committee. To this he would not seriously object, he said, but gentlemen might as well understand, first as last, that this war-debt question could not be ignored, — they could not stifle debate, nor could they bury his ordinance under a committee's table. The motion to refer to the Finance Committee prevailed.

On the seventh day an ordinance was offered which provided for issuing bonds in payment of the State debt incurred before the war. As no provision was made for the war debt, the ordinance practically denied the validity thereof, and it was tabled by 59 to 40.

On the eighth day the Finance Committee made report of Mr. Settle's ordinance, — recommending that no action be taken by the Convention on the war-debt question. Mr. Settle made a strenuous effort to get the rule suspended so that immediate action might be taken on the report, but was defeated by 60 to 47.

On the ninth day there was further effort to get action on this question; but while a motion was pending to that effect, an adjournment was carried by 57 to 53. The position of affairs at this juncture was such that this vote was regarded as being much nearer a test-vote than any other that had been taken. It seemed to indicate very

8

clearly that the Convention meant to do nothing that could jeopardize the prospects of the war debt for ultimate payment.

On the fourteenth day it was agreed that the Convention should adjourn *sine die* on the evening of the following day. Nothing had been done about the war debt since the ninth day, and everybody understood that nothing would be done. There were, to be sure, a dozen or more delegates anxious to settle the questions connected therewith; but, on the other hand, there was a strong party, including several of those who were foremost in the effort to annul the secession ordinance, which openly favored the assumption of that debt, and another large party which chose only to be known as opposed to any action in regard thereto. The pressure of the lobby was very strong. Its representative men were anxious to secure a formal acknowledgment of the validity of the debt, but were reasonably well content with defeating all efforts to formally annul it; and, on the evening of this fourteenth day, the whole lobby gleefully chuckled at its success.

On the fifteenth day, early in the morning hour, the resolution appointing a committee to determine what part of the debt of the State incurred since May 20, 1861, was for war purposes, what for other purposes, the best means of discharging the same, and of providing a sound currency, was called up, and tabled by a strong majority. This was the last measure touching the debt before the Convention, and its death was acknowledged to be the final stroke of victory in favor of the assumptionists.

An ordinance of local interest was taken up. The real Unionists of the Convention were not at all pleased with the situation; but the sentiment of the house had been so often declared, that they were determined to make no further effort on the debt question. At this juncture, and during the debate on this local ordinance, a message was announced from the Provisional Governor. The delegate on the floor gave way, and the message was read. It proved to be a simple announcement that he had received from the President the following telegram : —

" WASHINGTON, October 18, 1865.

" W. W. HOLDEN, *Provisional Governor :*

" Every dollar of the debt created to aid the Rebellion against the United States should be repudiated finally and forever. The great mass of the people should not be taxed to pay a debt to aid in carrying on a Rebellion to which they in fact, if left to themselves, were opposed. Let those who have given their means for the obligations of the States look for payment to that power they tried to establish in violation of law, Constitution, and the will of the people. They must meet their fate. It is their misfortune, and cannot be recognized by the people of any State professing themselves loyal to the government of the United States, and in the Union. I repeat, that the loyal people of North Carolina should be exonerated from the payment of every dollar of indebtedness created to aid in carrying on the Rebellion. I trust and hope that the people of North Carolina will wash their hands of everything that partakes in the slightest degree of the Rebellion which has been so recently crushed by the strong arm of the government in carrying out the obligations imposed by the Constitution of the United States.

(Signed)   " ANDREW JOHNSON,
                           " *President of the United States.*"

The scene which followed the reading of this Presidential message was extraordinary. The score of faithful Union men applauded it, and one excited delegate exclaimed, " Hurrah for Andy Johnson ! " Then silence fell upon the house, and every man looked to his neighbor for guidance. Mr. Conigland, of Halifax County, was the first to speak, and he announced himself as a free and independent man. " My conscience is my own, and I shall allow no earthly government to control my thoughts or form my opinions." Mr. Settle moved and carried a postponement of the subject-matter of the message till evening.

At the beginning of the evening session a motion to re-scind the order fixing the hour of adjournment was carried by 76 to 26; and Mr. Settle then moved to take up the ordi-nance he introduced on the sixth day of the session. An amendment was immediately offered, providing that the whole question in regard to the assumption of the war debt be left to a vote of the people. An excited debate of two hours followed, in which such men as Boyden, Moore, Winston, and Caldwell, all avowed Union men, took strong ground against the action which the President indicated would be advisable; while Settle and Phillips were the only delegates of any influence who spoke on the other side. Finally, Mr. Boyden — the leader of the fight against the secession ordinance — moved to lay the ordinance under consideration, as well as all questions connected therewith, on the table for the balance of the session. This defiant proposition was lost by a vote of 25 to 80, and the Conven-tion adjourned.

On the sixteenth and last day the contest was renewed, and continued for four hours. Great indignation was mani-fested at the turn which affairs had taken; and it was charged that the President's telegram came at the instigation of Gov-ernor Holden, and was intended for his benefit in the coming elections. During the day numerous amendments to the Settle ordinance were offered and urged, but none of them were accepted. Finally, Mr. Moore of Raleigh, chairman of the Business Committee, and therefore virtually the leader of the Convention, again proposed, notwithstanding the ad-vice of the President, to leave the whole matter to the peo-ple. This proposition, strange as it may seem, — and in view of the record of the Convention on the secession ordi-nance question it seems very strange, — this proposition was only defeated by four majority, the vote being 46 to 50.

The evening session showed that this was the final effort of the assumptionists. They made no more motions for

amendment, and the Settle ordinance was passed by a weak
viva voce vote, — only a few voices being heard in the nega-
tive, though about a dozen delegates afterward signed a protest against the action of the Convention. The ordinance as
passed is as follows : —

" *Be it declared and ordained by the Delegates of the State of
North Carolina in Convention assembled, and it is hereby declared
and ordained*, That it shall be the duty of the General Assembly
of the State, so soon as is practicable, to provide for the payment
of all debts and obligations created or incurred by the State,
other than in aid of the late Rebellion.

" *Be it further declared and ordained*, That all debts and obligations created or incurred by the State in aid of the Rebellion, directly or indirectly, are void ; and no General Assembly of this
State shall have power to assume or provide for the payment of
the same, or any portion thereof; nor shall any General Assembly
of this State have power to assume or provide for the payment
of any portion of the debts or obligations created and incurred,
directly or indirectly, by the late so-called Confederate States,
or by its agents, or under its authority."

XIX.

AFFAIRS IN CENTRAL NORTH CAROLINA.

GOLDSBORO, October 16, 1865.

IT is the ambition of Provisional Governor Holden to be
elected to the Governorship of the State by the people. The central counties will, however, pretty generally
vote against him, I judge, in the coming canvass. He is
intensely hated by the secession element, which will more
readily accept almost any other man. The loyalty of the

State is in the western part, the discontent is in the centre, the submission is on the sea-coast.

Who will be put into the field against Governor Holden for the executive office cannot yet be certainly said.   Efforts are making to bring out State Treasurer Jonathan Worth, and they promise to be successful.   His record for Unionism is as good, at least, as Holden's; but he favors the payment of the Rebel war debt, and would be voted for by all the Secessionists, — not that they love him, but that they hate Holden.   Mr. Worth is a small man, of moderate abilities, sterling honesty, and perfectly unassuming manners, whose integrity is an honorable by-word, but whose personal bearing would not particularly dignify the Governorship.   The only thing to fear from his election will be that the Secessionists may control him, and so control State affairs.   If he is strong enough to keep out of their hands after being elected by their votes, he will, I think, make a very fair Governor.

I had a long talk this morning with a Smithfield man. He said Holden was hated by one class of people and feared by the other.   He did n't believe in electing such men to office.   He himself was just as loyal as anybody now, but last winter he was as big a Rebel as there was in Johnston County.   He did n't take no 'count of these men who were sich good Union men all to once.   He meant to mind the laws now, and was willin' to ask Andy Johnson's pardon; but he did n't pretend that he was any better 'n anybody else.   He reckoned he 'd got to eat dirt some; but if he knew himself right well, he should eat it in the easiest way he could, and that would n't be by voting for Holden.

A Fayetteville merchant whom I met told me that he should have no hope of the future if the Black Republicans carried the day in the forthcoming Northern elections.   He considered it essential that they should be overthrown now and forever.   They forced the South into the war, and the

South would hardly believe the North wished peace unless they were beaten at the ballot-box.

I asked him if it seemed necessary that the North should consult the will of the South in respect to its own State officers.

Well, he thought it was the duty of the North to show that she really desired the South to come back into the Union, and he was certain that the election to office of men avowedly hostile to the South would not indicate any such desire.

But, I said, what would you have? What general policy does it appear to you we of the North should adopt?

He would n't dictate, he answered; but the North ought to rise above passion and elect conservative men.

The conversation reminded me of a little speech made last week in the Convention at Raleigh. During the debate on the secession ordinance, Honorable Bedford Brown, once in Congress from this State, introduced a resolution declaring that the war had forever settled that a State has no Constitutional right to secede. After that ordinance had been declared null and void, he urged the passage of his resolution as an appropriate sequel to the action on the other question, and said he thought it would much help the chances of the State before Congress next winter. He called attention to the fact that the idea of the resolution is in General Slocum's opening speech to the New York Democracy, and remarked that he believed it would furnish a common ground of brotherhood for all conservative men. He indorsed General Slocum as eminently national and soundly conservative, and expressed the hope that he might be elected, as that would be a triumph of conservative views full of promise for the South. His resolution went to the table, however, as being needless; and the great conservative party lost the benefit of its passage.

Two gentlemen of this town favored me with their views

at some length last evening in regard to the duty of the South and the duty of the nation in the present emergency. They were clearly of the opinion that the Southern representatives should be admitted to their seats at the assembling of Congress; that the President should revoke the twenty thousand dollar clause in his amnesty proclamation; and that the South should be relieved for at least five years from the payment of any national taxes. They thought it very cruel in the North to doubt the word of the South when she said, on her honor, that she accepted the results of the war, and would in good faith abide by them, and hinted that the South might wish she had not so readily given up the position she could have taken at the close of the war.

I asked the landlord of my hotel if there were many Northern men in this section of the State. "Not many," he said, "outside the large towns."

"Is there any feeling of hostility to them that would make it dangerous for them to try to live here?"

"O no, they can live in Goldsboro well enough, and we should like to have a hundred on 'em come in here at once."

"But how about living in the country?"

"Well, there are some towns where they could live; but the planters don't like 'em very well, I reckon."

I asked him if the leading men of the various counties could n't see that it would be for the interest of the State to encourage the influx of Northern spirit and labor and capital.

Yes, he thought all the best men saw that, and he did n't know as there was any trouble about such men. But the common classes was another thing, and they were n't fond of the Yankees. He believed any Northern man would get along well enough if 't was knowed that he was befriended by the best men in his neighborhood, however.

I am certain that there can be no lower class of people than the North Carolina "clay-eaters," — this being the local name for the poor whites. I have looked into the cabins of not a few of them, and have made inquiries concerning them of a considerable number of persons. I state a deliberate conclusion when I say that the average negroes are superior in force and intellect to the great majority of these clay-eaters. Many of them — all of those not married — must be simply called vagabonds. They are generally without fixed home and without definite occupation. They are always thinly clad, their habitations are mere hovels, they are entirely uneducated, and many of them are hardly above beasts in their habits. Very few families have fifty dollars' worth of property of any kind. The men live most of the time in the woods, and generally keep one or two dogs and own a cheap rifle. The women are slatternly and utterly without any idea of decency or propriety; they cultivate a little corn, and sometimes a little patch of cow-peas, collards, or sweet potatoes. The whole class is bigoted and superstitious to the last degree; they generally believe in evil spirits, but rarely in a Divine Father. They are lazy and thriftless, mostly choose to live by begging or pilfering, and are more unreliable as farm hands than the worst of the negroes.

I find here as everywhere the complaint that the free negro will not work. There seems considerable demand for labor, yet, strange as it may seem, the people are warm colonizationists. They talk much about importing white labor, which, of course, they can't get till they put it on such footing as it commands in the North. The idea of everybody is that labor must be kept out of good society; and so I hear much assertion to the effect that German laborers can be imported who will work for about ten or twelve dollars per month, and occupy the cabins which the negroes have vacated.

The fact, if not the name, of slavery remains in many of these central counties. An officer in our army, for twelve years a resident of the State, tells me that many of the people hope some system of peonage or apprenticeship will be established as soon as the State gets full control of her affairs; and an officer of the Freedmen's Bureau says that in some counties, from all he can learn, negroes are whipped almost as much now as ever.

"The war," says the Raleigh *Sentinel* in a late issue, "has settled a fact, that African slavery or involuntary servitude shall no longer exist in the United States, and we accept it as a fixed fact; but the principle whether African slavery is right or wrong, whether it is best, wisest for both races, that the slaves should be free, or whether it is just and right to the former slaveholders that they shall be free, or whether the slaves are of right entitled to be free, these are still open questions."

A Johnston County man told in my hearing, and with a great deal of gusto, how he managed his negroes. He could n't whip them, he said, because they 'd sneak off to the provost marshal and complain of him. "But I 'll be d—d if I don't get even with the cusses when they try to ride ahead; I jest tell 'em I 'm in for a fight, and then I go into 'em for about ten minutes; they understand it, an' come down on thar knees right sudden." He told this with plain indications that he considered himself smart in thus retaining the essential feature of slavery.

A Moore County man whom I met at Raleigh had much to say of the marital relations of the negroes. He believed two thirds of the men would abandon their wives whenever the notion took them, and he doubted if one woman in six was true to her husband. He had no idea that any law could be made to reach this people in this regard, and expected their condition in respect to virtue would be worse hereafter than when they were slaves. He told me a story of a negro who came to him, said he had two wives in Wilmington, but wanted to be married to a third for the war or so long as the Yankees held that city. This seemed to him such conclusive evidence of the negro's unfitness for freedom, that, though it proved nothing, I was glad to be able to match his story with one from the adjoining county of Harnett, to the effect that a white man, having a wife in Virginia, had applied to a magistrate to be married to another woman for forty days, and had tendered a bushel of sweet potatoes in payment for the job.

There is much hostility to the Freedmen's Bureau, — more hereabouts than I found in the western part of the State. The people claim that it "interferes with the regular operations of labor." I get this phrase from several different persons: just what it means is more than I can tell. I judge, however, from all I hear, that the farmers and small planters are disposed to retain their old relations to the negroes, and that the Bureau is acting as the black man's next friend.

Not a few persons seem to me to be trying to find a pretext for a general onslaught upon the negroes. They charge that the blacks are pretty generally organizing, and in many of the lower counties are drilling semi-weekly. I am not able to satisfy myself that there is any truth in these charges. That the negroes hold weekly meetings in some neighborhoods many of the delegates in the Freedmen's Convention told me; but they assured me that they were always of a social or religious character, and I have neither seen nor heard anything that causes me to doubt their word. Most of the blacks whom I meet seem to me unusually well informed as to the situation so far as it affects their race, and exceedingly anxious to bear themselves with propriety and decorum before all men.

As I have already said, there are the usual complaints about the idleness of the negroes. Some of them have, to be sure, left their old homes; but I estimate that the number who have wandered away does not exceed one tenth of the aggregate. The others are, for the most part, quietly at work on the plantations and farms. " From our experience and observation," says the editor of the *Progress*, of Raleigh, a native, and a former slaveholder, " we believe that by treating the blacks justly, and paying them promptly, more will be produced, by good management, under the free-labor system than was under the old slave system."

XX.

SUMMARY OF THREE WEEKS' OBSERVATIONS IN NORTH CAROLINA.

WILMINGTON, October 17, 1865.

SPINDLING of legs, round of shoulders, sunken of chest, lank of body, stooping of posture, narrow of face, retreating of forehead, thin of nose, small of chin, large of mouth, — this is the native North-Carolinian as one sees him outside the cities and large towns. There is insipidity in his face, indecision in his step, and inefficiency in his whole bearing. His house has two rooms and a loft, and is meanly furnished, — one, and possibly two, beds, three or four chairs, half a dozen stools, a cheap pine table, an old spinning-wheel, a water-bucket and drinking gourd, two tin wash-basins, half a dozen tin platters, a few cooking utensils, and a dozen odd pieces of crockery. Paint and whitewash and wall-paper and window-curtains are to him needless luxuries. His wife is leaner, more round-shouldered, more sunken of chest, and more pinched of face than her husband. He "chaws" and she "dips." The children of these two are large-eyed, tow-headed urchins, alike igno-

rant of the decencies and the possibilities of life. In this
house there is often neither book nor newspaper; and, what
is infinitely worse, no longing for either. The day begins
at sunrise and ends at dark; its duties are alike devoid of
dignity and mental or moral compensation. The man has
a small farm, and once owned six or eight negroes. How
the family now lives, the propping hands of the negroes
being taken away, is a mystery, even if one remembers the
simple cheapness of mere animal life.

I am not speaking either of the white resident of the
cities or of the " poor white," technically so named, but of
the common inhabitant of the country, — the man who pays
a tax and votes, but never runs for office; who was a private
in the Rebel army, but never anything more; who hates
the Yankees as a matter of course, but has no personal ill-
will toward them ; who believes in the Divine right of slavery, but is positive that a free negro cannot be made to
work. He is hospitable enough in words and manner, but
expects you to pay extravagantly in greenbacks or liberally
in silver for a seat at his table and the use of his odd bed.
His larder is lean, and his cookery is in the last degree
wretched. He tenders " apple-jack," as an evidence of
good-will, and wonders in a feeble way how a man can live
who don't drink it at least half a dozen times a day. He
likes to talk, and rarely has any work that prevents him from
hanging on the fence to chat with the chance traveller who
asks the road; but his conversation runs in an everlasting
circle round the negro, with an occasional pause for the
relation of personal adventures in the war. He receives two
or three letters per year, perhaps, and wonders why a man
should take a daily newspaper. He troubles himself very
little about schools or education, but likes to go to meeting,
and thinks himself well informed as to matters of theology.
He believes the " abolishioners " brought on the war; but
he does n't love Jeff Davis or Governor Vance. He " allers

dun hansumly by his niggers," and thinks them the " most ongratefullest creeturs on the face of the yerth."

The complexion of these country residents is noticeable, and suggests many inquiries. If you say that half the men and nearly all the women are very pale, you strike at the matter, but fail to fairly hit it. Their whiteness of skin is simply the whiteness of ordinary tallow. It is sallowness, with a suggestion of clayeyness. Unquestionably soap and water and crash towels would improve the appearance, but I doubt if they would give any bloom to the cheek. The skin seems utterly without vitality, and beyond the action of any restorative stimulants : it has a pitiful and repulsive death-in-life appearance. I am told the climate is in fault, but my judgment says the root of the matter is in the diet of the people. The range of eatables is exceedingly narrow, and swine's flesh constitutes at least half the food of all classes outside the towns and cities ; while the consumption of grease — of fat in one form or another — would, I am sure, aston-ish even an Arctic explorer. The whole economy of life seems radically wrong, and there is no inherent energy which promises reformation.

The amount of tobacco consumed by the people is beyond all calculation. I hardly exaggerate in saying that at least seven tenths of all persons above the age of twelve years use it in some form. Nearly every man and boy smokes or chews, and very many of them do both, while the country women chew and smoke to some extent, and women of most classes " dip." When I saw old Solon Shingle come into the witness-box to tell the story about his famous " bar'l o' apple sass " I thought the manner in which he disposed of his quid of tobacco the nastiest piece of business I should ever see. I was mistaken. To see a man take it from his mouth and put it in his hat when he goes to breakfast is by no means uncommon. I have even seen men lay it under the edge of their plate at dinner ; and one of the leading delegates in the Convention held an immense quid between the thumb and finger of the hand with which he abundantly gesticulated during a ten-minutes speech! Could nastiness go further? And do not these things mark the civilization of a people? In South Carolina, though seeing all classes, I did not once observe a white woman "dipping" snuff; but in this State I have seen scores, — I should scarcely exaggerate if I said hundreds. I saw them in Charlotte, the first town at which I stopped, within an hour after my arrival; and have seen them in every place I have visited since, — "dipping" in the porches of their own houses, on the streets, and twice in the public parlors of hotels. If barbaric life has a filthier and more disgusting custom than this, may I be excused from seeing it.

The labor system of the State is not so badly disorganized as that of South Carolina, but it is thoroughly demoralized. One sees here more white men in trades there almost given up to negroes, but he also sees negroes in trades here from which they are excluded there. The number of grown men, middle-aged men, who have no ostensible business but lounging and whiskey-drinking, is much greater in this State than in that. It is the complaint of papers in all sections of the State, that there never before were so many idle men, — vagrants, consumers, non-producers, non-taxpayers. The chief pity of the matter, however, is, that they seem to have no desire for work. "And who makes so much fuss about the negroes not working as these very white drones who hug the street-corners, lounge about dram-shops, and trust to chance for food and raiment?" asks one of the Raleigh papers, very pertinently. "We trust our law-makers will do all in their power," adds another journal, "to compel the freedmen to work for an honest living; but we consider it equally incumbent on them to take steps to reduce the amount of vagrancy among the whites." These extracts are not from papers edited by Northern or outside men, but the two writers are

men who have always lived in the State. The columns of
the Wilmington and Newbern papers, edited by new-comers,
bear witness, however, to the same state of facts.

It probably never will be settled whether the State did or
did not want to go out of the Union in May, 1861. That
she did not in December, 1860, nor in February, 1861, is
clear enough from the votes cast in those months; but the
condition of affairs had greatly changed by the following
May. "My situation, and not my will, consents," quoted
one delegate of the recent Convention in explanation of
North Carolina's course then. I am everywhere urged to
believe that the "geographical necessity" forced her out. I
have heard that phrase so much since I came into the State,
that I should be tempted to consider it a sort of byword if
it were not used by sober men of mature years. While
many seem anxious that the stranger should believe the
State did not voluntarily secede, there are others who insist
that it was h'er matured will to go out in that fatal May.
"If she did not believe in the constitutional right of secession, she at least believed the time had come for a revolution," said a gentleman to me here last evening. "The people desired the State to withdraw," said Delegate Ferrebee,
who was also delegate in the Secession Convention. "I am
convinced that not two fifths of the people ever favored secession in any form," responded Delegate Pool. When doc-
tors disagree, who shall decide? "My calm and deliberate
judgment," said a leading lawyer to me in Charlotte, "is,
that about five eighths of the people of the State sustained
the action of the Secession Convention." On the other hand,
Delegate Boyden says, "I don't believe one third of them
ever sustained it." How shall an outsider come to a conclusion?

It needs to be continually borne in mind that much of the
"Unionism" of the State is mere personal bitterness toward
Jeff Davis, or Governor Vance, or some less noted secession

leader. Thus, when the outspoken Raleigh *Progress* says, "it is remarkable that treason has become so rampant and defiant before the State has been readmitted," it is excited because somebody has proposed to ask the President to consider the utter worthlessness of old Governor Vance, and decide if he may not just as well set him free. Yet the *Progress* is quite right when it remarks that "there must be a great change of heart in North Carolina before Andrew Johnson, as a candidate for the Presidency, can carry it against any prominent leader of the Rebellion who may oppose him"; and also quite right again when it says that "the work of restoration in our State has been damaged by attempts to conciliate men who deserve nothing but stripes."

The action of the Convention in respect to the secession ordinance and the war debt pointedly marks the outlines of the situation. Over thirty delegates declared by a solemn vote that the ordinance never had any force whatever, and then turned squarely about and put themselves on record in favor of assuming the debt made in trying to sustain that pretended ordinance! In other words, a large number of gentlemen who consider themselves insulted if called by any other name than "Unionist" desire the State to pay her share of the expense of the war for breaking up the Union. Is there in this action an exhibition of what is technically called "cheek"? There is at least, as I have already said, startling proof that words are very cheap, and that Unionism in name is one thing, and Unionism in fact quite another thing.

The average sentiment of the State is very far from being up to that of the Convention, as shown by its action on the secession ordinance. Of course the declaration that it has always been null and void will be sustained by the vote of next December, but that vote will be smaller even than that just cast in choosing the Convention. That there will be further resistance to the government is not possible. I

do not forget that Delegate Phillips declared in debate that
"if the North and South ever again come into the position
they occupied in 1860–61, blood will be again spilled"; nor
do I forget that another delegate said he knew men of position who declared themselves "ready for further trial of the
present issue, if England and France would recognize the
confederacy"; yet against these signs of the hour I set the
declaration of Uncle Nat Boyden, "Neither principalities,
nor powers, nor things present, nor things to come, nor life,
nor death, nor any other creature, shall hereafter separate
us from the sisterhood of States!" That any possible separation may be prevented, we need only to help the Union
men of the State. That the average sentiment of her people may be brought up to the best sentiment of the Convention, we need to make haste slowly in the work of reconstruction.

The condition of the negro is in some respects worse and
in others better than in South Carolina. He is in such mi-
nority here that he cannot enforce his natural rights so easily
as he does there; but, on the other hand, because of that
same fact, the essential natural rights are generally more
readily granted to him here than there. The cold hunkerism of this people, however, stands immovably in his way,
and gives him little chance. It is greatly to his credit that
he has not been seized by such discontent as prevails below.
In the extreme western part of the State he got uneasy and
drifted over the line and off toward Charleston; and in the
eastern part he must needs go down to Newbern and Wilmington to find freedom. Elsewhere, however, with local
exceptions, he is staying on the old place, and working at
the old tasks; and I am convinced that, in the main, he has
not given serious cause of complaint.

"The chief ambition of a wench seems to be to wear a
veil and carry a parasol," said a ladylike-appearing woman
at the hotel in Salisbury. The mistress of the hotel in

Charlotte, at which chance travellers are fleeced at the rate of four dollars per day regular charges, and another dollar for extras, complained that "the nasty niggers must have a parasol when they ha'n't got no shoes." One of two misses who passed me on the street one day in Raleigh was scolding because her girl had stolen her veil, and she added, finally, "She got so crazy for it that ma had to get her one." A gentlemen of this place with whom I spoke this morning professed great amusement at a fact of his observation, — that full-blooded negro wenches carry a parasol and wear a white handkerchief around the neck to protect themselves from the sun. An officer of the Freedmen's Bureau told me the wearing of black veils by the young negro women had given great offence to the young white women, and that there was a time earlier in the season when the latter would not wear them at all. Does this matter of veils and parasols and handkerchiefs seem a small one? Yet it is one of serious import to the bitter, spiteful women whose passionate hearts nursed the Rebellion. I have, one way and another, heard so much about it, that I am not at liberty to suppose it a mere matter of local or temporary grievance. Wretched negro girls, you of sprawling feet and immense lips and retreating foreheads and coal-black color, cease from your vagaries! Cease from such sore troubling of the placid and miasmatic waters of good society!

"The nigger is crazy to ride, — to own an old mule and an old cart, and to be seen driving through the streets," said an ex-Rebel colonel to me at Charlotte. "A negro has reached kingdom come," remarked my seat-mate in the wearisome ride last night from Goldsboro, "when he's got on horseback." And it seems to give grave offence to the gentry of the State that the negro likes riding better than walking, that he will insist on buying a poor old mule and a poor old cart and going into business for himself! In this grief is indirect proof that Sambo appreciates the situation, and is anxious to be at work for himself as soon as possible.

To his average good disposition is due the fact that in many counties slavery still exists as a fact even if abolished as a name. I make this assertion only after much inquiry into the condition of things. The State is so large and sparsely settled, and means of communicating with some sections are so unfavorable, that even the Freedmen's Bureau has not yet found all the counties. When the Freedmen's Convention deliberately asks the general commanding the department to give some of its members safe return to their homes, there is such testimony to the existence of the old condition of slavery unconsciously furnished as no amount of negation can overweigh; and when one of the delegates to the Constitutional Convention chuckles over the fact that some of his constituents don't yet know that slavery is abolished, he furnishes proof unquestionable as to the actual situation.

"What my people wants first," said an intelligent colored man to me at Salisbury, "what dey fust wants is de right to be free." He compassed the whole case in few words. In other States, where their number in proportion to the number of whites is greater than it is here, or where the revolution made by the war has been deeper, they assume and hold this first right, to be free, — assume and hold it to their harm, doubtless, in thousands of cases; but here, in many counties, even this primary right is yet denied them. Some of the delegates to the Freedmen's Convention were obliged to sneak off from home in the night, and expected punishment on their return. The negro is no model of virtue, and he delights in laziness and the excitement of the city; but, on the whole, I think he is bearing himself very well in North Carolina, — with credit to himself and to his friends.

So far as I can learn, the intelligent colored men are pleading very little as yet for the right of suffrage, but very much for the right to testify in the courts. "We can live without a vote, but not without the right to speak for our-

selves," said one of them to me at Greensboro, — antici-
pating the sentiment of the lame barber here who observed,
as he brushed my hair this morning, and emphasized his
words with a thump of my head for which he made a hundred apologies, "To be sure, sah, we wants to vote, but, sah,
de great matter is to git into de witness-box." One of the
leading lawyers of the western part of the State, a former
District Attorney and member of the Legislature, told a
friend of mine that he knows no prominent member of the
bar who does not favor the admission to the courts of negro
evidence. I presume it is true that many leading men of
the State occupy this ground ; but the distance between
these leading men and the common people is very great ;
and I am sorrowfully certain that the latter are far from
being willing to allow the negro to be heard in court in his
own behalf.

"We are too poor to educate our own children now," said
Delegate Settle ; "and much as I wish for the education of
the negro, his help will have to come from the North at present." It is something to get a desire that the negro shall
be educated, — and Mr. Settle is one of those who want him
colonized. The North took Mr. Settle at his spirit before
he uttered his word, and this year has in operation, in various parts of the State, about fifty schools, under charge of
about sixty teachers, and embracing nearly five thousand
different pupils. Most of these teachers are ladies, not a
few of whom are from Massachusetts. The State Superin-
tendent reports a good degree of progress, and the most
indifferent inquiry anywhere among the negroes develops a
living and grasping interest.

The labor system, as I have already said, is in better
order than in South Carolina. The negroes are not, however, any better paid than there. Where they work for a
share of the crop they get from one fourth to one third.
Many of them, though, are working for regular wages, —

six to eight dollars per month with board, and nine to twelve dollars without board. The planters and farmers rather pride themselves on the liberality of these wages; but they are, of course, utterly insufficient for anything more than bare support. There is less complaint here than below that the negro fails to observe his contract. The local county police does much to keep down disorder, and doubtless is something of a terror to negroes of vicious tendencies who would like to desert their work.

Yet it cannot be denied that there are conflicts between employers and employed, and some careful and observant officers tell me they are increasing because of the injustice of some masters who strive to keep up the old authority of slave days. " It is generally known that the prejudice and bitterness is increasing between the whites and the blacks," says one Raleigh paper ; and " clashings between the races are unfortunately becoming more and more frequent," responds Governor Holden's organ. The real question of the hour is neither one of suffrage nor one of giving testimony, but one of establishing the true relations of employer and employed. The true course is luminously indicated by another paper of the State: " If the employers, and especially the late slave-owners, will treat the blacks kindly and justly, these troubles that now annoy us will soon pass away." Will the white man be wise in season ? For the negro, strong in his longing for freedom, gropes blindly and passionately, and will not be cheated of what the earth, and the very heavens themselves, assure him is his right.

XXI.

THE GREAT MILITARY PRISON OF SOUTH CAROLINA.

WITHIN THE STOCKADE,
FLORENCE, October 19, 1865.

DOES it seem affectation that I date my letter from "Within the Stockade"? At least I write it there, — write it in my note-book, on my knee, sitting on a block of wood, in one of the hut houses built by the hands of those who served the cause of Union and Liberty in the prisons of secession and slavery, — write it to the accompaniment of glaring lightning and crashing thunder and driving rain. Will these mud walls shelter me through the storm of this hot afternoon? I cannot forget that they have sheltered men who perilled vastly more than ease and comfort; and as I look through the hole that they called a "door," and see the acres of such barbaric but sanctified habitations, I lift reverent heart of thanksgiving to Him who gave us the victory, and blessed the struggle and suffering of that great army through whom we have national unity and the assured promise of universal freedom.

Florence is a name rather than a place ; or, say, a point at which three railroads centre, rather than a town. There is a hotel, and a church, and a machine-shop, and two so-called stores, and three bar-rooms, and twenty-five or thirty residences, and a great pine forest. There is a long, broad street ; at one end of which is the hotel, — a somewhat pretentious two-story wood building, with a wide and lofty piazza in front, and an ungainly tower in the centre. At the farther end of the street are the stores and the machine-shop. Midway are the apothecary's, and the hospital, and a vacant law office. Back of this street, in the pines, are the

dwellings which constitute the town. The three railroads
have a common starting-point just in front of the hotel.
Passengers from Wilmington to Charleston reach here
about seven in the evening, and leave about three in the
morning, after paying two dollars each for supper and lodging of a passably good character. Passengers from Charleston to Wilmington reach here at the same hour, leave at the
same time, and pay the same tax for the support of the
landlord. Those from Columbia get supper here, and are
taxed one dollar. Those for Cheraw are obliged to disburse
three dollars for supper, lodging, and breakfast. The town
is, therefore, a railroad eating-house, with sleeping-rooms
attached.

Situated at the intersection of the great cross-line of railroad with the great coast-line, about one hundred miles from
either Wilmington or Charleston, and about seventy-five
miles from either the coast or Columbia, it was peculiarly
adapted for the location and safety of a prison.

The stockade is about a mile and a half north of east from
the hotel, about a third of a mile from the railroad, and near
the centre of a great opening in the pine forest, which is
locally known as " the old field." The field is a sandy, rolling, fenceless, irregularly-shaped tract of five hundred acres,
more or less, which probably at some time formed the tillable portion of two or three plantations mostly given up to
turpentine and rosin making. The stockade is about thirty-
five rods wide north and south, and some seventy rods long
east and west; containing, perhaps, fifteen or sixteen acres.
Through the middle of this enclosure, from north to south,
flows a little stream of water, five or six feet in width and
four or five inches in depth. It is a swiftly running stream,
and the water has a not unpleasant taste. From either end
the prison-pen slopes off to this brook, — making five or six
acres of low, marshy ground, lying principally east of the
stream, full of sink-holes and stagnant waters and mias-

matic odors and malarial influences, — the breeding-place of agues and fevers and typhoids and rheumatic complaints, — the rank and pestiferous home of disease and death, than which hellish malignity could scarcely have fashioned one more fit to the purpose of that foul treason which laid its foundation in slavery and sought to enthrone Rapine and Anarchy as twin deities in the land of law and liberty!

Everything remains as the Rebels left it when they evacuated Florence, — remains almost as it was when these hillsides swarmed with our soldier prisoners. On the east and on the west, outside the stockade, twenty rods or so distant from the walls, are the long lines of earthworks reaching away to the timber on either side, and far down in front of these again are the numerous rifle-pits commanding the advance for nearly a hundred rods. The main entrance to the stockade was at the northwestern corner. Near this corner were the log-houses of the guard and half a dozen small ovens. The barracks stand almost as they did when last occupied, but the houses over the ovens have been burned. Just north of this entrance is a handsome little grove of a dozen trees, among which yet remain the benches and stools of the officers of the guard. Fifty feet in front of the middle of the western wall was the flag-staff whence floated the banner of treason and slavery. Its stump only remains, and loyal and disloyal alike cut chips of memento therefrom. Across the pestilential quagmire, beyond the northeastern corner, is another deserted village of log-houses, — houses of the guard for the rear of the prison-pen, not one of which has been touched. I went among them with the wonder if some long-haired, lean-bodied, leering-eyed Johnnie might not spring out with ready musket and bid me halt; and, sure enough, from one of them suddenly emerged a fellow in gray, who looked at me a moment, and then strode away with a swinging and defiant step. In the southeastern corner of the pen was the rear entrance. — thence the prisoners

9   M

went to fetch wood, a dozen cords of which yet lie piled only five or six rods away.

The walls of the stockade are sixteen feet high, built of unhewn logs some nine or ten inches in diameter, set deeply in the ground. This solid wall of oak and pine logs is un-broken, except by the gate openings and the quagmire, — the marshy ground necessitating the substitution of a stout board fence for the wall of logs. Outside the wall is, of course, a wide and deep ditch, the earth from which is thrown against the logs and forms a narrow path about three or four feet below their tops, whereon the guard walked and overlooked this prison-pen, and from whence fiends in human shape shot half-crazed boys who straggled over this dead-line, which runs just behind the hut within which I sit. A ditch could not be dug through the quagmire, and so there are picket platforms built on the fence there, — one, noticeably, on each side over the brook.

Inside the stockade there has been very little change save such as time makes. In the northwestern corner, near the main entrance, was the hospital, — seven log-houses, each some forty feet long and twenty feet wide. These the guard partially burned when they left. Through the centre of the enclosure from east to west is a narrow graded road; the bridge over the creek has partially fallen in, but the road-bed is as hard and smooth as it was six months ago. The Rebels attempted to burn the stockade wall by firing piles of wood thrown against it on the inside, but the fire refused its work, and only scorched the logs at seventy-five or a hundred points of the long line; and the half-burned sticks of wood and the little bundles of pitch-pine remain in their places to show how the most destructive of the elements enlisted in the service of the Union, and saved this prison-pen as an eloquent token of the cost of liberty.

Does any man, horrified by the stories told concerning it, believe that the famous and infamous " dead-line " was a myth? However it may have been elsewhere, here it is a hateful reality. It is about twenty feet inside the stockade walls. Part of the way it is marked by a light pole laid in crotches; elsewhere it is only marked by the line which distinguishes trodden from untrodden ground, — of earth rank with grass and of earth bare of grass. Just back of this hut, in the northeastern quarter, there is only this line of grass and no-grass. Doubtless this was the best of the Southern prison-pens; but even here, if current report among such of the towns-people as can be induced to speak at all of the stockade is true, the guards indulged in that very pleasant and exceedingly humorous amusement which consisted in tossing pieces of meat or bread into the stockade, between the wall and dead-line, in order to get a shot at some Yankee boy who was so hungry as to thoughtlessly rush for it. These fellows would have their joke, you see! Shall we mudsills complain thereat? If they serve who stand and wait, did not these also serve who died between the wall and the dead-line?

Go no more, even in dreams, to Pompeii and Herculaneum, buried cities of the Old World. Here is the city of the living dead, — city as populous as those, as fruitful as those in the signs and tokens of a life that was and is not. On these ten or eleven acres there were at least 2,500 houses, — perhaps 3,000 would be a more correct figure; and not less than three fourths of them are nearly as good as they were on the day of their sudden evacuation, and in hundreds of them are memorials of that life of want and woe which 13,000 men knew here, and from which 4,000 passed out through the door of the dead-house to the slope way yonder by the timber, and laid themselves down in long rows for the final sleep and for the glorious reward due unselfish souls.

In the construction of these habitations there is almost infinite variety on a common, general plan. This one in which I sit, and through which the still driving storm begins

to beat, furnishes that general plan, with very little elabora-
tion or decoration. Come in and see it. Do you find the
door low and narrow, and have you a horror of this squat
roof and these smoky walls and this earth floor? Yet here
lived three or four men, for many weeks, doubtless, and,
perhaps, for many months!

The hut is six and a half feet long, four feet and three
inches wide, and about five feet high in the centre. A hole
of fifteen inches depth was dug; at either end of it was set
a forked stick; in these two forks was laid a ridge-pole.
The wall of our house is the side of the hole; the roof is
thé slope of sticks or slabs of wood resting on the ridge-pole
and at the edge of the hole. This is the general plan. The
huts smaller than this are more numerous than those larger.

The back end is made of sticks driven into the ground,
against which earth has been thrown. The front end is
built with more care. Half of it is of mud brick, and the
door and the little chimney at the corner occupy the other
half. The door is simply a hole; the chimney is seemingly
built up of little bricks, and gives a tiny fireplace of about
fifteen inches square. The roof was first covered with pine
brush and then with six or eight inches of earth.

Perhaps a hundred of the huts are entirely above ground.
Possibly a score are so high that an ordinary man can stand
straight in them. But then there are a thousand built over
holes three feet deep, a thousand not more than four feet
high in the ridge, a thousand not more than four feet
square, some hundreds that show only such height above
ground as a well-filled grave. Do you deem it awful that
men should live in such habitations as these? Yet they
were palaces beside the burrows of Salisbury. The thousands of tiny brick used here were made from the reddish
earth of the hillside west of the brook. The graded flat, ex-
tending back sixty or seventy feet from the stream, suggests
a parade-ground; but it was only the bed on which these

little bricks were sun-baked. In the use of the brick there was sometimes a great deal of skill and ingenuity displayed. One sees with pleasure a score or two of chimneys that are models of architectural beauty; one finds not a few fire-places that are constructed with elaborate improvements. So, too, a few of the huts have doors curiously braided or woven of splinters. There is, indeed, over in the southwestern corner, one whole house above ground, woven, walls and roof, like a basket. These things, though, are exceptional; generally there was only so much as would answer the baldest utilitarianism.

I saw with gladness that there was plenty of wood. Some of it, as I have already said, is still piled in a long rank just outside the stockade. There is an abundance, also, scattered all about the enclosure, particularly east of the brook. Look into a hundred huts, and you shall see wood ready cut for the little fireplace in seventy-five of them surely. In a few cases it even yet lies nicely piled against the chimney on the outside.

They were Yankee boys, the inhabitants of this city. Here is a great pine knot fashioned into a barber's chair, for which many a man would be glad to bid a hundred dollars at a Sanitary Fair. It is nothing but a rough bit of log, but its purpose is evident enough. They pitched quoits sometimes, I judge; for over in the southeastern corner is even now the little post at which they aimed, with an old horseshoe lying near. So, too, they seem to have indulged in cricket in the sweet spring days when General Sherman and his forces were in the State above, for I found one wicket in its place. Did they indulge in games at bows and arrows? for I picked up what was clearly an arrow. That they played checkers is certain, for just down the hill a little is a hut in which is a rude checkerboard, and in the corner near the fireplace I tumbled out half a dozen of their pieces, — four round, and two square, cut from pine splinters. I guess they also played cards, for in one hut I picked up the ten of clubs, the five spot and the queen of hearts, and the ace and the jack of spades. You see life came to a sudden pause here, — there was no time for blotting out all the marks of this daily existence; and, walk where you will, you stumble against something that suggests it was but yesterday these prison-boys found liberty.

The occupant of one house was a German. Here is a scrap from some German newspaper, a leaf from a German Testament, — parts of the second and third chapters of Second Corinthians, — and a bit of German manuscript, probably a letter.

In another hut I found an old tin plate, part of an iron fork, the blade of a table-knife, and the bowl of a clay pipe. An Irishman lived here; he wrote his name on one of the posts, "Mic O'Lary"; and I have half a leaf from his Prayer-Book: "O Lord God, I would not only pray for myself, but for all men. Bless my relatives and friends wherever they are. Bless, too, my enemies, and may they become my friends. May universal peace soon prevail." So the simple heart lifted sublime prayer in the night-time, and consecrated his tent with the balm of forgiveness.

In this little square, deep hole-house was a page of Hazlitt's Table-Talk, a rude wooden spoon, a pair of wooden knives, a tin plate, and an armful of pine wood. Was it this morning that the tenant moved out into the large world?

In this adjoining cabin must have lived a boy direct from one of the New England States. It is six months since he last passed through the door, yet everything is as orderly and neat as if arranged but an hour ago. His wood is carefully piled in the corner next to the fireplace, his stool is sound and strong, his seat against the wall has not fallen down, the bowl of his brierwood pipe is sweet and clean. He was saving and thoughtful: here is the spring of a pocket-knife laid away against a possible need; carefully in the pine-bush covering of his roof is a little roll of blue army cloth for patches; on a string, tied in the corner, are strung three buttons. He read somebody's History of English Literature, for here is a leaf from the book, pages 229 and 230; he kept the roll of his mess, I judge, for here is a page, wet and dingy, from his diary, on which are a dozen names.

In still another hut I find a rude pipe-bowl, dug out of a sassafras-root, and a wooden spoon large enough for a giant. The boy was at home, too, to the tract distributor, for here is No. 80 — "Do you know the Way?" — "published by a South Carolina Colportage Board."

The boys who lived here — a most wretched hut, with its pile of straw in the centre — were also visited by the tract man, who left with them "An Old Blade in a New Scabbard," thus: "Deserted: This is to certify that, within the last twelve months, one Peter Weakhearted has deserted from the army of Jesus Christ. One of our scouts saw him last Sabbath walking arm in arm with Captain Lovesin, of the Whiskey Guards, in Cursing Grove, near Lake Perdition. A gracious reward will be given for the recovery and restoration of this deserter to the army."

In the house with a door at each end, — and there is but one such house, — I found the rarest treasure of the morning. It was tucked into the piny thatching, and concealed by a scrap of red woollen cloth. It is a daguerrotype, with the cases half worn away by long shuffling in the knapsack, and the whole tied together with a bit of black thread. It is apparently the picture of mother and two sisters. A goodlooking, sober-faced woman of forty-five, wearing black bonnet and veil and cape and dress, and holding a dark parasol; a young lady of nineteen or twenty, wearing a hat trimmed with black, a light spring or fall dress, and a gray cloth sack, and holding a fan; and, between and behind the two, a sweet-faced miss of large and loving eyes, who stands in such position that the only article of dress visible is a black silk cape.

Said I not that here was life arrested in the very pulse-beat? The tale of Florence can be half read even now by the dullest eye.

A quarter of a mile away from the entrance-gate are the eight long rows of mounds, to which so much of this life finally came. 2,352, that is the highest number of the graves; but there are many score unnumbered, and the negroes say the men were often buried at random in the old field. "Chucked 'em in like muttons," said an intelligent negro carpenter, who was often in trouble for trying to feed and help the boys in blue. The half-acre of ground occupied by these known and numbered graves is not enclosed, and vagrant cows wander at will over the low mounds. Of course the Rebels kept a record of this potter's field, else why the numbered graves? But that has not been, and probably never will be, found.

The storm has passed by, and the sun, now almost in its setting, suffuses the low west with a flood of golden glory. I have spent the entire day in the stockade. The little accessories of its prison life remain as I have drawn them; its body and substance are told in the fact that from one third to one fourth of the prisoners brought here are lying yonder in the sandy hill-slope.

XXII.

LIFE AND LABOR IN THE SOUTH CAROLINA LOW-COUNTRY.

CHARLESTON, October 21, 1865.

LET no man come into the Carolinas this fall or winter for a so-called pleasure-trip. Since the first week in September I have travelled over most of the stage and railway routes in the two States; and I assure you that, though I may have found some profit, I have not found very much pleasure.

The railroads are worn out, and there is not a single line in either State that should not be relaid with new iron at the earliest possible day. Half the freight cars are fit for a few months more service, but the other half and all the passenger coaches were ready months ago for condemnation; though I suppose they must be used another half-year at least, because the various companies are unable to buy new stock. The engines seem generally in rather worse order than the cars, and a careful inspection of almost any one of them is calculated to vividly impress the traveller with the uncertainty of life. That delays and accidents are numerous follows as a matter of course. It must be said, however, that the accidents do not very frequently result in loss of life or serious injury of person. The average rate of railway speed is about nine miles per hour in South Carolina, and about eleven miles per hour in North Carolina. The cost of travel is about seven and a half cents per mile; on one road it is only six cents, and on another it is about eleven cents.

The late election passed off without any serious disturbance. With respect to Governor, the vote of Charleston stands, — James L. Orr, 785; Wade Hampton, 661. An effort was made to get the latter to run against Orr; but, at

9 *

the last moment, he declined doing so.   Had he been a candidate, I think he would have received three fourths of the vote of this district.

The city elected two senators and twenty representatives for the Legislature.   The delegation is, generally speaking, weak; yet it is in one sense very strong, for it italicizes the fact that the people are disposed to break away from the old leaders and take up new men.   Judge Lesesne, who has been senator for a number of years, is defeated by a heavy majority, though he is an estimable gentleman of much influence in State affairs.   With three or four exceptions, the representatives are without legislative experience.   They were mostly nominated by the "Workingmen's Association," and of course there is considerable disgust at the result among the so-called aristocracy of the city.   In respect to the matter of Unionism, it is only to be said that some of them were Union men from the beginning to the end, some were original Secessionists, and some were men who took sides as little as possible.   In a word, the result is only significant as marking the triumph of the common people against the upper classes.

The city election takes place in less than a fortnight.   As yet very little has been said about it, "but I expect this d—d 'Workingmen's Association' will carry the day," complained one gentleman with whom I spoke.   There is only one candidate in the field for Mayor, — Mr. P. G. Gilliard, an ex-Rebel colonel, who lost an arm in the war.   The present incumbent of the office, Mr. Charles Macbeth, who has been in it for many years, "killed himself," as I am told by several persons, by moving in the late Convention to admit negro testimony to the courts, — "though why it should kill him," says one of the legislators elect, "when we all know we 've got to come to it in less than six months, I can't see."

The negro's prospects in the South Carolina low-country

are not flattering. The situation is in many respects already against him; and the Presidential order, under which General Howard is now here, is full of evil and woful portent.

Further observation of the agents of the Freedmen's Bureau, and of the way in which they do the business intrusted to them, confirms me more strongly in the opinion I expressed six weeks ago, — that at least half of them are wholly unfit for the positions they occupy. They cannot be trusted to administer justice between the planters and the freedmen, for they too generally side with the former, even in cases where the right course is not difficult to choose.

Official reports from Marion, Darlington, and Williamsburg Districts represent the negroes as quiet, well-disposed, and generally at work for mere starvation wages. My own observations in these three districts pretty fairly confirm these reports, and furnish some clew to the bearing of the whites.

I had opportunity to see many intelligent "fellows," as the workingmen are invariably called by the planters. The first complaint of all the whites is that the negroes will not work, that they are constantly violating their contracts, &c., &c. I asked the "fellows" about this. "Well, you see, boss," said one of them, "de fust dif'culty about de matter be dis yer, we gits no meat; and de secon' is, dat we gits de fum-tyin' too much." The whole case was epigrammatically stated in that sentence.

While we stopped a couple of hours at one station on the railroad for water, I strolled off to the house of a planter who had a dozen "fellows" and as many more women and children on his place. Men and women were at work in the cornfield, and he was smoking in his piazza, — everything in the nature of a porch being called a "piazza." He received me courteously enough, and asked me to "have a pipe," which I declined. "Did I come up from the kears?" he inquired. I told him I did. He had "heerd," he said, "that the kears was in trouble. 'Pears like they are in trouble most every day," he continued; "my neegurs is allus stoppin' in their work to run off and see what's the matter with 'em." That launched him into the usual stream. "Know much about neegurs, mister?" he queried. I told him I had never lived in the South. "Wall then, mister, ye don't know much about 'em." And he proceeded to enlighten me at some length. Incidentally I asked him how he fed them. "Corn and rice and such game as they can git," said he. Afterwards, while speaking on general subjects, I asked if there was much meat to be had for the white families. "O yes," he replied, "right smart o' meat yer abouts." Still later in the conversation I remarked, "I think you said you don't give the negroes much meat." "Jes so, mister; don't give neegurs bacon this year like we used to." "Why so?" said I; "I believe you said there was right smart of it in the country." He seemed a little puzzled at the turn of conversation, and suddenly "called to mind" that he had an engagement with a neighbor at about that hour. He invited me to walk with him, and also invited me to "turn in and lie out with us" if I ever came through the country.

At Florence I found a most intelligent negro carpenter who lived three miles out of town, but came in every day to his work. He had been travelling through the district lately, — in connection with the league, I judged. "What is the real cause of trouble between the plantation negroes and their employers?" said I. "Well, sah," he answered, "there's a many masters as wants to git de colored peoples away, ye see; an' dey's got de contrac's, an' dey can't do it, ye see, lawful; so dey 'buses dem, an' jerks 'em up by de two fums, an' don't give 'em de bacon, an' calls on 'em to do work in de night time an' Sun'ay, till de colored people dey gits oneasy an' goes off."

In the cars, between the Santee and this city, I asked a

man who was loudly complaining about his "niggers" if the planters generally gave their hands full allowance of bacon this fall. "Many of 'em don't give out any at all," said he, somewhat snappishly. So, too, while we lunched at the river, I asked of a countryman who got on at Kingstree, "I suppose now you give your negroes better meat than this?" alluding to some on the table. "Hav n't guv 'em any at all fur nigh on two months." "How 's that?" said I; "I don't see how you get much work out of them unless you give them meat." He answered that there was n't much in the country, and that the contracts did n't bind them to give the negroes meat. And so, too, the man on whose left I sat at dinner at the hotel to-day told his neighbor on the right of a row he had been having with the officers of his district about giving meat to his negroes; "an' he said I must let 'em have it twice a week," he remarked in conclusion.

A man who got on the cars at Marion "'lowed" he had been in jail for "whippin' a nigger, — bin in fifteen days, sir; was there ever such a d—d outrage!" he exclaimed. No one disputing him, he went on to say, "But I larnt a trick wuth two o' his'n," alluding, I suppose, to the officer who sent him to jail. "I jest strings 'em up by the thumbs for 'bout half an hour, an' then they are d—d glad to go to work." Another man whom I saw in the contract office at Florence had strung a woman up by the thumbs, and also whipped her, for which he also went to jail.

I infer from all I saw and heard while in the northeastern section, that the negroes at work in the pines are more generally contented than those on plantations anywhere in the State. There is more variety in the turpentine and rosin business than in cotton-growing; and though the work may be harder for one or two days in any given week, there are other days in which there is but little to do. The yield of rosin this season will be very small.

The negro's situation in the other districts of the so-called low-country is not so good as in those already named. From Georgetown there are many complaints that he is turbulent and "rebellious," and these are made the pretext for treating him with much severity. A gentleman from the town of that name tells me of a case in which a negro was cruelly beaten over the head and shoulders with a large club for insisting that an examination of his contract would show that he was under no obligation to perform certain work required of him. In the upper part of Charleston District the planters are quietly holding meetings at which they pass resolutions not to sell land to negroes, and not to hire negroes unless they can show a "consent-paper" from their former owner. In Beaufort District they not only refuse to sell land to negroes, but also refuse to rent it to them; and many black men have been told that they would be shot if they leased land and undertook to work for themselves. From Colleton District there are complaints that our own soldiers are being used as negro-drivers; and an old man from near St. George's showed me what he claimed was the wound of a bayonet, inflicted upon him by a soldier because he would not obey his orders in regard to the performance of a certain piece of work.

I have no hesitation in saying that the negro troops ought at once to be removed from the interior and put in garrison on the coast. I believe that the two Massachusetts regiments, and perhaps one New York regiment, have done their duty well, creditably to the States they represent, and honorably to the flag they bear; but, generally, the black regiments are wretchedly officered, and unless discipline is well kept up the presence of the negro soldiery is sadly demoralizing to the resident negroes. These have troubles enough without bearing those brought upon them by soldiers of their own race who are ruled by rude and rough and lawless white officers.

Not a little of the discontent among the blacks of Claren-

..on, Charleston, and Colleton Districts, and some of the hostility of the whites toward the negroes in these districts, has, I am confident, been engendered by the presence of these badly officered negro troops. If their removal seems a concession to notorious and unrepentant Rebels, it is yet a concession demanded by the interests of the only loyal population in the three districts.

All these low-country districts are filled with negroes from the up-country, — not with negroes raised there, but with those taken up there during the war. Many of them have drifted down here in search of freedom, but a large proportion have, after the summer's work, been turned away from the plantations, and sent hither to live by begging or stealing. The cruelty of the old planters in this regard is shocking, and the tales told of the conduct of some of them would be past belief if they were not well authenticated.

The better class of planters in the districts hereabouts very much fear serious difficulty before spring with these homeless and wandering negroes. Hunger will lead, they say, to theft, and theft will lead to organizations of white men for protection of property; and these organizations will lead to conflicts between the negroes and the lower class of whites, in which the negroes will be worsted. That such an issue of the present condition of affairs is possible, I can very easily see; that it is probable, I do not incline to believe; that the majority of the large planters will seek to prevent it, I am quite certain.

If a " war of the races " is brought on in South Carolina, it can have but one result, unless the United States troops are made a third party to it. " We 'ns smart nuff t' hold 'r own," said a scowling but intelligent negro to me at Orangeburg. And they are. Moreover, the whites of all these low-country districts know that fact, too.

Immigration is held to be the panacea for all present evils and troubles. One of the representatives elect from this city

will make strong efforts to secure legislative action at the
coming session of the General Assembly in favor of a bill
granting State aid to foreign immigrants.   The Yankee is
not wanted here, except by the enlightened few; but Germans who will consent to take a secondary position will be
welcomed.   Yet even they, with their liberal and democratic
ideas, are likely to encounter serious opposition during the
next two or three years at least.

I have already alluded to the presence in this city of General Howard.   The following is the order under which he is
acting : —

"WAR DEPARTMENT, ADJUTANT-GENERAL'S OFFICE,
WASHINGTON, October 9, 1865.

"*General Order, No.* 145.

"Whereas, certain tracts of land situated on the coast of South
Carolina, Georgia, and Florida, at the time for the most part vacant, were set apart, by Major-General W. T. Sherman's Special
Field Order, No. 15, for the benefit of refugees and freedmen that
had been congregated by the operations of war, or had been left
to take care of themselves by their former owners; and, whereas,
an expectation was thereby created that they would be able to
retain possession of said lands; and, whereas, a large number of
the former owners are earnestly soliciting the restoration of the
same, and promising to absorb the labor and care for the freedmen : It is ordered, that Major-General Howard, Commissioner
of the Bureau of Refugees, Freedmen, and Abandoned Lands,
proceed to the several above-named States, and endeavor to effect an arrangement mutually satisfactory to the freedmen and
the land-owners, and make report; and, in case a mutually satisfactory arrangement can be effected, he is duly empowered and
directed to issue such orders as may become necessary after a full
and careful investigation of the interests of the parties concerned.

"By order of the President of the United States.

"E. D. TOWNSEND,
Assistant Adjutant-General."

The publication of this order has produced considerable
excitement and anticipative satisfaction among the rebellious

portion of this community, and much anxiety among the friends of the freedmen. That the original intention of government in setting apart the Sea Islands was to either give or sell them to the freedmen I sincerely believe. That the negroes were allowed to receive the impression that this was the purpose of the government is beyond all question. That General Saxton colonized them in vast numbers on those islands, with this understanding on his part and theirs, is matter of record. If the faith of the nation was ever impliedly pledged to anything, it was to the assurance that the colored people should have a home there, — as witness the famous order of General Sherman, approved by the Secretary of War, and practically indorsed for nearly nine months by all branches of the government : —

" Head-quarters Military Division of the Mississippi, }
In the Field, Savannah, Ga., January 16, 1865. }

" *Special Field Order, No.* 15.

" I. The islands from Charleston, south, the abandoned rice-fields along the rivers for thirty miles back from the sea, and the country bordering the St. John's River, Florida, are reserved and set apart for the settlement of the negroes now made free by the acts of war and the proclamation of the President of the United States.

" II. At Beaufort, Hilton Head, Savannah, Fernandina, St. Augustine, and Jacksonville the blacks may remain in their chosen or accustomed vocations; but on the islands and in the settlements hereafter to be established no white person whatever, unless military officers and soldiers detailed for duty, will be permitted to reside; and the sole and exclusive management of affairs will be left to the freed people themselves, subject only to the United States military authority and the acts of Congress. By the laws of war, and orders of the President of the United States, the negro is free, and must be dealt with as such. He cannot be subjected to conscription or forced military service, save by the written orders of the highest military authority of the Department, under such regulations as the President or Congress may prescribe. Domestic servants, blacksmiths, carpenters, and other mechanics

N

will be free to select their own work and residence, but the young and able-bodied negroes must be encouraged to enlist as soldiers in the service of the United States, to contribute their share toward maintaining their freedom and securing their rights as citizens of the United States.

" III. Whenever three respectable negroes, heads of families, shall desire to settle on land, and shall have selected for that purpose an island or a locality clearly defined, within the limits above designated, the Inspector of Settlements and Plantations will himself, or by such subordinate officer as he may appoint, give them a license to settle such island or district, and afford them such assistance as he can to enable them to establish a peaceable agricultural settlement. The three parties named will subdivide the land, under the supervision of the Inspector, among themselves and such other as may choose to settle near them, so that each family shall have a plot of not more than (40) forty acres of tillable ground, and when it borders on some water channel, with not more than eight hundred feet of water front, in the possession of which land the military authorities will afford them protection, until such time as they can protect themselves, or until Congress shall regulate their title. The Quartermaster may, on the requisition of the Inspector of Settlements and Plantations, place at the disposal of the Inspector, one or more of the captured steamers, to ply between the settlements and one or more of the commercial points heretofore named in orders, to afford the settlers the opportunity to supply their necessary wants, and to sell the products of their land and labor.

" IV. Whenever a negro has enlisted in the military service of the United States, he may locate his family in any one of the settlements at pleasure, and acquire a homestead, and all other rights and privileges of a settler, as though present in person. In like manner, negroes may settle their families and engage on board the gunboats, or in fishing, or in the navigation of the inland waters, without losing any claim to land or other advantage derived from this system. But no one, unless an actual settler as above defined, or unless absent on government service, will be entitled to claim any right to land or property in any settlement by virtue of these orders.

" V. In order to carry out this system of settlement, a general

officer will be detailed as Inspector of Settlements and Plantations, whose duty it shall be to visit the settlements, to regulate
their police and general management, and who will furnish personally to each head of a family, subject to the approval of the
President of the United States, a possessory title in writing, giving as near as possible the description of boundaries; and who
shall adjust all claims or conflicts that may arise under the same,
subject to the like approval, treating such titles altogether as possessory. The same general officer will also be charged with the
enlistment and organization of the negro recruits, and protecting
their interests while absent from their settlements; and will be
governed by the rules and regulations prescribed by the War Department for such purposes.

"VI. Brigadier-General R. Saxton is hereby appointed Inspector of Settlements and Plantations, and will at once enter on the
performance of his duties. No change is intended or desired in
the settlement now on Beaufort Island, nor will any rights to
property heretofore acquired be affected thereby.

"By order of Major-General W. T. Sherman.

"L. M. DAYTON,
Assistant Adjutant-General."

If this order means anything, it means that the government intended to give the negroes "an expectation that
they would be able to retain possession of said lands"; and
if the President's order of the 9th does not break the implied national pledge, then everybody in Charleston fails to
comprehend its spirit and purpose.

The ex-Rebel owners of the islands are quite ready to
make promises, which one in five may perhaps keep. Yet
I talked with one this forenoon who does n't believe a free
negro will work, who expects to have control of his land by
Christmas or New Year's, and who is already devising ways
to get rid of the negroes upon it. The city property of the
most virulent Rebels is being restored to them as fast as
possible under executive orders; and the common conclusion of all classes that General Howard must find a "satisfactory arrangement" is held to be justified by the action

in respect to other property. In a word, the interpretation of the order is, that he is to make the best terms he can for the freedmen, and then surrender the islands to their former owners. If anything better than this results from his mission, the people of Charleston will have a new grievance, and the freedman and his resident friends a new cause for rejoicing, and for thankfulness to Him whose promises are yea and amen unto all men.

Three days ago General Howard went down to Edisto Island in company with a representative of the old owners thereof. They were met at a church by over two thousand freedmen, and a long and painfully interesting meeting was held. To say that the negroes were overwhelmed with sorrow and dissatisfaction is to state a fact in sober phrase. General Howard explained to them with careful and sympathetic words what he believed to be the wishes of the President, and asked them to appoint a committee to consider the terms proposed by the planters. This they did; and while the committee were in consultation, the assembly sang several of the most touching and mournful of the negro songs, and were addressed in broken and tearful words by some of their own preachers. The scarcely concealed spirit of all was that the government had deceived them, and it required the most earnest efforts of General Howard and his associates to keep this spirit from finding stormy outbreak. The result of the conference between representative Whaley and the Freedmen's Committee does not promise a speedy reconciliation of the negroes to their removal from the lands. They say that they will not, under any circumstances, work with overseers as heretofore, which is what the planters propose. Some few of them seemed willing to work for fair wages, but the great body were anxious to rent or buy the lands, to which the planters will not consent.

General Howard has represented the difficulties of the case to the President in strong terms. I am sure he will do his hard task with all possible consideration for the interests of the freedmen. He has issued some orders in the premises, the main features of which are, that the agents of the bureau on the several islands are to constitute boards of supervisors representing the government, the planters, and the freedmen; and that no lands occupied by negroes are to be restored till the planters engage to give the freedmen all the crops of this year, secure them in their homes, and pay them fair wages for the work of the coming year.

I have no idea this bargain will or can be carried out, because, first, the planters will not agree to their part of it; and, second, the negroes will not give up the islands on such terms. The South-Carolinians are reasonably well disposed toward the government, because they know the folly of further resistance to it; but their general hostility and antipathy to the negro is something remarkable to see. The planters believe they ought to have their old estates, and they also believe the President means that they shall have them; and hence the "fair terms" which they propose are such as will neither satisfy the freedmen nor the friends of the freedmen. The negroes, on the other hand, almost universally believe that the islands have been given to them, and they are not likely to very readily relinquish that belief. They long ago lost all faith in their old masters. An attempt to force them from the islands at present, or to compel them to the acceptance of the terms proposed by the planters, will overthrow their faith in the government, and then there will be — bloodshed.

XXIII.

LIFE AND LABOR IN THE SOUTH CAROLINA UP-COUNTRY.

BLACKVILLE, October 23, 1865.

THE trip from Charleston to Augusta is not one that can be recommended as agreeable to make. There are four routes by which you may travel, and no one in Charleston, so far as I could find, can tell which a traveller had better take. The air-line distance between the two points is about one hundred and ten miles. The routes are as follows: first, one hundred miles by sea, ninety miles by railroad, and forty-six miles by stage; second, one hundred and ten miles by railroad and forty-five miles by stage; third, ninety-four miles by railroad and fifty-one miles by stage; fourth, eighty-five miles by railroad and fifty-six miles by stage. The expense of the trip is about the same on each route. I chose the last named.

Leaving Charleston early yesterday morning, I reached Branchville at eleven o'clock, — sixty-three miles by rail. From ·that point the stage runs twice a week to Johnson's Turn Out, — fifty-six miles. Twice a week — in promise; whenever it is n't broken down — in fact. I believe, to speak cautiously, that I may say it makes the trip — occasionally! My day did n't happen, however, to be its day; and when I saw the thing this evening, I was very thankful for that happening. Finding the stage-coach broken down, there was nothing to do but to prove the virtue of patience by waiting to see what would turn up.

Branchville is a flourishing town of about nine buildings, situated in a swamp. Its principal attractions are enormously large mosquitos, ravenously hungry bedbugs, and smashed-up railroad engines. The railroad eating-house, however, sets a table excelled by only one hotel in South Carolina; and the bed furnished the Connecticut captain and myself by the lady in charge was both clean and comfortable.

This morning we all got off for Johnson's, — the gentleman and lady from New York in a North Carolina ark drawn by a pair of mules of extreme poverty; the cotton-buyer and the colonel in an old army wagon that came down with cotton; the captain and myself in a rickety carryall that could scarcely carry itself; and the other three in a tolerably comfortable family carriage. We are to pay fifteen dollars each, — the captain and I. Our team is a span of horses, both poor, and one very aged. Our driver, the owner of the establishment, is a refugee from the sea-islands, of one of the great South Carolina families, whose different branches have so long intermarried that the present generation is neither shrewd nor intelligent. By twelve hours' continuous driving, over roads moderately good, we made thirty-two miles! and at half past eight this evening we were put out at a small house in the suburbs of Blackville.

All day long we have travelled in the track of Sherman's army; and we come to our quarters to-night with the most profound admiration for the genius displayed by his troops in destroying railroads. Literally, their work must be seen to be appreciated. To wind a bar of iron twice around a telegraph pole or a small tree seems to have been but mere pastime, and to fuse a dozen bars together at the centre by an immense fire of ties appears to have been thought a happy joke. Our road has neither led us near many houses nor many ruins of houses; but of fences there are none worth mentioning, except such as have been built during the season. Blackville is a poor little village of perhaps six hundred inhabitants.

This district — Barnwell — is the home of Aldrich, the mover in the late Convention of the famous fire-eating resolution. I guess he well represented his constituents; for

I am told that they voted almost unanimously for Wade Hampton for Governor, and will not vote for General Samuel McGowan, the principal candidate for Congress, who, by the way, has issued an address to the voters of the Congressional District, in which occurs the following paragraph, reaffirming the significant declarations he made in the Convention concerning the Democratic party and the question of negro suffrage : —

"After the delegations from the Southern States shall have been received into Congress, many delicate and important duties will devolve upon them, especially in reference to the freedmen of the South, and the control which Congress, or a party in Congress, may desire still to exercise over them. It may not be improper, in this connection, to say that, whilst I have approved the course of the State in seeking to restore her old relations with the government of the United States, it has been upon the faith and expectation that the State, as soon as reconstructed, is to have entire control of the whole subject of her domestic affairs. The State, and the State alone, must be left to decide to whom she will give the right of suffrage or other political rights. A new code *noir* must be enacted to protect and govern the population lately made free, — to prevent idleness, vagrancy, pauperism, and crime. I am not prophet enough to foresee whether we can succeed, but I solemnly believe it will be impossible to live in the country at all unless the State has exclusive control of the whole subject. I have hope that this will be permitted ; and I think it is in accordance with our interests and true policy to sustain the President and the Democratic party in their efforts to restore the States to their position of equality, and to give them equal rights in the government."

One finds in this South Carolina up-country a strong feeling of favor toward Jeff Davis. Among the men to whom I spoke on the subject at Columbia and other points, at least two thirds were very confident that his release was advisable as a peace-offering to the South.

I had some conversation with a Fairfield man in regard

to the matter, and what he said is substantially what a dozen other persons have said to me.

"Mr. Davis," he observed, "is a very pure man and a sincere Christian. He had little to do with bringing on the war, and your people can't afford to hang him."

"But is he not very unpopular with your own people?" I asked.

"Not with the people at large, sir. Some of our leaders don't like him, and just before the close of the war there was much denunciation of him in some of our newspapers. But I assure you they did n't reflect the sentiment of our people."

"I suppose you know," said I, "that we generally hold him deserving of death for treason."

"Yes, I reckon most of you would like to see him hang; but you would shock the whole civilized world if you hung him, sir."

"But suppose we judge that he must be hung to make treason odious, as the President says?"

"I think Andy Johnson never will hang him. He is a Southern man, and he loves the South better than he does the North."

In further conversation he said the President had been more lenient toward the South than any one could have hoped he would be.

The order against wearing the Confederate button is neither so generally obeyed nor so vigorously enforced up this way as in the low-country. I notice it not only on old garments, but on coats made within a month; and whereas it appears to be elsewhere worn usually because of the poverty of the people, men sport it here as the badge of allegiance to the South. In some towns where the order in respect to it has been carried into effect, the young men accomplish their purpose of spite by ostentatiously wearing coats on which there are no buttons.

10

At Branchville I fell in with a gentleman from Newberry, who urged that the government ought to enforce the Monroe doctrine. I asked him if he thought this country needed any more fighting just at present. He believed, he said, that a very large body of men, South as well as North, would like to lend a hand to help drive Maximillian out of Mexico. But surely you of South Carolina, I said, ought to be at work here at home. Well, yes, there was work to do, but a foreign war would do more than almost anything else to restore good feeling in this country. Do you really suppose, I queried, that many of the Confederate soldiers would join an army to cross the Rio Grande? Your General Sheridan, he replied, could get a thousand from our State in two weeks if he called for them. " I reckon not," said a man who had been an attentive listener, — " I reckon not; I 've been a soldier three years, and I know I 've had fight enuff to last me my life, and I don't know of any old comrade who wants to shoulder his gun for anybody agen."

While in Lexington District I called on a planter who was exceedingly anxious to learn what the government was going to do about paying for the slaves.

I told him I did n't know as anything was to be done.

" I 'low the gov'ment won't take away all our niggers fur nothin'."

I answered that I had no idea a single dollar would ever be given as compensation.

" But the Cons'tution makes niggers prop'ty, and gov'ment is bound to pay for 'em."

I explained to him at some length what had been from time to time done by the authorities in respect to slavery and the freedmen, and repeated the expression of my belief that no action would ever be had even looking to the payment of money as compensation for emancipation.

Well, Congress had paid for niggers in Washington, he knew, and he thought 't would be a d——n shame if it did n't

pay for 'em in South Carolina. If everybody was to be
plundered in that way, he did n't know as he cared to come
back into the Union.

  One of the men stopping to-night at the house where I
am also urged at some length this evening that government
ought to pay for the slaves, and would do no more than the
fair thing if it granted the South a hundred millions for
damages to other property.

  Another man was quite certain that the President would
not require the South to pay any part of the national debt.

  " What, ruin us, and then make us help pay the cost of
our own whipping? I reckon not! "

  " What will you do about it? "

  " O, well, I reckon we won't have to help pay that debt,
no how."

  There is an uneasiness of feeling among the negroes of the
South Carolina up-country which promises no good to them.
The military arm was slow in making itself felt in this section generally, and, per consequence, the negroes were held
in actual slavery much longer than in the low-country.   It
was impossible but that such a state of facts should produce
discontent and anxiety among them, and collisions between
the two races are of much more frequent occurrence than
in the lower part of the State.   Speaking in general terms,
the whites are not so well disposed toward practical recognition of the negro's freedom as are those of the other section,
nor are the negroes so generally disposed to remain quietly
on the plantations where they have been living.

  This district, Barnwell, has gained an unenviable notoriety
throughout the State for the cruelty with which its negro
population is treated. If half the stories are true that I
hear, the resident agent of the Freedmen's Bureau is not
only unfit for his place, but is deserving of court-martial.   I
learn of many outrages upon the negroes; and to knock one
of them down with a club, or tie one of them up and horse-

whip him, seems to be regarded as only a pleasant pastime.
One of the men employed about the stables here cut off a
negro boy's ear last week with one blow of a whip, and tells
of the act as though it were a good joke.   In the lower section of the district, as a planter tells me, there is a regular
patrol-and-pass system, such as prevailed in the days of
slavery.   There is, I judge, much lawlessness on the part
of the negroes.   How much of it is induced by their treatment I am unable to say.   I have the statement from several parties that the blacks have organized a band of about
one hundred persons, which goes up and down the district
for the purpose of robbery.   One gentleman assures me that
the band is led by a white man.

The district above this, Edgefield, has also an undesirable
name.   At Columbia I heard two delegates speaking of
affairs therein.   They admitted that "many negroes" had
been beaten to death during the summer, and said the planters were very slow in discovering what emancipation meant.
Among the negroes whom I met at Orangeburg was one from
Edgefield, who showed me a back not yet healed from a
severe whipping given him in August.

In Greenville District, which is the home of Governor
Perry, there is, I believe, from what I can learn, a band of
so-called "regulators," who, on a small scale, are assuming
to govern the negroes.

In Anderson District, which is the home of Governor
Orr, a case has just occurred, of which I learned the particulars from head-quarters at Charleston.   On the night of
the 8th instant, three soldiers of a Maine regiment, who were
guarding some government cotton which a treasury agent
was shipping down the river, were brutally murdered, —
shot from behind, as is the custom of the country.   There is
not the least complaint that they were in any way specially
obnoxious or had been guilty of any wrong deed.   They
were simply killed because they were Yankees.   Investiga-

tions already made lead to the conclusion that at least a
score of persons were engaged in the murder, only three or
four of whom have been arrested. A negro who was supposed to have communicated some information to the authorities in respect to the matter has also been murdered ; and
anonymous letters have been circulated in which it is distinctly announced that any one will be killed who aids in
bringing the murderers to punishment.

In Newberry District a case has recently occurred in
which the negroes took justice into their own hands. It
appears that in a car which was standing on the track were
three or four women and two Rebel soldiers, — one of them
a Texan. A negro sergeant had occasion to enter the car,
and was roughly ordered out by the Texan. He responded
to the effect that he knew his business and should mind it.
The two Rebel soldiers thereupon seized him and undertook
to thrust him out. He resisted, and the Texan stabbed him,
inflicting what was supposed to be a mortal wound. In an
hour the two Rebels were caught by the negro soldiers of
the regiment to which the sergeant belonged ; and in three
hours more the Texan had been tried by drum-head court-
martial, shot, and buried. The other Confederate escaped
while they were taking him up for trial, and will not be
retaken.

During the early part of the season the whole up-country
was filled with negroes, brought up last fall by their owners
to keep them out of the way of the Yankees. These are
drifting back to the coast districts at the rate of two to three
hundred per week. In not a few instances they report that
they have been turned from the plantations, — which report
is, in some cases, probably true.

I find very few negroes who seem willing to make contracts for the coming year. Many appear to have a notion
that they can live more easily and comfortably by job work.
A considerable number are anxious to become landholders,

by lease or by time purchases. Large numbers are "waitin' fur Janawry," hoping, as near as I can learn, that some change for the better will occur at that time. The great body of the freedmen have worked during this season for wholly inadequate wages, and seem, under the circumstances, to have worked with reasonable faithfulness.

XXIV.

SOCIAL CHARACTERISTICS OF THE SOUTH-CAROLINIANS.

AIKEN, October 24, 1865.

THE importance of soap and water as elements in civilization have been much ignored or overlooked. I am satisfied that if the people of this State, with all their belongings and surroundings, — except such as would be damaged by water, — could be thoroughly washed at least once a week, a year would show a very material advance toward civilization. I do not now speak of inward or mental foulness, though doubtless a weekly cleansing in this regard would be beneficial; but I am convinced that he would be a great public benefactor who could prevail upon the common people of South Carolina to make good use of soap and water. Thrift and tidiness are handmaids of cleanliness; and if it were possible to bring the latter into the homes of the poorer classes of this State, I make no doubt that the next generation would find here the material prosperity of Massachusetts.

I am too much a traveller — not in foreign lands, but in my own country — to be upset in my equanimity by even a wide departure from the average cleanliness of New England housewives, and I very readily make allowance for difference of custom; but, after all this, I cannot help remarking what general negligence and slovenliness there is in the houses of the poorer and so-called lower class of inhabitants, and how easily people accommodate themselves to conditions that could not exist a week in any Northern community.

Personal cleanliness is much more general than household cleanliness, whence I conclude that there is something radically rotten in the labor system of the State. It would seem that negroes are natural slovens, or that the relation of master and slave has ruined them in this regard. It would also seem that master and mistress have either not cared, or have been unable, to insist upon the right and proper thing in this respect.

Any thoughtful traveller will notice that the aggregate number of white men in the State of ages ranging from twenty-five to forty-five is comparatively small; and he cannot help remarking with pain and sorrow that the majority of them are idlers or semi-vagabonds. I don't forget that the whole labor system of the State is thoroughly demoralized and disorganized; and the sad thing is, not that so many men are out of regular business, but that so many are using no endeavor to get into business. I have talked with hundreds who have done nothing since the war closed, and don't intend doing anything before next spring at best.

"I saw a very painful thing the other day," said an intelligent gentleman to me at Columbia one evening; "it was the only son of one of our first families driving an express-wagon. His father was killed in the war, your government has taken the house and grounds, and he is actually supporting his mother and sister by driving a hack!"

"Is labor honorable?" I asked.

"Well, but you see we are not accustomed to manual labor: it has always been counted degrading, and it is really humiliating that Henry should drive a hack!"

"Better that than starvation?" I queried.

" O, well, of course ; but then his friends would gladly have helped him along till he could find something less degrading than hack-driving."

I judge, from various conversations I have had with young men, that no considerable number are likely, just at present, to pain their friends by engaging in any useful employment. Lads of sixteen to twenty are plenty enough at all loafing-places, and their talk is not at all encouraging to one hopeful of the future.

The negro, bad as his condition is, seems to me, on the whole, to accommodate himself more easily than the white to the change of situation. He does n't like plantation work, and moves, day by day, in a great wave of life, toward the sea-coast. He can't tell you why he is going toward Charleston. It is vagabondism with some ; it is a blind instinct for freedom and proximity to the Yankee with others. Just how all these negroes who have deserted the plantation manage to live no one can tell ; but live in some way, and without very much stealing, they do. Half a dollar will start a whole family in trade, and a negro woman in Columbia, to whom that amount had been given, was next day selling corn-cake and peaches on a corner near the post-office, where I found her on every succeeding day of my stay. I asked a middle-aged colored man who had a little stand under a large tree near the church in which the Convention met, how all the negroes who had quit the plantations managed to get along. " Dun know, sah, but 'pears like dey got 'long some-how."

I should say that the real question at issue in the South is, not " What shall be done with the negro ? " but " What shall be done with the white ? " It is both absurd and wicked to charge that the negroes, as a class, are not at work. Their vitality is at least thirty or forty per cent greater than that of the average whites. They can support their cheap lives with very little labor, and the niggardly short-sightedness of the planters prevents them from becoming landholders: why should they concern themselves to do much work? Of course the whites are forever complaining. They demand that all labor shall be, as heretofore, in the hands of the blacks; and all ease and profit, as heretofore, in the hands of themselves.

If the nation allows the whites to work out the problem of the future in their own way, the negro's condition in three years will be as bad as it was before the war. All that force and spirit and energy which made them such bitter enemies of the government is now turned into a channel for the overwhelming of the blacks. The viciousness that could not overturn the nation is now mainly engaged in the effort to retain the substance of slavery. What are names if the thing itself remains?

There is, of course, another side to this labor question. White men don't know how to work, and the organization of society has been such that in many cases this is their misfortune rather than their fault. Take the useful occupations of mason, carpenter, blacksmith, by which so many men at the North find support, comfort, and even opulence, — more than half the blacksmiths, most of the brick-masons, and nearly all the hundred or more carpenters that I have seen were colored men. The few white men one meets who seem anxious to go into business really don't know what to do. The resources of tact, handicraft, and intelligence at the command of a Northern man are not at their command. They will get a wood contract, or will establish a line of hauling-wagons, or open a store. "Going into trade" seems a very common resort; and as a consequence, small shops are exceedingly numerous, and are daily increasing.

Really, the promise of the morrow is not wholly encouraging. Existence has supported itself so long on the shoulder of the slave that it has few resources of its own; and numbers of men who would be at something by which the lease on

10 *   o

life and comfort could be held, sit idly by without either ability or energy.   Of course, one may answer that it is their
own failing, &c.; but, as I said before, the case is sometimes
one of misfortune rather than fault.   The whole organization
of society was unsound, and the whole burden of its disease
falls upon the men of this generation: the few have inherent energy enough to make for themselves a place in the
ranks of labor ; but the many wait, half listlessly and half
hopefully, for time to bring them victory over necessity.

The strictest economy in personal expenditure is everywhere a pressing necessity.   The people are very poor.
Three fourths of the property which they had at the beginning of the war is gone.   Their slovenly method of living is
neither pleasant to see nor agreeable to share, but it would
be worth hundreds of millions of dollars if the same degree
of economy could be made to prevail throughout the country.
Not that this meagre and narrow life is in itself a good thing,
but that the salvation of a people lies in days of forethought
and a considerate expenditure of the gains of business.

South Carolina is just now an excellent place of residence
for one who is forced to the wearing of old clothes.   Any
possible style of garment is in full fashion ; and a week's
travel in the interior will give anybody the sight of coats,
for instance, in styles enough to drive a tailor crazy.   Southern homespun is doubtless a serviceable cloth, but it is very
rarely a handsome one.   How garments made from it at a
Broadway house might look is an open question ; in garments made after the scant patterns of the back-country
there is neither comfort to the wearer nor satisfaction to the
beholder.   Yet one cannot help rejoicing at seeing how proud
some of the people are of this same ill-looking homespun.   It
is in special cases the mark of Southern allegiance, but it is
at least the sign and token of native industry.   Possibly the
negroes spun and wove it, but mechanical skill in any class
is one of the elements of a prosperous future.

Education never was general in the State, and for the last two or three years it has been almost entirely neglected. The ignorance of the great body of the whites is a fact that will astonish any observer conversant with the middle classes of the North. Travel where you will, and that sure indication of modern civilization, the school-house, is not to be found. Outside half a dozen of the larger towns I have not seen a dozen in over six hundred miles of travel. A few persons express the hope that the Legislature will do something to set the College once more at work; but, generally speaking, the indifference of the masses to the whole subject of education is as startling as it is painful.

The negroes, on the other hand, though in a very ignorant manner, are much interested in the matter. They all seem anxious to learn to read, — many of them appearing to have a notion that thereby will come honor and happiness. Schools for their benefit have already been established at some of the principal points, and the intent of the Freedmen's Bureau is that there shall be at least one in each district before spring. The disposition of the whites toward the negro schools is not good, and in many localities the teachers would be subject to insult, and probably to outrage, but for the presence of the military.

The language of the common people of the State is a curious mixture of English and African. There is so little communication between the various sections that the speech of the northern part is in many particulars quite unlike that of the southern part. The language of the negroes is even more marked than that of the lower classes of the whites, and their isolation is such that each district of the State has a dialect of its own. To show how speech is corrupted, I may mention that I have met many negroes whose jargon was so utterly unintelligible that I could scarcely comprehend the ideas they tried to convey.

The negroes almost invariably drop the final *g* in words

of two or more syllables that end in *ing*, as *comin'* for *coming*, *meetin'* for *meeting*, &c. They also drop the final *d* in words of all syllables, as *an'* for *and*, *fin'* for *find*, *aroun'* for *around*, *behin'* for *behind*, &c. The final *t* is usually, but not always dropped, as *fas'* for *fast*, *mos'* for *most;* though by a change of vowel it is sometimes retained, as *fut* for *foot*, *fust* for *first*, &c. The *f* in *of* is, I believe, always dropped, as *o' corn* for *of corn*, and *o' my cabin* for *of my cabin.* For the letter thus dropped *b* is sometimes substituted, as *chil' ob Pete* for *child of Peter*, *ob life* for *of life*, &c.

Exceptions to this general rule in regard to final letters are ·numerous enough: thus *going* becomes *gwine*, *child* becomes *chile* or *cheel*, *set* becomes *sette*, &c.

The letters *w* and *v* are frequently interchanged: thus *very* becomes *werry*, and *well* becomes *vell*, &c. On the other hand, *ve* is often changed into *b*, as *forgib* for *forgive*, *lib* for *live*, &c. The letters *th* are never heard; their place in short words is filled by *d*, as *de* for *the*, *dis* for *this*, *dat* for *that*, &c.; while in longer words the *h* is lost and the *t* retained, as *tree* for *three*, *trow* for *throw*, *tings* for *things*, &c.

From dropping letters the way is short to dropping syllables, and *gentleman* becomes *gen'l'man*, *little* becomes *leel*, *government* becomes *gov'ment*, *plantation* becomes *plan'shun*, *tobacco* becomes *bacca*, &c.

From a change of syllables the way is short to a change of words, and *us* becomes *we*, *she* becomes *her*, and *he* becomes *him;* thus *all of us* is *all we*, *she runs* is *her runs*, *he has got a whip* is *him 's got vhip*, &c.

By a still more curious trick of words the pronoun *them* is used in the objective for any gender or number, but undergoes, among the low-country negroes especially, such a change itself as to be hardly recognizable. Tell me the meaning of the unique word *shum?* Yet it is in very common use among the negroes of this class, and is their corruption of the words *see them*.

The term applied by the negroes to their owners or employers is not, as generally printed, *massa* or *mass'r*. They use the long *a*, and the word is really, out of the cities, *mawssa*, and sometimes even *mawrssa*, though this last pronunciation is rarely heard.

The terms *cousin* and *brother* are in common use among the negroes, and seem to be expressive of equality. The older and more trusted blacks of a plantation never speak of a field hand as *cousin;* but the field-hands designate each other as Bro' Bob, Bro' John, Co'n Sally, Co' Pete, &c.

Of words whose pronunciation is without rule, so far as I can discover, take the following instances: *shut* is *shet, such* is *sich, drove* is *druv, catch* is *ketch, there* is *thar, car* is *kear, steady* is *studdy, another* is *nudder, hear* is *hare, sure* is *sho, both* is *boff,* &c., &c.

The particle *da* is curiously used; thus, for *John is coming,* we have *John da come;* for *he runs in the road,* we have *he da run,* &c. Is the word a corruption of *do,* and is it indicative of present action? I am unable to suggest any other explanation, and that this is the true one I am not at all certain.

The salutation *how do you do* is never anything more than *how-dy,* and with the lower class of negroes is simply *huddy.* The words *dun gone* are in very common use, as, "We 's jus' dun gone broke de co'n," "He 's dun gone to town," "Her 's done gone steal my gr'un'-nut," "All we gang o' nigger dun gone an' lef um," &c. The word *both* is not generally used, the phrase *all-two* taking its place.

The language of the lower classes of the whites is so much like that of the negroes that it is difficult to say where the English ends and the African begins. Very many of the strange words and phrases which I have mentioned as in use among the negroes I have also heard among the back-country whites. There are other instances, however, of a corruption of language in which the negroes have no part.

A South-Carolinian never *thinks* or *guesses*, but *'lows* or *reckons.* He *ha'n't got no use for a Yankee nohow,* and thinks him a *no-'count fellow,* or a *low-down triflin' cuss,* of whom he would like to *git shet;* and he will *feel obligated* to you if you will help him out of his *ill-fortunate* situation; and, *dog-gone-you,* as you are not an *ill-conditioned* man, and as he has *refugeed* from the Yankees, he will take a little whiskey with you *dry-so.*

XXV.

FIRST GLIMPSES OF GEORGIA.

MILLEDGEVILLE, October 26, 1865.

THE distance from Aiken to Augusta is twenty miles, and it is made by railroad in two hours and a half, at an expense of two dollars, on the narrow, pine-board, backless seats of a tolerably clean car.

Augusta is considered by many persons the handsomest city in the South, and I have often been told that I would find its general appearance much like that of a Northern city. It certainly is a pleasant place, and there are not many finer streets than the long, wide avenue on which most of its business is done; and yet in respect of beauty the city has no advantage over Raleigh, and cannot be compared with the Columbia that existed a year ago. That anybody should have fancied it had the appearance of a Northern city seems to me very remarkable. Everything about it, from the piazzaed cottages on its back streets to the great hotel in which it domiciles its guests, from the broad-doored cigar-shop on the corner to the dry-goods palace in its principal block, is distinctively Southern; and he certainly must have had a dull eye for local characteristics who could ever have found here any striking resemblance to either Portland or Worcester or Syracuse or Detroit or Columbus or Quincy or Dubuque.

The air-line distance from Augusta to Milledgeville is about eighty-five miles. There are three routes, and no one to tell the traveller which is the most expeditious, comfortable, or inexpensive. They are as follows: first, daily, three hundred miles by railroad; second, tri-weekly, one hundred and thirty miles by railroad and twenty miles by stage; third, semi-weekly, sixty-three miles by railroad and thirty-seven by stage. Being once here, I don't wonder everybody in Augusta is professedly so ignorant concerning the various routes ; for the truth is, come by which you will, you wish you had taken some other.

I chose the last-named of the three routes, and fifty miles of railroad travel brought me, at 10 A. M., to Camak, a lively railroad station of three private residences, a vacant store, and a deserted law-office.

In going up and down its busy streets I met a matronly and neatly dressed negro woman to whom I touched my hat, and an elderly and somewhat pompous white man of whom I asked my prospects for getting a dinner. He could guv me dinner up yon at his house, he said, when noon cum on. So I went there, and got a dinner of stewed beef, boiled sweet potatoes, hoe-cake, and buttermilk. Not being quite sure that I was an invited guest, I was a little embarrassed by the question of compensation. I found, however, on broaching the matter, that the old gentleman had no difficulty in charging me a dollar.

The gentlemen whom I met on the cars did not appear to believe that any honest jury in the country would, on trial, find Davis or Lee or any other Southern leader guilty of treason.

"Treason is a crime unknown to the genius of our institutions, sir," said one gentleman, in a lofty way; "and no act can be treason if it is sustained by any considerable body of the people."

"We were all for the war," responded a Convention delgate; " I was opposed to secession, but I could n't do any other way than follow the State; and what I did we all did, — we all did, sir, — we all were for the war; and if you try Mr. Davis you must try all of us, — all of us, sir."

"Mr. Davis was always a fourth-rate man," observed the judge; "and the government would give him more prominence than he deserves if it tried him for treason."

"He ought to be hung," answered the colonel, "but not for treason. He was the marplot of our revolution; his obstinacy ruined our cause, and he deserves hanging for that if for anything, though I 've no idea he will ever be harmed."

Several of us fell into a chat about the various generals of the two armies. Lee they all considered the greatest man of the age. Grant they did n't call much of a soldier; but one of them said he "told a d—d deal of truth" when he wrote that the South had recruited from the cradle and the grave. Sherman, one more observed, "is a child of hell; he could n't be a gentleman if he would, and I 'm d—d if I believe he would if he could." Slocum had always treated the South well, and they hoped he would carry the day in New York. Howard seemed a clever man and a good officer, but "is soft on the nigger." Kilpatrick is "a fine officer and a d—n mean soldier." Sheridan is "a lucky cuss." Of their own officers they said Jo Johnston was loved like a brother. Bragg is "an old ass who ought to be hung for blundering." Hardee is "only so-so." Beauregard knows something about forts and guns, but nothing about an army. Wheeler and his men were "the G—d d—est set of thieves and cutthroats out of jail."

At Camak three or four of us had some conversation about the freedmen. They will not work, I was told, and near

Augusta they have taken forcible possession of several plantations and will not allow any white persons thereon.   One delegate said a negro woman living ten miles above Augusta was nearly horsewhipped to death last week by her master; and another had heard that a negro man on a plantation some miles below the city was recently shot for claiming his freedom.

The gentlemen pretty generally agreed that Andrew Johnson had disappointed the South, being less harsh than it was expected he would be.   Two men thought he was figuring for the Southern vote in 1868, and one of them believed the South and the Democratic party could elect him then.

After five hours' waiting we took the cars for Maysville, and made our thirteen miles in an hour and a half, to find one small hack waiting to carry ten of us to Sparta, twelve miles distant.   We managed it, however, the five elderly gentlemen taking the inside.   They were all Convention delegates, — a railroad president and ex-State judge, a colonel and wealthy planter, a Methodist minister, a doctor, and a farmer.   We of the outside were, an ex-Rebel general, who sat with the driver; a negro boy, who sat behind on the baggage; and an ex-editor of one of the Augusta papers, an ex-Rebel quartermaster, and the Yankee correspondent, who sat atop.   Our driver was a wide-awake young fellow, who put us along at the rate of five miles an hour.   Our position on top the coach was pleasant enough, except that the roof was weak, and there was danger of breaking through; the road was in bad order, and there was a fair prospect that we should turn over; the evening was dark, and there was good chance that the numerous low-hanging boughs under which we passed might brush us off or hang us up like Absolom.   However, I made the trip with no worse accident than gaining a hole in my scalp and a bruise over my eye.

The editor and the quartermaster did most of the talking.

They gave an hour to the relation of personal incidents of service in the Rebel army. The quartermaster had barely escaped capture on two occasions. At one time he held a white handkerchief in his hand and was ready to surrender, but the soldiers whom he saw did n't see him. He remained in service till the end of the war, and was with Lee at the breaking up of the army of Virginia.

The editor said the war would have closed two years ago but for the women of the South, and the negroes could have closed it in six months at any time by laying down the shovel and the hoe.

The quartermaster expressed surprise that the negroes show so little gratitude to their old owners, and said that those for whom most had been done were now the most ungrateful.

The general remarked that the vote of the State in elect ing the Convention was light, — "everybody knew there was a certain disagreeable work to do."

It was about eight o'clock by the time we were unloaded at Sparta, and we left it at three o'clock this morning. The town itself may be very nice, but its hotel is very bad, and the landlord was very drunk last night, and the talk of the loungers in the office was very hostile to the government. The principal sober man about the house seemed to be Sam, a coal-black negro of twenty-five or thereabouts. He was lively and accommodating, and his orders secured us a passably good supper and a lunch before starting this morning.

A ride of twenty-five miles in an old ambulance in company with the colonel, the editor, and the negro boy, brought me into Milledgeville mid-forenoon of the sixth day from Charleston, at an aggregate expense of a good many bruises, a considerable lameness, a bad cold, a very sore throat, a moderate attack of chills and fever, and fifty-seven dollars in greenbacks. When I next make that trip I shall try some other route.

However, the view from the brow of the hill two miles northeast of town was a luxury to eyes and heart aweary of the dull, leaden, eternal monotony of Carolina pine-swamps and Carolina pine-barrens. It was almost a New England scene, — the Oconee River glimmering through green trees, woody hills, and rolling fallow lands on either side; forests and meadows alternating to the right and to the left; a gently rising hill beyond the river; the town embowered in its wealth of trees; windows glistening in the sunshine; a church lifting its spire serenely skyward; the white house corners showing among the trees; countrymen driving into town; cows feeding in the fields beyond; the darling New England charm of blue hills rising in the background; and, over all, the calmest and loveliest of October mornings!

Our driver was William, present freedman, former slave, who marched over our road twelve years ago in a negro-trader's chain-gang. "Dat ting come no mo'," said he, with some emphasis. Curiously enough, he found no trouble in making a living, and had no desire to be re-enslaved!

The two delegates concurred in the opinion that the government ought to pay the South at least one hundred million dollars indemnity money; and one of them expressed the belief that Congress would ultimately take this view of the case, and appropriate the money.

I asked some questions about the Georgia school system, and remarked that I hoped the time would soon come when school-houses would be as numerous in Georgia as in Massachusetts.

"Well, I hope it never will come," said one of them; "popular education 's all à d—d humbug, in my judgment."

"I think so too," answered the other. "I used to be in favor of it; but since I 've seen what it leads to in the North, I 'm opposed to it."

"That 's just it," concluded the first; "it 's well enough to give boys who are to be professional men a good education; but reading, writing, and arithmetic are full as much as ought to be taught the common people."

The capital of Georgia is simply the capital, and nothing more. It has no manufacturing establishments, and is the centre of no trade. Its only railroad connection is with the South; that is, a single track runs up here from Macon. Some time this line will probably be built through to a point on the Augusta and Atlanta Road, but even then the capital will be only a half-way station on a small cross-road.

The quiet and aristocratic little city is regularly laid out, with a deal more show, indeed, than is necessary; for all its business is done in one block, and most of its residences are on one street. It has three principal features, — the public square, the state-house, and the hotel. The square is large and rolling, and will unquestionably some time be handsome. In its centre is the state-house. At one corner is the ruin of the magazine. On one side is the ruin of the arsenal. On another side are the three churches of the place, — small, plain, cheap wooden buildings, occupied respectively by the Presbyterians, the Baptists, and the Methodists. The state-house is a solid and inelegant pile of brick, hidden beneath a dirty-brown stucco. It is at present very much out of repair, but could never have been either graceful or impressive. It would scarcely be an exaggeration to say that the city exists for the benefit of the keeper of the hotel, who has served his State in the army and in Fort Delaware, and is now anxious to serve it in the Legislature; who keeps a good house, unblushingly pockets twenty-eight dollars per week from each customer, and carries himself with the utmost nonchalance, knowing that, whether you will or no, you must be content with his terms or leave the city.

XXVI.

ORGANIZATION AND *PERSONNEL* OF THE GEORGIA STATE CONVENTION.

MILLEDGEVILLE, October 27, 1865.

THE State Convention met on Wednesday, the 25th instant, in the hall of the lower house of the General Assembly. Unlike the Conventions of either South Carolina or North Carolina, it was, as seemed to me most proper, called to order by the Provisional Governor.

After the list of the various counties of the State had been called, and the delegates had answered to their names, he said, " I am instructed to require of you to take the amnesty oath." There was no such oath-taking in either of the Carolina Conventions. On his making this announcement, the delegates came forward in companies of eight or ten, and the oath was administered by Provisional Judge Harris, of this city.

Herschel V. Johnson was then elected President of the Convention, — there being no other candidate, though twenty-seven delegates insisted upon voting for Judge Jenkins of Augusta. Mr. Johnson's speech on taking the chair was very brief, and its pith lies in this paragraph : —

" We are convened under extraordinary circumstances, and charged with grave and responsible trusts. The past, with its scenes of chastisement and of sorrow, the present, with its stern and tangible realities, admonish us to act with caution and wisdom. It is not for me to say what you ought or ought not to do. That is your province. Upon you rests the responsibility to a confiding constituency. I may be permitted, however, to suggest that the duty of the Convention is clearly indicated by surrounding circumstances. Let us do what those circumstances indicate. Let us do nothing more, lest, by attempting too much, we should engender schism and excitement, and hazard the usefulness of our deliberations. We cannot correct or cure the errors of the past ; but it is our duty, as far as possible, to rescue ourselves and our posterity from their consequences. Let us address ourselves to the task with the dignity of manly purpose, humbly relying upon the Father of light to illumine our understandings."

The Convention numbers exactly three hundred delegates, — of whom two hundred and seventy-seven have answered at roll-call, though two hundred and seventy-two is the aggregate of the highest vote yet cast. There are, apparently, many seedy politicians among them. The people have not so thoroughly broken away from their leaders as in the Carolinas. There are also not a few exceedingly rough backwoods fellows who never saw Milledgeville before, and probably never will see it again, and don't know how to live while here now. On the whole, the body does not give one a particularly favorable impression of the intelligence of the people of the State. It is so large, however, that all this may be true, and yet leave room for the fact that there are many able and intelligent men in it, — though they are not, generally speaking, the ones who do most of the talking.

The journal of the secret proceedings of the Secession Convention which met January 16, 1861, shows that the vote on the test resolution, declaring it the right and duty of the State to secede, was 166 to 130. The vote on the passage of the ordinance of secession was 208 to 89. It will be seen that in the three days intervening between these two votes, forty delegates who originally voted against the right and duty of secession gave way under the tremendous pressure of the time. Three days later in the session the engrossed ordinance was brought in and signed, in presence of the Governor, the commissioners from various States, the judges of the Supreme Court, and a packed gallery of the beauty and wealth of the city. A large number of the eighty-nine gave way under this pressure, but some still remained firm. On the following day six more gave way, though they entered a formal protest on the journal. Efforts then began to dragoon the refractory members into submission. Propositions were made to formally send a list of the delegates who refused to sign the ordinance to the governors of the several Southern States; to distribute photographic copies of the ordinance, with its signatures and blank spaces; to distribute twenty-five thousand copies of a list of the names of the stubborn delegates, etc. So far as appears of record, none of these propositions were actually put to a vote, but they produced their effect; and, day by day, the oppositionists were brought around and gave the document their signatures, so that finally it bore the names of all but about twenty. The position of this little band of the faithful was anything but pleasant. Even those who simply voted against the test resolution of the first day were snubbed on all sides. These others suffered all kinds of indirect, and some kinds of direct, insult; some of them kept a quasi connection with the Convention, but the leaders retired from the city and took no notice of its action.

Twenty-one of the delegates in the Secession Convention are here now, namely: D. R. Adams, of Putnam County; E. B. Arnold, of Henry; D. A. Cochran, of Terrell; R. J. Cochran, of Wilkinson; N. M. Crawford, of Greene; J. M. Giles, of Houston; A. H. Kenan, of Baldwin; Herschel V. Johnson and George Stapleton, of Jefferson; H. D. McDaniel, of Walton; Rowan Pafford, of Coffee; P. Reynolds, of Newton; Thomas P. Saffold, of Morgan; J. P. Simmons and R. D. Winn, of Gwinnette; D. Taliaferro, of Whitefield; N. Tucker, of Laurens; H. D. Williams, of Harris; William Willingham, of Oglethorpe; David Whelchel, of Hall; and Jacob Young, of Irwin.

Of these delegates, Mr. Giles was an original Secessionist, but the other twenty voted against the resolution declaratory of the right to secede. Of this twenty there were fifteen who voted against the passage of the ordinance of secession;

Messrs. Giles, Crawford, McDaniel, Saffold, and Williams voted for it; and Mr. Adams did not vote at all.

Honorable Joshua Hill, delegate from Morgan County, was in the Federal Congress at the time of the secession of Georgia. Honorable A. H. Kenan, of Baldwin, was a member of the first Rebel Congress, as well as of the Provisional Congress. Honorable Hines Holt, of Muscogee, was also in the first Rebel Congress. Honorable James L. Seward, of Thomas, was also formerly a member of the Federal Congress.

The inside of the state-house corresponds to its outside. The halls are low, narrow, and dark, with common plank floors. The stairways are of wood, and very narrow and cramped. The basement is a collection of old store-rooms, filled with all sorts of rubbish. In the second story are the library and the executive offices. In the third story are the legislative halls, — in the space between them being numerous apple, cigar, and peanut stands. The Representatives' Hall, in which the Convention meets, is large, square, and squat, the ceiling being about twenty feet. Opposite the speaker's desk is a little gallery, so far below the ceiling that a man of moderate height can nearly stand erect in it. Behind the speaker's chair is a full-length portrait of one of the early Governors of the State; on the right is a full-length of Franklin, and on the left a full-length of Lafayette, each remarkable for size rather than quality. The Senate Chamber is of somewhat more cheerful appearance than the other, and is ornamented with six immense full-length portraits of the job-work style, — Washington, Jefferson, Jackson, &c.

"I'll be d—d if I vote for any man who did n't go with the State," said one of the delegates while the canvass for officers was going on; in accordance with which spirit the secretary is a gentleman who was a colonel in the Rebel army, and the doorkeeper a gentleman who lost an arm in the service.

The Governor's message was sent in immediately after the election of officers had been concluded. It is a brief, practical, straightforward document. The Governor says nothing about secession or the war, and what he has to say about slavery and the freedmen is in this paragraph : —

" Slavery has been abolished in these States. Georgia, in Convention, is called upon to put on record an acknowledgment of the accomplished fact, to give assurance to mankind that involuntary servitude shall not hereafter, in any form, or by virtue of any device, exist within her borders; to enjoin on succeeding legislators that they shall guard by law the community from the evils of sudden emancipation; shall secure those emerging from bondage in the enjoyment of their legal rights; and shall protect the humble, the ignorant, and weak from wrong and aggression."

Provisional Governor James Johnson is a plain and unassuming gentleman of forty-five to fifty years of age, of medium size and height, who dresses throughout in black, has a regular and pleasantly inexpressive face, wears short chin and throat whiskers, and is slightly bald.

Herschel V. Johnson, late Governor and candidate for the Vice-Presidency, is a man who leaves his mark upon everything he touches. He is short, and of aldermanic build and proportions. He has a ponderous lower jaw, flabby cheeks, a large and sharp, though not a long nose, a cold, steely eye, and a high, retreating forehead, broad at the base and narrow above. The noticeable peculiarity in the shape of his head is that it is very large on a line drawn through the eyes and ears, and recedes on all sides toward the crown. His face is cleanly shaven, he wears gold-bowed spectacles, and he has long black hair. He looks like a man of great abilities, strong force, and immense vitality. His manners are courteous, but in no respect genial or winning. He seems reserved, and appears to have very few warm, personal friends, though everybody professes respect for him as a lawyer and a statesman.

11   P

Honorable Charles J. Jenkins is the leader of the Convention. He would have been made its President had he allowed his friends to have their way. The whole business is in the hands of one committee of sixteen, of which he is the head. He has been one of the members of the Supreme Court of the State, is everywhere respected and venerated, and is mentioned in connection with the Governorship and the United States Senate. He is a lame man, who must be considerably over sixty years of age, yet who has still great force and vigor. In figure he is under medium height, and of square and compact build. He has a full, strongly lined, fatherly face, and snow-white hair and whiskers. He ran for the Convention of 1860 – 61 as a Union man and was defeated, but was sent to this without a show of opposition. His home is in Augusta.

Honorable Joshua Hill is only second in influence to Judge Jenkins. He was a member of Congress in 1860 – 61, and his course in the stormy days of that session is matter of honorable record. "Had there been three other men as brave as Josh Hill we could have saved the State from secession," said a very intelligent gentleman to me yesterday. Mr. Hill is a fine type of physical manhood, over six feet in height, with deep chest, broad shoulders, erect figure, and a bearing that commands respect everywhere. He has a large mouth, large nose, high cheek-bones, forehead very prominent in the eyebrows, — in a word, his face is as rugged a one as could be found in a long day's travel. His intellectual ability is considerable; but his distinguishing characteristic, his friends say, is "plain horse sense." He lives at Madison, the county seat of Morgan County, and is a man of about fifty years of age.

The leader of the lobby, and therefore entitled to mention with the members of the Convention, is ex-Governor Joseph E. Brown. He has three points that the most unobservant observer catches at the first glance, — a large mouth, a long neck, and a narrow and hollow chest. Besides this, he is tall and very slim, has a pleasant face, a courteous smile for everybody, a large and strong nose, dark gray eyes, and a good forehead. His hair is just beginning to turn; he wears it rather long, and its end is rolled under in his neck. He is clean shaven, except his throat, on which he wears a short gray whisker. His manner is easy, and his talk is plausible and apparently sincere. He declares himself a firm supporter of the President's reconstruction policy, and has more personal popularity than any other man in Georgia. Everybody seems to concur in the assertion that he managed her finances better than any other Governor they ever had. He still occupies the Executive Mansion, Governor Johnson simply having rooms there.

The Convention attracts more public notice than did those at Columbia and Raleigh, — the lobby representation in the war-debt interest being larger than in either of the Carolina Conventions, and the excitement of the debates furnishing a grateful relief to the monotony of the city's dull life. The daily attendance thus far averages about one hundred and fifty persons, one fourth of them, perhaps, being ladies.

XXVII.

SECESSION AND SLAVERY.

MILLEDGEVILLE, October 28, 1865.

THE question of undoing the work of the Secession Convention, which occupied two wrathful days at Raleigh, here scarcely occupied two minutes. The committee of sixteen was named at the opening of the second day's session, and before night Judge Jenkins reported the following ordinance: —

"*We, the people of the State of Georgia, in Convention at our seat of Government, do declare and ordain,* That an ordinance adopted by the same people, in Convention, on the nineteenth day of January, A. D. eighteen hundred and sixty-one, entitled ' An ordinance to dissolve the union between the State of Georgia and other States united with her under a compact of government entitled the Constitution of the United States of America '; also an ordinance, adopted by the same on the sixteenth day of March, in the year last aforesaid, entitled ' An ordinance to adopt and ratify the Constitution of the Confederate States of America '; and also all ordinances and resolutions of the same, adopted between the sixteenth day of January and the twenty-fourth day of March, in the year aforesaid, subversive of, or antagonistic to, the civil and military authority of the government of the United States of America, under the Constitution thereof, be, and the same are, hereby repealed."

As soon as it was read, the chairman of the committee asked its adoption, and it was at once unanimously passed by a *viva voce* vote without debate, and with as little apparent interest as though it had been a mere resolution of inquiry.

There was no approving concourse of dignitaries, no ratifying roar of cannon, no packed gallery of beauty and applause, no parchment ordinance for all men to sign, and — Heaven give pity — not even a poor " yea and nay " record on the journal !

Joshua Hill rose as soon as its passage was announced, and gave notice that he should move to reconsider, in order to substitute for the phrase " be, and the same are, hereby repealed," the words " are now, and always have been, null and void." The former is the language in Mississippi and South Carolina, the latter that of North Carolina, while that of Alabama is " be, and the same is, hereby declared to be null and void." Mr. Hill's motion to substitute the strong language of the old North State gave promise of an interesting debate, and the gallery was crowded next morning when he called up his motion. But he bowed down and took upon his neck the yoke of the Secessionists for the sake of "harmony," and everybody went away disappointed, and to disappointment a few added disgust.

Mr. Hill said: "I gave notice on yesterday, that I would this morning move the reconsideration of the ordinance repealing the ordinance of the 19th of January, 1861, and subsequent ordinances and resolutions. I made this motion in no captious spirit, and with no desire to make a procrustean bed for any man to be laid upon. It was made with no purpose of producing schism between those who approved the secession ordinance and those who condemned it. My object was to give expression to my individual sentiment upon the subject. It is my habit to take little account of considerations of policy, and this is a habit which I think I shall adhere to; but on this occasion, at the solicitation of many friends who four years ago agreed cordially with me in opinion upon the subject of secession, and for a variety of reasons, the best of which is the harmony of this body, and the danger of distracting its counsels, I have been induced to reconsider my motion. The appeals of my friends, and the inducements they suggest, do not fall unheeded upon me. I declare upon this floor, that even after the sorrows and disasters which have come upon this land, I have no personal bitterness towards any man in heaven or on earth who contributed to bring about the secession of this State. There are to-day higher, nobler considerations than the mere discussion of this subject which weigh upon my mind; and it is not my purpose, nor is it my feeling, to limit my associations with men politically by the test of catholicity in regard to opinions upon this subject. I would not wound the feelings of any man. I am frank to say that my association with men who have disagreed with me upon this subject, both in my own county and elsewhere, is and has been of the most cordial character. My labors in this body shall be bent to one single purpose, and that is the earliest admittance of Georgia into the Union, and the restoration of her ancient rights, so far as may be permitted. That is my earnest desire. I have no friends to reward or enemies to punish. I have not yet combined with any political organization. I do not say what I shall do in the future. I am unwilling to be the first to produce dissension in this body, and I therefore withdraw my motion to reconsider."

Once more the people must lift the requiem for the Lost Leader. Possibly Mr. Hill could not have carried his point, but he could at least have made a gallant fight for the sound doctrine. I recall what brave old Nat Boyden said in the Raleigh Convention, when the trimmers appealed to him to accept the repealing phrase for the sake of "harmony": "Gentlemen, *unanimity in a good deed is a thing for praise ; but in any other, it is a public misfortune, for severest censure.*" Georgia went out of the Union by a mere repeal, and she comes back by another mere repeal. Who shall sit in the high place and keep the tally of repeals? Is there any abandonment, in her action, of the old heresy of State sovereignty? Did the war settle nothing but the nation's physical supremacy? And there was not vigor enough in this former leader to even insist upon a simple vote to reconsider!

The question of the language to use in acknowledging the abolition of slavery, and declaring its prohibition forever, which occupied one long and exciting day at Columbia, here scarcely occupied one minute. In the new Bill of Rights, as it came from the committee of sixteen, is this clause : —

" 20. The government of the United States having, as a war measure, proclaimed all slaves held or owned in this State emancipated from slavery, and having carried that proclamation into full practical effect, there shall henceforth be within the State of Georgia neither slavery nor involuntary servitude, save as a punishment for crime after legal conviction thereof; provided, that this acquiescence in the action of the government of the United States is not intended to operate as a relinquishment, or waiver, or estoppel of such claim for compensation of loss sustained by reason of the emancipation of his slaves as any citizen of Georgia may hereafter make upon the justice and magnanimity of that government."

The clause was reached at exactly five o'clock this evening. The clerk read it in his high monotone, — holding the paper in one hand and a candle in the other, for the hall is low and dark; the President responded, as he had nineteen times before in the last half-hour, " If there be no objection, and the chair hears none, the clause will be considered as agreed to, and the clerk will read the next in order." There was no objection, and the clerk went on with his reading. So, without a word to warm the blood of friend or foe, the great Empire State of the South grudgingly took up the banner of liberty and fell into the ranks of progression.

XXVIII.

ASKING PARDON FOR JEFF DAVIS.

MILLEDGEVILLE, October 31, 1865.

EARLY in the morning of the second day's session of the Convention, Mr. E. C. Anderson, of Savannah, late colonel in the Rebel army, moved a resolution for the appointment of a committee to memorialize the President in behalf of Jeff Davis and others.

The Convention took fire at once, and a motion was made to lay the resolution on the table. This was lost by 95 to 148, and an hour's excited debate followed.

Mr. Anderson hoped gentlemen would consider the condition of Mr. Davis and the other persons whose names were mentioned in the resolution. He could see no reason why they were held in confinement, and he thought the great government of the United States should be magnanimous enough to set them at liberty.

Mr. Joshua Hill believed this question should not be forced upon the Convention. The body had not met to ask pardon for anybody, but to do what was necessary to restore Georgia to the Union. Moreover, the President understands his business and does not ask our advice. He well knows why we are here, and the voice of the Convention on this question will pass him as the idle wind.

Mr. Ira E. Dupree, of Twiggs County, indorsed the President as a wise and merciful man, who was doing all for the South that she could reasonably ask. He himself had once hated Mr. Johnson, but now he believed him the man for the times. He was glad, however, that the resolution had been introduced. He believed it was right and proper to pass it. In order that the South might love the old flag once more, it was necessary that no more blood be spilled. He hoped everybody would be pardoned, and was certain no one could blame the people for asking the pardon of their late ruler.

Mr. C. H. Hopkins, of Pierce County, who will run for Congress as an out-and-out Union man, thought the government should be allowed to take its own course in regard to Jeff Davis. Mr. Stephens had already been discharged; and that was right, for he did all he could to keep Georgia from seceding, and truthfully warned the people of the consequences of so doing. As for Davis, he would never ask for his pardon. We need have no fears but that all will be properly done. We have an Andrew Jackson at the head of the government, whom nothing can sway from his purposes. If he intends to release Davis, he will do it. If he means to have him tried, he will be tried. The firmness of the Executive was recently shown in his refusing to interfere to save even a woman from the punishment due her crimes.

If we arrest the trial of Davis now, supposing our petition could have that effect, what would the world say? Why, that we knew he was guilty of treason, and endeavored in this roundabout way to shield him from trial and punishment. We were deceived by pretended statesmen into the dreadful contest from which we have just emerged. They told us there would be no war, no blockade, no bloodshed; that twenty men could whip a hundred. Now let the leader of all these so-called statesmen be tried. I want him tried, so that we may see if it will be decided that a State has no right to secede. If I were him, I would demand a trial, and if found guilty of treason would meet my fate like a man.

Mr. J. D. Mathews, of Oglethorpe, the leader of the impracticables, an ex-colonel of the Rebel army, and a man of most harsh and forbidding manners, would vote heartily for the resolution. The question involved was not one of principle, but of asking pardon for unfortunate gentlemen now languishing in prison. Once they were our representative men on the battle-field and in the council-chamber, — representative of a government to which we were all pledged. That government is so deeply buried that even the second resurrection cannot reach it, and these men now stand only as the representatives of a cause for which we all battled, — a cause which we and they alike thought sacred. (Applause on the floor.) Why should we not ask this favor? We have been pardoned by the national Executive, and by our pardon we become free and sovereign citizens, clothed with all the rights and privileges pertaining to Americans. Among the most sacred of these rights is that of petition; and all we mean to do in passing and carrying out this resolution is to exercise that sacred right. I understand that the President of the United States is inclined to mercy; that his policy is one of leniency; and I believe that the presentation of the petition proposed by this resolution will rather strengthen his hands than weaken and embarrass him. These

11 *

men, as I have said, are no more representative men of the Confederacy, but they represent the cause for which we battled. We have been pardoned, and have resumed all our rights as citizens of the United States; and I declare that I will not be deterred from asking pardon for these unfortunate gentlemen now languishing in military prisons. (Hearty applause throughout the house.)   Mr. Davis is no more a traitor than the rest of us.   Nor need he nor any of us be ashamed of our records.   We have illustrated Southern manhood on a hundred battle-fields, and we have shown that we can honorably submit to the decrees of God.   Now let us come up as men, not as criminals for a favor, but as men for our rights, and ask the pardon of our late and beloved leaders.

Mr. Hill again explained that it did not seem proper to him that a Convention called as this was should meddle with this question.   The differences between the people of the State should be allayed, not excited, and no good could come of this discussion.

Mr. Solomon Cohen, of Savannah, and late postmaster there, strongly urged the passage of the resolution.   True sympathy for the unfortunate gentlemen named in it demanded that it should be passed.   He thought the President had done nobly, and he could not believe a respectful petition would embarrass him.   If this resolution is not passed, after what has been said here, it will go forth to the world that Georgia, which did so much to place Mr. Davis in his position, utterly abandons him in his hour of defeat and calamity.

This closed the debate.   A motion to indefinitely postpone the resolution received 56 votes; and it was then passed by a *viva-voce* vote.

The committee was appointed, — Mr. Anderson, chairman, — and this morning the following memorial was reported: —

"To his Excellency Andrew Johnson, *President of the United States:* —

"The delegates of the State of Georgia, in Convention assembled, do earnestly invoke the Executive clemency in behalf of Jefferson Davis, Alexander H. Stephens, and James A. Seddon of Virginia, A. G. McGrath of South Carolina, David Yulee of Florida, and H. W. Mercer of Georgia, now confined as prisoners, and all others similarly circumstanced.

"Your Excellency has been pleased to restore Mr. Stephens to his liberty. He returns to the grateful people of this State as a solemn pledge of the magnanimity which rules the public councils; and his great name and influence will be potent to revive the amity of the past, and fructify the wise and generous policy which your Excellency has inaugurated. Emboldened by this example, impelled by the purity of our motives, and stimulated by the prayers of a numerous people, we appeal for clemency in behalf of the distinguished persons we have named. Restore them to liberty and to the embraces of their families, translate them from captivity to the light of freedom and hope, and the gratitude of the prisoners will be mingled with the joyful acclamations which shall ascend to Heaven from the hearts of this people.

"Jefferson Davis was elected to his high position by our suffrages and in response to our wishes. We imposed upon him a responsibility which he did not seek. Originally opposed to the sectional policy to which public opinion, with irresistible power, finally drove him, he became the exponent of our principles and the leader of our cause. He simply responded to the united voice of his section. If he, then, is guilty, so are we; we were the principals, he was our agent. Let not the retribution of a mighty nation be visited upon his head, while we, who urged him to his destiny, are suffered to escape. The liberal clemency of the government has been extended over us; we breathe the air and experience the blessings of freedom; we therefore ask that the leader, who, in response to the democratic instincts of his nature, the principles of his party, and the solicitations of his section, became the head and front of our offending, shall not now be bruised for our iniquities or punished for our transgressions.

"Mr. Davis was not the leader of a feeble and temporary insurrection; he was the representative of great ideas and the exponent of principles which stirred and consolidated a numerous and intelligent people. This people was not his dupe. They pursued the cause they adopted of their own free will, and he did not draw them on, but followed after them. It is for these reasons that we invoke the Executive clemency in his behalf. His frame is feeble; his health is delicate; all broken by the storms of state, he languishes out in captivity a vicarious punishment for the acts of his people. Thousands of hearts are touched with his distress, thousands of prayers ascend to Heaven for his relief. We invoke in his behalf the generous exercise of the prerogative to pardon which the form and principles of the Constitution offer. as a beneficent instrument to a merciful Executive. We ask the continuance of that career of clemency which your Excellency has begun, and which alone, we earnestly believe, can secure the true unity and lasting greatness of this nation. Dispensing that mercy which is inculcated by the example of our great Master on high, your name will be transmitted to your countrymen as one of the benefactors of mankind. The Constitution of our country, renewed and fortified by your measures, will once more extend its protection over a contented and happy people, founded as it will be upon consent and affection, and ' resting like the great arch of the heavens equally upon all.' "

The memorial was adopted without debate or objection. It indicates that the people of Georgia are not likely to fail of their desires through any excess of modesty.

XXIX.

AMENDING THE STATE CONSTITUTION.

MILLEDGEVILLE, November 4, 1865.

THE Convention has finished the work of amending the Constitution. I shall note but briefly what that work has been.

The first article embodies the Bill of Rights, from which the following significant clause has been dropped: "A government which knowingly and persistently denies or withholds protection from the governed, when within its power, thereby releases them from the obligation of obedience." The clause heretofore reported prohibiting slavery is in this article.

The second article relates to the Legislature, and it occupied the attention of the Convention for two whole days.

A strong effort was made by several leading delegates to secure a reduction of one third in the number of senators and one half in the number of representatives. The general question of a reduction was agreed to, after considerable debate, by a small majority. The proposed change in the Senate was readily made; but a four hours' discussion showed that it was impossible to reconcile the different views in respect to the House, and the whole subject was finally tabled by a vote of 164 to 107. The number of legislators, therefore, remains as heretofore, — 44 senators and 169 representatives. The sessions of the Legislature are to be biennial, beginning on the first Thursday of November, and continuing forty days.

The basis of representation is "representative population." Propositions to change this to "white population," and to "aggregate population," were lost without a division of the house.

The clause respecting the powers and duties of the Legislature in regard to the freedmen is in section five of this article, and reads in this wise : —

" 5. It shall be the duty of the General Assembly at its next session, and thereafter as the public welfare may require, to provide by law for the government of free persons of color ; for the protection and security of their persons and property, — guarding them and the State against any evil that may arise from their sudden emancipation, and prescribing in what cases their testimony shall be admitted in the courts ; for the regulation of their transactions with citizens ; for the legalizing of their existing, and the contracting and solemnization of their future marital relations, and connected therewith their rights of testamentary capacity ; and for the regulation or prohibition of their immigration into this State from other States of the Union or elsewhere. And it shall further be the duty of the General Assembly to confer jurisdiction upon courts now existing, or to create county courts with jurisdiction, in criminal cases excepted from the exclusive jurisdiction of the Superior Court, and in civil cases whereto free persons of color may be parties."

It will be observed that herein is an implied discrimination against the freedmen, " prescribing in what cases their testimony shall be admitted in the courts." Just how much this may mean depends of course upon the Legislature ; but it is clear that the Convention is of opinion that the negro's right to give evidence should be restricted in some degree.

The third article defines the executive powers. A proposition to make the Governor's term of office four years led to a protracted debate, and was finally lost by a vote of 117 to 161. The term, therefore, remains two years as heretofore ; but a new clause provides that no man shall be eligible for more than two terms till after the expiration of four years from the end of his second term. A proposition to create the office of Lieutenant-Governor was defeated without a division.

The fourth, or judicial, article occupied the attention of

the Convention for two days. The judges of the Supreme Court, three in number, whose term of office is not less than six years, heretofore appointed by the Governor, are hereafter, by a vote of 208 to 62, to be elected by the General Assembly; while the judges of the Superior, or Criminal Courts, heretofore elected by the General Assembly, are hereafter, by a vote of 142 to 109, to be elected by the people on the first Wednesday in January of every fourth year. The election of the State's attorney and the solicitors has also been given to the people. Heretofore the Superior Court has not had jurisdiction in criminal cases relating to negroes, but the restriction is now removed.

The fifth article embodies several general provisions.

The clause instructing the General Assembly to provide, by an adequate endowment, for the early resumption of exercises at the State University led to a two hours' debate. Happily for the future of the State it was adopted, but by the close vote of 138 to 131.

The question, Shall the State offices be vacated? which produced several hours' talk at Raleigh, could here find but one supporter, who was allowed to speak an hour, after which his proposition declaring them vacant went to the table all but unanimously.

The qualifications of electors remain as heretofore, — free white male citizens, of the age of twenty-one years, two years resident in the State, and six months in the county where offering to vote. A proposition requiring that the people shall vote *viva voce* was defeated by about three to one.

One new section of this article expressly declares that the supreme law of the State shall be the Constitution of the United States and the laws and treaties made in pursuance thereof.

Another section ratifies so much of the legislation of the last four years as is not incompatible with the Constitution of the United States and the laws thereof; and still another ratifies the judgments, decrees, orders, and other proceedings of the courts of the State since the passage of the secession ordinance.

This article and the Constitution ends with the following new and suggestive clause, which was adopted without debate : —

" The marriage relation between white persons and persons of African descent is forever prohibited ; and the General Assembly shall enact laws for the punishment of officers who solemnize such marriages, or knowingly issue licenses therefor, and all such marriages shall be null and void."

XXX.

THE MINOR WORK OF THE CONVENTION.

MILLEDGEVILLE, November 6, 1865.

AN ordinance was passed which legalizes and makes valid the criminal code of the State adopted about four years ago.

An ordinance was passed which gives validity to all private contracts made during the war, and provides that they shall be settled with due regard to justice and equity.

An ordinance was passed, requesting the General Assembly, at its first session, to provide for the support and maintenance of the indigent widows and orphans of the deceased soldiers of the State.

A resolution was passed requesting the Provisional Governor, by proclamation or otherwise, to provide for the organization in each county of the State of one or more companies of volunteer militia.

An ordinance was passed, after much debate, suspending

the sale of property seized on execution till after the adjournment of the first session of the Legislature, or until the Legislature by law otherwise directs.

There is an excited state of feeling on the subject of Congressional representation, in which all classes of men in the Convention share. "We must have our representatives at Washington on the opening day," says Matthews of Oglethorpe; "and I believe the Administration will sustain us against the radicals and fanatics of the North in our effort to get into Congress." There was a good deal of remark to this effect; but another set of men found voice through a delegate named Kenan, who was in the first Rebel Congress. "I would not be in such haste," said he, "but would take time for due consideration; and when we have elected our best men, let them go there in a dignified manner, not to ask favors of any party, but to demand their rights." However, there was still another class which found voice in what was said by Mr. Wright, of Coweta: "We are living under a military despotism which can't be endured; let us get our rights first, and attend to our dignities afterward." Joshua Hill, who appears to be anxious to get a seat in the United States Senate, thought there was great need that the delegation should be present at the opening of the session, in order to help elect the speaker, — believing that "there never will be so good a time to get the test oath repealed as then, when everybody is anxious for office, and of course for votes."

The State has been redistricted for seven members of Congress, and the districts are as follows by counties: —

First District, — Chatham, Bryan, Liberty, McIntosh, Wayne, Glynn, Camden, Charlton, Ware, Pierce, Appling, Tatnall, Bullock, Effingham, Scriven, Emanuel, Montgomery, Telfair, Coffee, Clinch, Echols, Lowndes, Berrien, Irwin, Laurens, Johnson, Brooks, Colquitt, and Thomas.

Second District, — Decatur, Early, Miller, Baker, Mitchell,

Worth, Dooly, Wilcox, Pulaski, Houston, Macon, Marion, Chattahoochee, Sumter, Webster, Stewart, Quitman, Clay, Calhoun, Randolph, Terrell, and Dougherty.

Third District, — Muscogee, Schley, Taylor, Talbot, Harris, Troup, Merriwether, Heard, Coweta, Fayette, Clayton, Carroll, Campbell, Harralson, and Paulding.

Fourth District, — Upson, Pike, Spaulding, Henry, Newton, Butts, Monroe, Crawford, Bibb, Twiggs, Wilkinson, Baldwin, Jones, Jasper, and Putnam.

Fifth District, — Washington, Jefferson, Burke, Richmond, Glasscock, Hancock, Warren, Columbia, Lincoln, Wilkes, Talliaferro, Greene, Morgan, Oglethorpe, and Elbert.

Sixth District, — Milton, Gwinnett, Walton, Clarke, Jackson, Madison, Hart, Franklin, Bangs, Hall, Forsyth, Pickens, Dawson, Lumpkin, White, Habersham, Rabun, Towns, Union, Fannin, and Gilmer.

Seventh District, — DeKalb, Fulton, Cobb, Polk, Floyd, Bartow, Cherokee, Gordon, Chattooga, Walker, Whitfield, Murray, Catoosa, and Dade.

The Freedmen's Bureau was brought before the Convention by a message from the Provisional Governor, covering a letter from Brigadier-General Davis Tillson, State Commissioner, setting forth the necessity of having an agent of the bureau in each county, and stating that it was with the utmost difficulty that he had been able to get suitable officers for each section, even; and thereupon asking the Governor to authorize such of the county officers as the bureau might select, and as might be willing to serve, to act as its agents. This proposition the Governor indorsed as likely, if accepted and executed in good faith, to tend much toward removing martial law. The message and documents were sent to the committee of sixteen.

During the pendency of the matter before the committee, General Tillson met the delegates at the hall one evening, and explained to them the purposes and desires of the government and the bureau in respect to the freed people. He was kindly received, and listened to with great attention.

On the following day the committee made a report, accepting "the wise and liberal proposition" of General Tillson, and authorizing any civil officer, or any citizen of the State, to act, by his appointment and under his direction and instructions, as agent of the bureau "in adjusting difficulties between the white and colored population of the State, in maintaining the police of the country, and in other similar matters."

This goes one step beyond the General's request, but not beyond his desire, in that it authorizes him to constitute any citizen as his agent. Simple as is the whole proposition, — offering to the people a prospect that their own neighbors, instead of military officers, will, in many cases, be put in charge of the freedmen's interests, — their intense hatred of the bureau and the government led some men into opposition to this report.

Matthews, the inevitable, of Oglethorpe, thought he discovered terrible things in it. It was the entering wedge of nigger equality, — it legalized nigger testimony, — it savored of nigger suffrage, — it obliged a white man to stand beside a nigger in the witness-box, — it obliged every court in the State to admit nigger evidence, &c., &c., &c., — to all and several of which things he and his people were inflexibly opposed.

Several delegates endeavored to make him see the matter in its true light, but without avail; and the report was then adopted, with about twenty dissenting voices.

It should be borne in mind that these agents, whether county officers or mere civilians, will not be under the State laws, but under the instructions of the bureau, and their functions can at any time be suspended by the Assistant Commissioner. General Tillson is confident that he will be able to prove the practical wisdom of the proposed plan in a very short time.

XXXI.

HOW REPUDIATION WAS ACCOMPLISHED.

MILLEDGEVILLE, November 7, 1865.

THE leading question before the South Carolina Convention was that respecting the prohibition of slavery. The leading question before the North Carolina Convention was that respecting the legality of the ordinance of secession. The leading question before the Georgia Convention was that respecting the assumption of the war debt.

Knowing very well what had been required of the conventions of Alabama and North Carolina, and seeing what would probably be required of the Legislatures of South Carolina and Mississippi, in respect to the debt, the delegates here were, to use a homely but expressive word, very touchy on the subject. They would talk calmly enough with an outsider on other questions; but as soon as conversation turned to that many of them became excited, not to say violent, in their language.

When the Convention came together I doubt if there were over seventy delegates out of the two hundred and ninety present who opposed the assumption of that debt. I think there were also at least one hundred to one hundred and twenty-five who favored its assumption at the face value of the bonds and notes in which it exists. The balance of those who favored its assumption would have been content to reduce it to a specie basis on the value of gold at the time the various bonds, &c., were issued. In a word, there were at least three, and quite likely four would be a more correct figure, — at least three to one in favor of assuming that debt.

The Comptroller-General of the State, Honorable Peterson Thweatt, in his report of the 16th of October, took strong ground in favor of paying the debt, which he said "rested on the highest moral and legal considerations." A couple of paragraphs from that report will show his feeling and judgment on the question: —

"What have the political questions of the war to do with this matter? Whether the war was right or wrong, was it not at the call of the State and by the coercion of the Confederate government that tens of thousands of our men went to battle, perilling health, limb, and life in a cause which they believed to be just, and leaving behind them wives and children and mothers, dependent upon the maternal care of the State? How could the State refuse to make provision for those men and their families? And how can the State now drive away from the door of her treasury the public creditors who enabled her to discharge so sacred a duty? If the State did her duty to the suffering soldier in the field and his famishing little ones at home, it was because public-spirited men furnished the provisions, clothing, and money, and took in exchange the treasury notes or bonds of the State. These treasury notes and bonds *were issued* with the *unanimous* assent of the representatives of the whole State; there was *no division, no opposition, no objection* from *any quarter whatever to their issue*, to meet the appropriations made, and thereby the promise to pay them was the solemn pledge of the whole people of the State; and can these creditors now, without infinite dishonor to Georgia, be sent away loaded down with repudiated paper?

"Should Georgia's good name and credit and fame go down, however, and she be held as a 'REPUDIATOR,' — should the good old State that gave me birth be charged with the violation of her most solemn promises and pledges in matters of dollars and cents, — should she be charged with having *deliberately borrowed money* of her banks, of her citizens, of her widows and orphans, and of others, by issuing bonds and treasury notes with solemn promises to pay the same, and then, without any default on the part of those who gave her their money and credit, *deliberately refused to repay* the same, or any part thereof, and that she did this, too, because there was no power to *compel* her to *do justice*, — should the good old State that we have all ever been so proud of be charged with *thus treating* her own citizens, (including helpless

women and children,) or any one else who *trusted, alone,* to her
HONOR, and in consequence of the same, she shall never have the
credit and high character she once possessed, — I desire to 'put
it on record' that I had 'no part or lot' in thus placing her, but,
that, as an officer of the State, and a true and loyal citizen, I
contended, from the beginning to the end, for the INTEGRITY and
HONOR OF GEORGIA !"

The Provisional Governor, on the other hand, took strong
ground against paying the debt, as the following paragraph
from the message delivered to the Convention on its organization will show : —

"It is of no legal or moral obligation, because it was created to
aid in the prosecution of a war of rebellion against the United
States. The purpose sought to be accomplished was unconstitutional, and all who participated in any wise in the effort to sever
the country were violators of law, and can therefore set up no
claim, either legal or equitable, for money advanced or for services rendered. Furthermore, these contracts, from which a liabil-
ity is said to result, were made with Georgia in revolt, — with
Georgia as a member of the Confederate States government. The
government to which she then belonged has been overthrown, and
with its overthrow all Confederate debts became extinct. Georgia, as a component part of it, no longer exists, and her debts then
incurred have in like manner been extinguished. She is now no
longer in revolt. She is one of the States of the Federal Union ;
and in her return to reconciliation her allegiance to the government requires that the act of secession be cancelled, and all other
acts done and performed in aid of the Rebellion be declared void
and of no effect. The ultimate redemption of the currency, both
State and Confederate, was made dependent in fact and in terms
upon the result of the fatal struggle. No one expected payment
if finally defeated in our efforts to secure independence, and therefore no plighted faith is violated by a refusal on the part of Georgia to assume to pay an indebtedness dependent on the issue.
The currency and the cause flourished together while in life ; and
now that the cause has no longer a being, the currency that sustained it may well be interred in the same grave. Let the record of your action on this subject discourage, in the future, all

premature efforts to overthrow long and well-established governments. In a word, ordain solemnly and deliberately that no Legislature, now or hereafter, shall, directly or indirectly, in whole or in part, assume to pay, in any manner, these demands, unconstitutional in their creation, and many of them without even the countenance of equity to support them."

This report and this message were the standards round which the fight on the debt question raged. The amount of debt contracted during the war was a trifle over seventeen million dollars, of which some four millions were for the civil expenses of the State. Of the whole amount, about eight and a half millions were payable "six months after a treaty of peace shall have been ratified between the United States and the Confederate States." I propose to show in considerable detail the action and debate of the Convention on the great questions involved in the overthrow of this war debt.

On the third day of its session an ordinance was introduced declaring void so much of the State debt as was made in aid of the Rebellion against the United States.

Two motions were at once made, — to lay the ordinance on the table for future action, and to send it to the Business Committee of Sixteen.

Mr. J. R. Parrott, of Cass County, argued against laying on the table. The people are anxious for an expression in regard to the matter involved. It should go to the committee for a report, and then the whole question of the legality of that debt should be met and settled here and forever.

Two or three delegates thought the matter was already before the committee, by the reference thereto of the Governor's message.

General A. J. Hansell, of Marietta, concurred in this opinion. For himself, he would say that he was opposed to repudiation. He thought this war debt was justly due, and should be paid on the basis of the gold value of the bonds when they were issued.

Honorable James L. Seward, of Thomasville, former member of Congress, held that the whole debt had no legal existence; and he was amazed that anybody could pretend that such part of it as was payable six months after a treaty of peace is made was valid. He did n't care what was done with the ordinance in question, but the subject involved in it could not be slurred over in any possible way.

The ordinance then, and without further debate, went to the committee by general consent.

On the fourth day Mr. J. L. Warren, of Pulaski County, moved a resolution for a committee of five to wait on the Provisional Governor and learn whether he has any information from the President to the effect that the repudiation of the State debt, created during the late civil war, is essential to a resumption of amicable relations with the United States.

This mere resolution of inquiry fell into the Convention like a bombshell, and a dozen delegates rushed into hasty speeches on the question. It was not a grapple with the main point, — the payment of the debt, — but a lively skirmish around it, which lasted about two hours and a half, and was exceedingly entertaining.

Mr. Warren was opposed to repudiation, and did n't want any Presidential telegrams sprung on the Convention at the last moment. If the Governor had information of the kind indicated in his resolution, he wanted it before the body at once. If the authorities at Washington require this thing of us, we must submit as we did to the emancipation of our slaves; but let us know beforehand what we are compelled to do, so that if we must repudiate the responsibility may rest upon the government of the United States, and not on the escutcheon of Georgia.

Mr. C. T. Goode, of Houston County, an ex-Rebel colonel, said he had no doubt as to the entire legality of the debt, and to any voluntary repudiation of it he was utterly opposed;

but Georgia is desolated, and all the elements of her enterprise are paralyzed. A military despotism is marching with iron tread over our Constitution and laws, and grinding out the rights of our citizens. This thing must cease or we shall die, — we must get rid of this despotism or Georgia cannot survive. We are at the mercy of the conqueror, and must submit to his dictates, however hard or unjust we may deem them.

Judge Simmons, of Gwinette County, the leading Unionist in the Convention of 1861, earnestly opposed the passage of the resolution. He would not even seem to admit that the debt could be repudiated. We have submitted to a disgrace deep enough and dark enough already. Our meeting here as we do under the proclamation of a military governor is humiliation enough to satisfy any reasonable man. Let us act in a dignified manner, — act for ourselves and not admit that we are utterly without rights. Secession was not my fault; every delegate here will bear me witness that I never favored it in any shape. But when the State went out of the Union we all went with her, — her people stood as one man for her defence; and now it would not be fair, would not be decent and honest, for us to turn around and repudiate the debt we all helped her to create. I never saw the day when I believed the South would be gainer in asserting her independence, and I believe we are better off now than we would have been had we gained it; but I would as soon steal as repudiate this debt. We have lost about everything but honor, — let us save that. Let us do our work here as becomes men who have consciences. The President stands as a wall between us and the radicalism of the North; and I am sure he would not ask us to repudiate this debt if he knew how anxious we all are to pay it, and keep the fair name of the State untarnished. If the Congress requires of us to repudiate precedent to the admission of our representatives, then we must do it. But let us wait and see if that

12

further disgrace is required of us. If we must drink still
deeper of the cup of infamy, let those who require it of us
take the responsibility of putting it to our lips. *Let us repudiate only at the express command of military power; and
then, when we are again in the enjoyment of our rights in the
Federal Union, and are once more a free and independent sovereignty, let us call another Convention and assume the whole
debt.*

Honorable A. H. Kenan, of this city, who was in the
Rebel Congress, was opposed to the resolution. If Georgia
paid her proportion of the taxes laid by the general government, he thought no one had a right to say what she should
do with her own debt. At all events, the Legislature, and not
the Convention, was the proper body to take action in regard
to the subject if any action was needed.

Mr. A. H. Chappel, of Columbus, one of the few real
Union men of the Convention, took exception to the idea
that there was any disgrace in the defeat of the South. We
made the war like men, we fought it like men, and when we
were conquered we surrendered like men. In all this there
is not to me, and should not be to any true Georgian, any
disgrace, any humiliation. I regard the President's telegram to Governor Holden simply as a hint, not as a dictation, but as a friendly warning. And I remark that he is but
carrying out the policy heretofore enunciated both by the
Federal Congress and President Lincoln, that no part of the
debt incurred in carrying on the war must be paid. After
having swallowed the camel, let us not strain at the gnat.
After having unanimously ratified the decree of emancipation, which buried all our fortunes, will it debase us to accept this smaller condition that the conqueror requires?

Ex-colonel J. D. Matthews, of Oglethorpe County, followed the hostile speech he made on the Jeff Davis pardon
question with another quite as objectionable on this. He
said he should vote against the resolution. He denied the

right either of the President or of Congress to interfere in
this matter. The President certainly cannot decide upon it.
We shall not be back in the Union till our representatives
are admitted to their seats, and if Congress requires us to
repudiate, it will be time then to act. Don't let us do more
than is required of us. True, we have no rights but such as
the conqueror chooses to give us; but I will not yield one
inch more than military force requires me to yield. The
Convention is the representative of what is left of the sovereignty of Georgia; let us do what in us lies to assert that
sovereignty. I shall never give my vote to add the damning disgrace of repudiation to the humiliation of subjugation. Let our members go to Congress and be refused before we even take it into consideration. I will never consent
to do so sooner. I will then entertain the proposition, and
not before. I think it is unbecoming in us to seek this information of the President. His private views upon it we
already know. His public policy he has boldly proclaimed;
and that is to let us manage our internal affairs in our own
way. It is only those who are bankrupt in argument upon
this matter, that seek to frighten us by citations of the President. I am free to admit that, in my judgment, Georgians
have not been disgraced by the results of the war. The
Southern men have made a history of gallant deed and doing
which commands the respect of mankind and of which our
most distant posterity will not be ashamed. But there is a
disgrace which can forever mar the beauty of character,
however high and noble it may previously have been. There
is a disgrace, which, like murder and the loss of virgin purity,
can never be effaced, can never be washed out. That disgrace is the infamy of dishonesty. Repudiation of honest
debts contracted by the constitutional authorities of the State,
bound upon our plighted faith for a valuable consideration,
is dishonest. I have no soft term to apply to the term of
repudiation. The war debt of Georgia was so contracted,

and I hold that the people of the State are bound by every principle of honor and justice, manhood and magnanimity to pay the debt. I fully realize our condition as a people. I would not embarrass, unnecessarily, the State in her effort to return to the Union; but where the honor of the State is involved, where the solemn faith of her people is pledged, where the principles of justice and equity are asserting their claims and demanding to be heard, I will never submit to the policy of disregarding our solemn duty, except under the compulsion of irresistible power. You may repudiate now, you may pass a solemn ordinance here that declares the war debt of Georgia to be unconstitutional and void, that it was contracted, if you please, for the purpose of carrying on a wicked and rebellious enterprise, and that at no time shall it ever be paid; and yet your children who may come after you, when you have passed from the stage of action, would have a perfect right to resume and pay the debt. For one, I declare, should you pass an ordinance of repudiation, and should Providence grant to me the term of a thousand years on earth, I would, as one of the last acts of my life, use all the influence and power I possessed to arouse my countrymen to a sense of justice and honor, and ask them to denounce your action, and to meet the claims of justice and right, by paying the debt.

General Hansell said repudiation would shock the moral sense of every right-thinking man and be an act of ineffable disgrace. He would vote against the resolution. True, we have swallowed the camel, but I am in no mood for a dessert, even if it be a gnat. I look upon this inquiry as a *quasi* request to impose further terms of humiliation. I mean to meet those already imposed in good faith and as becomes a man, but I beg gentlemen to ask for no more at present.

Mr. Joshua Hill said he thought there was a great deal of needless feeling existing. The resolution is a simple one of inquiry, which it is every way proper to pass. I must add, however, that whatever may or may not be the dishonor of repudiating this debt, it would be an everlasting stigma for any future convention to assume it if we set it aside.

Mr. Solomon Cohen, ex-postmaster of Savannah, and probable candidate for Congress from that district, found the whole question of State rights involved in this issue. He honored the President for his course in endeavoring to stay the waves of Northern fanaticism, and would uphold him all he could; but there is a limit beyond which I cannot go, and I never, no, never, can vote for repudiation, even at the conqueror's command. We know very well what the fanatical portion of the North require of us. They would not be satisfied with repudiation, unless joined with negro evidence, negro suffrage, negro equality, social and political. Do what we may, we cannot get over that test-oath which they have on their statute-book, and which no honorable man in Georgia can take. Charles Sumner and Thaddeus Stevens have already indicated what they require of us. We must meet them somewhere, and I propose to meet them right here. If this test is now made a prerequisite to our restoration, I for one will resign, and let my constituents, if they choose, send another man to fill the seat I now hold.

The debate here ended, and the obnoxious resolution went to the table by a vote of 162 to 113.

On the fifth day Joshua Hill moved a resolution, asking the Governor to communicate from time to time such facts in his possession as might be of public interest.

Nothing could be more proper than this, certainly; but one delegate made a furious assault upon it, on the ground that it was intended, under it, to bring in Presidential instructions on the repudiation question. No one denied this, but there was so little in the resolution itself, that the Convention could not refuse to pass it. In half an hour there came up from the Governor a brief message, enclosing and indorsing the following telegrams : —

"WASHINGTON, October 28, 1865.
"TO GOVERNOR JAMES JOHNSON : —

"Your several telegrams have been received. The President of the United States cannot recognize the people of any State as having resumed the relations of loyalty to the Union that admits as legal obligations contracted or debts created in their name to promote the war of the Rebellion.

"WM. H. SEWARD."

"WASHINGTON, October 29, 1865.
"TO JAMES JOHNSON, *Provisional Governor of Georgia :* —

"Your despatch has been received. The people of Georgia should not hesitate one single moment in repudiating every single dollar of debt created for the purpose of aiding the Rebellion against the government of the United States. It will not do to levy and collect taxes from a State and people that are loyal and in the Union to pay a debt that was created to aid in taking them out, thereby subverting the Constitution of the United States. I do not believe that the great mass of the people of the State of Georgia, when left uninfluenced, will ever submit to the payment of a debt which was the main cause of bringing on their past and present suffering, — the result of the Rebellion. Those who invested their capital in the creation of this debt must meet their fate and take it as one of the inevitable results of the Rebellion, though it may seem hard to them. It should at once be made known, at home and abroad, that no debt contracted for the purpose of dissolving the Union of the States can or will be paid by taxes levied on the people for such purposes.

"ANDREW JOHNSON."

To say that this produced consternation is to put the fact very mildly indeed. The fluttering in the gallery was quite as bad as on the floor of the Convention. "D—n the thing!" said a delegate who sat near me. There was nothing for it, however, but to send the message and accompanying documents to the committee of sixteen, and that was done.

An ordinance was immediately introduced by Mr. Chappell, of Muscogee. The first section declared the whole war debt null and void ; the second provided for the payment by subsequent Legislatures of "any particular debts incurred for other purposes than that of carrying on, aiding, or abetting the war, directly or indirectly"; the third provided that "all evidences of debt whatever issued by the State, payable only in Confederate currency," should be forever prohibited from being paid; the fourth made the ordinance a part of the Constitution. This followed the Governor's message and went to the Business Committee.

On the sixth day the question came up again on the introduction of a resolution appointing a commission of three to inquire and report to the General Assembly what proportion of the debt of the State was created for strictly war purposes. The temper of the Convention in favor of paying all the debt was sharply indicated by the general unanimity with which it refused to consider this proposition.

The Convention thought to make a strong point against somebody by calling on the Provisional Governor for copies of his telegrams to Washington. He sent them in before the resolution of inquiry could be engrossed. A hundred delegates affected to laugh contemptuously when they found he had said, "We need help to reject the war debt; what ought the Convention to do?" There did not, however, seem to be anything funny in the matter, except the nervous eagerness of the Convention to save the war debt.

Later in the day, Mr. W. F. Wright, of Coweta County, introduced an ordinance to divide the debt, with a view to reject all that part incurred directly in prosecuting the war, and to pay all of it that went to soldiers' families, civil officers, and for general civil expenses. It followed the other documents and was sent to Judge Jenkins's committee.

On the seventh day, Mr. Matthews, of Oglethorpe County, moved a resolution directing the committee of sixteen to inquire as to the propriety of selling the Atlantic and Great Western Railway, with the view of enabling the State to pay her debts. The house refused by a decisive vote to suspend the rules and consider this resolution.

This railway is the line from Atlanta to Chattanooga, is the exclusive property of the State, and yielded in the three or four years last preceding the war a yearly income of nearly a million of dollars.

Immediately on the refusal of the house to consider the Matthews resolution, Mr. Cohen, of Savannah, introduced an ordinance, understood to have been drawn by ex-Governor Brown, for the sale of the Great Western and Atlantic Railroad, and for the incorporation of the purchasers thereof. It valued the road at ten million two hundred thousand dollars, proposed to fix the shares at one hundred dollars each, and to receive in payment for such shares national currency at par, Georgia bonds issued before the war at ninety-five cents on the dollar, and the various issues constituting the so-called war debt at rates ranging from twenty to seventy-five cents on the dollar. The peculiar feature of the bill was, of course, the indirect proposition to pay the war debt.

Mr. Joshua Hill said the bill was very ingeniously drawn; but he thought its purpose was easily enough apparent, and he proposed to meet the issue it raised at once. He was alike opposed to the sale of the road and to the payment of the so-called war debt. He believed, moreover, that the Convention had nothing to do with the subjects thus presented, and he was sorry any one had seen fit to bring forward such a disturbing measure. He could truthfully say he had no part in bringing on the war, and he wanted no reference here to the questions involved in it. The President had said to him long ago that the State must ignore the war debt, and nothing could be made by attempting to avoid that conclusion. Gentlemen would do well to bear in mind that the Convention existed simply by the will of the President, and that the power which created it could very easily dissolve it.

Mr. J. R. Parrott, of Bartow County, a lawyer, a gentleman of thirty-five years or thereabouts, with the blackest of eyes and hair and beard, a man who has served in the Legislature, and was conscripted in the army, next got the floor. He alone, of all the speakers, put the question on its true basis. He was utterly and unalterably opposed to the assumption of this illegal and unconstitutional debt, and he would resist here and everywhere all efforts to tax the poor people of the State for the benefit of the Shylocks who hold it. He said no one proposed to pay Georgia's share of the Confederate States debt. No one proposed to pay for the lost slaves, for the burned houses, for the ruined fortunes of the thousands, — no one proposed anything but the payment of these bonds in the hands of men, fat and sleek, who never saw the forefront of battle, and were careful to keep out of harm's way in the hour of conflict. There was one debt the State should pay, — that to the orphans whose property it had, by legislative enactment, forced into State securities; but beyond that it never should, with his consent, pay a dollar of the debt created in the effort to debase the old flag. There are hundreds of men who were in the bullet department of the war, whilst others were in the speculating or stay-at-home department. The former had no chances at State six-per-cents, the latter class got them all. In many cases those in the bullet department had their houses burnt, their fencing all destroyed, their horses, cows, mules, hogs, and other property taken from them. In the name of all that is fair and honest, I ask, gentlemen, if it is right to tax this bullet department, — man's naked land and the industry of himself and his homeless family, for all time to come, — to put money into the pocket of him of the speculating department or to swell the wealth of the favorites of power? Let gentlemen vote for such injustice if they wish, and go home and meet the condemnation of an outraged people. Over three hundred millions invested in negroes, over one hundred and fifty millions of other property, and all our Confederate money, went down with the war; and now I say, let

12 *   R

our State debt created by the war, and for the war, and which was dependent on the war, go with all the balance. Let us have no favorites, no preferred debt, but let every man, so far as the war debt is concerned, whether State or Confederate, stand upon an equal footing. If you will propose any plan by which our people can become educated, the resources of our State developed, our fields cultivated, our barns filled with plenty, and happiness and prosperity bless the whole people, I will go for it heart and hand; but my conceptions of honesty and justice will not warrant me in throwing the burden of the war on the widowhood and orphanage of my State, in taxing the toiling thousands of my suffering countrymen to pay off a debt which I consider unconstitutional and void, and that should pass away with the unfortunate war just ended.

After a brief personal explanation by the mover of the ordinance, in which he avowed his purpose to secure the payment of the entire debt, the bill was tabled by a strong majority.

Here the war-debt question rested for four days. The telegrams from Washington were as leaven in the lump. The subject became one of still more grave importance. Committees sat upon it, caucuses deliberated upon it. It was the common theme of conversation everywhere. The morning was troubled with it; it disturbed the digestion of noon; and the pillow of night was disquieted by it. Slowly, but nevertheless very surely, men came to see the matter in a new light. They were not convinced of the illegality of the debt, and they insisted that their acquiescence in the results of the war ought not to be judged by their position in regard to this matter; but they began to admit that it would not do to disregard the admonitions of the President, — began to see that they could, under certain circumstances, vote for repudiation.

On the eleventh day the contest was renewed with great

vigor, and the battle raged for four hours in such confusion that one can hardly report everything that was done.

Judge Jenkins reported from the committee of sixteen that they had been unable to agree upon any report touching the war debt, and he asked that they be discharged from its further consideration. The discharge was granted.

Mr. Chappell at once called up his ordinance introduced on the fifth day, declaring the war debt null and void. Among the substitutes and amendments proposed were the following: —

By Mr. Uriah Dart, of Glynn County: To issue seven per cent bonds at ten, twenty, and thirty years, in payment of the whole debt according to the gold standard. Lost by a *viva voce* vote.

By Mr. J. R. Alexander, of Thomas County: "Whereas official information has been received that Georgia cannot be restored to her relations in the Union till she repudiates her war debt, therefore the said debt is hereby declared null and void." Lost by 111 to 135.

By Mr. G. R. Black, of Scriven County: Declaring the desire of the State to pay the debt, directing the General Assembly to provide for its payment in full, and providing that if Congress shall require repudiation precedent to readmission, then it shall be the duty of the Legislature to repudiate as of necessity. Lost by 86 to 182.

By Mr. N. J. Hammond, of Atlanta: That even if the people were compelled to ackowledge the illegality of the debt, it was an obligation of honor that ought to be discharged. Lost by a *viva voce* vote.

By Judge Simmons: "That it shall be the duty of the Legislature, at the next session thereof, to ascertain the specie value received by the State for each class of bonds, notes, &c., when negotiated or issued from the treasury during the late civil war, and to provide by law for the payment thereof, with such interest as may be found just and right on each class, at such specie value; which payment may be provided for by a sale of such portion of the State property as may be necessary for that purpose, by issuing new treasury notes, such as could be circulated as money among the people, for the redemption of those now outstanding, or State bonds, payable at such future time as that the profits of the State road and other public property would be sufficient to pay the same at maturity, or both, or by levying a tax payable in kind, upon such outstanding treasury notes, for their redemption in whole, or in part, or by such other means as that body may see fit to adopt, provided that no tax, except such tax in kind, payable in such outstanding treasury notes, shall be levied upon the people to pay said debt, or any part thereof; and provided further, that if the government of the United States shall require of the State of Georgia, as a condition precedent to her restoration to all her civil and political rights, as a constituent member of the Federal government, that she shall repudiate a part or the whole of her war debt, then, and in that event, said war debt, or such part thereof, and all bonds, notes, certificates, and other securities issued now and outstanding for the payment of the same, is and are hereby declared to be null and void to all intents and purposes whatever." This strange proposition for cheating the people, the President, and the nation, came from one who claims great consideration as a bold Unionist in 1860 – 61; but it was lost by a *viva voce* vote.

By Mr. Cohen: "That the consideration of the whole subject be postponed for the present, and be specially referred to the Legislature to be elected in October, 1867." Lost by a *viva voce* vote.

This finished the amendments and substitutes, and paved the way for debate, which came up on a motion to strike from Mr. Chappell's ordinance the fourth clause, making the whole a part of the Constitution.

Mr. Chappell wanted the ordinance made a part of the

Constitution. If this were not done, the members of the Legislature, sworn to support the Constitution but not the ordinance, would look upon the two in a very different light, and might easily be persuaded that they were under no legal or moral obligations to observe the latter. The only security we can have for their keeping inviolate a decree of this Convention is their oaths to that effect, and this we could not get unless the decree is incorporated into the Constitution. Put it in there and it will stand forever as an enduring reminder to posterity of the consequences of Rebellion.

Mr. Matthews made another bitter but eloquent speech against the whole ordinance, and against the proposition to incorporate it into the Constitution. He regarded the debt as a debt of honor, as a solemn pledge, which Georgia made to the people of the State; and if there is no honor in that transaction, there is no honor under Heaven. It cannot be repudiated without the violation of the most sacred pledges of Georgia. I do not wish to be represented here as charging the President of the United States with being a tyrant, but it is little less than tyranny to make this demand upon us. I will not crawl in the dust to lick the hand of power. We are not yet slaves; we are the same men we were four years ago; and I bid my associates stand as we stood when we flung the flag of Rebellion to the breeze, as we stood through the long and bloody years in which we upheld that flag! (Hearty applause.) I see no necessity for putting this thing into the Constitution, for an ordinance of this body is just as much a part of the fundamental law as that document itself. I ask gentlemen to be satisfied with a simple repudiation. Let the damning instrument which records our everlasting shame and disgrace be kept as inconspicuous as possible, let it go into darkness among the musty archives of the State, so that our children need not be called upon to blush at its sight, so that future generations must seek long to find it, and, haply, not discovering it, may cherish the hope that we were found to be not slaves, but men of honor, even in our hour of sorest distress!

Mr. Hammond thought the fears of the friends of the original ordinance were groundless. A debt once repudiated would never be assumed. Besides, he did not like this distrust of the Legislature. Georgians were not scoundrels, and their word was good as any man's oath. If the Legislature was disposed to disregard the action of the Convention they could do it, Constitution or no Constitution. Let the Convention do its work with proper respect for those who sent them here.

Mr. Hill rebuked the gentlemen who kept up the fight in favor of the war debt. He thought the course of the Secessionists who fled the country much more honorable than that of those who remained, got pardoned, and were continually renewing agitation. As for himself, he was not acting at the dictation of the President or any one else, but from his own sense of right and duty. He opposed the motion to strike out the last clause of the ordinance. He wanted it to stand in the Constitution as a landmark for all coming generations of Georgia's children, to warn them against the mischiefs, evils, and curses of secession. He would have all classes keep it continually before them, so that they may see if in the future any man is inclined to break faith upon the subject.

Mr. Seward had no doubt of the illegality of the war debt. If secession was null and void, all contracts under it were null and void also; and that it was null and void is the very thing decided by the war. If there is no right of secession, then secession is treason, and all obligations issued to sustain it, being likewise treasonable, are wrong in morals as well as in law. He could see no valid reason for declining to make the ordinance a part of the Constitution.

The previous question was then called by Mr. Seward, and the words, "This ordinance shall be a part of the Constitution and fundamental law of the State," were stricken out by a vote of 156 to 107.

On the twelfth day, that is, this morning, Mr. Chappell moved to reconsider the vote by which this clause was stricken out; but the motion was lost by 89 to 117.

And then, without further words, the great contest came to a close, and the ordinance as amended passed by a vote of 135 to 117. It is in the following words: —

"*Be it ordained by the people of Georgia, in Convention assembled*, That all the debts contracted or incurred by the State of Georgia, either as a separate State or as a member of the late partnership or confederacy of States styled the Confederate States of America, for the purpose of carrying on the late war of secession against the United States of America, or for the purpose of aiding, abetting, or promoting said war in any way, directly or indirectly, be, and the same are, hereby declared null and void; and the Legislature is hereby prohibited forever from, in any way, acknowledging or paying the same debts, or any part thereof, or from passing any law for that purpose, or to secure or provide for the said debts, or any part thereof, by any appropriation of money, property, stocks, funds, or assests of any kind to that object.

"*Be it further ordained*, That inasmuch as the annual income of the State, before and during said war, from taxation and other sources of revenue, was amply sufficient for the support of the ordinary civil government of the State, and for the payment of all its expenses incident to a state of peace, and as the extraordinary expenses which led to the creation of a debt were the offspring and results of the war, it is therefore the judgment, ordinance, and decree of this Convention, that all debts of the State incurred during said war shall be considered, held, and treated as debts incurred for carrying on the war; *Provided*, that nothing herein contained shall prevent any Legislature hereafter to assemble from making appropriations of money for the payment of any claim against the State originating after the 19th January, 1861, where it shall be made clearly to appear that such claim was founded upon a consideration disconnected with any purpose of aiding or assisting the prosecution of the late war against the United States, and not incidental to a state of war.

"*Be it further ordained*, That all bills, bonds, notes, or evidences of debt whatever, issued by the State, payable only in Confederate currency, or on a contingency or contingencies which have never happened, and can now never happen, have ceased to be debts at all, either in whole or part, and are hereby wholly prohibited from being paid, even though originally issued for other purposes than that of carrying on the said war, or aiding or establishing it, directly or indirectly."

This ordinance came originally from Honorable A. H. Chappell, of Columbus; but it was shorn of its strength by an amendment moved by Mr. Hill, viz., the proviso of the second section, in place of which Mr. Chappell had the words, "Except in cases where it shall be satisfactorily shown by impartial and disinterested proof that any particular debt or debts were incurred for other purposes than that of carrying on, aiding, or abetting the war, directly or indirectly." It will be noticed that the vague words of the proviso, "shall be made clearly to appear," can, in the hands of a Legislature of the proper stamp, be made to cover a very wide range of claims; and leading delegates tell me that they will be made to cover at least half the seventeen millions of the so-called war debt. This proviso was adopted by a large majority, without count.

It is noticeable that the men who voted against assuming the debt live in the mountainous and wire-grass regions of the State, where, indeed, the loyal men of 1860–61 were found. Yet it must not be forgotten that the ordinance finally passed could have received scarcely seventy-five votes on the opening day of the Convention. Among those who voted against it are Judge Jenkins, probable Governor, Messrs. Matthews, Cohen, Cabannis, and Cook, each of whom is likely to be elected to Congress, and Messrs. Arnold, Kenan, Reynolds, Simmons, and Stapleton of the Union men in the Secession Convention.

XXXII.

REVIEW OF THE PROCEEDINGS OF THE STATE CONVENTION.

MACON, November 8, 1865.

THE State Convention adjourned at noon to-day, subject to the call of its President, having held a session of thirteen days.

The delegates were enabled before leaving town to settle the gubernatorial question quite to their own satisfaction, and I presume to the general satisfaction of the people. Alexander H. Stephens appreciates his position, and declines to run for any office, thus leaving the field clear for Judge Charles J. Jenkins, of Augusta, whose election will take place on the 15th instant.

It would be a mockery to say that this was a Convention of loyal men. The flag was neither raised on the State-House where the Convention met nor on the hotel where nine tenths of the delegates boarded; and I know, of my own knowledge, that when an outsider remarked one morning to a knot of four delegates that it would look well to hoist the flag on the Capitol, he was answered, "No, I'll be d—d if anybody gets that up there."

It was found easy enough to invite ex-Rebel generals and ex-Rebel colonels and ex-Rebel politicians to seats on the floor of the Convention, but no motion was made to invite to such seats either Major-General Steadman, commanding the department, or Brevet Major-General Wilson, commanding the district, or Brigadier-General Tillson, State Commissioner of the Freedmen's Bureau, all of whom were obliged to find seats as best they could in the dirty and miserable little gallery. Furthermore, the report getting out that one delegate

of some Union propensities meant to move a resolution
giving these officers such courtesies, he was waited upon by
another delegate who said to him, "I give you fair warning, you can do as you please, but if you do move such a
resolution you 'll see a d—d pretty little row right away."

The course of Mr. Joshua Hill in declining to move a reconsideration of the secession ordinance, because such motion
would disturb the harmony of the body, typified the spirit of
the best men.   They were willing to do just as little as would
be needful to meet what they supposed are the requirements
of the government.   The other side only differed from these
in the fact that they were anxious to do just as little as would
be needful to restore the State to her relations with the
Union.

The excessively modest opinion of the Convention in respect to its labors is apparent from the following address,
adopted just before the adjournment : —

"To HIS EXCELLENCY ANDREW JOHNSON, *President of the
United States of America :* —

"The people of the State of Georgia, now in Convention, having repealed all ordinances and resolutions by them heretofore
adopted with a purpose to separate themselves from the United
States, and to enter into another confederacy; and having adopted
a Constitution strictly republican, wherein the supremacy of the
Constitution, the constitutional laws, and treaties of the United
States of America are distinctly affirmed; having therein recognized the emancipation by the United States government of persons previously held as slaves in this State, and ordained, in the
fundamental law, that neither slavery nor involuntary servitude
(save as a punishment for crime) shall hereafter exist in Georgia;
and having, as they conceive, done all things necessary and proper,
on their part, to the full and complete restoration of their State to
her rights and privileges as a State, and as a member of the American Union, respectfully request that all needful executive and
legislative measures be taken to effect such restoration as speedily
as possible.

" We, the delegates of the people, fully informed as to their purposes and desires, assure your Excellency that it is their fixed intention to perform their whole duty as citizens of the United States; that their desire is to live under the Constitution in peace and harmony with the whole people, and to see sectional strife banished forever from the national councils.

" We moreover express to you, Sir, their entire confidence in your just and kind intentions towards them, and their anticipations of your conciliatory and trustful consideration of their acts and doings in this Convention."

Newspapers came but infrequently to Georgia's out-of-the-way capital, and I have seen little indicative of the opinion held by the sound heart of the North of the Convention's work. For myself, with every disposition to charity of judgment, I must pronounce it very far from being good. Of the semi-rebellious, semi-defiant spirit manifested by individual delegates in private conversation I do not now speak, — the present concern being wholly with their acts and speeches as public men. Dealing therewith, I can only echo the words of Joshua Hill, the old Union leader, — words uttered after he had sacrificed his great opportunity and surrendered the lofty principle of nationality for the sake of harmonious action in respect to the secession ordinance. Having given up the vital point at issue in the whole war without the least struggle to save it, he was yet forced to declare: " Seeing what I see, and hearing what I hear, I am bound to conclude that the spirit of enmity to the United States government is not yet extinct."

The State-rights heresy was as dominant in this Convention, almost, as in that of 1861. True, there is a clause in the new Constitution that acknowledges the Constitution of the United States and all laws created in pursuance thereof as the supreme law of the State; but the natural belief and feeling of members crops out, nevertheless, in the before-given memorial to the President. " With a purpose to separate themselves from the United States and *to enter into another Confederacy*," is the noteworthy language of this document, by which it is virtually declared that the United States is not a nationality, not a government one and indivisible, but only a "confederacy" that may be broken up at any moment. Yet, in the face of this language, and in face of the fact that the secession ordinance is only repealed, and of the other grave fact, that no part of the Convention's work is submitted to the people for ratification, this address to the President brazenly claims that everything necessary and proper has been done to entitle the State to a full and complete restoration of her rights in the Union.

It seems to me, in view of the language of all classes of delegates, a very grave matter that the constitution and the ordinance repealing the act of secession are not submitted to the people. One of the best of the so-called Union men openly suggested, if he did not strongly advocate, the repudiation of the war debt by this Convention and its assumption by another convention, called as soon as the State resumes her privileges in Congress. Delegate Simmons representing the element which never acquiesced in the war, said: "Our meeting here by military proclamation as we do is a disgrace and humiliation." Delegate Goode, representing the element which opposed secession, but heartily engaged in the war on behalf of the State, said: "The office of Provisional Governor is a military office, and all his acts and appointments are of a military character; and with them we as a people have nothing to do except as we are compelled by military force." Delegate Kenan, representing the element which favored co-operation in the winter of 1860–61, yet was at heart urgent for secession, said: "We are living under a tyrannical military despotism; our hands are tied; we have no free will of our own; we must do whatever the conqueror bids us do." Delegate Matthews, representing the element which was hot for secession and is now very malignant, said: "It is an insult to the proud State of Georgia to call this a free Convention of her people, if we are to be governed in our course by the views of the President." The argument from all these utterances is plain enough, — if this was simply a military Convention, how long before we shall have a party here advocating a repudiation of its action in one or more particulars?

The action of the Convention on the slavery question was consonant with that on the secession question. It accepted the fact as accomplished by the arms of the nation, but put in a claim for compensation. We may be thankful for its broad affirmation that the Presidential proclamation was not the useless paper that some men would have us believe; but it is scarcely less than an insult to even indirectly assert an obligation on the part of the government to pay for the slaves it declared free.

The Convention directs the Legislature to provide for the government and protection of freedmen, but adds that " the General Assembly shall prescribe in what cases his testimony shall be admitted into the courts," and thereby impliedly says he shall yet be a slave in fact if not in name.

It is this indifference to manhood, — low, dwarfed, ignorant, pitifully poor manhood, if you will, but still manhood, — it is this indifference to the man in the negro that shocks my moral sense everywhere in the South, and nowhere more than here. There is a lower deep than the Levite reached in going by on the other side, for he only shunned the wounded man; and these Georgians reach it by ignoring the very existence of the wounded man.

I am told by a dozen delegates — am even told by no less than three Superior Court judges of the State — that there is nothing in the code of Georgia to prevent the admission of negro evidence in the courts. Indeed, one of these judges, who has much influence in the State, tells me that when slavery fell everything resting on it fell; and that the negro, by virtue of his status as a free person, has just the same legal rights that the white man has. The revolting and humiliating feature of the situation is, therefore, the cool indifference with which everybody ignores those rights.

In the matter of asking freedom for certain persons, the animus of the Convention was also apparent. There was slight opposition to memorializing in favor of Jeff Davis, but its character showed less love for the government than chagrin at the overthrow of the Rebellion. So, too, when the resolution asking pardon for ex-Commodore Tatnall came up, a unanimous vote for it was urged because he deserted a very high place in the navy of the United States in order to war upon the flag under which he had sailed for more than forty years ; and after this vote had been urged solely on this strange ground, only four or five delegates had manhood enough to vote against the resolution !

The war debt of the State was repudiated, yet here the usual doublefacedness of the Convention again appeared. In spite of the strong words of the first section of the ordinance, the final clause, which made it a part of the Constitution, was stricken out by a vote of 156 to 107, so as to leave the whole subject open for action at a future session of the Convention. Furthermore, there was inserted, by an almost unanimous vote, a proviso giving the Legislature power to pay any claim "where it shall be made clearly to appear that such claim is founded upon a consideration disconnected with any purpose of aiding or assisting the prosecution of the late war against the United States." Will a claim for four years' service as Governor be allowed under that proviso? Will the two millions necessary to pay the Legislature for four years' service be disallowed? If the war-debt bondholders can make it appear that their bonds were issued to pay for corn and bacon to be given to starving women and children whose husbands and fathers were fighting the government, will not a pliant Legislature appropriate the necessary money?

There were many earnest men in the Convention who sincerely mean, as the address to the President says, "to perform their whole duty as citizens of the United States"; but with three or four exceptions, they were lacking either in force or disposition to attempt to control the Convention toward good ends. Possibly the aggregate of the individual opinions and purposes of the several delegates is better than the aggregate of the action of the Convention, but of that neither the government nor the people of the North can judge. In all her relations to the Union, the State must be judged by the action and words of her delegates in Convention assembled. What is that judgment?

There is no hearty acquiescence in the result of the war. There is no love of the nation as a unit. There is a formal assent to certain terms of restoration, but the promise is kept to the ear only to be broken to the heart. These delegates sue for pardon for their late leaders, but they most praise the worst traitors of them all. They prohibit slavery, but they file their claim for compensation for the emancipated slaves. They instruct the General Assembly to provide for the protection of the freedman, but they say he shall have only partial rights in the courts. They declare the war debt null and void, but they devise a cunning proviso through which speculators may drive a chariot and four. They admit the supremacy of the Federal Constitution, but they reaffirm the legality of secession.

Have they a right to declare that their new Constitution is "strictly republican" in form? Have they a right to assert that they have "done all things needful and proper, on their part, to the full and complete restoration of their State to her rights and privileges as a member of the American Union"?

XXXIII.

A VISIT TO THE HOME OF JUDGE LYNCH.

ALBANY, November 10, 1865.

I HAVE reached the Southern point of my Southern trip. This town is in the southwestern corner of Georgia, about forty miles from the Alabama line, and about sixty miles above the Florida line.

Winter seems scarcely nearer now than when I left New York on the 1st of September. I write this afternoon in a room with northern exposure, without a fire, and with my two windows wide open. The landlord said to me this morning that he reckoned he would have to get a stove into the office of the hotel pretty soon if this cold snap continued. There has yet been but one frost here this fall, and that was so slight it did no damage. A dozen varieties of roses are in full bloom and fragrance in the gardens and dooryards of the town; wild-flowers blossom in the old fields and by the roadside; the grass still shows freshness and greenness; the leaves of the mulberry are beginning to fall, but those of the oak and china and willow have hardly lost any of their summer color.

Albany is the shire town of Dougherty County, and contains a population of twenty-five hundred persons. It is on the bank of the Flint River, and is the terminus of the Southwestern Railroad. A tri-weekly line of stage-coaches runs hence to Thomasville, ten miles above the Florida line, at which point connection is made with another line for Tallahassee and with the Atlantic and Gulf Railroad for Savannah. The town is reached from Milledgeville, one hundred and forty miles distant, by fourteen hours of railroad riding, in cars wretched beyond Northern conception, over a road

on which not more than an average of one train per day is
disabled by breakage or being thrown from the track. The
"accident" to the train on which I came down was trifling,
and only detained us an hour. I expect, however, to be
thrown from the track on my return. Albany has three
small churches, two small hotels, half a dozen very large
cotton warehouses, a good many groggeries, and one small
schoolhouse. Its private residences are neither large nor
pretty, and the general aspect of the town is dirty, slovenly,
and shiftless. It has a filthy river on the east, and lowland
piney woods on the south, west, and north.

During the war the town was a place of considerable importance. Its remote distance from any point held by our
forces or easily accessible to them rendered it a safe store-
house; and the Confederate quartermaster and commissary
departments had here, during the years 1863 and 1864, an
immense bakery and many millions of dollars worth of supplies of all kinds. "If any of Sherman's raiding parties could
have pushed through in the fall of 1863 or the spring of 1864,
and destroyed what we had here," said an ex-Rebel quartermaster to me, "it would have crippled us more than the loss
of half of Johnston's army." But none of our forces got
here during the war, and so the town suffered no damage,
and appears about as well, I understand, as it did four or five
years ago.

I was told by several persons in the upper country that I
would find Albany one of the worst places in the State both
in regard to morals and Unionism. It was a rabid secession
town in 1860–61, and sent many soldiers very early to the
war. Such of the returned soldiery as I have met seem,
as a general thing, quiet and well disposed; but many of the
towns-people who did not go into the field are exceedingly
bitter, and do not accept the new order of things in either a
wise or kindly spirit. "I have my pardon in my pocket, and
have taken the oath three times," said one of them in my

hearing last evening, "but I'll be d—d if I a'n't as big a
Rebel as I ever was!"   Whereunto another responded,
"That's jest my case, only I ha'n't got my pardon yet." I
judge that these two men are representatives of a considerable element in the population.

I reached the place at five o'clock last evening. Half an
hour later I sat on the steps of the hotel waiting supper.
There were five of us talking with each other as travelling
acquaintances will. While we sat there up came an ex-Rebel
colonel and a county judge. Both were tipsy. The colonel
singled me out, — perhaps because I was the youngest and
smallest of the party, — and asked me to drink with him. I
declined. He pressed his invitation, and the judge joined his
importunity. I declined again and again, telling them that I
never drank, and would not begin now. The colonel swore
I should drink with them, and threw his arms around me as
I sat in my chair. I rose and disengaged myself and stepped
into the hotel. He asked each of the other gentlemen to
drink, and each of them also declined. "I'll get my pistol,
somebody shall drink with me," he added with an oath, as he
started for his store five or six doors away. "He means you,"
said one of the gentlemen, as I resumed my seat. I answered
that I thought he would n't trouble me. Directly he came
out of the store with a revolver in his hand, exclaiming,
"Now show me the man who won't drink with me!"   The
landlord seemed to anticipate trouble, for he stepped out and
met the colonel, and persuaded him that some one on the
opposite side of the street was calling him.

That the judge and one of the leading merchants should
be on a drunken spree appeared a very good beginning, even
for Albany.   Another day was to show me that this was a
small matter, albeit it involved the possibility of being shot
at by a half-drunken colonel.

Last night there was a ball in the upper part of the town.
One of the boarders at the hotel courteously invited me to

accompany him to it. Anxious as I was to see the beauty
and grace of the town, I declined the invitation, pleading
extreme weariness, that I might not again give offence. This
morning we all learned that the dance broke up soon after
midnight in a drunken row. Pistol-shots were fired, but no
one was hit, though two or three persons were somewhat
beaten with clubs, and one man was wounded with a knife.

This morning, while walking on one of the back streets, I
was suddenly confronted by a man with bruises and blood
on his face, and a stout dagger in his hand. "Now I've got
ye!" he exclaimed, as we met at the corner. I dodged from
the encounter, and assured him he was mistaken in his man.
"Be you Pete Beeson?" he inquired. I told him I was not
Mr. Beeson, and had not the honor of Mr. Beeson's acquaintance. "Then give me your hand and take a drink." I shook
hands with him, declined the invitation to "try a little whiskey" which he pressed upon me, and left him making drunken
apologies to the fence.

I began to suspect that Albany would be an excellent location for a temperance society. Yet all this was but the
beginning of my experience.

About noon half a dozen of us sat on the hotel steps waiting dinner. I was talking with an ex-Rebel captain. Down
the sidewalk, some twenty-five yards from where we sat, we
suddenly became aware that a quarrel was progressing. It
was between a negro man and a young fellow with his left
arm in a sling. I noticed that the latter wore an army blouse,
and of course supposed him to be a soldier. He struck out
three or four times, but the negro was much the taller of the
two and kept out of his reach. Nothing coming of this, he
disengaged his arm from the sling and turned and seized a
long-handled shovel from half a dozen in front of a store.
The negro stepped into the store, the soldier striking a blow
at him as he went, and following him up. In an instant he
shuffled out, one of the clerks striking him about the head

and shoulders with a small stick. Thus far the matter had not become serious and no one interfered.

The old negro walked down past the hotel, but soon stopped to excitedly explain the affair to three or four men standing there. While he was doing so, the soldier rushed out of the store above with a large and ugly looking knife in his hand. Seeing this, the clerk of the hotel said to the negro, " Come, come, old Bill, if you don't want to get into trouble you 'd better get out of town at once." Old Bill did n't heed the warning, however. Thinking he might be moved by a stranger, and desiring to prevent a possible conflict between the soldiers and the negroes, I stepped to him, took him by the arm, and said, " There, John, that 'll do for this time ; now go home." He at once started, while I resumed my seat, and half a dozen fellows rushed across from the opposite side of the street, shouting, " Kill him ! " " Kill the d—n nigger ! " " Somebody shoot him ! " He soon turned the corner and was out of sight, the whole affair having occupied scarcely two minutes.

In a moment more one of the three or four men to whom the negro had volunteered his excited explanation stepped up in front of me and demanded why I had interfered in the business. I answered, " Simply to stop the quarrel."

" What business was the quarrel to you ? ".

" The same as to every good citizen."

" Well, by G—d, we don't 'low any outside interference yerabouts, — do you hear ? "

" O yes, I hear very well."

He passed along a few steps, and I supposed he had concluded his advice. Not so, however, for he returned with, " Did you interfere for the white man or the nigger ? "

" For neither. I simply interfered to stop a quarrel."

" Well, by G—d ! I 'm the responsible party in this business, and if you 've got anything to say you kin jest say it to me."

"I've nothing to say except to hope that if you are the responsible party, you'll do just what I was trying to do, — prevent any fighting."

"You interfered on the side of the nigger, and no one don't do that yere while I'm 'round, — do you hear?"

"Certainly, sir; but you make a mistake, — I interfered on nobody's side. I merely told the negro he had better go home; and I did that only to break up a quarrel and prevent a street fight; and that, I'm sure, any one, whether a citizen or a stranger, had a perfect right to do."

The fellow would not be satisfied, and I sat for full five minutes and heard one unbroken stream of half-drunken taunt and invective and billingsgate. When he said he could jest lay me down and stamp on me, I could n't help remarking that, as he was four inches the tallest, and weighed one hundred and eighty to my one hundred and thirty, he was probably correct in his judgment in regard to the matter. I thought he might strike me, but he did n't, and I kept my seat. Having assured me that I was no gentleman, and that if I had any pluck I would know how to resent an insult, he allowed a couple of companions to lead him away.

I have been thus minute in detailing this ridiculous affair because of the importance to which it grew in the course of a few hours.

Coming out from dinner half an hour later, the landlord told me that the negro had always been free; that the young fellow with the blue army blouse was no soldier, but one of their citizens; and that my assailant was an ex-major of the Confederate service. He added that he was a very fierce man when in liquor, and had recently horsewhipped a person. He further added that perhaps I had better keep out of the way this afternoon. I told him I did n't anticipate any trouble. I had hardly taken my seat among the gentlemen on the steps before one of the major's friends passed into the hotel. He soon sent the clerk to call me, and then warned me that the major was always armed, and that I had better keep out of sight unless I was prepared to defend myself. I thanked him for his service, and reiterated that I did n't believe there would be any difficulty. He had scarcely gone before I was waited upon by a citizen of the town, who, in courteous phrase, informed me that my interference on behalf of the negro as against a white man would not be readily overlooked by all persons. I replied to him that I had supposed the white man to be a soldier; and I presumed no one would undertake to say that I might not interfere between a soldier and a negro. "But," said I, "there was no interference in behalf of any one, my whole purpose being to save the town from a conflict between the soldiers on one side and the negroes on the other side." The explanation was entirely satisfactory to him, he said, and he would endeavor to put the matter in its proper light before the major and his friends, of whom I had better keep clear all the afternoon. I said I had been already warned. In less than ten minutes I was waited upon by citizen number two, who asked my name, residence, and business. I gave him my card, and told him my business was my own affair, with which I recognized no one's right to interfere. He also warned me to beware of the major, and added that he had just bought a horsewhip and was drinking pretty heavily. I assured him that I should go about my business as if nothing had happened. And so I did: that business being, first, to keep an appointment at head-quarters; second, to write the first part of this letter; and, third, to nurse my regular tri-weekly turn of chill and fever.

In going to head-quarters and returning therefrom I saw nothing of my friend the major with the pistol and knife and horsewhip. I met citizen number one, however, who told me I was doing a very foolhardy thing in being on the street unless I was prepared to give as well as take. He said the major would horsewhip me at sight, and finally advised me

to leave town forthwith. I answered that I came here expecting to remain till to-morrow morning, and had not yet
seen any reason for changing my original determination.

Writing quietly in my room, lying buried under a warmth-
less mountain of bedclothes while the ague shook me, sleeping a hot and disturbed sleep while the fever burned me, —
so the afternoon wore away.

I woke a few minutes before six, and found the clerk of
the hotel waiting. He came to advise me as a friend, he
said, not to leave my room. I asked him for a detailed account of the situation. The afternoon had been very lively,
and the evening was quite promising. My friend the major
had been joined by my friend the colonel and my friend the
judge and several other high-toned Southern gentlemen, all
of whom were somewhat in liquor and deeply incensed at
"the d—d Yankee" for "taking a nigger's part." Various
members of the gang had been to the hotel and done me the
honor of inquiring for my room, and had severally been told
that I was out. Now that supper time was near, they had
come in a body, and were anxious to have me show my
"d—d Yankee face."

It further appeared that the old negro had made complaint
at head-quarters of the man who drew a knife on him, — the
little fellow whose arm was in a sling and whose body was
in a blue blouse. The captain had sent out a corporal and
four men to arrest him, the negro going along to point him
out. In front of the hotel the military had fallen in with the
major's gang, and a conflict had ensued in which his new
horsewhip was worn up on the negro's head and shoulders.
The soldiers were powerless to protect the negro, and retired
without being able either to effect the arrest of the lame man
or the major. The gang now stood in an attitude of defiance, swearing that no one should be arrested by the "d—d
Yankees," and the post commandant had taken no measures
to assert his authority or to put down the disturbance.

I dismissed the clerk and took the matter into consideration. Clearly, it would be useless to appeal to the military, of whom there are but thirty stationed here. Should I borrow a revolver and use it if attacked?

While I debated the question with myself, — one voice saying "yes" and the other arguing that it would be foolish to get into a quarrel with a gang of drunken ruffians who ruled the town, — citizen number three presented himself. He also came to advise me as a friend. The crowd, he said, was very much excited. If I was seen on the street or in the hall of the hotel I might be shot at once; or I might be seized and carried out of town and "strung up"; or I would at least be assaulted and much bruised unless I shot two or three men at sight. Was n't this a pretty dish to set before a little Yankee whose only weapons were a pen and inkstand! I suggested to the good citizen that I thought he was exaggerating the danger very much.

Just then the landlord himself entered my room. He asked me if I was going down to supper. I responded that I wanted nothing but a cup of tea, and intended to go down for that. He begged to send it to me, saying that it would not be advisable to appear in the dining-room. I asked him if he expected to allow a gang of drunken brawlers to insult the guests of the house. He replied that he would close the doors against them, but that the excitement was so great he could not be responsible for the consequences. So I consented to take a cup of tea in my room, and my visitors and advisers retired.

It seemed to me that everybody had conspired to raise a bugaboo for my benefit, and I was inclined to treat the whole thing as a piece of pleasantry, though I could not but admit that it had frightened half a dozen gentlemen. I had not seen a man of the gang since the major left me before dinner, and I proposed to myself to go down the back way and come upon the street for a reconnoissance.

Just then, while I finished my tea, I heard an excited shout in front of the hotel; and, going into the hall to see what it meant, I met the clerk, who advised me to leave the house as soon as possible, offering, himself, to conduct me by the back way to a safe retreat.

Before I made answer the landlord again appeared. He had been a captain in the Confederate service, and is a very courteous and well-disposed man. He was apparently much embarrassed, but finally made me understand that he, too, thought it advisable for me, on his account as well as my own, to leave the house. He had already been set upon by the gang for declining to show them the way to my room, and expressed the belief that they would " go through the house" before ten o'clock, unless he could be able to prove to them that I had vacated the premises. He would bolt and block the doors if I insisted on remaining, and would defend his guests to the last; but he hoped I would not deem it necessary to insist upon meeting a gang of twelve or fifteen drunken men. He sincerely regretted that I had been disturbed, and said he had endeavored without avail to explain the affair in its true light. He would have me conducted to a quiet private house, and hoped to see me again on a more auspicious occasion.

Was it worth while to remain and insist upon my rights? I had not seen one of the gang of ruffians; but I had been told that a dozen or more leading men of the town were in it, backed, of course, by the usual crowd of idle fellows of the baser sort. Should I allow myself to be forced into a quarrel on an issue that I had not made? I finally concluded to retire from the field.

The clerk, a slight but wiry young man who had served three years as a private in the Rebel army, offered again to see me out of the difficulty. "I know nothing of you," he said, " except that you are the guest of the house, and appear to be a gentleman, and no one shall disturb you unless

13 *

over my dead body." I smiled at his fervor, and told him I had no idea that any one would trouble me, and I could n't think of taking his services as a guard. He insisted on going with me, however, and stepped into an adjoining room and borrowed a pistol.

It was now eight o'clock, and as we passed into the lower hall I could hear the noisy surging of the drunken crowd in front of the hotel. The landlord reconnoitred at the main door, and reported that it would not be safe to attempt to leave by that. So we filed out through the back yard and the back gate. Reaching the street, we marched in solid column, two abreast; the clerk on the right with pistol in hand, the Yankee on the left with overcoat and blanket, and the negro boy in the rear with my valise on his head.

Through how many back streets did we march? say, rather, through how many did we not march! I had no idea there were half as many in the whole town. I was possessed with a strong desire to sit down and have a hearty laugh; but when I asked my guard if I might shout, he said, "Hist, there 's some of 'em!" Sure enough, there were three tipsyish men blundering along in the darkness scarcely twenty yards away. "I heerd 'em say dey shoot de G—d d—n Yankee if dey gits de chance," said the negro boy in a low voice. I heard the clerk's pistol click, and he pushed me to the middle of the street. "I 'll stand by you," he said, and I have no doubt the hot blood jumped in his veins. He breathed more freely when we and they had passed, and vouchsafed the sole remark, "I know the ways here better than you do." After that we marched in solemn silence through the heavy sand, and finally halted at a large white house just in the edge of the town.

Here he left me, with the simple explanation that the hotel had no accommodations, and wished me to have a bed till morning. The old lady had evidently received lodgers from there before, for she said it was all right, and at once sent me up to this pleasant room in which I write.

AMERICUS, November 11.

I ran the blockade this morning, and am now thirty-seven miles from Albany and my friends of knives and pistols and horsewhips.

It appeared to me that if I was in such danger as my advisers represented, I might be waited upon at the depot about the time of leaving the city. Having already fallen back once, it did not seem advisable to get into further trouble at the last moment. Wherefore, I concluded to take the advice of the hotel-clerk and give my friends the slip, by taking the freight train at half-past five instead of the mail train at half-past seven.

While I walked on the platform of the depot in the breaking morning, laughing at the ridiculous position in which I found myself, one of the train hands spoke to one of the station hands: "Jest be 'round when the mail goes out, an' I reckon you 'll see fun." "Why?" said the other. "O, wa'al I do' know, but there 's a Yankee he 's got in trouble with some o' our folks, an' they 's comin' down to see him off this mornin'."

"Thank you, good friends," said I, to myself, "but I shall not be here when you come down." We made the run hither in about four hours, stopping half an hour for breakfast.

An hour and a half after my arrival the passenger train came along up. Finding that one of the men who stopped here was from Albany, I engaged him in conversation; and finally, telling him I had heard something about a fuss down there, led him along to give me the whole story.

He had n't seen the Yankee, he said, but gentlemen told him that he seemed a civil enough sort of fellow. He 'lowed the Yankee might ha' interfered on the nigger's side if thar 'd been any 'casion to do so; but gentlemen told him he 'd only told the nigger to go 'long home and mind his business and not get up a row with the soldiers. He did n't know for certain where the Yankee slept last night; some said he went off with the Federal captain, and some said he cum up to next station horseback, and some said the landlord had hid him away; and for his part he could n't tell nothin' about it 'cept that he did n't stay at the hotel. He knew about that; the men they went up to his room and got some newspapers he left, some Yankee papers; and then they kinder sarched the house all over like, but they could n't find nothin' of him.

" I don't know," he continued, " whar he stayed, sir. The Yankees is right smart, and I reckon he knew what he was about, like, all the time. Some on 'em reckoned as how they 'd find him at the depo' this mornin', but somebody else said he 'd gone off on the freight train, and they did n't come down. I ha'n't got no feelin' agin the Yankees, but some o' our folks has, and they don't like them interferin' so much with the niggers."

From another source I have also learned that there was much noise and excitement about the hotel till midnight; that there were twenty or more half-drunken men around there for a long time; that some of the rooms were searched for the offending Yankee. So many of the leading men were in the spree that very little could be done to put down the row, which exceeded any that had occurred there for a dozen years.

Thinking of the affair now and at this distance, it still seems as if everybody had conspired to exaggerate its proportions to me. Three days ago I should have deemed it utterly impossible for anything I could say or do to produce such an exhibition of feeling. While the result indicates the under-current of passion, I cannot believe that any sober citizen of Albany sanctions the work of his townsmen on yesterday.

XXXIV.

THE GREAT MILITARY PRISON OF GEORGIA.

ANDERSONVILLE, November 13, 1865.

A GENTLEMAN who came down from Macon this morning tells me that a private telegram to Major-General Wilson announces the hanging of Wirz on Friday last. The man seems to have no friends even in the little village where he lived so long. In that he has passed beyond the praise and blame of men is new hope for the Republic and new source for confidence in the sovereign people. Let me without harsh words and with plain phrases paint you the Andersonville of to-day, — draw it for you as it stood on the day when he died who made its name a world-wide synonyme of cruel barbarity.

I sat in the cars talking with an ex-Rebel major, formerly on the staff of Howell Cobb when he had command of the Georgia Reserves. Suddenly he broke into something I was saying with, "There's where Captain Wirz lived," pointing to the right of the track as we came southward. I looked and saw a large unpainted wooden house, two stories high in the ridge, and scarcely one in the eaves, — a plain Southern dwelling of the average country sort, with negro-quarters in the rear and a turnip-patch on the left. A sallow-faced white woman looked from the window, and a large-eyed negro child stood on the doorsteps.

"We are near Andersonville, then?" said I. "Yes, Anderson is only a mile and a half distant," he responded. I learned afterwards that the place is generally called Anderson hereabouts, the affix *ville* being of recent origin. Years ago it was simply Station Number Eight, and received its present name, I am told, in honor of General Robert Anderson of Sumter fame.

Five minutes more and there flashed upon us through the trees the white line of the cemetery fence, and in another instant we caught a glimpse of the long rows of white headboards standing brightly in the noonday sunshine and within the retired circlet of lofty trees. It was but a glance, and then the high bank of the railroad-cut shut out the view. In a moment more, however, we rolled out to the level, and a score of persons rose to look through the windows and see the famous stockade of dreadful memory.

Before the war Anderson numbered the following houses: first, a small white church without steeple; second, Dyke's house, with its adjoining saw-mill and grist-mill; third, a small white depot building; fourth, a small, square, unpainted building of one room, in which the post-office was kept; and fifth, a two-room log-cabin. This is all there was of the village, though there were half a dozen houses not over a mile away, of which the Widow Turner's was in sight. These six buildings yet remain, but the old post-office and the Turner house are unoccupied.

The village now contains about fifty buildings, great and small; the great ones being two or three houses built for the chief officers of the post and prison, and the buildings put up for the commissary and quartermaster departments, and the small ones being those erected for the soldiers and minor officers of the guard. All were cheaply built, none are painted, and the general appearance of the place is squalid and forbidding. The various buildings are scattered about on a tract of over a hundred acres, which has a general slope from the northwest toward the southeast. The whole village lies west of the railroad.

The great stockade was the central feature of the famous Andersonville prison, technically known to the Rebels as "Camp Sumter." Connected with this were the cook-house, the bake-house, the numerous forts, the officers' stockade, the hospital stockade, the dispensary, the vegetable garden, the Confederate hospital, the general cemetery, the pest-house, and the small-pox cemetery. The great cemetery is nearly north of the large stockade; and the hospital stockade, with its accessories of dispensary and vegetable garden, is nearly south thereof. The whole prison lies east of the railroad.

One hundred and twenty rods nearly due east of the little depot building is the southwest corner of the main stockade. It originally contained fifteen acres, about five acres of which were swamp. Eleven acres were afterward added to the northern end, so that it now exists as a parallelogram, rather less than twice as long north and south as it is wide east and west. Some seven or eight acres are south of the little stream which crosses it. The swamp is mostly in that part north of the brook. The extreme southern end is eighteen or twenty feet above the level of the water, and the slope down to it is quite gradual. The bank north of the stream is very steep, and the farther end of the stockade is at least forty-five or fifty feet above the water level.

The stockade has a double wall, the outer one being about one hundred and sixty feet from the inner one, and each being built of logs ten or twelve inches in diameter, set five feet in the earth, and standing twenty feet above the surface. The logs are mostly pine. Those of the outer wall retain the bark. Those of the inner wall are all peeled, and those of the original stockade are also hewn. As if this double wall were not sufficient to guard against escape, a deep ditch was dug along the southern and eastern sides, outside the outer wall of course; and for a part of the distance on the northern and eastern sides there is even a third wall of logs.

The sentry-boxes, built just below the top of the inner wall, are mere frames, covered with a board roof, and reached by rude ladders. The boxes were forty-four in number, — thirteen on each side, seven on each end, and one at each

corner. These all remain as though they were but yesterday occupied, except one on the western side near the northern end. Much use has broken some of the ladders, but the
greater part still stand beneath the sentry-boxes.

There is but one gate in the outer wall. It is in the
western side, not far from the southern end. In the inner
wall are two gates, one on each side of the brook. They
are strong and heavy, and turn harshly on their hinges. In
the right-hand fold of each is cut a small door for single
passage. The staples and bars remain, but some one has
carried away the locks.

Within the stockade proper there is, as compared with
Florence, scarcely nothing to see. In the days when it was
packed with from thirty to thirty-five thousand men, the
whole surface was covered with tents and mud-and-stick cabins. Of these not more than fifty remain, and they are all
south of the brook.

In the northern end there are only the five long sheds
originally built as barracks for men not sick enough to be
sent to hospital. They are simply roofed frames, without
either siding or flooring. Each is thirty by one hundred
and twenty feet in size. There is nothing about them to
indicate their latter-day use. The famous caves were in
the bank north of the brook and swamp, but the rains have
so cut away the bank that not more than a dozen of them
can be found, and of these only small sections remain. Here,
too, were the equally famous springs, but the washing down
of the bank has also ruined them. Little brooklets find their
way out from the red earth and mottled clay; but where
"Love's Delight" and "Jacob's Well" and "Heart's Ease,"
and all the other comforting springs were, can never more
be shown. Just in the brow of the bank were the wells;
one can find a dozen or more of them, cut trimly down into
the firm red earth for thirty or thirty-five feet, but now water-
less and liable to engulf unwary wanderers.

In the southern end were gathered the last prisoners, and here, accordingly, are abundant evidences of life. Though not more than fifty of the huts remain, there are fragments and ruins of at least a couple of hundred more. The gate on this side the brook was the main gate. Just inside it, on the left, is a small, square log-cabin, whose use is suggested by the counters and platform scales within. On the right of the gate are five open sheds, running north and south. Each is twenty by one hundred feet in size, and the slope of the ground makes them about four feet high in the eaves in the end toward the wall, and about nine feet in the end toward the brook. The rear of each is scarcely four feet distant from the dead-line. Far down in front of the gate, almost over to the eastern wall, is another shed of the same general character as those nearer the gate. Under these six sheds is the record of an heroic struggle for existence. Here is gathered everything all these prisoners had for house-building, — three or four wagon-loads of bits of board and split slabs. As the number in prison decreased, those who remained brought hither what the departed had left, choosing to build their rough bunks under a roof out of sun and rain. Nothing in the whole prison is more touching than this palpable evidence that these sons of the nation were so eager to get even the covering of these miserable roofs. Some of their bunks and benches remain intact; but, generally, the little all that constituted everything is scattered at random. Complete as is the general destruction, the ruins are of wonderful suggestiveness. You find half a stool, a broken knife, the handle of a huge wooden spoon, a split checker-board, an old pipe, a wooden hook, a bit of cunning carving on a beam, and, finally, — is it a barber's chair? — for, improbable as the presence of such a luxury seems, this combination of a seat and legs and braces and sloping back could hardly have been anything else than a veritable barber's chair.

In the whole stockade there is not a single tree. The

T

ground was originally well-wooded, but Winder cut away everything. In the northwestern corner, near the outer wall, he left a single tall pine, whose grateful shade could never fall within the stockade proper, — left it as if to tantalize the weary and fevered prisoners through the blazing summer days.

How dared any one ever deny the existence of a dead-line here? It is twenty feet inside the inner wall. For a part of the distance it was a palpable thing, — four inch strips of twenty feet siding, nailed on the top of posts three feet high. For another portion of the distance it was, however, marked only by these little posts twenty feet apart. That men in such a packed prison should not crowd beyond this undefined line between these posts was simply an impossibility. Hellish malignity could not have devised a surer way to lead half-crazed men to swift destruction than was found in thus establishing this unmarked line. A small portion of the finished line remains intact; elsewhere the posts still stand, but the strips of board have been torn off. That much of the line has disappeared for a memorial of the place scarcely needs to be said.

The stocks was an institution much in use during the earlier days of the prison, but discontinued after some months. The instruments were in the extreme southwestern corner, between the inner and the outer walls of the stockade. Nothing now remains of it but a couple of log sheds in a tumble-down condition.

The bake-house stands on the south bank of the brook, between the inner and the outer walls of the stockade. It is thirty by eighty feet in size, with two rooms below and a garret above. It contained two ovens, each twelve feet square. One of them remains in pretty fair condition, but the other is ruined. Some of the shelves and cases can still be seen. The bunks in the loft yet retain the straw on which the workmen lay. The well at the corner of the building is partly filled with rubbish; and of the dozen little slab cabins near by only four or five are in condition for inspection.

The enclosure for sick call was also between the inner and outer walls. It was a long pen at the right of the main gate of the inner wall, discontinued before the closing days of the prison. No trace of its existence remains.

The bridges were two in number, one on the eastern side and the other on the western side of the stockade proper. The one on the east is in good order, as is the corduroy road up the northern bank of the stream. That on the west is passable, but needs much repair, or would need it if there were use therefor.

Connected also directly with the stockade, though not within it, is the cook-house, a building standing forty or fifty rods north of the northwestern corner of the stockade walls, near the road to the cemetery. It is a roofed frame, forty by one hundred and twenty feet in size. In it were twelve great iron kettles, which the military authorities took away some time ago. It is now an empty shed, around which are many whitened bones.

The officers' stockade exists merely as a pen two hundred feet long by one hundred and fifteen feet wide, situated about twenty-five rods from the depot, and half that distance from the railroad track. In it were one or two barrack buildings, which were burned at the time of the evacuation. This stockade was not much used, the captured officers being generally confined in Macon.

The hospital stockade, sixty or seventy rods directly south of the general stockade, is an enclosure of eight acres, its length east and west being about double its width north and south. It is built with logs, only ten feet high, which, considering that no one went to the hospital till he was past walking, seems a needless waste of good lumber that might have been given to the boys in the general stockade for firewood in the

winter time. Posts were set within this enclosure for twenty-
two buildings, each twenty by one hundred and fifteen feet
in size. Seven of these appear to have been finished; that
is, roofed and sided. Nine more were roofed, but not sided.
The remaining six never got further than the corner-posts.
Twelve of the whole number now exist as mere sheds. None
of them ever had any floor but the earth, and eight never
were sided. Of these twelve only nine have chimneys, —
mere piles of sticks and clay, with a huge fireplace facing
either end of the building. A score of broken bunks are
scattered about, but the beds seem mostly to have been
spread on the earth. The other four buildings, wholly or
partly completed, have been torn down, mainly to use the
lumber in building the cemetery fence. There are three
deep wells in the stockade, and a small kitchen or cook-
house just without the single gate.

The dispensary is a plain two-story building, about twenty
rods west of the hospital stockade. It has three rooms on
the lower floor, and two on the upper floor, with a second
floor piazza on the western front. Under the southern end
is a cellar about fifteen feet square, in which is now collected
considerable rubbish. The central lower room of the house
was the shop. It is arranged with a counter through the
middle, and shelves on either side and at the farther end.
The medicines in use appear to have been principally such
roots, seeds, and barks as could be found in the Confederacy.
They were put up in packages about three inches square
and six inches long, each bearing a label of the following
character: "*Pinckneya Pubens* (Georgia Bark). Proper-
ties, Tonic and Anti-periodic. Directions, Infusion made
with one ounce of the bark to one pint of boiling water; let
it stand till cold, and then strain. Dose, From two to three
fluid ounces. From the C. S. Medical Laboratory, Macon,
Ga." There seem to have been two or three hundred of
these packages in store when the dispensary was given up,

every one of which has been broken open ; and the floor of
this small middle room is covered four or five inches deep
with a mass of bark, seed, paper, sticks, and roots. I was
able to find the labels of nine different preparations, to wit:
prickly elder, pink root, sumach berries, queen's delight,
poplar bark, worm seed, wild cherry bark, wild ginger, and
Georgia bark. Each was made ready for use by steeping
in water, and the dose was from one to three fluid ounces.
That there were other medicines than these is evident enough
from the fact that I found prescriptions for portions of qui-
nine, camphor, and one or two other articles.   In the mass of
rubbish and medicine I also found several scraps of paper
containing lists of men admitted on different days to the different divisions of the hospital. They give the name, the
regiment, company, and rank, and number of the detachment
to which they were assigned. I have part of the list of the
fifth division for October 21, 1864, which also gives the di-
agnosis of the disease. The men were mostly from New
England, New York, and Pennsylvania regiments, and of
the aggregate number a fraction over three fourths were admitted for treatment of scurvy. Four were admitted from
Massachusetts and two from Maine, and the bodies of these
six were lying in the cemetery before the end of the month.
Possibly the same mortality existed with respect to men from
other States, but I have no means of comparison.

A somewhat diamond-shaped tract of ground just west of
the dispensary is called the garden. It contains five or six
acres, and is enclosed by two deep ditches, four feet apart,
the earth removed being thrown up between them.   Beyond
digging these ditches and grubbing out a few stumps, nothing
was ever done with the garden. If it was proposed to allow
the scurvy prisoners to make use of the plat for vegetable
raising, the scheme came to an early death.

They buried their dead, these prisoners of Andersonville,
in the pleasantest field of all the section hereabouts. It is

in the heart of the pines, and gives serene resting-ground for men worn down in the battle. All about the graves the wild-flowers of the country blossom, — all around them most stately trees keep sturdy guard.

The cemetery covers forty-seven acres, and is nearly square in form. It occupies a tract somewhat larger than the old field, a portion of the timber on the north and the east having also been enclosed. The whitewashed picket fence is completed on three sides; on the eastern side is a rough board fence, which will soon, however, give way to a picket like that on the other sides. In direction, the cemetery is west of north from the stockade; in distance, it is about one third of a mile from the northern line thereof. The cemetery is laid out in four nearly equal sections, by cross-roads intersecting near the centre of the enclosure. The north and south road is partly graded; the east and west road is merely staked out, and is not likely to be soon finished. The entrance is by a plain gate about midway in the southern line. Inside the fence, on the right of the gate, on the transverse section of a cross, is the inscription: —

NATIONAL CEMETERY.
ANDERSONVILLE.

On the left of the gate, inscribed upon a similar neat white board, is this impressive and appropriate inscription : —

> " On FAME's eternal camping-ground
>   Their silent tents are spread,
>   And GLORY guards with solemn round
>   The bivouac of the dead."

On the eastern side of the road from this gate, that is, in the southeastern quarter of the cemetery, are three sections of graves, separated by broad alleys running east and west. Each of these sections contains about fourteen hundred graves, in long rows of over a hundred each. On the western side of the road, that is, in the southwestern quarter, are

two similar sections, separated also by an alley, and having
about the same number of graves in the long rows.   Where
the first of these alleys crosses the main road, on the right
and on the left, are these inscriptions : —

> " Whether in the prison drear
>   Or in the battle's van,
>   The fittest place for man to die
>   Is where he dies for man."

> " The hopes, the fears, the blood, the tears,
>   That marked the battle strife,
>   Are now all crowned by victory
>   That saved the nation's life."

Where the second alley crosses are similarly set up, on the
right and on the left the following memorial passages : —

> " A thousand battle-fields have drank
>   The blood of warriors brave,
>   And countless homes are dark and drear
>   In the land they died to save."

> " Then shall the dust
>   Return to the earth as it was;
>   And the spirit shall return
>   Unto God who gave it."

In the northwestern quarter, in the extreme corner of the
cemetery, are the graves of the guard, one hundred and fifteen in number, from the 1st, 2d, 3d, and 4th Georgia Reserves.   In the northeastern quarter is a solid section of over
five thousand graves, in rows of about two hundred each ;
and here stands the following motto : —

> " Through all Rebellion's horrors
>   Bright shines our nation's fame:
>   Our gallant soldiers, perishing,
>   Have won a deathless name."

In the centre of the enclosure, at the crossing of the roads,
is the forty-feet pine flag-staff, erected in July, by the burial
party which came out from Washington with Miss Clara
Barton, of Massachusetts.   Nearer to this than any other

are the graves of the six prisoners hung July 11, 1864, by their companions, for rascalities within the stockade.*

These 12,882 soldiers' and sailors' graves are each marked with a plain white head-board thirty inches high and ten inches wide, inscribed on the inside with name, regiment, company, rank, and date of death. At first the bodies were buried so far apart that there is often more than a foot of space between the edges of the head-boards; but in the large section in the northeastern corner, where those who died last winter and spring are buried, the space is never more than four inches and in many cases is scarcely two. The first recorded death was February 27, 1864, the last April 28, 1865, giving an average of about nine hundred and twenty deaths per month for fourteen months. In the months of August and September, 1864, the average of deaths appears, however, to have been nearly five hundred per week; and there were many occasions when the number exceeded one hundred per day.

Across the Sweet Water Creek, in the oaks, about a hundred rods distant, and south of east in direction from the hospital stockade, was the pest-house. It simply consisted of three log cabins, each about ten by fifteen feet in size. One of the number has been torn down, but the other two remain, and one of them is occupied by a " cracker " family.

The bodies of those who died of small-pox are buried in an old field about thirty rods northeast of the pest-house. There are sixty-four graves, a large proportion of them being of members of Tennessee regiments. The white head-boards show that the first death from this disease took place March 12, 1864, within a month after the occupation of the stockade, and the last on July 19, 1864. The graves will be enclosed in a little cemetery five rods square.

The troops on duty here were, as I have already indicated, the 1st, 2d, 3d, and 4th Georgia Reserves. They occupied

* See Postscript, page 315.

a collection of log-cabins near the depot, and another collection west of the hospital stockade, say one hundred in the aggregate, some of which are now vacant, while others are occupied by the negroes.   For the use of their sick two comfortable buildings were erected near the railroad, seventy-five rods from the depot, each two stories in height and twenty by one hundred feet in size.   They are now occupied for the hotel.

There were but two storehouses.   They are close by the depot, one on either side the railroad track.   The quarter-masters' building is thirty by one hundred and five feet in size, and eight feet high in the eaves; the commissary building is of the same height, and forty-five by two hundred and sixty feet in size.   It can very readily be seen that the Rebels were utterly unable to keep a week's full rations on hand, even when the stockade contained no more than twenty thousand prisoners.   These buildings now furnish a temporary home for various persons, and contain the freight rooms, a shoemaker's shop, a groggery, and the commissary supplies for the negroes at work in the cemetery.

The forts are nine in number.   The largest is at the southwestern corner of the stockade.   It mounted twelve guns, had three magazines, and enclosed the house and yard of the Widow Turner.   At the southeastern corner is a double fort, or perhaps I should say two single forts, one fronting south and the other fronting east, and each mounting three guns. Midway on the eastern side, not far from the wall, is a small fort mounting three guns; and far out in front of that, on the hill, the beginning of a larger one, which never was finished, though two guns were mounted there.   At the northeastern corner is a fort of five guns, and another of the same size is at the northwestern corner, while between the two is a smaller one of three guns.   On the western side is a long line of rifle-pits, and a square fort of five guns.   Here, then, were forty-one guns, so mounted that nearly every acre of

14

the stockade could be swept with grape and canister. The forts remain with walls and ditches and platforms and magazines intact, but the cannon have been removed by the military authorities.

The head-quarters of Captain Wirz were at first in the house already mentioned as near the railroad above the village. They were afterwards in the log-house of the Widow Turner, enclosed in the large fort. It has two rooms and is now a gaping skeleton. Finally they were in a large frame building erected for that purpose over in the village, not far from the church. A piazza has recently been added to it, and it is now occupied by a white family.

In the northern part of the slope on which the village is built are springs whose outflow forms a little stream running off to the southeast. Just south of the village are other springs, which make a little stream flowing off to the northeast. These two form a junction in the marsh just west of the bake-house, and thence flow eastwardly through the stockade, giving a sluggish stream with an average depth of ten or twelve inches and a width of four or five feet. It appears much larger in the stockade, because the partial damming of it by the eastern wall gives it a back-flow. If I add that five thousand men would have found it scantily sufficient for their uses, the condition of thirty thousand men compelled to find it sufficient will be very readily apparent.

"We had it pretty tough sometimes at Camp Chase," said a young fellow who had been a Rebel soldier, and with whom I talked at Fort Valley the other evening; "we had to tote our wood nigh onto half a mile in the winter time." Before I could answer, another young fellow, sitting on the opposite side of the fireplace, responded, "Well, s'pose you'd been in Andersonville, as my father was, where you did n't have to tote it at all; where you could see a thousand acres within a quarter of a mile, and was n't allowed to have a stick of it!" There seemed no occasion for me to speak to that point.

Andersonville was a good place for the prison. There is plenty of wood and plenty of water, and the section is generally healthful. I have spoken of the water privilege that was occupied; the one that was rejected can be seen by the most unobservant tourist. The little stream that runs through the stockade forms a junction, half a mile or less from the eastern wall, with the Sweet Water Creek. On this creek, a short mile above this junction, a merciful man might have located the stockade. The site is as good as that chosen by Winder; the labor of preparing it would not have been materially greater; the end of it might have adjoined the railroad track; its gate could not have been over half a mile from the station; there would have been half a dozen springs; and, best of all, there would have been the fish-fruitful and rapidly flowing current of the Sweet Water, a stream at least twenty feet wide and sixteen inches deep.

POSTSCRIPT.

In a small book recently published, entitled "Nineteen Months a Prisoner of War: by Lieutenant G. E. Sabre, Second Rhode Island Cavalry," I find the following interesting account by an eyewitness of that most remarkable and significant affair, — the trial and execution within the stockade of the six base creatures on whose graves is the record, "Hung July 11, 1864": —

" A preliminary examination drew from the arrested man an acknowledgment of his crime; and at the same time the names of a number of others implicated in the same acts were elicited. The entire party was arrested, and a trial called.

" On the next morning the sergeants of the different messes were assembled, and out of this number twelve were chosen to act as a jury. Several officers were brought down from Macon to witness the trial. Those of the sufferers by the depredations of the 'raiders,' who were able to attend, were summoned to appear as witnesses, and the accused were permitted to choose their own counsel and witnesses.

"The trial of the 'raiders' was conducted with the strictest impartiality. After hearing all the evidence, the respective cases were argued with considerable ability. The verdict given was for the leading 'raiders' to be hanged by the neck until dead, and the remainder to suffer such other punishments as the extent of their crimes deserved.

"The following were the names of the men condemned to death : —

"William Collins, 88th Pennsylvania Volunteers.

"Patrick Delany, 83d Pennsylvania Volunteers.

"Andrew Meever, United States Navy.

"Terrence Sullivan, 72d New York Volunteers.

"John Sarsfield, 140th New York Volunteers.

"Charles Curtis, 5th Rhode Island Artillery.

"On Monday, July 11th, 1864, a rude gallows was erected by our own men on a rising ground at the southwestern portion of the stockade. The gallows was a rude piece of workmanship, built out of material which the Rebel officials, but too willingly in this case, provided. It was composed of two heavy, forked logs, which were fixed perpendicularly in the earth, with a strong cross-beam resting in the forks at the top. A platform, about six feet from the ground, was built and supported upon props, which, at the final moment, were to be cut away, and the unfortunate men launched between heaven and earth. Six men from the camp were designated to adjust the ropes about the necks of the condemned, and a seventh was detailed to execute the dropping of the platform.

"At five o'clock in the afternoon the southwestern gate was thrown open, and the prisoners were marched in under guard of Rebel soldiers, commanded by Captain Wirz, accompanied by the colonel commanding the post. The solemn procession moved in front of the gallows and halted. By this time several thousand prisoners had assembled to witness the execution.

"When the culprits were formed in line, the Rebel captain stepped forward, and, as near as I could note them after the affair was over, made the following remarks to those in charge : —

"'PRISONERS, — I now hand over to you, in the same manner I received them, the men whom you have condemned to death on the gallows.'

" Then turning to the culprits he said : —

" 'You have been arrested and condemned by your own comrades; I now turn you over to them, and leave them to carry out the sentence or do as they may see fit.'

" After this, the colonel, captain, and guards immediately left the enclosure.

" The condemned now received the consolations of religion, administered by a Catholic priest, who was permitted by the Rebel authorities to visit the stockade on different occasions. The priest accompanied the culprits to the foot of the gallows, and engaged in prayer. In the midst of these holy offices, Curtis took occasion to make an attempt at escape. He succeeded in breaking through the crowd, but was immediately pursued and returned.

" The prayer being finished, the six criminals, each accompanied by the persons appointed to execute the sentence, stepped upon the platform. The criminals each said a few words, which were scarcely audible, proclaiming their innocence and begging for mercy.

" When they had concluded what they had to say, the ropes having been previously adjusted, a sack was drawn over their heads, and the six men who accompanied them descended.

" At a given signal the platform was cut away, and five of the unfortunate men were struggling in mid-air. The rope, however, of the sixth broke, and the culprit fell to the earth. He begged piteously to be released, but his comrades were inexorable. Another rope was secured, and, when the five bodies were removed, he was hanged alone.

" The bodies of the six men were removed from the stockade, and buried in a separate part of the graveyard, distinct from those who died in camp.

" During the execution, I observed outside of the enclosure the whole of the Rebel troops on duty at Camp Sumter drawn up facing the gallows. This was, as I understood afterwards, a precautionary measure, supposing some treachery on the part of the prisoners."

XXXV.

FORT VALLEY, November 15, 1865

THIS is a pleasant little town of some sixteen hundred to two thousand inhabitants, situated thirty miles below Macon and about one hundred miles above the Florida line. It is the principal place in Houston County, though not the county seat, and is the junction of the Muscogee and the Southwestern Railroads. It is not a point for the cotton trade, but does a large retail business with the surrounding country.

The section of the State below here, of which Albany may be called the centre, constituting Southwestern Georgia, is one of the finest cotton-growing regions of the South. It was not much traversed by either army, had no chance at running the blockade, and could get very little shipment on the railroads; consequently the surrender of the Southern army found in the country about all the cotton that had been raised in five years. Various gentlemen whom I met in the Carolinas from time to time told me there was probably more cotton in Georgia at the close of the war than in any other Southern State; and many gentlemen of this State tell me that the great bulk of the amount was in the southwestern section. The estimates of the amount in forty counties of this quarter average about two hundred thousand bales. The estimates of the amount made this year in the same counties average near ten thousand bales.

The men who did the fighting are everywhere the men who most readily accept the issues of the war. "I can whip any three Yankees in town," blustered an ex-Rebel officer at Americus the other day; but when I inquired about his record in the army I found that he was generally "seriously unwell" on the day of battle. So, too, one of the most malignant men I met at Milledgeville served during the war in the home guard, and, afterwards, as the commandant of a prison.

The late Rebel privates of this section are, generally, doing quite well. They mourn over the defeat of their armies, and are very fond of showing that but for this little mistake, or that little accident, or that other little blunder, the Confederacy would now be a great nation; but they appear, on the whole, to accept the issue of the war in good faith and with a determination to do their duties hereafter as orderly citizens. I should add, however, that there are more exceptions to this general fact than I found in South Carolina.

However strongly the Carolinian clings to his State-rights doctrine, he knows and feels that his State has been punished as a criminal for promulgating and upholding that dogma. The people of this section hold to the old faith on the abstract question, and do not seem to recognize that they have been beaten in the contest; and hence there is much scolding at what is termed "Presidential interference in the affairs of the State." Most noticeable as this is, there are very few who desire any further war on the subject. "I am as good a Calhoun man to-day as ever I was," said a gentleman to me at Smithville, "but you Yankees are too strong for us; and now I propose to keep my opinions to myself and do my duty as a good citizen."

An Americus merchant told me he was a hot Secessionist all through 1860, and, though sixty years of age, shouldered his musket early in 1861 and saw two years of service before he broke down. "We staked everything on the result, and for my part I submit to the issue without a murmur"; but. before our conversation closed he said, "We have all taken the amnesty oath; we have just as many rights now as Mr. Johnson himself has; Georgia is again a member of the

Federal Union, and I should like to see any Massachusetts or New York congressman get up and deny her sovereignty!" and, warming with his subject, he soon added, "We're not going there to ask favors, by G——d, but to demand our rights!"

There is a pretty general contempt everywhere for the "Yankees," the word standing for the resident of any Northern State. Passing by a piazza in Americus on which three or four men sat, I overheard one of them remark, "Well, hell's the place for Yankees, and I want 'em all to go thar as soon's possible, and take the niggers 'long with 'em." Talking with a very intelligent Macon gentleman, I asked him how Northern men would be likely to succeed in business if they were to come into the State this winter; and his answer was, "I think they would get along well enough in the upper-country, but in the lower part of the State there is such ignorance and prejudice that I reckon they would see hard times a long while before they made a living." I must add, that in a general way I hear much expression of a desire for an influx of Northern energy and Northern capital. "Yet when the Yankees come down here," said a man from Columbus, whom I sat next at the tea-table, "they'll have to be Georgians if they reckon to make money."

I have seen not a little of feminine bitterness since coming into the South; but the women of this section have favored me with some unusual exhibitions during the past week. One who took the train at Montezuma remarked to an acquaintance that the Yankees had all left that place, and she hoped to the good gracious that none would ever be seen there again; to which her friend responded, "I wish we could git shet of 'em forever up to our place." While going through the hotel hall to my room, one evening, from the parlor came a woman's voice asking Henry, the man of all work, if any Yankees came on the train. He reckoned not. "I'm thankful for that," answered the voice. When we went down past Andersonville the other day, a genteel young lady who sat in the seat in front of mine said to the gentleman who was her seatmate, " Do you know, I 'm not sorry so many Yankees died here, for they 'd no business to come down and fight the South ! "

I found many negroes below here who were run out of the northern part of the State and out of South Carolina, on the approach of Sherman's army. The beauty of the old " patriarchal institution " appears in the fact that none but the able-bodied negroes were brought away, — the love of the late masters for their servants so prevailing that the aged and infirm were left to the tender mercies of the Yankees!

These refugee negroes generally seem anxious to return to their former homes, though the whites profess to think it an indication of shiftlessness that they desire to see fathers and mothers and children. I saw a party of eleven one morning just starting out to walk over to Barnwell District, South Carolina, a distance of at least two hundred and fifty miles ; and the members of another gang of fourteen told me they were going to start for North Carolina so as to get there by Christmas.

The idea that the whites and the blacks cannot live to- gether is unusually prevalent throughout all 'this section. " The negroes were the ignorant cause of the war, and are bound to be exterminated before the conflict closes," said one gentleman, a member of the late Convention ; and I have heard the same idea a dozen times expressed within a week. " We must go down or they must," says another man ; and his associate responds, " D—d if it 's us, though." The colonization scheme has no supporters, I judge ; for I 've not heard it mentioned since coming into the State.

I sat an hour or more in the Freedmen's Bureau agency office at Albany one day last week. A planter from Mitchell County came in with the stereotyped phrase, " Niggers won't work, and everything is all going to ruin." He

14 *   U

wanted the captain to send him a dozen good fellows who would work right along. I don't at all wonder that he has trouble with his negroes, — white men would n't work for him if he talked to them as he said he did to his present hands. While he sat there, in came a planter from Lee County, an ex-Rebel colonel, who works twenty men and twelve women. He said he had found no trouble with his negroes. As soon as he came home from the army he called them together, explained to them that they were free and could go where they pleased; said to them that he would like to have all of them remain on the place, and would pay them fairly for their work. He gave them a week for consideration, and then every one was ready to contract with him. The contract gives them house room, firewood, medical attendance, and one third of the crop. None of his hands have left him, and all are ready to contract for the next year. In the statement of these two cases lies the whole problem: give the negro fair treatment and there will be very little cause for complaint against him.

The cases in which the planters turn the negroes off the plantation as soon as the crops are gathered are somewhat numerous. Here is one that comes under my own observation. The planter worked seven men and six women. I met the men on the street one forenoon, wandering aimlessly about. When I talked with them they told me their story. " Ole mass'r had 'greed to give we one tird de craps, an' we dun got 'em all up, — got de corn shucked, an' de tatees digged, and de rice trashed; an' ole mass'r he dun gone sold all de craps, an' he bringed we all up yere yes'er-day, an' gif we seven dollar fur de man an' he wife to buy de cloth wid to make we clofes, an' he say may be he gif we some shoes; an' he dun gif we'n none o' de craps, none o' de rice, none o' de corn, none o' de tatees, on'y de seven dollar fur de man an' he wife; an' den he tell we ter come on de plantation no mo'; an' he say we all bof mus' make livin' on we'ns freedom ; an' we got not'ing fur all de work on'y de seven dollar fur de man an' he wife, an' we got no corn nor not'ing for de winter." I have some satisfaction in knowing that this wretch is ordered to appear before the provost-marshal at two o'clock to-morrow afternoon.

An intelligent boy of about twenty touched his old cap to me, and asked the way to head-quarters. I went there with him and heard his story. He was a refugee from C'lina, — brought down last spring by his old master, who had since died. He had been doing job work this season, and had got fifty dollars laid up. He was a blacksmith, and worked at his trade. " A month ago, sah, — next Monday 's four weeks, sah, — I goes to work fur Mr. Bell ; an' he promise to do well by me ; an' I make no reg'lar bargain with him, but jes' work right 'long ev'ry day from sun to sun ; an' he say to me yes'day mornin', sah, ' Henry, you go up to town with me an' I reward you well for your work ' ; an' I dun cum up in his wagon, an' he drive round town an' say ag'in he gwine to reward me well ; an' when he git ready to go home, he jes' give me dis yer old pipe an' say he don't want me no more ; an' when I ax'd him where was de reward he gwine to give me, he cut at me wid de whip an' tell me to go 'bout my business ; an' den I comed yere, an' I tell you de whole story." That old pipe did not seem to the captain a sufficient compensation for a month's work at blacksmithing, and Mr. Bell was also ordered up for settlement with Henry, the aforesaid freedman.

In the South Carolina Convention one of the leading up-country delegates, during the debate on the slavery-prohibition clause of the Constitution, said, substantially, that the condition, as well as the name, of slavery should be prohibited ; and in this view he took exception to the phrase, "neither slavery nor involuntary servitude shall exist except as a punishment for crime," &c. ; for, he argued, it will be very easily possible for the Legislature, if so disposed, to re-establish the condition of slavery by a system of crimes and punishments impliedly authorized by that clause.

Down here in Southwestern Georgia is the man who furnishes the practical illustration for this argument. He is called General John T. Morgan, and he has been making a speech on the negro question, which the editor of his county paper indorses as "sensible." "The grand point in his speech," says the editor, "was that in order to wield the bone and muscle of the negro effectively in the various industrial pursuits of the South, we must put him in competition with white laborers, and we thought he was very successful in its demonstration." The abstract of his views on this point is brief, but it is full enough on the main question, as the following paragraph shows : —

"He urged that, as the Constitution gives the power to inflict involuntary servitude as a punishment for crime, a law should be so framed as to enable the judicial authorities of the State to sell into bondage again those negroes who should be found guilty of certain crimes; and in conclusion said he thought that this, in connection with the whipping-post and the pillory, would do more to check vagrancy, theft, robbery, and other crimes among the negroes than all the penitentiaries which could be built."

I cannot doubt that some simple-minded persons really apprehend trouble with the blacks about Christmas. I have talked with hundreds of the negroes since I left Milledgeville, but am utterly unable to find any feeling among them that seems to me to threaten a revolt. On the contrary, they appear to believe that their only chance for decent treatment during the winter lies in the protection which the presence of the military will give them. If the troops are all removed they fear just what this General Morgan advocates, — a virtual re-establishment of slavery.

XXXVI.

THE STATE ELECTIONS.

COLUMBUS, November 17, 1865.

THE general election of this State took place yesterday. In this city and county it passed off quietly enough, — the vote being about one fifth larger than that cast for delegates to the late State Convention.

The election of Judge Charles L. Jenkins, of Augusta, to the governorship of the State is cause for congratulation. I had frequent occasion to speak of him during the session of the late Convention, of which body he was the undisputed leader. The office to which he is now elected has been more than once at his disposal; but, though he served his county often in former years in the Legislature, he never had much desire for office, and latterly has given himself to the duties of his profession and of his position as Judge of the Supreme Court. Everybody concedes his entire personal and official integrity, and he has always been especially free from the contamination of party or legislative intrigue. That a man of such universally acknowledged probity and uprightness of character has been elected to the high office of Governor of a great State is in itself cause for congratulation. It must also be added that Judge Jenkins appreciates the present situation much better than the majority of the people of the State. He was defeated as a Union man, in spite of the great repute in which he was personally held, for the Convention of 1861. His position on the bench kept him aloof from active affairs during the war; but though, like almost every one else, he " went with the State," it was known by all who cared to inquire his views, that he never ceased regretting the course of the

South.   He was the choice of many of the best men of the
State for Provisional Governor, and was elected to the late
Convention without opposition.   His course in that body is
well known.   As chairman of the committee of sixteen, he
reported the obnoxious clause of the new Constitution which
sets up the claim for compensation for emancipated slaves,
but one of his friends asserts that he very decidedly opposed
the adoption of that clause in committee.   As chairman of
that committee, he also reported the bill *repealing* the ordinance of secession; but I have his own assurance that he
desired to declare it *null and void.*   As chairman of that
committee, he also reported the equivocal measure respecting the rights of the freedmen in the courts.   How far it
concurred with his own views I am unable to say.   He
voted against the repudiation of the war debt; his position
being that the people ought to be left free to do as they
pleased in regard to its payment.   A better man for the
office and the crisis might possibly be found, but it is a good
deal to get one into that position of such stamp as he is.
He has been elected without opposition, each of the other
gentlemen mentioned for the office having formally declined
being candidates.

In the Second Congressional District, comprising the
extreme southwestern section of the State, — twenty-two
counties, — there were two candidates for Congress, — General Phil Cook and Dr. J. E. Blount.   General Cook was
originally opposed to secession, but went into the war as
soon as the State went out of the Union, and remained in it
to the end, — receiving some slight wounds.   He was one
of the silent members of the late Convention; and is, I
judge, reasonably well disposed toward the government.
Dr. Blount opposed secession, opposed the war, and now
says that " the only hope for the peace, happiness, and prosperity of our people is in the free and cheerful support of
the Union and the President."   Of course General Cook is
elected.

In the Third Congressional District, comprising the fifteen counties of Middle Western Georgia, including that in which Columbus is situated, there were also two candidates, — Colonel Hugh Buchanan, of Coweta County, and Judge Benjamin H. Bigham, of Troup County.

Mr. Bigham has many times been a member of the lower house of the Legislature, and generally occupied important positions on the committees of that body. He is now judge of the Atlanta Circuit. He defined his position in a lengthy card, of which the substance is in the following paragraph : —

"I opposed the secession of Georgia from the Union; but I nevertheless regret to see that we have a candidate for Congress in this district who commends himself by saying he thinks he can take the test oath, to which he especially refers. Speaking for myself, I am not ready to write ' traitor' over the graves of the honored dead. I would not, if I could, thus insult the survivors of the recent severe conflict of arms. I am fully committed to the firm and substantial support of the President, reserving to myself the manly right to discriminate, and to disagree with him where I may conscientiously think he is wrong. I will not cringe to power nor sacrifice principle; nor by any act or expression of mine countenance the proscription of any man for past opinions ; and I speak in all sincerity when I say the fate of our people shall be my fate."

Mr. Buchanan is a lawyer by profession, who has served two terms in the upper house of the Legislature. He was an original Secessionist, and entered the Rebel army in April, 1861, as a third lieutenant. He rose through the intermediate grades to a lieutenant-colonelcy; and at the battle of Pavillion Station, in June, 1864, was so severely wounded that it was thought for months he could not recover; and in fact he was not able to return to his command when the Confederate armies surrendered. His card contains the following precious paragraph : —

"It may not be amiss or improper to state, for the information of those not acquainted with me, that, at the commencement of the late war, I volunteered my services, and, through the executive of the State of Georgia, entered into the army of the Confederate States, served in the army of Virginia, and did all in my power to sustain the cause of the South, and secure the independence of the Confederate States. No law was ever passed by the Congress of the Confederate States by which I could be required to take up arms during the whole struggle. I was exempt by the laws of the Confederate States. I refused to avail myself of the exemption, and continued in the service to the last. The cause failed, the Confederacy fell, and our expectations of a separate and distinct nationality passed away. I feel that I am not responsible for that failure in any way. As a citizen, a soldier, and a man I did all I could to insure success."

You see, it was no question between a Unionist and a Disunionist, but a mere contest between two Rebels. Of course the one who went into the army carried the day. His county organ says of him, that "he will be the peer of any member from this State in intellect and every virtue that adorns the human character."

In the Seventh Congressional District, composed of the fourteen counties in the extreme northwestern corner of the State, and constituting what is locally known as "Cherokee Georgia," there were three prominent candidates.

Mr. H. G. Cole, of Atlanta, was the candidate of the original Union men who never gave in their adhesion to the defunct Confederacy and who never acquiesced in the decision of the Secession Convention. He was everywhere known from the beginning to the end of the war as an out-and-out enemy of the Rebellion and a friend of the Union, and suffered a year's imprisonment at the hands of Howell Cobb and other malignants of the State on that account.

Mr. James P. Hambleton, the Atlanta editor who got up the famous "black list" against New York merchants, in the fall of 1860, was the candidate of the original Secessionists and all the present Rebel malcontents. A single paragraph from his card clearly reveals his status and eminent fitness for a seat in the Congress of the United States: —

"From the date of the ordinance of secession to the dark days of the surrender of the Southern armies I did all and everything in my power for the establishment of Southern independence and a separate and distinct nationality. Would to God the cause for which we all suffered so much had been crowned with success; but as it was otherwise ordered, I accept the decision of the sword."

General William T. Wofford, of Cass County, was the candidate of the men who were not original Secessionists, but who acquiesced in the action of the Convention of 1861, and supported the State in her efforts in behalf of the Confederacy. He published no card, but allowed his friends to speak for him, and a paragraph from their plea will show his position: —

"General Wofford is not an extreme man in any sense. He is eminently conservative in all things. We need men in Congress in whose honor and integrity we can repose confidence, who will contend to the last for all we can now ask for in support of the policy of President Johnson, and who are as little obnoxious as possible to those in power. The reason for this is plain. We can expect but little from those we so recently regarded as our enemies, if we send men to them whom they regard with suspicion and distrust. In General Wofford we have a man in whom all have confidence, the purity of whose motives no man North or South can question, upon whose record there is not a blot, and from whose influence we have more to expect than almost any man in the South."

The returns from this district will, I am confident, show the election of General Wofford. He is a lawyer by profession, and a cavalry soldier of the Mexican war. He has served one term as clerk, and two terms as member, of the lower house of the Legislature. He strongly opposed Secession in the winter of 1860–61, and voted against the passage of the ordinance of secession in the Convention of May, 1861. But, as one of the cards in his behalf says, "The State went out, and as a true Georgian, believing in the honesty of the people and in the principle that the majority ought to rule, he went with her." He was made colonel of the 18th Regiment, was promoted to a brigadier-ship, and was in command of the district of Northern Georgia at the time of the surrender of the Confederate forces last spring. From all I can learn respecting him, I judge that he is not very badly disposed toward the government and the new order of things.

Without waiting for the returns, I can safely say that the local elections in nearly all the counties of the western and southwestern sections resulted in favor of the men who "went with the State." I do not hear of the success of a single candidate who opposed the war or was even lukewarm in its support, while as between war men the result is generally in favor of the most radical.

In most of these counties wherever an issue was made during the canvass for delegates in the late Convention, the election resulted in favor of men who were co-operationists in 1861 and against those who were original Secessionists. There was a certain disagreeable work to do in the Convention, and the people seemed to think that *quasi* Union men were the proper parties to haul the chestnuts out of the fire. Now the case is different. The Legislature will be composed of men of another stamp, — generally of men of more ability, but also of less original Unionism than those in the Convention.

I everywhere encounter more or less of the feeling which a Cuthbert man expressed in this terse and forcible language : " I hope every district in the State will elect a man for Congress who can't take that d—d test oath ; I want to see the Yankees try it on ; if Georgia is n't a free sovereign State, I think, by G—d, it 's time we knew it ! " This

practical reaffirmation of the dogma of State rights is something of every-day witness to any one travelling here. The
people hold to it just as strongly to-day as they did five
years ago; and the moral of this election is, that the supremacy of the State is above that of the nation.

XXXVII.

MATTERS IN WESTERN GEORGIA.

NEWNAN, November 20, 1865.

AS I looked up the streets of Newnan from the windows
and platform of the railway car, it seemed a charming
place, — a gentle slope toward the east, three or four white
stores, the corner of the court-house with its surroundings
of luxuriant China trees, the hotel with its broad and high
piazzas, a wealth of trees and shrubbery everywhere, on all
sides handsome cottage houses embowered in greenness and
rose blossoms, to the right and left numberless oaks with
their crimson and golden frost-touched leaves, and then in
the dim background the dreamy and uncertain outline of
wooded hills with their blue beauty shimmering in the low
sun of a glorious Indian summer afternoon!

Yet Newnan is just like every other Southern town, —
streets full of mud-holes and wallowing swine, fences in
every stage of tumble-down ruin, sidewalks in every condition of break-neck disorder, yards full of sticks and stones
and bits of every conceivable rubbish, — everywhere a grand
carnival of sloth and unthrift and untidiness and slovenliness,
— everywhere that apathy of shiftlessness so pitiful to the
soul of a New-Englander!

'T is n't Nature's fault. She is infinitely more bountiful

than under our Northern skies. Wild-flowers beautifying every grove and creek-side, and roses and half a dozen strange blossoms tempting into every garden, — and snow on our Massachusetts hillsides! One may well say the war did not produce its full and proper fruitage if the year 1870 does not show this fair South-land redeemed from the careless mistreatment of all these long years, — this Southern people educated to a love of order and cleanliness, and an appreciation of thrift, industry, and the royal dignity of labor!

Newnan is the county seat of Coweta County, and has a population of about twenty-seven hundred. It is on the 'ine of railroad from Atlanta to Montgomery, — forty miles 'elow Atlanta, thirty miles from the western line of Georgia, and rather above the middle of the State north and south. It is the home of very many rich planters, boasts numerous handsome suburban residences, is said to have a more elegant and cultured society than any other place in the western part of the State, prides itself on its early and constant devotion to the cause of secession, and has just elected radical Secessionists and unconquered Rebels to the Legislature.

"If your party carries the day in the forthcoming elections in the North," said a Convention delegate to me at Milledgeville, three weeks ago, "I shall think it perfectly useless for us to send congressmen to Washington." These Georgians thought the President had gone over to the Democratic party, and one man assured me that he wished the success of their nominees in New York and New Jersey!

Surprised as most of them are at the result, not one man in fifty seems to have any true conception of the real significance of the late elections in the North. The merchant of Columbus who said in the public parlor of the hotel one evening so loudly that half a dozen persons heard him, "I'm in favor of having our men go to Congress and take their seats any way, whether the d—d Yankees are willing or not," only put in strong phrase an idea I have heard half a dozen times in more cautious language. If there are fifty' good Union men in all the towns where I have stopped within two weeks they live so quietly that neither observation nor inquiry can find them; and the great mass of the people characterize the result of the recent political campaign in the North as sectional.

Through this part of the State the moral standing of the citizen seems to be measured by his war record. The chief requirement in respect to any man is that he shall "go with the State." The supremacy of the Constitution of the United States is formally acknowledged, but the common conversation of all classes asserts the supremacy of the State. The Calhoun doctrine is pushed to its last conclusion. There is not merely a broad assertion of the rights of the States, but an open enunciation of the supremacy of the State over the general government, — an enlarged reaffirmation of the doctrine declared in simply repealing the ordinance of secession.

A gentleman whom I met in the eastern part of the State said to me: " If there had been three bold and true leaders in the winter of 1860-61, we could have saved the State from secession, in my judgment; but Benj. Hill forsook us, and then Alex. Stephens forsook us, and we had only Josh. Hill left, and the State swung into Rebellion."

Benjamin H. Hill lives at LaGrange, some twenty miles below here. He has long been one of the leading men of the State. He acquiesced in secession, but did not go into the army, I believe. Pending the recent election, he was asked his opinion as to the duty of the people in the present emergency, particularly with reference to the expediency of electing gentlemen to Congress who cannot take the test oath. The following letter is his answer: —

" The oath is unconstitutional, because it adds to and varies from the oath required by the Constitution. This is settled by several adjudications.

" The oath is unwise, unnatural, and unprecedented, because it is retroactive in its requirements. It does not seek to procure proper conduct in the officer while discharging the duties of his office; but does seek to exclude him from the office altogether by reason of something done or not done long before the office was conferred.

"If Congress can prescribe one test it can prescribe another test; and thus, by legislation, destroy the right of representation.

"I would vote for no man to represent Georgia who *could* take this oath, because it is the highest evidence of infidelity to the sentiments of the people of the State.

"I would vote for no man, anywhere, who *would* take this oath, because it is the highest evidence of his infidelity to the Constitution. The man who takes that oath admits a power in Congress to destroy every department of the government as well as every right of representation.

"I am a candidate for no office, and will seek none and desire none. The man who wishes now to be a representative in Congress from the South either does not comprehend the very unpleasant and very heavy duties of that position, or has made up his mind to hold the position without discharging the duties. In either case he is not fit to be trusted.

"There is no danger now from any spirit of resistance in Georgia. The only danger comes from an opposite direction, — servility. I intend to be loyal myself, and I have not been faithless to any obligation I ever assumed, even when unwillingly assumed. I resisted secession until resistance was hopeless, and then I resisted subjugation until resistance was hopeless. I would not, if I could, change my record.

"But I will help no man to represent Georgia whose fidelity to the State is doubted, or whose ability and willingness to maintain and vindicate the honor of her people, living and dead, is suspicious. I will vote for no man to administer the Constitution who, in the very beginning of his work, would take an oath which admits a power in Congress to subvert that Constitution.

"Each house of Congress is *sole judge* as to whether persons seeking seats have the qualifications prescribed by the Constitution, and have been elected and returned according to the laws. THE PEOPLE are the *sole judges* of every other qualification. Otherwise, Congress can nullify or even *destroy* the right of election

Secured to the people alone, and thus make a congressional despotism.

"The right of the States to representation in Congress is the clearest of all rights under the Constitution. It is the right without which no other right can exist and no obligation can be imposed. I have an abiding faith that the President will not permit its destruction by test oaths or otherwise. He was for the Union against the South; and it is my opinion that he will show himself for the Union against *Massachusetts* when the issue comes."

I have only to add that the italics of this remarkable letter are Mr. Hill's. I believe it expresses the feeling of four fifths of the men and of all the women of Georgia. If it is not a formal declaration of war against the nationality of the government I am unable to comprehend the force of its very plain and explicit language; and if it does not indicate an insolence and dictatorial spirit without precedent I have read history to little purpose.

Let Congress dispense with the test oath, and give us back the good old times! Let it admit all these Rebel generals and colonels and politicians, and so restore universal harmony! Let us all join hands and cover the nakedness of the land, and assure the world that it is not scarred with a million graves, and that there has been no war for lofty principles and the natural rights of man, but only a friendly contest of strength and endurance, in which the victors concede everything to the vanquished on the sole condition that the latter pronounce the former magnanimous!

Whether the North Carolina "dirt-eater," or the South Carolina "sand-hiller," or the Georgia "cracker," is lowest in the scale of human existence would be difficult to say. The ordinary plantation negro seemed to me, when I first saw him in any numbers, at the very bottom of not only probabilities, but also possibilities, so far as they affect human relations; but these specimens of the white race must

be credited with having reached a yet lower depth of squalid
and beastly wretchedness. However poor or ignorant or
unclean or improvident he may be, I never yet found a
negro who had not at least a vague desire for a better condition, an undefined longing for something called freedom, a
shrewd instinct of self-preservation. These three ideas —
or, let me say, shadows of ideas — do not make the creature
a man, but they lift him out of the bounds of brutedom.
The Georgia " cracker," as I have seen him since leaving
Milledgeville, seems to me to lack not only all that the
negro does, but also even the desire for a better condition
and the vague longing for an enlargement of his liberties
and his rights. Such filthy poverty, such foul ignorance,
such idiotic imbecility, such bestial instincts, such grovel-
ling desires, — no trick of words can make plain the scene
in and around one of these " cracker " habitations, no fertil-
ity of language can embody the simple facts for a Northern mind, and the case is one in which even seeing itself is
scarcely believing.   Time and effort will lead the negro up
to intelligent manhood; but I almost doubt if they will be
able to lead this " white trash " even up to respectability.

Ex-Governor Herschel V. Johnson closed the late Convention with a brief speech. It brought tears to the eyes
of many delegates, was ordered to be spread upon the
journal, and has been very generally printed in the newspapers of the State. During my journeyings since the adjournment of the Convention, I have often been referred to
it as an epitome of Georgia feeling and judgment. It is
scarcely less noticeable for what it contains than for what it
does not contain ; but I note now only a single paragraph
in which he speaks of the freedmen. It is as follows : —

" We are now to enter upon the experiment whether the class
of people to which we are in future to look as our laboring class
can be organized into efficient and trustworthy laborers. That
may be done — or I hope it may be done — if we are left to our-

selves. If we cannot succeed, others need not attempt it; and I trust that in the future we will have the poor privilege of being let alone in reference to this class of our people."

I bear you sorrowful witness that there spoke the true Georgian. He is sublimely ignorant of the fact that the negro is also a child of the Republic; sublimely ignorant of the other fact, that the war has restored to him certain human rights. He only sees so many machines, the mission of which it is to do his work; and he asks you to let him alone in their management. He begs of you to give him this "poor privilege," and gravely tells you that they cannot be made to work at all if this be denied him!

I also bear you sorrowful witness that every Georgian despises the negro. As a slave he was well enough; but as a man he is only a poor, pitiful creature, from whom little or no good can be expected. Secessionists and Unionists are just alike, so far as I can see, in contempt for him, and alike in wanting him out of the way.

"I hope you will remain in the State long enough," said a very intelligent gentleman of Northern Georgia to me, nearly a month ago, — "I hope you will remain in the State long enough to see what a miserable thing the negro is, the poor creature who brought on the war and is bound to be exterminated before it ends; for it won't end till they or we are gone." There also spoke the true Georgian, a kindly man, a sober judge, and a professed Unionist.

From the average Georgia stand-point, he is half insane who talks of educating the negro. "What, build school-houses for the niggers!" exclaimed a citizen to a Cincinnati gentleman with whom I sat in the public room at the Macon hotel. "Well, when we do, I'll just let you know." Some of the leading men see and say that the interests of the State will be promoted by educating the freedmen; but nine tenths of the people sneer just as the Macon man did. Yet within four blocks of that same hotel I saw the negro porter of a store

15   v

laboring at his spelling-book in the corner, when no custom-
ers were in; and a young negro woman with her spelling-
book fastened to the fence, that she might study while at
work over the wash-tub.   Still I'm everywhere told that
the nigger can't learn, and money spent in educating him
would be money thrown away!

Georgia is the richest and most enlightened of the Gulf
States.   It asks Northern capital, but it holds out no induce-
ment for the development of the mental and moral capital
dormant in its negroes and poor whites.   For which of these
classes there is the best chance in the coming years it is
hard to say.   There certainly can be no more wretched
human beings than the "crackers."   The adults of this
class can have no hope for this life, and the children will
grow to the estate of their parents unless the spirit of caste
is broken down and common schools are built up.   The
universal prophecy that the negro will not work is under-
mining his humanity and forcing him to its partial fulfilment.
The universal contempt in which he is held is driving him
into hatred of his contemners and such vagabondage as leads
by swift steps to the grave.

XXXVIII

MATTERS IN NORTHWESTERN GEORGIA.

ATLANTA, November 23, 1865.

ATLANTA is built on something less than a hundred
hills; and, excepting Boston, is the most irregularly
laid out city I ever saw.   In fact, the greater portion of it
seems never to have been laid out at all till Sherman's army
came in here.   That did the work pretty thoroughly, — so
thoroughly, indeed, as to prove remarkably destructive ability in his men.

Coming here has dispelled two illusions under which I rested : first, that Atlanta was a small place ; and second, that it was wholly destroyed. It was a city of about fourteen thousand inhabitants two years ago, and it was not more than half burned last fall. The entire business portion, excepting the Masonic Hall building and one block of six stores and a hotel, was laid in ruins, and not a few of the larger residences in all parts of the city were also burned. But the City Hall and the Medical College, and all the churches, and many of the handsomer and more stylish private dwellings, and nearly all the houses of the middling and poorer classes, were spared ; and on the first of last June there was ample shelter here for at least six or eight thousand persons. Of course, however, when the entire business portion of the place had disappeared, the city had been practically put out of the way for the time being, even if nothing be said of the fact that it was depopulated by military orders.

The marks of the conflict are everywhere strikingly apparent. The ruin is not so massive and impressive as that of Columbia and Charleston ; but as far as it extends it is more complete and of less value. The city always had a mushroom character, and the fire-king must have laughed in glee when it was given over into his keeping. There is yet abundant evidence of his energy, — not so much in crumbling walls and solitary chimneys, as in thousands of masses of brick and mortar, thousands of pieces of charred timber, thousands of half-burned boards, thousands of scraps of tin roofing, thousands of car and engine bolts and bars, thousands of ruined articles of hardware, thousands upon thousands of tons of *débris* of all sorts and shapes. Moreover, there are plenty of cannon-balls and long shot lying about the streets, with not a few shell-struck houses in some sections ; and from the court-house square can be seen a dozen or more forts, and many a hillside from which the timber was cut so that the enemy might not come upon the city unawares.

From all this ruin and devastation a new city is springing up with marvellous rapidity. The narrow and irregular and numerous streets are alive from morning till night with drays and carts and hand-barrows and wagons, — with hauling teams and shouting men, — with loads of lumber and loads of brick and loads of sand, — with piles of furniture and hundreds of packed boxes, — with mortar-makers and hod-carriers, — with carpenters and masons, — with rubbish removers and house-builders, — with a never-ending throng of pushing and crowding and scrambling and eager and excited and enterprising men, all bent on building and trading and swift fortune-making.

Chicago in her busiest days could scarcely show such a sight as clamors for observation here. Every horse and mule and wagon is in active use. The four railroads centring here groan with the freight and passenger traffic, and yet are unable to meet the demand of the nervous and palpitating city. Men rush about the streets with little regard for comfort or pleasure, and yet find the days all too short and too few for the work in hand. The sound of the saw and plane and hammer rings out from daylight till dark, and yet master-builders are worried with offered contracts which they cannot take. Rents are so high that they would seem fabulous on Lake Street, and yet there is the most urgent cry for store-room and office-room. Four thousand mechanics are at work, and yet five thousand more could get immediate employment if brick and lumber were to be had at any price. There are already over two hundred stores, so called, and yet every day brings some trader who is restless and fretful till he secures a place in which to display another stock of goods.

Where all this eagerness and excitement will end no one seems to care to inquire. The one sole idea first in every man's mind is to make money. That this apparent prosperity is real no outsider can believe. That business is planted on sure foundations no merchant pretends. That there will come a pause and then a crash, a few prudent men prophesy.

Meantime Atlanta is doing more than Macon and Augusta combined. The railroad from here to Chattanooga clears over one hundred thousand dollars per month, and could add fifty thousand more to that enormous sum if it had plenty of engines and rolling stock. The trade of the city is already thirty per cent greater than it was before the var, and it is limited only by the accommodations afforded, and has even now spread its wings far out on streets heretofore sacred to the privacy of home.

Wonderful as is the new growth of the city, its original existence is still more wonderful. It is two hundred and fifty miles from the sea-coast, in the midst of a country but moderately productive, not in the vicinity of any navigable river, and without facilities of any kind for manufacturing purposes; yet it was founded less than twenty years ago, is now the fourth place in population in the State, and bids fair to be the second in less than five years.

It can never be a handsome city, but its surrounding hills and slopes offer beautiful sites for elegant residences. Many of the buildings now going up are of frail and fire-tempting character, but in several instances owners are putting in solid one or two-story brick blocks, — intending at some future time to add two or three stories more. Few of the present merchants were here before the war, — few of them are yet to be considered as permanent residents of the city. The streets never were either neat or tasty; now, what with the piles of building material and the greater piles of *débris* and rubbish, and the vast amount of teaming and hauling over them, they are simply horrible. The former residents are coming home, and in the private portions, as

well as the business section, there is great activity of repair
and refurnishing.　The place has no decent hotel, — no one
has yet found time to build a large house.　Of small and
wretched fifth-rate hotels there are half a dozen; but better
than any of these are several of the very numerous so-
called private boarding-houses, which send their porters
and runners to every train, receive all classes of transient
guests, charge the usual four dollars per day, and are hotels
in everything but name.　The city handsomely supports two
of the largest daily newspapers in the State, has five or six
churches, a medical college, two or three select schools, and
is talking about an academy.

These northwestern counties were all strongly opposed to
secession in 1860 – 61, and this Congressional district furnished several hundred soldiers to our armies.　Its disposition toward the government is now, as a whole, probably
better than that of any other district in the State.　Its
slaves constituted less than one fourth of its aggregate population before the war, and in general there is much less
complaint here than elsewhere as to the disposition of the
freedman.　The people pretty generally quietly accept the
decision of the sword, and the men who prate of State
supremacy are far less in number than in the district
below.

The social condition of affairs is deplorable in the extreme.　It results mainly from the bitter feud between the
two classes of people, — those who "went with the State,"
and those who remained true to the Union.　While the
country was under the control of Johnston and Hood, the
Union men suffered almost every conceivable wrong and
outrage.　Their families were turned out of doors, their
wives were abused and insulted, their daughters were maltreated and ruined, their farms were pillaged and desolated,
their houses were sacked and burned, and they themselves
were imprisoned and tortured; nay, many of them were

hunted down like wild beasts, and shot like dogs when at the point of death by starvation. That the Union men now seek to strike a balance for the indignities and barbarities of other days is only most natural. Whence a constant turmoil in all sections, which results in the sudden death of not a few persons and the arrest and imprisonment of large numbers. The leading delegate of this section went so far as to say, in the late State Convention, that three fifths of the men in all Cherokee Gèorgia are now under indictment. I hope this is an exaggeration; but my own observations convince me that the truth is at least so bad as to present a picture of civil commotion only less painful than the commotion of war itself.

The people of this section are generally hardy and industrious, and in many respects are so much unlike those of some other sections of the State, that "Cherokee Georgia" is a term of contempt and reproach with the aristocrats and land monopolists of the southern and southeastern parts. I found the delegates from this quarter lacking in something of the polish of those from the cities, but no class of men in the late Convention showed a wider range of general information. I find the common people no more ignorant than elsewhere in the State, and it is certainly to be said in their favor that they are not sitting in sullen indifference nor idling in helpless poverty. Poor they are, having little left but lean bodies and homespun garments; but I judge that the whites of these twenty counties in the northwest have done more work since the close of the war than the whites of any fifty counties below the middle line of the State.

I am very certain that the President's course in granting pardons so freely to leading Rebels in this State has not strengthened the faith nor upheld the hands nor encouraged the hearts of these mountain men who were always our friends. They should receive such favors as government has to give; but I am everywhere told that the golden apples

are cast into the laps of men not yet cleansed of love for the
Rebellion, while the original Unionists, who kept the faith
unto the end, are generally cuffed and sent away empty-
handed.   As I have already said, hundreds of these men
suffered every possible outrage at the hands of the Rebels.
You need n't undertake to tell them who is to blame for
their treatment, for they know that Joe Brown and Howell
Cobb could have prevented it by a word.

Scores of women, whose husbands were abused or imprisoned, went to Brown or Cobb for protection or relief,
only to be insulted or coldly turned away.   Now when these
men and women see Joe Brown put forward and accepted
as Presidential adviser for this State, and see Howell Cobb
restored to all his rights of person and property, is it any
wonder that they manifest little love for the government, —
nay, any wonder that some of these men swear roundly, and
exclaim, " D—n your government, if it has no favors for
anybody but black-hearted Rebels! "   When I talked with
one of them, he cut me short with, " Treason a crime? D—n
it, loyalty 's the only crime, I think ! "

XXXIX.

MATTERS IN CENTRAL GEORGIA.

GREENSBORO, November 25, 1865.

FINALLY I have found what I began to fear I should
not see in this Southern trip, — evidence that it is possible for at least some persons in this section of the country
to know and appreciate order and beauty and taste and
neatness and home-like comfort.

Greensboro is the only place of thirty or forty in which

I have stopped that may challenge comparison with Northern towns on the score of general appearance. It is the shire town of Greene County, has a population of sixteen hundred to two thousand persons, and is often mentioned in the State as the place where Mr. Secretary Seward once taught school. It is situated on the Georgia Railroad, about midway between Atlanta and Augusta, in the heart of a high, rolling, productive country, in which there are many good farms under fair cultivation. It formerly had a cotton factory, which is now used as barracks for the one hundred and fifty soldiers stationed here; a handsome brick college in grounds luxuriant with vines and flowers and evergreens, in which an academy is now kept; and two or three small hotels, which are now all closed. It has half a dozen substantial brick stores, and is doing a moderate trade with the well-peopled surrounding country. Its court-house is the best I have anywhere seen in the State; and two of its half-dozen churches are buildings both tasteful and costly. Its beautiful yards and gardens are not so numerous as in some other towns I have visited, but there is everywhere a noticeable absence of that glaring showiness so common in the South. In general, the little town has a very Northern appearance, — looking not indeed so much like a New England town as like a quiet county seat of Northern New Jersey or Central New York.

Finally, I have also found what I began to fear I should not see in this Southern trip, — evidence that it is possible for at least some Southern women to know and appreciate the dignity of domestic life, and to comprehend the subtile mysteries of thrifty and orderly and cleanly housekeeping.

The house of this widow lady, in which I am domiciled for a day or two, is the one house of all in which I have stopped that may challenge comparison with the house of any New England dame under the sun. It is a small cor-

15 *

ner-lot house, set round with vines and evergreens and china-trees, and having the usual cook-house and servants' quarters in the rear. Every one of its four rooms below and its three chambers above is as neat and tastefully and appropriately furnished as any house I ever saw in Massachusetts. There is a place for everything, and everything is in its place. The room assigned to me is without carpet, but its bare floor is as clean as water and soap and scrubbing-brushes can make it; its furnishing is old and quaint, but every way proper and in order; its bed will bear the most careful inspection, from the snowy counterpane to the solid cotton mattress; and in one corner is an old-fashioned reel, —evidence of how much well-ordered household economy! I confess that I am charmed and delighted, — for how much sloth and apathy and filth and shiftlessness and slovenliness has vexed and saddened my New England soul for twelve long weeks!

Nor is the comfort and good order of the household due wholly to the servants, either. There appear to be a couple of them, and they well do their work, but the head of the house is the widow lady herself; and she and the married daughter living with her superintend household affairs to their minutest detail; and I am sure that if the servants were to leave to-morrow, the home would neither fall in pieces nor go into bankruptcy. The table is well supplied, and the manner in which it is served demonstrates what my general experience in the South contradicts, — the capacity of a negro woman to be a good cook. Need I say, after all this, that the ladies of the house are ladies in the good sense of the word? It is a private boarding-house, at which chance travellers are always at liberty to ask for accommodations, and I expect to pay the usual four dollars per day; but the boarders are apparently at home, and I am treated like the guest of the family. The mistress of the house owned a few slaves, and is not very hopeful regarding free negro labor;

but in that respect she does not differ from every other native resident of the State, and I am very sure no one can be kinder to this black man working out his great destiny than she was to her slaves.

Does all this matter seem merely personal or unimportant? It is neither. The son and son-in-law of the house were both soldiers, and both suffered long imprisonment at our hands. They are now good citizens, who live by honest work. If any member of the household has any bitterness of feeling because of the war, I have failed to find it, after a good deal of conversation on all branches of the subject. They mourn the loss of property, but they accept that as part of their defeat. They wish the soldiers were out of the way ; but peaceable citizens of no town like the presence of the military. They have some prejudices against the Yankees, but they are not offensively apparent, even to one who avows himself a Yankee of the Yankees. It is not a small matter that there is even one town in the whole of this great State that may court measurement by a Northern standard ; for herein is the promise of many more such towns to be built up, when the land is purged of the spirit of slavery. It is not a small matter that one traveller has found a pleasant stopping-place ; for in that fact is proof enough how little slavery cared either for the comforts or the economies of home, and proof also of the future homes that shall rise here under the new heavens. It is neither merely personal nor unimportant that twelve weeks of travel in three of the late slave States should find but one village and one household that would lose nothing in comparison with fifty villages and some hundreds of households in Massachusetts alone. Give this people Freedom and all her handmaids, and the traveller of a dozen years hence will not need to draw such pictures as I have drawn of Southern shiftlessness and slovenliness.

Visiting many of the wretched towns of this State and

the Carolinas, and seeing how all the inhabitants live, one can scarcely wonder that the negroes sought early opportunity to break away from their old homes, and begin life on their own account. If they said, " Anything will be better than this," they exaggerated very little. The new life might bring them poverty and trouble, but it at least gave them freedom, and the poverty was no strange thing.

In such towns as Greensboro, and proportionately in others as they approximate toward it, one cannot help seeing most vivdily the other side of the question involved in their course. That freedom should bring desire for change was most natural, as all human experience testifies. Yet, seeing what that change has worked in many of the best towns of Central Georgia, one cannot help wishing the poor negro could have been content, for a time, in his old situation. His removal has reduced hundreds of these Southern women to even such necessary work as will support life, and thousands more to a certain amount of manual labor. Let no one regret this.

If there is one thing more needed in the whole South, — in the three States, I mean, which have come under my observation, — more needed here than loyalty, it is respect for labor as labor ; not merely respect for it as a means of sustaining life, but respect for it as a branch of Divine economy, respect for it as a means of human elevation. And if there is one thing more needful than to teach the *men* of the South that labor is *noble*, it is to teach the *women* of the South that labor is not *degrading*. Therefore, as one who would see the problem of man's capacity wrought out in this country to most beautiful results, I welcome the necessity which the course of the negro has forced upon so many women here. Let them work, — let them begin as children, and learn to do housework.

It is pitiful that, in this age and in this country, one should find occasion to say what is thus impliedly said ; but we shall

not see the full fruit of the war till labor is dignified in every
town and village of the whole South; and if the negro must
ignorantly many times sacrifice his own ease and comfort
now for the good of this people, as they have heretofore sacrificed his freedom and his life for their pleasure, there will
only be given another proof that "God works in a mysteri-
ous way His wonders to perform."

Yet that the negro should thus ignorantly sacrifice his ease
and comfort is none the less touching. That he does do this
is apparent to any one who looks upon the situation with un-
prejudiced eye. He does it everywhere in individual cases,
however hard that fact may be of acceptance to any of our
theorists; but in all Central Georgia he does it on a wholesale
scale. He is a human being, and it was not easy to believe
that he would do what all my experience had proved human
beings would not do except in isolated cases; yet that thousands of negroes in this section, where slavery was less a
burden than in almost any other part of the South, that thousands of negroes have left homes wherein they had every
needful care and comfort, for the uncertain chances of life by
themselves, is a fact that I cannot refuse to see. In Greensboro, in Madison, in Sparta, in Milledgeville, in Macon,
in Athens, in Washington, — go where you will in Central
Georgia, and you cannot fail to come to this conclusion. It
is neither supposition nor speculation; it is a hard, unpalpa-
ble fact.

In the Carolinas and in other parts of this State I found a
few negroes who had clearly let go the bird in hand without
any prospect of finding even one in the bush; here I find
thousands of such. I know very well that every white man,
woman, and child in the whole State is ready to swear that
every negro is worse off now than before he was freed. I
accept no such evidence; but hundreds of conversations with
negroes of every class in at least a dozen towns of this section have convinced me that the race is, on a large scale,

ignorantly sacrificing its own material good for the husks of vagabondage.

In South Carolina, as I have already said, where slavery reached its lowest estate, it was not easily possible for the negro to make his condition worse by striking out for himself. There was scarcely more than a choice between two evils, and he chose that which promised him most independence. Hereabouts his situation was different, and he has too often made the bad choice.

This must also be borne. For if the privileges of freedom are given to the negro, must he not also take its duties and responsibilities? If his exercise of the privilege of choice leads him into want and suffering, will you again enslave him with the requirement that he shall live with the old master or mistress who treated him well? You may advise him to such course, but you cannot compel him thereto. If you would secure his freedom to him, you must let him have his own way in this regard, even if you see that it will bring him to the utmost misery.

I went into the outskirts of Macon and hunted up many of the negroes who had left old homes in the city and surrounding country. I did the same thing at Madison and Milledgeville. Hundreds and hundreds of them will feel the pangs of cold and hunger this winter who might have kept every necessity and many of the comforts of life, if they had chosen to remain with those who formerly held them as slaves. Who shall have the heart to blame them? For they were in search of nothing less noble and glorious than freedom. They were in rags and wretchedness, but the unquenchable longing of the soul for liberty was being satisfied. Pity them I did, but blame them I could not; advise them I did, but scold them I could not.

Over by the half-built Confederate arsenal in Macon I found a little hut in which were eleven negroes, — an old man, a middle-aged man, three women and six children.

There was beside in the hut only a couple of bundles of old rags, which answered, I suppose, for beds, three or four rude stools, a single chair, a bag of meal, four or five pounds of bacon, and half a dozen cooking utensils.

"Well, Uncle," said I, after he had told me that he was raised near Knoxville, some thirty miles away, — "well, Uncle, what did you come up to the city for? Why did n't you stay on the old place? Did n't you have a kind master?"

"I 's had a berry good master, mass'r," he said, "but ye see I 's wanted to be free man."

"But you were just as free there as you are here."

"P'r'aps I is, but I 's make a livin' up yer, I dun reckon; an' I likes ter be free man whar I 's can go an' cum, an' nobody says not'ing."

"But you would have been more comfortable on the old place: you would have had plenty to eat and plenty of clothes to wear."

"Ye see, mass'r, de good Lo'd he know what 's de best t'ing fur de brack, well as fur de w'ite; an' He say ter we dat we should cum up yer, an' I don't reckon He let we starve."

I had some further talk with the family, but could only get for answer to my many times varied question, that they came to the city to get freedom.

Near Milledgeville I found another of these crowded cabins, in which lived a man and his wife and seven children, the eldest of whom could not have been over twelve or thirteen years of age. He was an intelligent fellow, and there was a certain air of spruceness about his cabin rather uncommon. I had much talk with him. He came up from Fort Valley country, he said, an' he reckoned he could get something to do after a bit. 'T was rather hard times, he knew, an' good many black people was comin' to de city, but he reckoned they 'd all git through the winter some way.

"But don't you think," said I, "that it would have been better for a great many of them to remain on the plantations or with their old masters and mistresses in town?"

"Wa'l now ye see, sah, das a Scriptur' what says if de man hab a little to eat, an' he eat with a 'tented mind, he be better off dan de man what hab de fat ox an' is n't 'tented."

There seemed no further occasion to argue the case with this man at least. Elsewhere in the same neighborhood I talked with other negroes. Many of them had left comfortable homes, but all seemed to think they could get along somehow through the winter. It was a warmish day, and many of the women were sitting on the ground on the sunny side of their huts, engaged, as so many negro women everywhere are, in knitting socks or stockings.

This morning I walked out to the little negro village near Greensboro, where are living many blacks who were houseservants in the town, as well as some who have come in from the country. Their average condition is better than that of those in the neighborhood of large cities, but yet it is impossible but that many of them must either suffer or steal before spring. I am convinced that many of those who were servants in town had pleasant homes, and did not want for any of the simple comforts of life.

"Well, Auntie," said I to one of them, a weather-beaten old creature, who looked as though she had seen at least sixty years, but was as vigorous about her small housework as a girl of twenty, — "well, Auntie, how do you get along in your freedom?"

"No reason to make complaint, sah. I has sum soin' and some washin', and 'pears like I had nuf ter do."

"But you are getting to be an old woman, and your old mistress would have given you a good home as long as you live. Would n't it have been better to stay with her?"

"Well now, honey, ye don't see only one side 'pears like. I be an ole woman as ye say, but I 's mighty peart yet, and

I don't reckon I'll want fur nothing dis yer winter; and when de wa'm season cum agin, mebbe I go back to town ter live."

"What did you leave the old place for, Auntie, any way?"

"What fur? '*Joy my freedom!*'"

The directness and exultation of this answer half puzzled and half disconcerted me. I knew how this old woman had lived, — knew what a favorite she had been in the family in which she had formerly been owned, — knew what large liberty had been always given her in everything. What is the "freedom" that war has brought this dusky race?

XL.

MATTERS IN EASTERN GEORGIA.

AUGUSTA, November 28, 1865.

AUGUSTA is a fine point for business; and when it is once more brought in connection with Charleston and Savannah by railroad, Atlanta, busy as she is now, and confident as she is of the future, will need to have sharper eyes and even yet more restless energy if she would not be distanced.

The close of the war found more cotton, probably, stored in and about this city than at any other point in the South. One feels justified, from all that is said, in estimating the amount at fully fifty thousand bales; and many dealers put the figure at sixty thousand, while a few even fix it as high as sixty-five thousand. Very little of this was burned, and most of it was in the hands of private parties. Consequently, there has been a large business here in the article all the fall, in which there is not yet very much abatement.

w

In this Congressional District, the Fifth, the contest at the recent election was more animated than in any other district in the State, — and one of the worst Rebels in the district carries the day.

Colonel James D. Matthews, of Oglethorpe County, is a lawyer by profession, and was a colonel in the Rebel army. He is the most uncompromising malcontent in the congressional delegation from this State, was by all odds the noisiest and bitterest Rebel in the late Convention, and is about as badly disposed toward the government and the new order of things as any man I have met in all my tour. He is of very cold, hard, severe, inflexible cast of countenance, has a taunting and aggressive manner, and speaks in a high, falsetto, sarcastic, impassioned tone of voice. His appearance, his manner, and his voice alike attest his individuality. He made many speeches during the Convention, and each of them was galling and venomous. He was the most audacious of those who demanded pardon for Jeff Davis, the most haughty of those who advocated the dogma of State sovereignty, the most galling of those who sneered at the supremacy of the nation, the most insolent of those who denounced the government for requiring a repudiation of the Rebel war debt, the most domineering of those who fought everything looking toward a recognition of the legal rights of the negro, the most stubborn of those who resisted the effort to establish co-operative action between the people and the Freedmen's Bureau.

The moral of this election is so plain that he who runs may read.   And the city of Augusta, which would have General Steedman believe she is loyal, cast three fourths of her vote for this malignant Matthews!

In the stage between here and Milledgeville I rode a month ago with two gentlemen of considerable local weight and prominence, who were both anti-Secessionists in 1860 – 61. They talked of the approaching Convention, and of its prob-

able action in redistricting the State for representatives.
"Well, Colonel," said the younger, himself a man of over
forty years, — "well, Colonel, what will be our proper
course when we are once more fully restored to the
Union?" The answer came, after a moment's consideration, "We must strike hands with the Democratic party
of the North, and manage them as we always have." There
was a pause while we rattled down the hill, and then the
questioner responded, "That's just it; they were ready
enough to give us control if we gave them the offices; and
I reckon they've not changed very much yet." There was
then conversation on other matters; but half an hour later,
after a mile or so of silence, the Colonel suddenly resumed,
"Yes, sir, our duty is plain; we shall be without weight
now that slavery's gone, unless we do join hands with them.
Andy Johnson will want a re-election, and the united Democratic party must take him up; it shall be a fair division,—
we want the power and they want the spoils."

"I hate the Yankees with my whole heart," said a gen-
teelly dressed woman who sat just behind me in the cars the
other day coming to the city. "And I hate them so bad
that I'm going off to Texas to live," answered the gentleman with whom she talked.

At Atlanta I saw a family of seven persons, from the
county above this, on their way to that region; at Greensboro I saw a family of thirteen, including the old folks, with
daughter, son-in-law, and grandchildren, and having a wagon-
load of trunks, bound for that State; at Berzelia, twenty
miles west of here, I fell in with a man who had just returned from an inspection tour, and would start for there
next week at the head of a company of twenty. I asked
him if he did n't like it in this State. To which he answered,
"I am going to see if I can't get shet of the Yankees." A
man whom I sat opposite at breakfast this morning told his
neighbor that a common acquaintance from Athens left last

week, and he knew of another family near Washington who would go in a few days. I have heard of very few persons who fall in with the Alabama scheme for emigrating to Brazil; but I am convinced that in the Central and Eastern sections of Georgia there are many who purpose moving to Texas, and only in one or two instances have I heard any reason assigned but a desire to get away from the Yankees.

Yet not all the people of this section are of such antagonistic spirit, — not all of them are so at war with common sense and the conquering Yankee.

"I don't believe I'll ever vote again in my life," said a young man from Athens to me; "the first vote and the only vote I ever cast was for the revolution candidates from our county to the Convention of 1861. I left college and went into service two days after Sumter was fired on, and I stayed in the army to the bitter end. I've got enough of war, and if there is ever another in this country I shall emigrate."

"I'm d—n glad the war's over, any how," said a Madison gentleman to me. He was dressed like a gentleman and mostly spoke like one, but profanity is much more common down here than in the North. "I did all I could for the revolution, and now I'm going to do all I can for the Union. You mustn't ask me to give up my idea of State rights, — that's in my bones, and never can be got out; but I assure you it shall never give any more trouble, so far as I am concerned."

When Federal soldiers died in the South, while held as prisoners, they were very rarely given burial in the cemeteries of the town or city in which they died, but were generally packed away outside the walls, if, indeed, their bodies were not ignominiously buried in by-places. Here, however, the bodies of such men were all given decent burial in the large and beautiful city cemetery, — a fact which must be infinitely grateful to the friends and relatives of the two hundred boys who finished their warfare in this city. They

lie in three long rows in the southeastern corner of the
cemetery, and can readily be identified by a reference to the
sexton's books. When the first ones were laid there, now
two years ago, some of the extra-finished Rebels of the city
were very much offended, and complained of the sexton for
his action in the matter, saying that it was an insult to bury
Yankees there.   With gratitude and admiration I set down
the answer of the sexton: " If you ever get to heaven,
you 'll find plenty of Yankees there; and 't wont hurt anybody to lie alongside a Yankee in here, I reckon."

Down on the river-bank yesterday afternoon I had some
talk with a middle-aged gentleman, who said he had always
been a Union man.   He kept out of the war, but only at the
expense of all his property.   He thought there were not
over one hundred men in this whole county who could be
trusted as Union men ; he was very certain the President
ought not to pardon Howell Cobb, and reckoned it would
have been a good thing if General Wilson had strung him
up the first time he got eyes on him ; he wanted South
Carolina blotted out of existence as a State, and allowed it
would suit every Union man in the South if she was turned
over to the niggers ; he could never vote for a man who was
a Secessionist, and had n't voted at the recent congressional
election ; he was glad the President had paroled Alexander
Stephens, though he wanted a man to be one thing or t' other,
not half Union and half Secesh, and he hoped C. C. Clay
would soon be paroled ; as for Jeff Davis, he did n't know,
though he reckoned the old fellow might as well be set loose
on t' other side the ocean ; and, finally, he thought we should
have more peace in the country if each side, the North and
the South, just hung about a thousand parsons !

The people of this city and vicinity are unusually exercised about the pardon of Jeff Davis.   There are two classes.
A young man, representative of one class, who had been a
major in the Rebel service, said to me last evening, " I be-

lieve President Davis and General Lee the two greatest men of the present generation, and I feel like fighting every time I think how Mr. Davis is kept shut up in Fortress Monroe, and every time I hear the great and good Lee maligned by the Yankees." An elderly gentleman who lives a few miles below the city, and who was a delegate in the late Convention, said the other day, in a stage wherein I also was a passenger, "Mr. Davis ought to be hung, but not by the Yankees; he was the Marplot of our cause, and he ought to be hung, not for treason, but for his cursed mismanagement in the Presidential office of the Confederacy. We should have succeeded but for his obstinacy; and his favoritism toward every man we distrusted and every man who proved himself incompetent, did us more harm than Yankee guns ever did." This gentleman represents the second class, which is just as anxious for Mr. Davis's pardon as is the first named. I have heard much talk about his pardon in all sections, but in none more than this; and I learn that some of the ladies of this city, stimulated by the recent example of their sister-sympathizers in Baltimore, are canvassing the expediency of getting up a monster petition of the women of Georgia in his behalf.

I saw Alexander H. Stephens to-day, — a little old man with most marvellous eyes, looking not so much like a human being as like a character from one of Dickens's stories. Yet if Georgians reverence anybody it is Mr. Stephens; and there is n't the least question but that his presence in the State is beneficial in the best sense. He resists all importunities to make a public speech; but I am told that he converses freely with all who call upon him, and that he urges everybody to accept the issue of the war in the most cheerful and liberal spirit. While in Columbus, two weeks ago, I was told of a letter he wrote to a friend in that city immediately after the famous Hampton Roads conference. I tried in every way to get a sight of it, but without success.

The gentleman who told me of it had read it, and used these words in respect thereto : "*He said that peace could be obtained on terms not humiliating to the South, and that it ought to be made at once, but Mr. Davis and his principal advisers did not want peace.*"

I hear much talk about Wirz during the last three or four days, because the last of the illustrated papers chronicles his execution, I suppose. Winder is generally considered the chief brute, but Wirz is held to have been a willing tool. Of course the people don't readily own that the Andersonville cruelties were practised in their State, and occasionally I find a man who seeks to justify them. The great majority of the people, however, condemn them ; and I am constantly assured that such models of Christian manhood as Howell Cobb and Robert Toombs did all they could to improve the condition of the prisoners. Most persons claim that there was much perjured testimony given at the trial, but many admit that General Wilson would have been justified in hanging Wirz as soon as he caught him. On the whole, — though one young man said to me, "He was a bully fellow and died game," — I believe there is a general sense of relief at Wirz's execution. "There 's one wretch the less left to remind us of the terrible war," earnestly said a very intelligent Macon gentleman.

I have talked with many of the planters of this section. Most of them complain of the negroes ; and General Tillson, State Commissioner of the Freedmen's Bureau, says he is satisfied that the blacks are not generally doing more than about half the work they might, though he considers this quite a good proportion when all the facts of the situation are taken into account. Many of the planters, however, are making arrangements to introduce white labor. I have, within the last four days, heard of no less than nine leading men, in their respective localities, who either have already made contracts for white labor or are soon going

North to secure it.   One of these planters left here yesterday for New York, to arrange for sixty men for himself
alone, and for thirty more for some of his neighbors.   He
will get Germans if possible, and does not doubt but that
they can readily be taught to make cotton with proficiency.
" The only way in which we can control the labor of the
free negro is to bring him in competition with the white
laborer," is the language of scores of men.

WAYNESBORO, November 29, 1865.

" There are two places in the State," said an acquaintance
to me at Augusta, " where they 'd as soon shoot a man as a
dog, — Albany and Waynesboro.   I 've been in Albany
nine times in the course of three or four years, and have
seen a big row every time I was there.   Waynesboro is
just as bad, only it is n't so large a place.   They manage to
shoot half a dozen men a year there, though, without much
trouble."   It was a hint to walk very circumspectly, and,
remembering Albany, I am giving it due heed.

Waynesboro is n't a lovely place, by any means.   In
fact, I don't see why anybody should desire to live here;
and a forced residence of half a year might very well make
a man long to be shot.   Happily, though the town is the
county seat of Burke, but few persons do live here, — five
hundred, perhaps.   From Greensboro to Waynesboro is
about one hundred miles, but those miles space the distance from civilization to barbarism.   Not to be unjust to
Waynesboro, let me say that it has a hotel, and a church,
and two or three stores, and a good many dram-shops, and
at least a hundred residences.

The town is the present terminus of the railroad from
Augusta to Savannah, and therefore every traveller must pay
it at least small tribute.   It is thirty miles below Augusta,
and stages run from here to make connection with the
Savannah end of the railroad.   About sixty miles of the

line was destroyed by Sherman's army, and that sixty miles of staging was probably the worst in the whole South. Fortunately,—for I must make the trip to-night and to-morrow, — fifteen miles of the gap have been filled, and there are now but forty-five miles to make in these terrible old ambulance coaches. That will take ten hours at least, beginning at eleven P. M. The ride of six or seven hours in the chill November night, over a new and wretched road, through the low and marshy piny woods, will be very pleasant — for those who like it!

Most of the counties in this section elected original Secessionists to the Convention, and have not changed their course of action in respect to the Legislature. Some of the men sent to the Convention were such notorious Rebels that the story was started immediately on their election that they would be arrested. Of course it had no other foundation than mere rumor. Yet, if I am not wrongly informed in regard to several of those elected to the lower house, almost the last place in which they should be is in a body called to legislate so as to restore the State's relations to the Union.

I scarcely need add that there is hereabouts a strong surface hatred of the Yankees. Officers on duty tell me some very curious stories illustrative of this fact. I am assured by one whose veracity no man can question, that in an adjoining county there is a public league of young women who have vowed not to speak to a Federal soldier under any circumstances whatever. Insolent treatment of soldiers and officers on the street is so common that it excites little or no remark. One of the drivers of the stage-line tells me that only three days ago a man refused to ride in his coach because an officer of the army had a seat therein. It is confidently reported that in one neighboring county young ladies have been seen within a fortnight wearing little secession flags in their hats; but I am slow to believe this

16

story, though it circulates on what appears to be good authority. While my acquaintance with some of the better class of citizens furnishes no cause for the assertion that there is unusual hostility to the government or to people from the North, the every-day language of the lower classes is clear proof of the existence of what I have designated as surface hatred.

As a curious specimen of what one hears, take the following little speech made by an apparently intelligent man to a group of half a dozen persons, of whom I was one : —

"I've sent an advertisement to the paper for a job of overseeing some plantations next year. I reckon I could do that right lively. O, I tell you, I can do up some tall cussin' when I get started. Can't lick free niggers, but I don't know if there's any law ag'in cussin' 'em, and I believe it does 'em a heap o' good. It's next best to lickin'. Jest cuss one o' 'em right smart for 'bout five minutes, and he'll play off peart. Probably the Yankees don't like that style, but I ha'n't no use for a Yankee no how. I had a lot of likely negroes, but they're all gone; had Confederate money, but that's all gone; and I've got a heap o' Confederate bonds, but they a'n't worth a damn. I reckon God Almighty fought on the other side in this war. He used to smile on us, but He has n't given us anything but frowns lately. I don't care a damn, but I don't like to see my friends all so cut up about it. I can git along well enough. I should like to lick a hundred free negroes jest once all 'round. If I did n't bring 'em to know their places, I'd pay ten dollars apiece for all I failed on. But the Yankees give us our orders, — we mus n't lick the freedmen, they say. Free-damn-cusses I call 'em. I reckon 't a'n't ag'in no law to swa'r at 'em, and damn me if I can't do that ar. Yes, sir, God Almighty was ag'in us, but I 'low 't won't be wrong to cuss the free niggers. Yes, sir, God Almighty was ag'in us. . . . Waal, I ha'n't no use for a Yankee, — they're low-down, triflin' fellows, any how, and I reckon I shall have to play a lone hand and git 'long the best I can by myself."

The State-rights doctrine flourishes here much more vigorously than in the northern part of the State. "I don't vote

for no man as long as I live, who did n't go with the State
in the revolution," said one man to me. I should scarcely
exaggerate, if I said that the test of a man's moral worth is
his position on this question. State allegiance is made a
sine qua non, apparently, by everybody. " I ha'n't got no
use for a man who went ag'in the State, though," said one
who had been telling me at some length how he opposed secession. " We shall have to knuckle down a little more, I
reckon," remarked one gentleman to another, in the hotel at
Augusta, " but I shall be a Calhoun man as long as I live."
No one argues the point, as some do in South Carolina. It
seems to be the common average sentiment that only a secondary allegiance is due to the general government.

I asked one of the delegates to the late Convention what
the war had settled, and his answer was, " Well, it settled
that the North was the strongest, and that the negroes are
free."

" But did it settle nothing in regard to State rights ? " I
continued.

" It settled that you are able to enforce your belief on that
question, but I don't believe it has changed the opinion of a
single Southern man," said he; and after a moment he added, " but I 've no idea we shall ever go to war on that point;
we down here have had war enough, and you may hold your
opinion just as I hold mine."

The planters hereabouts are not generally hopeful in regard to the availability of free negro labor. I had some
conversation with a knot of them, in which the question of
white labor came up.

" We shall have to have control of the free nigroes, or
import white men to do the work," said one of them.

I asked if the negroes would n't work if they were treated
exactly as white men would be in the same circumstances.

" No, a free nigroe is a free nigroe, any how."

" But," said I, " that way of talking and feeling cannot be

beneficial either to him or to your interests. Why not use him fairly, like a man?"

"The trouble is jest here," said another, "he don't know his place. If you let us alone, we 'll teach him, and then I reckon we 'll git along with him better."

"But what do you mean by teaching him his place?" I asked.

A third man took up the question, and answered: "Our people are restive at what they call outside interference. The negro is n't to blame for his freedom. He served us faithfully all through the war, and I sincerely believe very few planters have any desire to see him injured. We know his ways; and if you give us time, I think we shall be able to get him back into his place again, — not as a slave, but as a good producer."

They kept up a conversation among themselves, till the first again responded, "A free nigroe is a poor cuss, any how."

To which a fourth one answered, "I 'll tell you how 't is: a free nigger 's jest like any low-down white fellow, — pull off your coat and work with him, and he does well enough; put it on and go off to town, and he shirks." Numbers one and two seemed a little puzzled at this, and he continued: "Now I don't have a d—n bit of trouble with my fellows when I work right 'long with 'em."

"But your people don't generally go into the field and work, as our Northern farmers do," said I.

"That 's just it," said the third; and the fourth concluded, "Yes, that 's just it; we 've had too many d—n fine notions, and one of our new notions is, that we must have white labor; I go in for white labor, — yes, I do; and I 'm agoin' to put some on my plantation. I 'm goin' to work myself!"

XLI.

MATTERS IN SOUTHEASTERN GEORGIA.

SAVANNAH, December 2, 1865.

THE destruction of railroads in this State was as complete as in South Carolina, but the energy of the people in repairing damages is much greater, and, therefore, communication between the different sections ever reached by the cars is much more readily made here than there.

I have travelled over most of the stage lines in the State; and while I can't say that either the vehicles or the animals are respectably good, I can fairly own that neither are quite so bad as those in Carolina. I must decline, however, to recommend any of the lines to the patronage of the travelling public, though I will add that the use of either will furnish many new sensations to travellers from civilized countries.

In many towns there are no hotels, chance travellers finding accommodations at so-called private boarding-houses. The almost invariable charge, whether at these houses or at regular hotels, is four dollars per day, — three and a half being the rate in only two of the many towns I have visited. In the large cities, and in one or two of the large towns, I have found the table reasonably well supplied, that is, from a Southern stand-point; but elsewhere the standard is hardly up even to that of the Carolinas.

Western Georgia and Northern Georgia I found full of " runners " from Louisville and Cincinnati. They represented all branches of trade, and pretty generally reported that they were getting many orders. In this section I find more representatives of Eastern houses. I believe the delivery of goods already ordered will give a stock in the State sufficient for the coming year. Everybody seems to have a passion for keeping store, and hundreds of men are going into trade who should go into agriculture. If the coming season brings a "smash" in many towns, the prophecies of numerous business men will not be unfulfilled.

Business in the city has been very brisk all the fall, and many a merchant has had all he could do who moaned last spring for the "good old days." One of them said to me yesterday, "There's been more done in the last six months than I believed last winter would be done in two years." I have found no other place in the South where early faith in the recuperative energies of the people has met with such large reward as here. Many men seem inclined to believe that the promise will not be kept, and are prophesying a dull season next year. Others are more hopeful, and say that when the railroads connecting with Augusta, Macon, and Thomasville are repaired, the trade of the city will be fifty per cent greater than ever. This latter view seems to me the correct one; but it can hardly be appreciated by any one who is uninformed as to the numbers of Northern, and particularly Northwestern men moving into the upper and western sections of the State.

There are already many Northern men in business here, and I am told of many more who propose coming out during the winter. A considerable portion of these are men who were in the army, and not a few of them are ex-soldiers who did more or less duty in the city, and of course come here now with some social and business relations already formed. The feeling toward persons from the North is very far from being what is desirable, but several who have been here through the year say it is improving.

In the First Congressional District, Solomon Cohen, of this city, has been elected representative. He is, as his name indicates, of Hebrew descent, though a native of this country, I believe. He is a lawyer by profession, and stands among the leading members of the bar in his section. He was a delegate in the famous Charleston Democratic Convention, and was one of the few Southern men who refused to secede from that body. He was Buchanan's postmaster here, and an opponent of secession. State allegiance carried him into the post-office under the Rebel government, however, and he gave a son to the army thereof, who was killed shortly after going into service. He was a delegate in the late Convention, and was prominent in the action to secure an assumption of the Rebel war debt.

I record with pleasure that I have found two men who are eminently sound on the State-rights question. One of them has been a Rebel sergeant, and is now a railroad fireman. He stood by while three or four of us were carelessly chatting about the subject. "Dun know anything 'bout the matter myself, but old Uncle Sam says as how States ha'n't any right to kick out o' the traces, and that's enough for me." The other one of my couple is a planter, and he put this word into the conversation of a couple of his neighbors who were hair-splitting about reserved rights, &c.: "Well, I reckon it's one of the reserved rights of the Federal government to put down a rebellion, and I don't happen to know any man down to my section who proposes to dispute that right agen."

I also record with pleasure that I have found one man who is eminently sound on the negro labor question. He keeps a hotel, — the most systematic and orderly house, with one exception, that I have found in the South. He has no help but that of negroes. I asked him how he got along so admirably with them, when so many persons complained that nothing could be done with them. "Why, I treat 'em just as I would white men; pay them fair wages every Saturday night, give 'em good beds and a good table, and make 'em toe the mark. They know me, and I don't have the least trouble with 'em."

There is much want and suffering among the residents of

Southeastern Georgia. I judge they did not very readily accept the situation last spring. However that may be, there is no question about two facts, — they were despoiled of nearly all their property by the Rebel army, and have made but insignificant crops of all kinds during the present season. I am told that there are at least two thousand respectable·white persons in and around Savannah alone who must live mainly on charity through the winter. I know, too, from conversation with many of the Convention delegates from this section, that there are numbers of such persons in nearly all the twenty-five or thirty nearest counties.

Of course this general destitution affects the negroes even more seriously than the whites. I shall not exaggerate if I say that hundreds of them have already died in and about Savannah of actual starvation. What the combined effect of increased scarcity of food and increased severity of weather will be in the course of the next three months is easily conjectured. The military authorities and the officers of the Freedmen's Bureau have done, and will continue to do, all that is possible to relieve this widely-spread suffering; but they work at a double disadvantage, — the prejudice of the whites and the ignorance of the blacks hindering their labors.

The negroes are badly treated in some of the counties west and northwest of the city. I fell in, on yesterday, with a gentleman who has been making a horseback tour in six or eight of them, in search of cotton. He says hundreds of negroes have been turned off the plantations during the month, with little or no money, and but a few bushels of corn, and that many of them will be actually forced into thieving to support life. He saw one negro woman horse-whipped very severely for some offence, and saw a negro man who had been shot in the arm for declining, at first, to be turned off the plantation where he had worked all summer. He also tells me that some of the members elect of the Legislature are pledged to resist all efforts to give the negro the right to sue or be heard as evidence in the courts.

I heard one man tell another, as I sat in the car while coming down from Augusta, that his father had just turned over forty negroes off his plantation, " with corn enough for a month or so." A South Carolina lady, a refugee in this State, told me of a case in the county adjoining this, on the north : she knew a planter who had turned all the old people off his place, and among them was a very aged woman, without children, who died in less than a week from want.

I hardly need add that the freedmen throughout this section are somewhat disinclined to make contracts for another season. The rice plantation negroes are very slow to comprehend the fact that freedom does not mean idleness, — being the most degraded specimens of the race I have anywhere found. They generally seem without conscience in respect to the sin of theft, and almost infinite patience will be required to bring them out into an intelligent appreciation of their rights and responsibilities. One large planter tells me that he has offered twelve dollars per month for the season, without being able to get all the labor he wants. This case, however, I believe to be exceptional.

I have fallen in with a gentleman of middle age who was in the Rebel army about three years. He is a lawyer by profession, and is among the leading members of the bar in his section. He has been in the Legislature, and before the war was one of the most popular speakers in his district. He is a man of such ability that he was often invited to speak with Howell Cobb, Ben Hill, Lucius J. Gartrell, and other leading politicians. He claims to have been always a Union man, and says his service in the army was compulsory. He is now, at least, acting the part of a quiet, well-disposed citizen ; and his advice is found of value by the officer in command in his city. I speak thus particularly, because I do not deem it advisable to give either his name or

his residence. On a certain Sunday morning we two fell
into some talk on the condition of the State and the prospects of the future. I found him, after a time, quite ready
to speak, and he found me equally ready to listen. And
this, almost word for word, is what he said : —

"I think you are mistaken, sir. Giving suffrage to the negro
would not accomplish the ends you desire to reach, I'm afraid.
Perhaps I'm prejudiced against him, but I doubt if suffrage would
secure his freedom to him, for I know too well how he can be
wound round the finger of a plausible white man. You've been
about the State considerable, I reckon, but let me tell you just
how I see things ; and remember, I'm a native Georgian, and
expect to live and die in my State.

"The negro's first want is, not the ballot, but a chance to live,
— yes, sir, *a chance to live.* You say the government has given
him freedom, and that many good men in the North believe he
must have the ballot to secure that freedom. I tell you he's not
got his freedom yet, and isn't likely to get it right away. Why,
he can't even live without the consent of the white man! He has
no land ; he can make no crops except the white man gives him
a chance. He hasn't any timber; he can't get a stick of wood
without leave from a white man. We crowd him into the fewest
possible employments, and then he can scarcely get work anywhere but in the rice-fields and cotton plantations of a white man
who has owned him and given up slavery only at the point of the
bayonet. Even in this city he can't get a pail of water from a
well without asking a white man for the privilege. He can
hardly breathe, and he certainly can't live in a house, unless a
white man gives his consent. What sort of freedom is that?

"He has freedom in name, but not in fact. In many respects
he is worse off than he was before you made him free, for then
the property interest of his master protected him, and now his
master's hand as well as the hand of everybody else is against
him. True, he has the military here for his protection ; but there
are a thousand things done here every day under the colonel's
very nose that he don't know anything about, and that he can't
know anything about, — things he couldn't remedy if he did
know about 'em. Then, besides, there are hundreds of wrongs

of which he knows, that he can't reach and can't make right. 'T is n't such whippings as he told you about that most wrong the negro; it 's the small, endless, mean little injustice of every day that 's going to kill him off. He 's only partially protected now; take the troops away, and his chance would n't be as good as a piece of light-wood in a house on fire.

" Yes, I know there 's talk of selling them into slavery again, but I don't see how you got hold of it. I know a good many of these men they 've sent to the Legislature; and I know there 'll be private talk this session, even if there is n't open effort, to make the penal code take him back into the condition of slavery. It 'll be called 'involuntary servitude for the punishment of crime,' but it won't differ much from slavery. Why, I know men right here in this very town who believe in making the breaking of a contract a crime for which the nigger may be sold. They can do it. They can establish any system of crimes and punishments they please. I don't say they will do that, but I know many men who would vote for doing it. You Northern men can't see much of the real feeling here. Get the troops away and the State into Congress, and I give you my solemn word that I believe three fourths of the counties in the State would vote for such a penal code as would practically reduce half the negroes to slavery in less than a year.

" No, I have n't much faith in the idea that capital and labor will reconcile themselves. Things are exceptional here. Our capital is all in the hands of a few, and invested in great plantations. Our labor is all in the hands of a race supremely ignorant, and against whom we all have a strong prejudice. In my opinion, you can't reconcile these two interests unless you put the labor in subjection to the capital, that is, unless you give the white man control of the negro. Of course that can't again be allowed, and therefore there 's an almost impassable gulf between the negro and freedom unless the government aids him.

" I 'll tell you what I think you should have done. The policy of confiscation should be rigidly carried out at once. Mercy to the individual is death to the State; and in pardoning all the leading men, the President is *killing the free State he might have built here.* The landed aristocracy have always been the curse of the State, — I say that as a man born and reared in Georgia and bound to her by every possible tie. Till that is broken down there can be no real freedom here for either the negro or the poor white. The result of the war gave you a chance you never will get again to overthrow that monopoly. The negroes and the poor whites are bitter enemies in many respects, but they agree in wanting land. You should have carried out your confiscation policy, — divided up the great plantations into fifty-acre lots, and sold them to the highest and best bidders. That would have thrown some of the land into other large plantations, but it would have been fair, and would have given the poor whites and the negroes a chance. Give a man a piece of land, let him have a cabin of his own upon his own lot, and then you make him free. Civil rights are good for nothing, the ballot is good for nothing, till you make some men of every class landholders. You must give the negroes and the poor whites a chance to live, — that's the first thing you should do. The negro has a great notion to get a piece of land, and you should help him along by that notion. What does he want of a vote ? He would n't know how to use it, and 't would n't bring him anything to eat or wear if he had a dozen. Give him land, and then you touch his case exactly. He can get none now. There is n't one planter in a thousand who would sell him any ; but if you 'd carried out your confiscation policy he could have bought it like anybody else.

" I said in a speech on last Fourth of July that we had always boasted of our country as the land of the free and the home of the oppressed, while in fact it had been the land of the oppressed and the home of the slave. I said, too, that I hoped the war had made it possible for men to be free without regard to color, so that we might boast more truly than England that our flag floats over no slave. I spoke very cautiously, but what little I said was enough to kill me politically in this county. I have sometimes thought I would go North and urge your people to take the first fruits of the victory, but I should not dare to come back here after speaking up there. I 've wanted to write a letter to some leading newspaper ; but if I should say what I honestly believe, I should be killed if it ever got out that I wrote it. There is n't any freedom of speech here, or anywhere in the State, unless you speak just as the Secessionists please to let you. I should be shot before to-morrow morning if I were to publicly say what I 've said to you. Take the troops away, and off the great lines of travel there would be a reign of terror in a month. Your test oath is a bad thing. It sets an ugly precedent, and it will keep our best men out of Congress. I wish you could have reached your ends in some other way. But you've got it, and you'll have to enforce it. It will punish many who are not guilty, but it will accomplish final results which I want brought about as much as you do."

I have not met many men in this State who are more competent to speak upon the condition of the people than this captain. His remarks do not apply to this section alone. It seems to me that they are a powerful argument out of the mouth of a Southern advocate of the opposite policy, that the ballot in the hand of every man, white and black, is the only method of securing the rights of the humbler classes of all colors in the South. It will give them the power and eloquence of numbers. It will give them what party leaders will covet, and what the bitterest slave oligarchist in the whole list will not be above stooping to secure. To be sure, some should be owners of land; but the citizen, with the ballot in his hand, is a king in his own right, to whom all things are possible. Ownership of land in fee-simple does not necessarily include command of the ballot; but put into the negro's horny palm the simple right to vote, and he is at once installed into ownership of houses and lands and comforts and luxuries, from which only his own idleness or improvidence can dispossess him.

XLII.

SUMMARY OF FIVE WEEKS' OBSERVATIONS IN GEORGIA.

SAVANNAH, December 4, 1865.

"A KIND Providence has cast our lot in the midst of a land unparalleled in the richness of its soil and resources, and unsurpassed in the material elements necessary for a great, happy, powerful, and prosperous State," said ex-Governor Herschel V. Johnson, in the brief address with which he closed the session of the late State Convention. There was something of State pride in the words, and yet they are true in a very large sense. Moreover, their truth can scarcely be recognized by any one more forcibly than by the traveller fresh from the dreary wilderness of the Carolinas.

Very much of Georgia reminds one of Central New York. Not that there are pretty villages and prosperous towns, nor that there are churches and school-houses and multiplied evidences of thrift and industry and intelligence; but that Nature has been very kind in her gifts of soil and surface, setting rich acres into a beautiful and comfortable diversity of hill and valley, upland and lowland, open country and thrifty timber. The extreme southern section is much like the Carolinas in its general features, — sand and swamp, piny woods and piny barrens; but even there the soil is richer and more easily worked than in the country farther up the coast. Elsewhere, however, with local exceptions, the State is much more inviting than any part of the Carolinas to the man from the North or the West. Given perfect freedom of speech and a hearty acquiescence in the new order of things, and even the New England farmer could easily find a home within Georgia.

I note, also, that for one Northern man coming into the Carolinas to live there are at least twenty coming into this State. They come mainly from the States of Ohio, Indiana, and Illinois, though I have met men from New York, Connecticut, Michigan, and Wisconsin. The greater proportion of all these are men who were soldiers; and among those yet in service I found not a few who declare their intention of coming back here before winter is over if they are mustered out prior to Christmas.

Atlanta seems to be the centre from which this new life radiates; it is the great Exchange, where you shall find everybody if you only wait and watch. I saw it with wonder, and think of it with ever-increasing wonder. The very genius of the West, holding in the one hand all its energies and in the other all its extravagances, is there; not sitting in the supreme ease of settled pause, but standing in the nervous tension of expectant movement. What is thus affirmed of Atlanta is to a less extent true of twenty other places in that quarter of the State. That these new men will make good settlers who shall doubt?

I believe the contempt for labor and the laborer is at least quite as strong in Georgia as even in South Carolina. In the office of head-quarters at Americus I met an ex-colonel, a man of forty-five years, who had a plantation and worked thirty-four negroes. I asked him how he and his neighbors were getting on with the fall work. "I know nothing about the work, sir," said he with a lofty air, in which there was a fine sneer. At Macon I found a man who mourned for the State because her "gentlemen" had all been ruined, and she must hereafter be the home of "greasy workingmen."

It has not been held degrading to "be in trade," and accordingly hundreds of men are opening little stores in localities where those already existent find but precarious support. Since the war it has not been held degrading to superintend a plantation, and accordingly many men are looking for easy supernumerary places among the planters. But woe to the upper-class white man who proposes to come down from his proud idleness and put his own hand into farm work! And woe to him of that class who talks of learning a trade! — " What, work with niggers and Yankees ! "

The people, as a class, are much more intelligent than those of the other Southern States I have visited, though an exception in this regard must be made respecting the residents of several counties in the lower section. The State once had a good system of common schools, and, though it could not be made to live, it was productive of much benefit for a time. There is also noticeable here a certain degree and quality of energy that I did not find to the northeast. It does not manifest itself in varied industries so much as in the victory over despondency consequent upon the downfall of the Confederacy. Give the people a right mind upon the question of the dignity of labor, and you shall see here what Governor Johnson covets, — " a great, happy, powerful, and prosperous State."

I also find here, in a certain proportion, what gives the North its superiority, — a middle class of people. The Georgia aristocrat is not always, as in Carolina, a great landholder; but his aristocracy takes even a more lordly tone than that of the other State. The poor white, the " cracker," is certainly as low in the scale of human existence as anything can be in this country. Between these two far-apart extremes is a great class whose presence assures the future of the State. Altogether too many of its members despise manual labor and covet a professional life; but time will bring them good sense, and with that will come the new era in which Georgia may rightly call herself the " Empire State of the South."

The prevailing vice of the whole people seems to be whiskey drinking. I have seen three times as much here in a month as I saw in the Carolinas in two months. That the native, on starting out for a ride in the cars or stage, should take a bottle of "Bourbon" or "old rye" or "sod-corn" or some other similar liquid, is a deal more in keeping than that he should take a lunch or a clean shirt. Not to drink is to separate yourself from the mass and frequently bring upon yourself personal criticism of an unpleasant sort.

There is scarcity of food everywhere; in many whole counties the merest necessaries of life are all any family have or can afford, while among the poorer classes there is great lack of even these. Of course this poverty falls most hardly on the negroes. The Freedmen's Bureau reports something less than two thousand pauper blacks in the State; but I know it will find ten thousand as soon as the cold weather comes, if it has agencies in most of the counties. But the suffering will not by any means be confined to the blacks. Hundreds of the "cracker" families will have a hard fight to keep the lean wolf of starvation from the doors of their wretched cabins; and not a few of those who before the war never knew any want, will now know that sharpest of all wants, — the want of food.

The people accept the repudiation of the Rebel war debt quite cheerfully, considering the doleful prophecies of the gentlemen of the late Convention. So many of the delegates there so earnestly assured me that their constituents were so exceedingly anxious to pay that eighteen millions of dollars, that I was half led into believing that the President had imposed a hard condition upon the Georgians. Haply, I doubted and did n't waste much sympathy, for I find that it was all a grand game of speculation. Men who had bought the bonds at ten to twenty cents on the dollar were anxious the State should be held to the payment of their face value, but, strange as it may seem, I have n't found a single man, except those thus pecuniarily interested, who finds fault because of the repudiation!

The feeling toward Northern men is very far from being liberal or kindly. Many of them are, as I have already said, coming in here; they are tolerated, but, generally speaking, not welcomed. Having once fought to overcome resistance to the government, they must fight again to overcome prejudice against the spirit of the nation. There are many counties in the State in which Northern labor and capital would not be safe but for the presence of the military. I know that this is a broad and serious assertion. I make it with full consciousness of its meaning.

The worst feature of the political situation is that the secondary character of the authority of the general government is everywhere virtually asserted. "Our defeat was the necessary result of superiority of numbers and resources," says ex-Governor Johnson gravely, without any recognition of the fact that he and they had warred against the supreme law of the land. The one thing I have had to report from all sections, as well as the lesson taught in the earlier elections and now thunderingly echoed in the later elections, is that the general sentiment asserts that every man's fealty is first due to the State. Not to have "gone with the State" in her late struggle is now to be scorned and contemned.

That a State has the right to secede is a doctrine not so generally held in Georgia as I supposed. Of course it follows from the doctrine of State supremacy, but the common people have not pushed this latter dogma to its conclusion. The average and common talk designates the late war as "the revolution," this being a phrase I did not more than once or twice hear during my trip in South Carolina, and a phrase very little used even in North Carolina.

The Georgians like to contrast themselves with the South-Carolinians. "They are all miserable cusses," said a gentleman to me at Augusta when I talked with him about the people on the opposite side of the river. "The chief danger now is that we shall show too much servility," says Ben Hill in his everywhere-lauded card respecting the test oath. "I reckon your folks found us standing up for our rights better than they did in C'lina," queried a man of me at Columbus. "It's all very well to require certain things of South Carolina, but the President makes a mistake when he undertakes to dictate to us," observed a Macon gentleman to me. And, "Tell your people not to suppose we are of the same blood as they are," responded his companion.

The idea broached by one of the speakers in the late Convention — that a subsequent Convention could undo its work — seems to have many supporters in the State. How far any of these would like to have that work undone is more than I can say. I only know there are plenty of men who argue that it is not of binding effect because done under duress. The Convention was called in violation of the Constitution, they say, and did its work at the point of the bayonet. It is not the voice of a free people, and may be repudiated as soon as we are in the Union again.

The aggregate vote of the State in the recent election was greater for members of Congress than for Governor. "I said I never would vote again in the United States," remarked a man to me at Fort Valley, "and I'm not ready yet to do so." This person represents a small class of the voters. Another class is represented by the Atlanta man whom I heard say, "I will not vote again till I can do so without knuckling to the d—d Yankees." A larger class than either of these is represented by the young fellow in the Macon and Milledgeville cars who loudly exclaimed, "No, by G—d, I never'll vote for a man who did n't go with the State in the revolution!" The votes of that class were not cast for Governor Jenkins, but were all given for some of the congressional candidates.

The citizens of the State are excessively anxious to be let alone with regard to the freedman. Ex-Governor Johnson spoke the average sentiment of the people, when he said,

"If we cannot succeed in making an efficient laborer of him, I think it will be useless for any one else to attempt it; and I trust that we may hereafter have the poor privilege of being let alone in reference to this class of our population." In South Carolina, nearly everybody spoke of the negro as though he had become the special charge of the Yankees; here, however, with the exception of an occasional remark to the effect that Greeley ought to come down and look after his family, there is much of this talk which indirectly asserts the continued supremacy of the whites over the blacks.

That many of the leading men desire to see the negro have a fair chance is beyond all question. I have met some such men. They take pains to tell me that he was very docile and trustworthy during the war, that he is not to blame for being free, and that he ought to be justly treated now. A few men even go so far as to urge that he must be educated. This is the bright side of the picture.

There was an exciting season in the recent Methodist Annual Conference, at Macon, over the case of a certain Rev. J. H. Caldwell, whose offence appeared to be that he had preached two sermons on the "Abuses of Slavery." One would think a minister of the Gospel might speak upon that subject, but the native Georgian loves the spirit of slavery as well now as he ever did, and the action of the presiding elder in removing Mr. Caldwell was sustained by the Conference. And this in the month of November, 1865!

The complaint that the free negro will not work is even more common than in South Carolina. There I found many persons anxious to argue the point, anxious to show me why he would not work; but here the fact is assumed in a somewhat lofty manner that precludes discussion.

That the negro will not work simply because he is free is the most insolent of all the humbugs of Southern society. Thus, a Macon gentleman, who has a plantation below Albany, told me of his experience. He was in the army of

Johnston, and came home in the early part of June. He heard that many planters were losing their help, and at once went down to his plantation, called his negroes together, made them a little speech, told them they were free, and could go where they pleased, said he would be glad to have them remain where they were, and would pay them fair wages for fair work. Some conference followed, resulting in arrangements mutually satisfactory. The negroes were faithful to their work all through the season, he has fairly set off to them their share of the crops made, and everything on his plantation has prospered. He has added about fifty to the hands thereon, and made a contract for the coming year with the whole number. Yet his neighbors, proceeding on the assumption that the freedmen will not work, have, of course, found all kinds of difficulty with them, and are generally unable to make contracts for next season. I have yet to hear of a single instance in which the method adopted by this gentleman has failed in securing work.

Everybody tells the Northern man that the negroes all expect a gift of lands or mules at Christmas. I have made numberless inquiries among them, bearing upon this point, and I declare my confident conviction that the assertion is untrue. There are some negroes in the southern, or perhaps I should say the southeastern section, who do expect some division of land at that time; and there are some in the western part who appear to have hopes that Christmas will bring them mules and carts; but the aggregate number of both these classes is comparatively small, and is very far from warranting the talk which one everywhere hears.

The truth in respect to the situation is, that the negroes are uncommonly ignorant of their rights and responsibilities. The State is very large, and the regular agents of the Freedmen's Bureau are very few in number. The old negro at Macon, who said to me, " One say dis, an' one say dat, an' we don' know, an' so hol' off till Janerwery," expressed the feeling of his people. The negro is lazy, he is improvident, and he prefers job work to season-contract work ; but where he is honestly informed and fairly treated, I believe he does quite as well as any one had a right to expect that he would.

The negroes of this State seem more suspicious and distrustful of the whites than those of the Carolinas. I judge that the Western troops did not use them quite fairly, and failed to strengthen their confidence in the Yankees. Moreover, not a few of the numerous post-commandants have been men utterly unfit to deal with the blacks, while I fear that some of them have been only less pro-slavery than the natives themselves. The appointment of local agents of the Freedmen's Bureau will give the blacks an opportunity to appeal to some responsible authority ; and when these are good men, it will do much to bring about a proper relationship between the two classes of people.

In some sections a new method of crime is developing. In almost any of the larger places it is matter of daily report that negroes have been guilty of theft for which bad whites are primarily responsible. In a few counties there are reported gangs of which white men are leaders and negroes are members, whose purpose is systematic plunder ; and at Macon I heard of a gang thus organized for the murder of men against whom the leaders had spite or prejudice. I believe this state of affairs prevails more generally in the northwestern section than elsewhere.

The negro's prospects are not, on the whole, as good as they ought to be in this great State. He has freedom in name, but it will be some time before he gets it in fact. His hope lies in the continued military occupation of the State and the continued existence of the Freedmen's Bureau. Even with these for his aid and protection, his condition is bad enough ; take these away, and in a good portion of the counties he would very soon not even have left the name of freedman.

XLIII.

SOME GENERAL CONCLUSIONS ON THE SITUATION IN GEORGIA AND THE CAROLINAS.

ON SHIPBOARD, December 7, 1865.

IF the representatives elect from the Southern States have been admitted to their seats in Congress, then has the South been victorious. But if the House has organized without their help, and if the whole reconstruction question is left open for general discussion in that body and in the public press, then indeed is there cause for most devout thanksgiving on this day set apart by the President.

My fourteen weeks' tour is at an end, and I am returning to New York. I have travelled over more than half the stage and railway routes in the States of North Carolina, South Carolina, and Georgia. I have been generally treated with civility and occasionally with courteous cordiality. I judge, from the stories told me by various persons, that my reception was, on the whole, something better than that accorded to the majority of Northern travellers.

I went South to study the political situation. I did not go to view the country, and consequently my letters have given but meagre information regarding the soil and climate and productions of the States visited. In pursuance of the plan marked out from the beginning, I sought conversation with all classes of Southerners, — my object being to gather information at first hand and to keep my reports free from the bias and prejudice of Northern sojourners. I was not obliged to write in the interest of any party or any person, and was not required to furnish arguments for upholding or breaking down any particular theory of reconstruction. In a word, my duty was that of a reporter. I meant to tell the truth, and I hoped to find the truth pleasant to tell.

Yet the conclusion of the whole matter is, that a very grave mistake, not to say a criminal blunder, has been committed, if the Southern representatives have been admitted into Congress.

It will not be safe to admit them to their seats at present. Some of them ought never to be admitted. They have no business in a Congress of the United States, for they are either of bitterly rebellious spirit or are encased in the poisonous bigotries of State supremacy. Against these the doors of our legislative halls should be forever closed. Other men there are of better disposition and larger views; but the time has not come for even their participation in the national counsels. If they are really fit for the places to which they have been chosen nothing will be lost if they prove anew that those also serve who stand and wait.

For it must be said that public sentiment is changing very rapidly in the South, and not wholly in the right direction. The President went to the extreme limit of magnanimity; but the more he gave the more was demanded. I have recently seen an article in one of the Southern papers in which the removal of Secretary Stanton is asked as a good-will offering to the people of the South; and a knot of gentlemen at the hotel in Augusta argued to me that the unconditional release of Jeff Davis was necessary to prove the kindly disposition of the North! So far as the people of Georgia and South Carolina, and a large proportion of those of North Carolina, are concerned, the indorsement of President Johnson, of which so much is said in their newspapers, is merely a grateful sense of favors to be received.

Possibly we were wrong to hope that one season could sow the grain of reconstruction and gather its fruitage of good order and fair respect for human rights. At least this season has not done that. I am sure the nation longs for nothing else so much as for honest and heroic peace; yet let not the representatives of the nation mistake this longing for weakness of faith or faintness of purpose in respect to the final triumph of justice.

It cannot be said that freedom of speech has been fully secured in either of the three States which I have visited. Personally, I have very little cause of complaint, for my *rôle* was rather that of a listener than of a talker; but I met many persons who kindly cautioned me, that at such and such places, and in such and such company, it would be advisable to refrain from conversation on certain topics. Among the members of the better class of people, resident in the cities and large towns, I found a fair degree of liberality of sentiment and courtesy of speech; but in travelling off the main railway lines, and among the average of the population, any man of Northern opinions must use much circumspection of language.

It follows, of course, that safety of person is not assured. Very likely one might travel through every county of either State without harm; but any Union man must expect to hear many insulting words; and any Northern man is sure to find his principles despised, his people contemned, and himself subjected to much disagreeable contumely; while any man holding and openly advocating even moderately radical sentiments on the negro question, stands an excellent chance, in many counties of Georgia and South Carolina, of being found dead some morning, — shot from behind, as is the custom of the country. Of course the war has not taught its full lesson till even Mr. Wendell Phillips can go into Georgia and proclaim " The South Victorious."

The leading men generally invite immigration, and are honest and sincere in their expression of desire for the influx of new life. They will, I am sure, do all they can to make the States safe and inviting for immigrants. In time even South Carolina will be as free as New York; but at present the masses of the people have little disposition of welcome for Northerners.

The late private soldiers of the Rebel army are the best class of citizens in the South. Generally speaking, they are disposed to go to work, though few of them know what work to do or to undertake. The bad classes are nearly all the women, who are as rebellious and as malignant as ever; most of the preachers, who are as hostile now as they were three years ago; many of the Rebel ex-officers who did n't see active service; and more than half the young men who managed in one way or another to keep out of the army.

I often had occasion to notice, both in Georgia and the Carolinas, the wide and pitiful difference between the residents of the cities and large towns and the residents of the country. There is no homogeneity, but everywhere a rigid spirit of caste. The longings of South Carolina are essentially monarchical rather than republican; even the common people have become so debauched in loyalty that very many of them would readily accept the creation of orders of nobility. In Georgia there is something less of this spirit; but the upper classes continually assert their right to rule, and the middle and lower classes have no ability to free themselves. The whole structure of society is full of separating walls; and it will sadden the heart of any Northern man, who travels in either of these three States, to see how poor and meagre and narrow a thing life is to all the country people. Even with the best class of townsfolk it lacks very much of the depth and breadth and fruitfulness of our Northern life, while with these others it is hardly less materialistic than that of their own mules and horses. Thus Charleston has much intelligence and considerable genuine culture; but go twenty miles away and you are in the land of the barbarians. So Raleigh is a city in which there is love of beauty and interest in education; but the common people of the county are, at least, forty years behind the same class of people in Vermont. Moreover, in Macon are many very fine residences, and the city may boast of its gentility and its respect for the nourishing elegances of life; but a dozen miles out are large neighborhoods not yet half civilized. The contrast between the inhabitants of the cities and those of the country is hardly less striking than that between the various classes constituting the body of the common people. Going from one county into another is frequently going into a foreign country. Travel continually brings novelty, but with that always came pain. Till all these hateful walls of caste are thrown down, we can have neither intelligent love of liberty, decent respect for justice, nor enlightened devotion to the idea of national unity. "Do men gather grapes of thorns, or figs of thistles?"

It has been the purpose of the ruling class apparently to build new barriers between themselves and the common people rather than tear away any of those already existing. I think no one can understand the actual condition of the mass of the whites of Georgia and the Carolinas, except by some daily contact with them. The injustice done to three fourths of them was hardly less than that done to all the blacks. There were two kinds of slavery, and negro slavery was only more wicked and debasing than white slavery. Nine of every ten white men in South Carolina had almost as little to do with even State affairs as the negroes had. Men talk of plans of reconstruction. That is the best plan which proposes to do most for the common people. Till civilization has been carried down into the homes and hearts of all classes, we shall have neither regard for humanity nor respect for the rights of the citizen.

Any plan of reconstruction is wrong that does not assure toleration of opinion and the elevation of the common people to the consciousness that ours is a republican form of government. Whether they are technically in the Union or out of the Union, it is the national duty to deal with these States in such manner as will most surely exalt the lower and middle classes of their inhabitants. The nation must teach them a knowledge of their own rights, while it also teaches them respect for its rights and the rights of man as man.

Stopping for two or three days in some back county, I was always seeming to have drifted away from the world which held Illinois and Ohio and Massachusetts. The difficulty in keeping connection with our civilization did not so much lie in the fact that the whole structure of daily life is unlike ours, nor in the other fact that I was forced to hear the Union and all loyal men reviled, as in the greater fact that the people are utterly without knowledge. There is everywhere a lack of intellectual activity; while as for schools, books, newspapers, why, one may almost say there are none outside the cities and towns!

Had schools abounded six years ago, I doubt if the masses of the South could have been forced into the war. "Why, d—n it," said an Americus man to me, "the Union never hurt me, but I was the hottest Secessionist I reckon you ever saw. Howell Cobb made me so." Talking with a Columbia gentleman about sectional characteristics he said, "We had one advantage over you: your people knew all about the war, while ours only knew they were fighting for their homes." I asked, "But could you have made your men fight at all if they had understood the whole question at issue?" He answered, "O, when I said we had the advantage, I spoke from a military stand-point."

In the important town of Charlotte, North Carolina, I found a white man who owned the comfortable house in which he lived, who had a wife and three half-grown children, and yet had never taken a newspaper in his life. He thought they were handy for wrapping purposes, but he could n't see why anybody wanted to bother with the reading of them. He knew some folks spent money for them, but he also knew a-many houses where none had ever been seen. In that State I found several persons — whites, and not of the "clay-eater" class either — who never had been inside a school-house, and who did n't mean to 'low their children to go inside one. In the upper part of South Carolina I stopped one night at the house of a moderately well-to-do farmer who never had owned any book but a Testament, and that was given to him. When I expressed some surprise at this fact, he assured me that he was as well off as some other people thereabouts. Between Augusta and Milledgeville I rode in a stage-coach in which were two of the delegates of the Georgia Convention. When I said that I hoped the day would soon come in which school-houses would be as numerous in Georgia as in Massachusetts, one of them answered, "Well, I hope it 'll never come; popular education is all a d—n humbug, in my judgment"; whereupon the other responded, "That's my opinion too." These are exceptional cases, I am aware, but they truly index the situation of thousands of persons.

The Southern newspapers generally have a large advertising patronage, and appear to be prospering quite to the satisfaction of their proprietors. But they are all local in character, and most of them are intensely Southern in tone; while as sources of general information, and particularly of political information, they are beneath notice. The Southern colleges have mostly suspended operations on account of the war. Efforts are making to reopen them, and those in Georgia will probably be in working order by next spring. But that best fruit of modern civilization, so plentiful in the North, — the common-school house, — is almost wholly unknown in the Carolinas and Georgia. I have scarcely seen a dozen in my whole journey, while a trip of the same number of miles in New York and New England would probably show me five hundred. Underneath this one little fact lies the whole cause of the war.

The situation is horrible enough when the full force of this fact is comprehended; yet there is a still lower deep,

— there is small desire, even feeble longing, for schools and books and newspapers. The chief end of man seems to have been "to own a nigger." The great majority of the common people know next to nothing, either of history or contemporaneous affairs; either of the principles of government or the acts of their own government; either of the work or thought of the present age; either of the desires or the purposes of nations. They get their information and their opinions mainly from the local office-seekers. It is therefore inevitable that the one should be meagre and the other narrow. It is this general ignorance, and this general indifference to knowledge, that make a Southern trip such wearisome work. You can touch the masses with few of the appeals by which we move our own people. There is very little aspiration for larger life; and, more than that, there is almost no opportunity for its attainment. That education is the stairway to a nobler existence is a fact which they either fail to comprehend or to which they are wholly indifferent.

Where there is such a spirit of caste, where the ruling class has a personal interest in fostering prejudice, where the masses are in such an inert condition, where ignorance so generally prevails, where there is so little ambition for betterment, where life is so hard and material in its tone, it is not strange to find much hatred and contempt. Ignorance is generally cruel and frequently brutal. The political leaders of this people have apparently indoctrinated them with the notion that they are superior to any other class in the country. Hence there is usually very little effort to conceal the prevalent scorn of the Yankee, — this term being applied to the citizen of any Northern State. Any plan of reconstruction is wrong that tends to leave these old leaders in power. A few of them give certain evidence of a change of heart, — by some means save these for the sore and troubled future; but for the others, the men who not only brought on the war, but ruined the mental and moral force of their people before unfurling the banner of Rebellion, — for these there should never any more be place or countenance among honest and humane and patriotic people. When the nation gives them life and a chance for its continuance, it shows all the magnanimity that humanity can in such case afford.

In North Carolina there is a great deal of something that calls itself Unionism ; but I know nothing more like the apples of Sodom than most of this North Carolina Unionism. It is a cheat, a will-o'-the-wisp, and any man who trusts it will meet with overthrow. There may be in it the seed of loyalty, but woe to him who mistakes the germ for the ripened fruit. In all sections of the State I found abundant hatred of some leading or local Secessionist ; but how full of promise for the new era of national life is the Unionism which rests only on this foundation ?

In South Carolina there is very little pretence of love for the Union, but everywhere a passionate devotion to the State ; and the common sentiment holds that man guilty of treason who prefers the United States to South Carolina. There is no occasion to wonder at the admiration of the people for Wade Hampton, for he is the very exemplar of their spirit, — of their proud and narrow and domineering spirit. "It is our duty," he says, in a letter which he has recently addressed to the people of the State,—"it is our duty to support the President of the United States so long as he manifests a disposition to restore all our rights as a sovereign State." That sentence will forever stand as a model of cool arrogance, and yet it is in full accord with the spirit of the South-Carolinians. The war has taught them that the physical force of the nation cannot be resisted, and they will be obedient to the letter of the law ; but the whole current of their lives flows in direct antagonism to its spirit.

In Georgia there is something worse than sham Unionism or cold acquiescence in the issue of battle : it is the universally prevalent doctrine of the supremacy of the State. In South Carolina, a few men stood up against the storm, but in Georgia that man is hopelessly dead who doubted or faltered. The common sense of all classes pushes the necessity of allegiance to the State into the domain of morals as well as into that of politics; and he who did not "go with the State" in the Rebellion is held to have committed the unpardonable sin. At Macon I met a man who was one of the leading Unionists in the winter of 1860 – 61. He told me how he suffered then for his hostility to secession, and yet he added, " I should have considered myself forever disgraced, if I had n't heartily gone with the State when she decided to fight." I believe it is the concurrent testimony of all careful travellers in Georgia, that there is everywhere only cold toleration for the idea of national sovereignty, and but little pride in the strength and glory and renown of the United States of America.

Much is said of the hypocrisy of the South. I found but little of it anywhere. The North-Carolinian calls himself a Unionist, but he makes no special pretence of love for the Union. He desires many favors, but he asks them generally on the ground that he hated the Secessionists. He expects the nation to recognize rare virtue in that hatred, and hopes it may win for his State the restoration of her political rights; but he wears his mask of nationality so lightly that there is no difficulty in removing it. The South-Carolinian demands only something less than he did in the days before the war, but he offers no plea of Unionism as a guaranty for the future. He rests his case on the assumption that he has fully acquiesced in the results of the war, and he honestly believes that he has so acquiesced. His confidence in South Carolina is so supreme that he fails to see how much the conflict meant. He walks by such light as he has, and cannot yet believe that destiny has decreed his State a secondary place in the Union. The Georgian began by believing that Rebellion in the interest of slavery was honorable, and the result of the war has not changed his opinion. He is anxious for readmission to fellowship with New York and Pennsylvania and Connecticut, but he supports his application by little claim of community of interest with other States. His spirit is hard and uncompromising; he demands rights, but does not ask favors; and he is confident that Georgia is fully as important to the United States as they are to Georgia.

The fact that such a large proportion of the offices in the gift of the people of these States have been filled with men who were officers in the Rebel army does not in itself furnish any argument against the good disposition of the people. The sentiment which voluntarily confers honor on a man who has shown personal bravery, who has been plucky and daring and gallant, is one we cannot afford to crush, — it is one of the strong moral forces of a nation, and deserves nurture rather than condemnation. Moreover, in not a few cases these ex-officers are of better will and purpose toward the government than any other men in their respective localities. It may not be pleasant to us to recognize this fact; but I am confident that we shall make sure progress toward securing domestic tranquillity and the general welfare just in proportion as we act upon it.

The other fact, that almost every candidate was defeated who did n't "go with the State" during the war is one of serious import. It indicates a spirit of defiance to the nation, of determined opposition to the principle of national unity. So long as this spirit prevails, we can hope for no sound peace. It will not again marshal armies in the field. Such a thing is utterly beyond the range of possibilities so far as this generation or the next is concerned. A few untamed fire-eaters will bluster, and local politicians will brag, but the leaders are wiser than they were, and the people have had enough of war. But there are things quite as bad

17 *

as open war; and one of these is a sullen and relentless antagonism to the idea of national sovereignty, — from which will breed passionate devotion to local interests, unending persecution of the freedmen, never-ceasing clamor in behalf of State rights, and continual effort to break away from the solemn obligations of the national debt.

That is the true plan of reconstruction which makes haste very slowly. It does not comport with the character of our government to exact pledges of any State which are not exacted of all. The one sole needful condition is, that each State establish a government whereby all civil rights at least shall be assured in their fullest extent to every citizen. The Union is no Union, unless there is equality of privileges among the States. When Georgia and the Carolinas establish governments republican in fact as well as in form, they will have brought themselves into harmony with the national will, and may justly demand readmission to their former political relations in the Union. It is no time for passion or bitterness, and it does not become our manhood to do anything for revenge. Let us have peace and kindly feeling; yet, that our peace may be no sham or shallow affair, it is painfully essential that we keep these States awhile within national control, in order to aid the few wise and just men therein who are fighting the great fight with stubborn prejudice and hidebound custom. Any plan of reconstruction is wrong which accepts forced submission as genuine loyalty or even as cheerful acquiescence in the national desire and purpose.

Prior to the war we heard continually of the love of the master for his slave, and the love of the slave for his master. There was also much talk to the effect that the negro lived in the midst of pleasant surroundings, and had no desire to change his situation. It was asserted that he delighted in a state of dependence, and throve on the universal favor of the whites. Some of this language we conjectured might be extravagant; but to the single fact that there was universal good-will between the two classes every Southern white person bore evidence. So, too, during my trip through Georgia and the Carolinas they have generally seemed anxious to convince me that the blacks behaved well during the war, — kept at their old tasks, labored cheerfully and faithfully, did not show a disposition to be lawless, and were rarely guilty of acts of violence, even in sections where there were many women and children, and but few white men.

Yet I found everywhere now the most direct antagonism between the two classes. The whites charge generally that the negro is idle and at the bottom of all local disturbance, and credit him with most of the vices and very few of the virtues of humanity. The negroes charge that the whites are revengeful, and intend to cheat the laboring class at every opportunity, and credit them with neither good purposes nor kindly hearts. This present and positive hostility of each class to the other is a fact that will sorely perplex any Northern man travelling in either of these States. One would say, that, if there had formerly been such pleasant relations between them, there ought now to be mutual sympathy and forbearance, instead of mutual distrust and antagonism. One would say, too, that self-interest, the common interest of capital and labor, ought to keep them in harmony; while the fact is, that this very interest appears to put them in an attitude of partial defiance toward each other. I believe the most charitable traveller must come to the conclusion that the professed love of the whites for the blacks was mostly a monstrous sham or a downright false pretence. For myself, I judge that it was nothing less than an arrant humbug.

Individual cases of real attachment to individual servants were doubtless common enough before the war, and an honest observer finds not a few of them even now. But, having seen the present relations of the two classes, I wonder that I or any one else could ever have believed that the common white people, as a class, had any real love for the blacks as a race. Some of the better men are now willing to concede to them the minor rights of humanity, but not one man in five thousand proposes to give them all the rights of men and women, and scarcely one in twenty thousand would invest any of them with the rights of citizenship. To dream that any of these States will voluntarily grant the ballot to the negro during this generation seems to me to qualify yourself for the insane asylum. The plainest of all plain requirements is that the freed negro shall have the right to be heard in the courts; and the fierce and bitter opposition to meeting this requirement gives the sharp and unequivocal lie to all professions of love for him.

The negro is no model of virtue or manliness. He loves idleness, he has little conception of right and wrong, and he is improvident to the last degree of childishness. He is a creature, — as some of our own people will do well to keep carefully in mind, — he is a creature just forcibly released from slavery. The havoc of war has filled his heart with confused longings, and his ears with confused sounds of rights and privileges: it must be the nation's duty, for it cannot be left wholly to his late master, to help him to a clear understanding of those rights and privileges, and also to lay upon him a knowledge of his responsibilities. He is anxious to learn, and is very tractable in respect to minor matters; but we shall need almost infinite patience with him, for he comes very slowly to moral comprehensions.

Going into the States where I went, — and perhaps the fact is also true of the other Southern States, — going into Georgia and the Carolinas, and not keeping in mind the facts of yesterday, any man would almost be justified in concluding that the end and purpose in respect to this poor negro was his extermination. It is proclaimed everywhere that he will not work, that he cannot take care of himself, that he is a nuisance to society, that he lives by stealing, and that he is sure to die in a few months; and, truth to tell, the great body of the people, though one must not say, intentionally, are doing all they well can to make these assertions true. If it is not said that any considerable number wantonly abuse and outrage him, it must be said that they manifest a barbaric indifference to his fate which just as surely drives him on to destruction as open cruelty would.

There are some men and a few women — and perhaps the number of these is greater than we of the North generally suppose — who really desire that the negro should now have his full rights as a human being. With the same proportion of this class of persons in a community of Northern constitution, it might justly be concluded that the whole community would soon join or acquiesce in the effort to secure for him at least a fair share of those rights. Unfortunately, however, in these Southern communities the opinion of such persons cannot have the same weight it would in ours. The spirit of caste, of which I have already spoken, is an element figuring largely against them in any contest involving principle, — an element of whose practical workings we know very little. The walls between individuals and classes are so high and broad that the men and women who recognize the negro's rights and privileges as a freeman are almost as far from the masses as we of the North are. Moreover, that any opinion savors of the "Yankee" — in other words, is new to the South — is a fact that even prevents its consideration by the great body of the people. Their inherent antagonism to everything from the North — an antagonism fostered and cunningly cultured for half a century by the politicians in the interest of slavery — is something that no traveller can photograph, that no Northern man can understand, till he sees it with his own eyes, hears it with his own ears, and feels it by his own consciousness. That the full freedom of the negroes would be acknowledged at once is something we had no warrant for expecting. The old masters grant them nothing, except at the requirement of the nation, as a military or a political necessity; and any plan of reconstruction is wrong which proposes to at once or in the immediate future substitute free-will for this necessity.

Three fourths of the people assume that the negro will not labor except on compulsion; and the whole struggle between the whites on the one hand and the blacks on the other hand is a struggle for and against compulsion. The negro insists, very blindly perhaps, that he shall be free to come and go when he pleases; the white insists that he shall only come and go at the pleasure of his employer. The whites seem wholly unable to comprehend that freedom for the negro means the same thing as freedom for them. They readily enough admit that the government has made him free, but appear to believe that they still have the right to exercise over him the old control. It is partly their misfortune, and not wholly their fault, that they cannot understand the national intent as expressed in the Emancipation Proclamation and the Constitutional Amendment. I did not anywhere find a man who could see that laws should be applicable to all persons alike; and hence even the best men hold that each State must have a negro code. They acknowledge the overthrow of the special servitude of man to man, but seek through these codes to establish the general servitude of man to the Commonwealth. I had much talk with intelligent gentlemen in various sections, and particularly with such as I met during the Conventions at Columbia and Milledgeville, upon this subject, and found such a state of feeling as warrants little hope that the present generation of negroes will see the day in which their race shall be amenable only to such laws as apply to the whites.

I think the freedmen divide themselves into four classes: one fourth recognizing very clearly the necessity of work, and going about it with cheerful diligence and wise forethought; one fourth comprehending that there must be labor, but needing considerable encouragement to follow it steadily; one fourth preferring idleness, but not specially averse to doing some job work about the towns and cities; and one fourth avoiding labor as much as possible, and living by voluntary charity, persistent begging, or systematic pilfering. It is true that thousands of the aggregate body of this people appear to have hoped, and perhaps believed, that freedom meant idleness; true, too, that thousands are drifting about the country or loafing about the centres of population in a state of vagabondage. Yet of the hundreds with whom I talked, I found less than a score who seemed beyond hope of reformation. It is a cruel slander to say that the race will not work except on compulsion. I made much inquiry wherever I went, of great numbers of planters and other employers, and found but very few cases in which it appeared that they had refused to labor reasonably well when fairly treated and justly paid. Grudgingly admitted to any of the natural rights of man, despised alike by Unionists and Secessionists, wantonly outraged by many and meanly cheated by more of the old planters, receiving a hundred cuffs for one helping hand and a thousand curses for one kindly word, they bear themselves toward their former masters very much as white men and women would under the same circumstances. True, by such deportment they unquestionably harm themselves; but consider of how little value life is from their stand-point. They grope in the darkness of this transition period, and rarely find any sure stay for the weary arm and the fainting heart. Their souls are filled with a great but vague longing for freedom; they battle blindly with fate and circumstance for the unseen and uncomprehended, and seem to find every man's hand raised against them either for blows or reproaches. What wonder that they fill the land with restlessness!

However unfavorable this exhibit of the negroes in respect to labor may appear, it is quite as good as can be made for the whites. I everywhere found a condition of affairs in this regard that astounded me. Idleness, not occupation, seemed the normal state. It is the boast of men and women alike, that they have never done an hour's work. The public mind is thoroughly debauched, and the general conscience is lifeless as the grave. I met hundreds of hale and vigorous young men who unblushingly owned to me that they had not earned a penny since the war closed. Nine tenths of the people must be taught that labor is even not debasing. It was pitiful enough to find so much idleness, but it was more pitiful to observe that it was likely to continue indefinitely. The war will not have borne proper fruit if our peace does not speedily bring respect for labor as well as respect for man. When we have secured one of these things, we shall have gone far toward securing the other; and when we have secured both, then, indeed, shall we have noble cause for glorying in our country, — true warrant for exulting that our flag floats over no slave.

Meantime, while we patiently and helpfully wait for the day in which

> " All men's good shall
> Be each man's rule, and Universal Peace
> Lie like a shaft of light across the land,"

there are at least five things for the nation to do : make haste slowly in the work of reconstruction ; temper justice with mercy, but see to it that justice is not overborne ; keep military control of these lately rebellious States till they guarantee a republican form of government ; scrutinize carefully the personal fitness of the men chosen therefrom as representatives in the Congress of the United States ; and sustain therein some agency that shall stand between the whites and the blacks and aid each class in coming to a proper understanding of its privileges and responsibilities.

Cambridge : Stereotyped and Printed by Welch, Bigelow, & Co.